# My Dearest Enemy, My Dangerous Friend

Stories about siblings abound in literature, drama, comedy, biography, and history. We rarely talk about our own siblings without emotion, whether with love and gratitude, or exasperation, bitterness, anger and hate. Nevertheless, the subject of what it is to be and to have a sibling is one that has been ignored by psychiatrists, psychologists and therapists.

In *My Dearest Enemy, My Dangerous Friend*, Dorothy Rowe presents a radically new way of thinking about siblings that unites the many apparently contradictory aspects of these complex relationships. This helps us to recognise the various experiences involved in sibling relationships as a result of the fundamental drive for survival and validation, enabling us to reach a deeper understanding of our siblings and ourselves.

If you have a sibling, or you are bringing up siblings, or, as an only child, you want to know what you're missing, this is the book for you.

**Dorothy Rowe** is a psychologist and author of 12 books, including the worldwide bestseller *Depression: The Way Out of Your Prison*. She is Australian, lives in London, and has a Big Sister.

# My Dearest Enemy, My Dangerous Friend

## Making and Breaking Sibling Bonds

Dorothy Rowe

Routledge
Taylor & Francis Group

LONDON AND NEW YORK

First published 2007 by Routledge
27 Church Road, Hove, East Sussex BN3 2FA

Simultaneously published in the USA and Canada
by Routledge
270 Madison Avenue, New York, NY10016

Reprinted 2007

*Routledge is an imprint of the Taylor & Francis Group,
an Informa business*

Typeset in New Century Schoolbook
Printed and bound in Great Britain by
T J International Ltd, Padstow, Cornwall
Cover design by Lisa Dynan

*British Library Cataloguing in Publication Data*
A catalogue record for this book is available from the British Library

*Library of Congress Cataloging in Publication Data*
Rowe, Dorothy.
    My dearest enemy, my dangerous friend : making and
breaking sibling bonds / Dorothy Rowe.
        p. cm.
    Includes bibliographical references and index.
    ISBN 0-415-39048-6 (pbk)
    1. Brothers and sisters.   I. Title.
    BF723.S43R69 2007
    306.875--dc22

                                      2006021782

ISBN: 978-0-415-39048-4

*See how we grew up in the same house but lived in different countries?*

(Nadia on her big sister Vera: Marina Lewycka, *A Short History of Tractors in Ukrainian*, 2005)

# CONTENTS

# PREFACE

All of my life I have been studying siblings. When you read this book you will know why. One thing I have learnt is that there is only one thing you can say about all siblings. This is that there is no one thing that you can say about all siblings. They are as various as snowflakes. No doubt this is the reason that psychologists have not studied sibling attachment with the same enthusiasm and productivity as they have studied the mother–child relationship. Where studies have been done of groups of siblings, questionnaires which cannot by their nature pick up the huge variation in sibling differences have been used. Few researchers have studied siblings in their own home over their childhood, though Judy Dunn has studied infant siblings in their home[1].

Yet, for most of us, our sibling relationship is the longest relationship we have over our whole lifespan. Whether the relationship is long or short, it is so fraught with emotion that we cannot put it aside in the way we can ignore an erstwhile friend. When a person does find it hard to sever forever their relationship with a faithless friend, it is often the case that the friend occupied a sibling-like position in that person's life. Moreover, for the first time in human history, the political stability of the whole world is under threat, not from some power hierarchy but from a brotherhood, the brotherhood of Islam, a movement, not an organisation, which operates as brothers do. They fight among themselves but come together against an enemy, a non-brother. If ever there was a time to study siblings, this is it.

The word 'sibling' is defined as two children who have the same parents, but in practice the children in a family often

include half- and step-siblings. In cultures which allow poly-
gamy this would be more often the case than not. Also, in many
families cousins are regarded as brothers. Throughout the history of Christendom a family was likely to include half- and
step-siblings because when the wife died, as women then were
prone to do from childbirth and disease, the husband would
marry again, sometimes to a younger woman who could bear
more children or to a widow who had money and perhaps a
child or two. Nowadays the popularity of divorce has ensured
that many families contain children from the couple's previous
relationships. Hence in the book when I use the word sibling
I mean siblings who have the same parents, half-siblings who
share one parent, and step-siblings who have been drawn, willingly or unwillingly, into a family where there are already one
or more children and the adults in the family expect or hope
that all the children will regard themselves as siblings. In a
family that contains full siblings, halves and steps, one sibling's feelings towards a full sibling may be somewhat different
from his or her feelings towards a half- or step-sibling, but all
these siblings are presented with much the same complexities
in having to live together.

The best accounts of sibling relationships come not from
psychological research but from memoirs and biographies, and
from literature where the writer has translated his or her sibling experience into fictional form. Not all biographers dare to
venture into the dangerous territory of childhood and siblings.
Many skip quickly past what they call their subject's 'happy
childhood'. Penelope Fitzgerald's biography of her father and his
brothers, *The Knox Brothers*, is highly regarded, but it contains
only a few pages on the childhood of these brothers, and then
in terms of theirs being a happy childhood.[2] No explanation is
given as to why the Knox brothers as adults were so eccentric.
In some biographies siblings get little more than a place in
the family tree. This can also happen in autobiographies. In
his extraordinary autobiography *Germs*, Richard Wollheim
mentioned his brother only in scenes where his brother's presence is a necessary part of the story which Wollheim wishes to
tell about himself.[3] It is clear from these brief glimpses of his
brother that Wollheim and his brother did not enjoy an entirely
harmonious relationship. Wollheim was too truthful a man to

pretend a good relationship where none existed, and he would never have produced anything approaching a hagiography of his brother, the kind of thing some siblings write about their famous sibling. John Faulkner's study *My Brother Bill* shows William Faulkner as the ideal older brother and their parents as endless in their love and wisdom.[4] There is no mention of the father's drinking and the fights which the father had with his wife who devoted much of her time to domestic martyrdom.

In my selection of biographies and fiction I have drawn on those where the writer has tried to capture the pain and pleasure of being and having a sibling. By ranging as widely as I could I have tried to show that, while in different cultures and at different times the demands made on children in a family vary tremendously, the central themes of sibling experience are universal. Each of these themes I have made the subject of a chapter.

The first and major theme applies to all of us, whether we are a sibling or not, namely the overarching need to preserve our sense of being a person and our terror of being annihilated as a person. All our sibling relationships, whatever their nature, are based on this. Even indifference to a sibling can be a way of defending one's sense of being a person. Sibling relationships are very much about being validated or invalidated as a person.

The second theme is about how we form attachments, loving or otherwise, to our siblings.

The third theme concerns how, for some neurological reason which is far from being understood, every person falls into one of two groups. There are those who experience their sense of existence in relationship to other people, and there are those who experience their sense of existence in gaining clarity, organisation, control and a sense of achievement. For the first group, the fear of annihilation of their sense of being a person arises from the threat of total rejection and abandonment. For the second group, the threat comes from losing control and falling into chaos. We can express these different forms of how we experience our sense of being a person in an infinite number of ways. In families these basic differences are always a source of mutual irritation and incomprehension, and thus always the source of possible invalidation.

The fourth theme is about how all of us, siblings or not, are dominated by the need to behave in such a way that we can feel safe both physically and as a person. This I call 'needing to be good'. To earn our parents' attention and love we have to compete with our siblings over who is the 'goodest' of us all.

Fifth, when people are together as a couple or as a group there is always some kind of power struggle, sometimes muted, sometimes fierce. As well as competing over who is the 'goodest', siblings struggle over who has power over the others. Power validates: impotence invalidates.

Sixth, siblings can play such an important part in our life that if our sibling dies we suffer a loss different from, but as important as, the death of our parents.

Seventh, sibling differences are not resolved in childhood. In adulthood siblings battle over who has the most truthful, accurate memory of their shared past. Memory is a construction, and so each sibling constructs a memory which best maintains their sense of being a person.

Eighth, loyalty and betrayal amongst siblings has to do with maintaining or undermining the sibling's sense of being a person.

Ninth, if reconciliation is to be achieved it has to be based on mutual trust. There has to be no threat to the sense of being a person in the sibling relationship.

Most of us are siblings, and most of us know how painful, wonderful and extraordinary the sibling relationship can be. My thanks to those siblings who shared their experiences with me, both those who talked to me and those who told me about themselves through their writings and the testimonies they left behind them.

Dorothy Rowe
London
August 2006

# Acknowledgements

The author and publisher are grateful to the following for their permission to reproduce passages from copyright material as follows:

A P Watts Ltd for extracts from *A Very Close Conspiracy: Vanessa Bell and Virginia Woolf* by Jane Dunn; BBC for extracts from http://www.bbc.co.uk/comedy/theoffice/gareth/ (© bbc.co.uk); Berg Publishers for extracts from *Heinrich Böll: A German for His Time* by James Reid; Bloomsbury Publishers for permission to use extracts from *Long Shadows: Lies, Truth and History* by Erna Paris, and extracts from *Sister Brother: Gertrude and Leo Stein* by Brenda Wineapple; Brenda Wineapple for permission to use an extract from *Sister Brother: Gertrude and Leo Stein* by Brenda Wineapple; Constable & Robinson Ltd for extracts from *Ackerley* by Peter Parker; David Higham Associates for extracts from *Ivy When Young* by Hilary Spurling (published by Hodder & Stoughton), for extracts from *My Father and Myself* by J. R. Ackerley (published by the New York Review of Books); for extracts from *My Sister and Myself* by J. R. Ackerley (published by Hutchinson); and for extracts from *Matisse the Master* by Hilary Spurling (Published by Penguin); Extract from *JM Barrie and the Lost Boys* by Andrew Birkin reproduced with kind permission of Great Ormond Street Hospital for Children, London; Faber and Faber Ltd for extracts from *Istanbul: Memories of a City* by Orhan Pamuk; Excerpts from *Almost a Childhood* by Hans Georg Behr, Translated by Anthea Bell. Reprinted by permission of Granta Books; Extracts from *Life of Contrasts* by Diana Mosley (Hamish Hamilton, 1977) Copyright © 1977 by Diana Mosley, Reproduced by Permission of Penguin Books Ltd; Extracts from *The Mitford Girls* by Mary S. Lovell.

*Behaviour* by Don McCullin (from *Unreasonable Behaviour* by Don McCullin, published by Jonathan Cape. Reprinted by permission of the Random House Group Ltd), extracts from *Deceived with Kindness* by Angelica Garnett (from *Deceived with Kindness* by Angelica Garnett, published by Chatto & Windus. Reprinted by permission of The Random House Group Ltd), extracts from *On The Run* by Greg and Gina Hill (from *On The Run* by Greg and Gina Hill, published by Hutchinson. Reprinted by permission of The Random House Group Ltd), extracts from *The Pecking Order* by Dalton Conley (from *The Pecking Order* by Dalton Conley, copyright © Dalton Conley. Used by permission of Pantheon Books, a division of Random House Inc), and for extracts from *Don't Let's Go To The Dogs Tonight* by Alexandra Fuller, Copyright © 2001 by Alexandra Fuller. Used by Permission of Random House, Inc; Serpent's Tail for extracts from *Zacarias Moussaoui: The Making of a Terrorist* by Abd Samad Moussaoui; The Society of Authors for Extracts from *Eustace and Hilda* by L.P. Hartley (The Society of Authors at Literary Representative of the Estate of L.P. Hartley); Spellmount for extracts from *A Hitler Youth* by Henry Metelman, ISBN: 1862272522; Text publishing for extracts from *Swimming Upstream* (reproduced with permission from *Swimming Upstream* by Anthony Fingleton, first published by The Text Publishing Company Pty Ltd, Australia, www.textpublishing.com.au); Virago for extracts from *Ordinary Families* by E. Arnot Robertson; Virginia Ironside for extracts from *Janey and Me* by Virginia Ironside (Copyright © Virginia Ironside 2003); From *A Circle of Sisters: Alice Kipling, Georgiana Burne-Jones, Agnes Poynter, and Louisa Baldwin* by Judith Flanders. Copyright © 2001 by Judith Flanders. Used by permission of W. W. Norton & Company, Inc; Warner Books for extracts from *On The Run* by Gina Hill. Copyright © 2004 by Gregg Hill and Gina Hill. By Permission of Warner books, Inc; Zed Books for extracts from *A Daughter of Isis* by Narwal Saadawi (Zed Books, London, 1999) and *Walking Through Fire* by Narwal Saadawi (Zed Books, London, 2002).

There are also extracts from the following:

*The Catcher in the Rye* by J.D. Salinger; *The Double Bond: The Life of Primo Levi* by Carole Angier; *No Bed of Roses* by Joan

# Chapter 1

# OUR GREATEST NEED: OUR GREATEST FEAR

For all of his life the great painter Henri Matisse dreaded falling asleep. He said: 'I am inhabited by things that wake me, and don't show themselves.'[1]

In her *Memoirs of a Dutiful Daughter*, Simone de Beauvoir described a night in her teens when she was in conflict with her parents:

> One night, just as I had laid myself to sleep in a vast country bed, I was overwhelmed by a terrible anguish; I had on occasion been terrified of death, to the point of tears and screams; but this time it was worse. Life was already tilting over the brink into absolute nothingness; at the instant I felt a terror so violent that I nearly went to knock on my mother's door and pretend to be ill, just in order to hear a human voice. In the end I fell asleep, but I retained a horrified memory of that awful attack of nerves.[2]

Matisse's demons and Simone de Beauvoir's terror arose from the fear of becoming absolute nothingness, that is, the dissolution of the carefully constructed entity which we call 'I'. We all fear death but we can imagine 'I' continuing on in some form – our soul, our spirit, our children, our work, other people's memories – but to feel that 'I' is falling apart, disappearing, that is absolute terror.

We create all kinds of defences against this terror, but when we fall asleep the defences melt away. If our life is going along steadily, turning out to be what we expect it to be, then the terror recedes into the far distance. But when our life is not proceeding steadily, when the 'I' constructed by the brain out of our experiences cannot fit easily with what our world presents to us, our 'I' begins to crumble and we cast around for stronger, more effective defences to hold ourselves together. However, while the threat remains, no matter how good our defences are, they require our constant attention. If the ill fit between our 'I' and our world arises from our current circumstances – an unhappy marriage, an unsuitable job, being caught up in a war – we may be able to leave the marriage or the job, or extricate ourselves from the war, and thus find ourselves enjoying serenity again. But if the mismatch began in our childhood the threat remains with us no matter where we go and what we do, and the defence endlessly necessary. For Matisse and Simone de Beauvoir the mismatch began at birth.

Matisse was born in 1869 into a family of generations of weavers in northern France just as that area was undergoing industrialisation. As a child all around him was 'the remorseless, mind-numbing, drudgery of the weavers and farm labourers.' His ambitious father, Hippolyte Henri, escaped such drudgery by starting a seed merchant business but drove himself, his wife and his sons exceedingly hard in order to succeed. Their second son died when he was two and Matisse four. A third son, August Emile, was born in 1872. Hippolyte Henri expected much from his sons, but especially from Matisse as the elder boy. Had Matisse not had a younger brother, his father would likely have treated him all the more harshly and demanded more from him. As a schoolboy Matisse had periods of illness which look suspiciously like a useful defence against the more unpleasant aspects of his life, particularly the sheer hard labour involved in the seed merchant business. His brother August Emile did this work in Matisse's place. Without him Matisse might not have been able to leave his family and go to Paris to study art. Fortunately for him, and for us, August Emile was prepared to go into their father's business. Appalled as he was at his son's defection, his father very grudgingly gave Matisse a small allowance, but Matisse's community never forgave him. Hilary Spurling, Matisse's biographer, wrote, 'It would be hard to exaggerate the shock of Matisse's defection in a community which dismissed any form of art as an irrelevant, probably seditious and essentially contemptible occupation to be indulged in by layabouts, of whom the most successful might at best be regarded as a clown.'[3]

Matisse changed how we see the world, and so it is hard for us today to understand the almost universal contempt which Matisse's paintings provoked. He, his wife Amélie and their children lived in poverty for many years. Matisse could have made an excellent living if he had painted conventionally, but he could not betray his 'I', the person he knew himself to be.

As a small child Simone de Beauvoir was a delight to her parents. She was very bright, she loved her little sister Poupette, and she was good. In her early years she had been prone to temper tantrums, but when the Germans invaded France in 1914, 'It had been explained to me that if I were good and pious God would save France.' The chaplain at the Cours Désir congratulated her mother 'upon the radiant beauty of my soul'.[4] However, she was too clever and too observant not to see that the adults who judged her did not set the same high standards for themselves as they did for her. In her teens and writing about an argument with her parents she said, 'I tried to pretend, to lie, to give soft answers, but I did it all with ill grace: I felt I was a traitor to myself. I decided that I must "tell the truth, the whole truth, and nothing but the truth": in that way I would avoid disguising and at the same time betraying my thoughts. This was not very clever of me, for I merely succeeded in scandalising my parents without satisfying their curiosity.'[5] Her parents compared her unfavourably with her sister. '"Now, Poupette – *she'll* find a husband," my parents confidently predicted.'[6]

For both Matisse and Simone de Beauvoir there was an ill fit between the person they knew themselves to be and the world in which they lived, but they had two great advantages. One was that they each had a sibling who accepted (or in August's case 'put up with' might be a better description) what the other was. The other was that they each had enormous talent out of which they could both construct a defence against the fear of being annihilated as a person and produce their works of art. After she had lost her Catholic faith Simone de Beauvoir made a decision about her future. She wrote:

If at one time I had dreamed of being a teacher it was

because I wanted to be a law unto myself; I now thought that literature would allow me to realize this dream. It would guarantee me an immortality which would compensate me for the loss of heaven and eternity; there was no longer any God to love me, but I should have the undying love of millions of hearts. By writing a work based on my experience I would re-create myself and justify my existence.[7]

When Matisse married Amélie he warned her that, as much as he loved her, he would always love painting more. He worked almost incessantly. In great old age, when he no longer had the physical strength to paint, he cut brilliant shapes from coloured papers. There was always an enormous urgency behind his work. When in 1942 he was asked by Louis Aragon why he worked as he did, he answered simply, 'I do it in self-defence.'[8]

Neither Matisse nor Simone de Beauvoir was talking about a rare and special event. They were talking about the kind of events which inhabit our lives, that break in upon the quiet tenor of our days. We all know such events only too well. Suppose you are at home waiting for the person who gives shape, security and purpose to your life to arrive. The minutes tick by. The person does not come. You start to feel anxious and you comfort yourself with explanations, 'held up at work,' 'traffic's bad', but such comfort soon evaporates. You feel a constriction in your chest, your palms become damp with sweat, images of accidents come into your mind. You try to divert yourself with little tasks but you cannot concentrate. You can hear your heart beating fast and the constriction in your chest turns into a fierce pain. You want reassurance that everything will be all right, but the only person who can give you this reassurance is the one you are waiting for. You can try to tell yourself that even if the very worst has happened you will manage, but you know you will not. Life will be meaningless and you will fall apart, just as you are falling apart now as the waves of fear sweep over you and swirl you about. You feel yourself breaking into pieces, falling apart like a porcelain vase shattered by a blow. Then the door opens and there is your beloved. There is a moment of stillness and then the fragments of you that were whirling chaotically come back together again. You are whole and safe.

Or suppose you hear on the office grapevine that the firm is going to be reorganised. You are part of a team that has worked together well for a long time. You are sure your boss thinks highly of you but perhaps you have got this wrong. There is a sudden stab of sharp pain in your chest and your heart starts racing. You try to chat to people but you cannot get your breath and your palms stick to whatever they touch. You go to your boss's office as you would to an execution. When your boss delivers the blow by telling you that your team is being disbanded and your work is to be done by someone else, you do not take in his assurances that the references he will give you will praise you and that you will be certain to get another job very soon. How can you hear anything when you know that you are about to disappear like a puff of smoke in the wind? Your reflection in the mirror does not reassure you that you are still there. If all the people who are the structures that sustain you disappear, you will surely disappear too. You try to be sensible, be practical, get busy, but no amount of activity will extinguish the terror you feel.

Perhaps you have been going along quietly, your life unfolding in the way that you happily anticipated and then suddenly, without warning, something happens which shows you that your life is not what you think it is.

Michael Leunig is an Australian cartoonist whose work often asks the kind of questions which offend those people who believe that their views are absolutely right and must never be questioned by anyone else. Gentle soul that he is, Michael has made many enemies who may strike when he least expects it. After a Danish newspaper had published some cartoons which depicted the Prophet Mohammed a great many Muslims were outraged, and an Iranian newspaper started a competition for cartoons which made fun of the Holocaust. One summer evening Michael was about to water his garden when a call from a colleague alerted him to the fact that one of his own cartoons had been sent to the Iranian cartoon competition. Later he wrote:

I went into the harsh light of the internet and there,

on the Iranian website, as described to me on the
telephone, was a well-worn cartoon of mine prominently
displayed as the first entry in the famous international
competition. Local boy makes good. Furthermore, a
fake text bearing my name and expressing support for
the Muslims of the world glared eerily before me on
the screen. It was quite a sudden disillusionment.

There is a moment of confusion that is almost religious
as the mind tumbles about grasping for meaning and
reference points but, really, you are in free-fall at this
moment and the stomach feels weightless for a time
as you descend suddenly into a special underworld
where you must now spend some unscheduled time.

This is what happens when the fact slams into me
that I have been secretly and maliciously set up and
framed and that the story will soon be on the wire and
the twisting and distorting of my life is about to become
extreme and that the consequences for me and my family
could be dire.[9]

The Iranians who had organised the competition agreed to
remove the cartoon and the forged text, and eventually all the
media who had descended on Michael went away, but experiences like those described here always change us. Some people
become stronger; some do not. Some people live in fear that
the experience will happen again and they will not be strong
enough to survive it. Some people feel that the experience has
shown them that they cannot be the person they know themselves to be. They cannot fight back in the way that Matisse
and Simone de Beauvoir did and so all that is left of them is
a façade, a false self that other people acknowledge and talk
to, but behind the façade is nothing, just a wraith, a ghost of
what used to be. Many people live like this, feeling quite unable to present the person that they are to the world because
to do so would invite yet another threat of annihilation. Many
of these people feel that they no longer know who they really are. Some feel very guilty because they are not the person
their family or their society expects them to be: others feel very
resentful because other people have thrust a role upon them
which is at odds with who they are. Surviving the threat of

annihilation only to live as a façade leads to loneliness and great unhappiness.

It can also lead to physical illness. The unity of mind and body is now being demonstrated in the extensive research on the effects of troubling events on the efficient functioning of the immune system. In a review of this research Suzanne Segerstrom and Gregory Miller found that the 'stressors' which had the greatest physical effect were the chronic stressors, the ones that 'pervade a person's life, forcing him or her to restructure his or her identity or social roles', where 'the person does not know whether or when the challenge will end or can be certain that it will never end'. Studies of people suffering a chronic stressor such as 'a traumatic injury that leads to physical disability, providing care for a spouse with severe dementia, or being a refugee forced out of one's native country by war', all situations where the person is no longer in control of his own life, showed: 'The most chronic stressors were associated with the most global immunosuppression, as they were associated with reliable decreases in almost all functional immune measures examined.'[10] Not being the person you know yourself to be makes you ill.

What adds to the stress of the threat of annihilation as a person is our reluctance to talk about it. When we survive the threat of physical death we often talk about the experience afterwards, but when we survive the threat of being annihilated as a person we usually tell no one. Sometimes a reference to our fear just slips out. When the television presenter Graham Norton was interviewed by Sue Lawley on *Desert Island Discs* and she asked what luxury he wanted on his island he replied, 'I've always said that the luxury I'd bring was a mirror. It would be quite good to save your sanity, that you could see that you exist, rather than just be kind of lost in the trees.'[11]

Sometimes, in trying to explain what other people have called his 'breakdown', a person will give a description of how he experienced the near-annihilation of his sense of being a person. In a television programme about himself, Alastair Campbell, once director of communications for Tony Blair, did this. He said, 'It's like your mind is like a very fragile plate glass. And it's very large, you're trying harder and harder to hold this plate glass together. You can feel pressure on your mind and pressure on your body, and eventually it literally shatters, it explodes. It's a kind of cacophony of noise and of memories and of music and of people talking and different conversations, and you're trying to get some order into it, and you can't.'[12]

However, most of the time we find the fear of annihilation far too terrible to talk about. We feel that, if we spoke of it, the fear we had felt might come back in all its ferocity. We do not want to remember that we had had such an experience many times in childhood. If we had siblings it was often one or other of them who delivered such blows.

Perhaps you were just three years old and often felt confused and frightened by so many things that you could not comprehend. People came and went and picked you up and put you down and no one explained what was happening and why. The only person you could rely on was your teddy bear. Holding him you felt safe and at night, when he was tucked in beside you, you knew he was keeping at bay all those things out there in the dark. Then one day your big brother who was so much taller, stronger and quicker than you grabbed your teddy from you and held him over the railing of a bridge below which flowed a deep, dark river. You screamed and screamed in fear. When your brother relented and lifted your teddy back over the railing and gave him to you, your screams turned to sobs and you could not be consoled. How could you be consoled when there was no you but little bits of you spinning about in chaos? These bits came together eventually but you were not the same as you were before your brother took your teddy from you. That experience had changed you.

Perhaps you had been an only child for four years. Your world was made up of Mummy, Daddy and you. Then Mummy and Daddy started to talk about the little baby that was in Mummy's tummy and you had your hand there and felt the baby moving. You had seen some babies and they looked like dolls that moved. Then Mummy went away and came back with a baby. When Grandma took you into Mummy's bedroom you got a shock. Mummy was in bed holding the baby and Daddy was sitting beside her with his arm around her and both of them were looking at the baby, and the way they were looking told you that they loved the baby more than you. Even though Mummy called you over and you sat on the bed with them, you knew that now they had the baby they did not want you. A gigantic empty space opened up inside you and you felt that you had disappeared for ever.

We do not forget such childhood experiences. We may try to forget them but, remembered or not, their effects are profound. Our security is undermined and we resort to defences that, like all defences, impede our progress.

The experience of our greatest fear, being annihilated as a person, has always been the stuff of great literature. Whatever the story, it always turns on the characters' defences against annihilation while the crisis in the story is often the experience of the fear of the annihilation of the person. At the beginning of J. D. Salinger's *The Catcher in the Rye*, Holden Caulfield is making his way to his teacher's home on a bitterly cold afternoon:

> I ran across Route 204. It was as icy as hell and I
> damn near fell down. I didn't even know what I was
> running for – I guess I just felt like it. After I got
> across the road, I felt like I was sort of disappearing.
> It was that kind of crazy afternoon, terrifically cold,
> and no sun out or anything, and you felt like you were
> disappearing every time you crossed a road.[13]

At the end of the book he again feels he is disappearing, only this time it is much more frightening. He has spent five days wandering around New York, trying to make contact with people and failing, wishing that his dead brother Allie were with him. Now he is physically exhausted. He wanders up Fifth Avenue, watching the little children with their mothers and thinking about his kid sister Phoebe and of how the previous Christmas they had gone shopping and had 'a helluva time':

> Anyway, I kept walking and walking up Fifth Avenue,
> without any tie or anything. Then all of a sudden something
> spooky happened. Every time I came to the end of a block
> and stepped off the goddam curb, I had this feeling that I'd
> never get to the other side of the street. I thought I'd just
> go down, down, down, and nobody'd ever see me again. Boy,
> did it scare me. You can't imagine. I started sweating like
> a bastard – my whole shirt and underwear and everything.

Then I started doing something else. Every time I'd make it
to the end of the block I'd make believe I was talking to my
brother Allie. I'd say to him, 'Allie, don't let me disappear.
Allie, don't let me disappear. Allie, don't let me disappear.
Please, Allie.' And then when I'd reach the other side of
the street without disappearing, I'd thank him. Then it
would start again as soon as I got to the next corner.[14]

To be able to write about the experience of the near-annihilation
of the sense of being a person, J. D. Salinger must have known
that fear not once but many times. The fear is there again and
again in the writings of Virginia Woolf, in her diaries and in
her novels. In 1926 she described in her diary what she called
'A State of Mind'. Other people might call it 'nameless dread'.
She wrote:

Woke up perhaps at 3. Oh it's beginning it's coming – the
horror – physically a painful wave around the heart –
tossing me up. I'm unhappy unhappy! Down – God, I wish
I were dead! I've only a few years to live I hope. I can't face
this horror any more – (this wave spreading out over me).[15]

Here she described the fear as a wave; in other places she spoke
of her fear of being 'reduced to a whirlpool'.[16] Images of water
recur often in her writing. It was not just by chance that she
chose to die by drowning. As a young child she experienced
what her biographer Hermione Lee called 'moments of profound
horror or desolation', and in the years that followed there was
a series of deaths in her family which 'intensified her anticipation of a hidden enemy waiting to deliver "a sledge-hammer
blow"'. She had to develop 'some form of fight or resistance'. It
was this, as she later said, that made her a writer, someone
who would explain the purpose of these shocks or blows as she
called them. The blow became 'a revelation of some order'. 'It is
a token of the real thing behind appearances and I make it real
by putting it into words.'[17]

We have to find defences against the threat of annihilation.
When Holden feels himself in imminent danger of disappearing he turns to the only person he could trust, his brother Allie.
His parents have rejected him, his sister Phoebe is too young
to help him, only Allie has the moral strength and courage to

save him. Except that Allie was dead. The blows which Virginia Woolf suffered destroyed the security and order in her life. It was not just the deaths in her family when she was young but the sexual assaults she suffered at the hands of her two step-brothers, George and Gerald Duckworth. The defence she chose was to see the world around her as being merely appearances. Behind this illusion was a hidden order and security which she could find through her writing.

The problem with all defences is that they are no more than ideas which we construct out of our needs and wishes. They are all guesses about what is happening and what may happen, and, while they may be based on what we know, they are also based on what we want to deny. Holden's defence is based on a denial that his brother is dead and, as much as he may desire Allie's continued existence in some form, he knows that Allie is dead. His hatred of sentimentality and hypocrisy does not allow him to comfort himself with a belief in an afterlife with saints and angels. As his story comes to an end we discover that he is telling his story from the doubtful security of a psychiatric hospital.

Virginia Woolf's defence was to see order behind appearances, but, although she knew that order is essential to her survival, chaos being what she feared the most, her keen intelligence told her that we live in a world where things fall apart, as they did when in 1941 the German army was poised to invade Britain. Her defence of the hidden order no longer worked and, unable to bear the horror anymore, she killed herself.

Events in the world around us can threaten us with annihilation as a person. A war can destroy the structures which made our life secure, other people can show us by their criticism, betrayal or neglect that we are not the person we thought ourselves to be. Even more dangerous is what the psychoanalyst Justin Frank called 'the darker side of our internal reality – our aggression and envy, the reality of grief and loss, the knowledge that we are going to die'.[18] This is the hidden disorder from which we cannot escape but against which we always defend ourselves.

Unlike psychiatrists, psychoanalysts have always recognised what Justin Frank called 'an innate fear of falling apart'. 'The baby's most threatening terror is a fear of fragmentation, of losing his nascent, fragile sense of self.'[19] Psychoanalysts knew this because this was what their patients talked about, but psychoanalysts were not believed by most people. Psychoanalysts did themselves no favours by creating an exclusive jargon and writing in what often seemed to be a very condescending way for readers who were not part of the analysts' inner circle. Since their subject matter was what people feared the most, few people were brave and persistent enough to read the psychoanalysts' books and papers, and so their wisdom was dismissed by most people as far-fetched nonsense. How could babies have complex ideas about their mothers and their own needs and wishes? But since then the scientific study of the brain and its development has shown the psychoanalysts to be right.

Scientists who study the brain have done more than show that psychoanalysts were right about what babies know. They have also shown that two very different philosophers, born many centuries apart, were right. They were Epictatus and Spinoza.

Epictatus was an ancient Greek philosopher who observed what people did and noted that: 'It is not things in themselves which trouble people but their opinions of things.' He saw that what people did depended on how they interpreted events and not on the events themselves. This insight explained why individuals reacted so differently to the same event. No doubt Epictatus arrived at this conclusion by talking to people about why they did what they did, and in doing so different people would explain how their interpretation of an event derived from their past experience. Since no two people ever have exactly the same experience, no two people ever interpret an event in exactly the same way. Epictatus had no knowledge of how memories are stored in the brain and how the brain perceives, but all that is known now about the brain shows that Epictatus was right. What determines our behaviour is not what happens to us but how we interpret what happens to us. The neurologist Antonio Damasio explained how the brain operates:

The neural patterns and the corresponding mental images of the objects and events outside the brain are creations of the brain related to the reality that prompts their creation rather than passive mirror images reflecting that reality . . . There is no picture of the object being transferred optically from the retina to the visual cortex. The optics stop at the retina. Beyond that there are physical transformations that occur in continuity from the retina to the cerebral cortex. Likewise, the sounds you hear are not trumpeted from the cochlea to the auditory cortex by some megaphone.[20]

What this means is that we are incapable of perceiving reality directly. All we can perceive are the meanings, or images as Damasio calls them, which our brain has constructed.

Spinoza was a Portuguese-Jewish philosopher, born in 1632, who spent his short life in the Netherlands. He studied but rejected Descartes' proposition that the soul (or mind) was separate from the body, a concept which has been an enormous impediment to our understanding of ourselves. It is only in the last 20 years that the medical profession has had to make some guarded recognition of the fact that the way we think can affect the efficient functioning of our body. In his great work *The Ethics*, Spinoza proposed that the mind and body came from the same substance and are, in effect, one. He saw too that the self, what you call 'I', 'me', 'myself', and what Damasio has shown to grow slowly as the brain develops, strives to survive, and out of such striving comes a notion that dominates our lives, the idea of the necessity to be good. (If you are a sibling, remember how much time you spent trying to prove to your parents that you were 'gooder' than your siblings, and how dreadful you felt when you failed to achieve that.)

The quote comes from Proposition 18 in part IV of *The Ethics* and reads: 'the very first foundation of virtue is the endeavour to preserve the individual self, and happiness consists in the human capacity to preserve itself.' In Latin the proposition reads: '*Virtutis fundamentum esse ip sum conatum proprium esse conservandi, et felicitatem in eo consistere, quod homo suum esse conservare potest.*'[21]

Spinoza wrote in Latin and the words he used have connotations slightly different from their equivalent in English. *Virtutis* is translated as virtue, but it also means in Latin having power and the ability to act. We all want to think of ourselves as being good, and we all know the importance of being in charge of our lives and getting things done. Also, the Latin word *conatum* is translated here as endeavour, but it means more than just trying. There is a sense of seeking and striving.

The animal scientist Temple Grandin, drawing on the work of the neurologist Jaak Panksepp, pointed out that the emotion of seeking is a primary emotion along with anger and fear. She wrote: 'Animals and humans share a powerful and primal urge to *seek* out what they need in life. We depend on this emotion to stay alive, because curiosity and active interest in the environment help animals and people find good things, like food, shelter, and a mate, and it helps us stay away from bad things, like predators.'[22] Human beings not only look for good things to stay alive but they also seek those people and situations which will support their sense of being a person.

In the nineteenth century most people considered that babies experienced no more than what psychologist William James called 'a booming, buzzing confusion'. Now we know that this is not the case. Research by developmental psychologists has shown that babies are born into a world which they find immensely interesting. They arrive with certain talents that direct their interest to the areas of their environment which they most need. They are fully engaged with making sense of their environment. This ability to make sense of what happens to them does not come into being at the moment of their birth; rather it develops slowly while they are still in the womb. As their brain grows, babies become able to distinguish pleasure from pain. They begin to notice that one particular event always follows another particular event, and then they start to use the occurrence of the first event to predict the second. For instance, in the womb a baby may notice that a particular music is always followed by a pleasurable sense of ease as the baby's mother sits or lies down. Once born, the baby shows the alerting response, which is the baby's interpretation 'something nice is about to happen' whenever a particular piece of music is played. Thus a great many mothers in the UK discovered that their baby was born already knowing the theme tune of the popular television series *Neighbours*.

We create meaning in order to predict what will happen. We are meaning-creating creatures in order to be prediction-creating creatures. If we can predict what is going to happen we can keep ourselves safe. We interpret what is happening and we want our interpretations to be validated by events and by other people. For instance, you cook a meal for your friends and as you serve it your interpretation of the meal is 'I'm sure they will enjoy this.' You wait for the praise that will validate your interpretation, but you will also watch how your friends eat the meal to see whether they are just being polite when they tell you how good it is. We want our meanings to be validated because that makes us feel secure. Invalidation makes us anxious. We feel that not just our ideas but we ourselves have been invalidated

This feeling of being invalidated as a person arises from the way all the meanings we create coalesce into a structure of meaning which we experience as our sense of being a person, what we call 'I', 'me', 'myself'. The neuropsychologist Paul Broks wrote:

> The brain has evolved systems dedicated to social
> cognition and action. It constructs a model of the organism
> of which it is a part and, beyond this, a representation
> of that organism's place to other, similar, organisms:
> people. As part of the process it assembles a "self", which
> can be thought of as the device we humans employ as
> a means of negotiating the social environment.[23]

That is, there is no little you sitting inside yourself busy creating meaning. You *are* your structure of meaning; your structure of meaning *is* you. Your structure of meaning creates meaning.

Only a very small portion of the meanings in your meaning structure are in words. Most are in the form of images. Some are visual images, others sounds and voices. You can have an image of your body adopting a particular position, or a tactile image where someone touches you or you touch them. Our images of scents and smells can be a powerful trigger to certain memories which are themselves images. Damasio wrote:

> Images are constructed either when we engage
> objects, from persons and places to toothaches, from
> the outside of the brain towards its inside; or when
> we reconstruct objects from memory, from the inside

out, as it were. The business of making images never
stops while we are awake and it even continues during
part of our sleep, when we dream. One might argue
that images are the currency of our minds.[24]

Many of these images were created long before we had a language in which to create meanings. Psychologists who study
infant development have devised experiments to see whether
babies develop certain concepts and whether the concepts
babies develop relate directly to the language the baby hears
spoken by those around him. In Korean there is a verb for placing something in a box where it fits tightly and another verb for
placing something in a box where it fits loosely, but in English,
as I have just shown, a string of words is needed to convey
each idea. Five-month-old infants were shown successive pairs
of objects where each pair was put together in either a tight-
fitting way or a loose-fitting way. Being curious, babies look
long and hard at something new but grow bored and look away
from things they have seen before. So by measuring how long a
baby looks at something psychologists can tell whether a baby
sees one thing as being different from another. The English
babies, having been shown loose-fitting boxes for so long they
got bored, looked with interest at a tight-fitting box because
they could see it was different. It was clear that at five months
babies who heard only English still grasped the concepts of
'tight fit' and 'loose fit'.[25]

Psychotherapists working with young children often report
that a child in play re-enacts what have been called implicit,
behavioural or enactive memories. Phil Mollon wrote:

Although absent from consciousness and from the
linguistic system, these memories may be startlingly
accurate; by contrast, verbal memory is dependent on
conscious awareness and is subject to a great many
distortions and creative embellishments. For example,
Terr found that amongst 20 children with documented
histories of trauma, none could give a verbal description
of events before two-and-a-half years, but 18 of these
showed evidence of a traumatic memory in their
behaviour and play; e.g., a child who had been sexually
molested by a babysitter in the first two years of life

could not, at age five, remember or name the babysitter
and also denied any knowledge of being abused, but
in his play he enacted scenes that exactly replicated
a pornographic movie made by the babysitter.[26]

We all have implicit memories from the first years of our life.
In the scale of possible horrors these memories may not be of
anything particularly traumatic, but, as they were of first-time
encounters, we found them surprising and perhaps shocking.
They may be memories of being inexpertly but lovingly held by
an older sibling at the start of what was to become a lifelong
friendship, or they may be of a lucky escape from death at the
hands of a firstborn angry at being displaced. As an adult the
firstborn may tell an amusing story about how he had tried to
rid the family of this interloper. The younger sibling does not
consciously remember the incident, perhaps where, at the top
of a steep hill, the older boy let the brake off on a pram in which
his baby brother slept, but he listens unsmiling and knows why
he has never trusted his brother.

Damasio uses the words *feeling* and *emotion* in order to distinguish between what we experience consciously and what
goes on unconsciously. Feelings are conscious and develop only
with the development of consciousness, but in the developing
brain emotions come early and continue to operate even though
we may have not conscious memory of them. Damasio was able
to demonstrate this with one of his patients, David, 'who had
one of the most severe defects in learning and memory ever
recorded, [and who] cannot learn any new fact at all.' Even so,
when David was subjected to a good guy–bad guy routine where
one member of staff was helpful to him and another member
not, and then given a task of selecting from four photographs
which of the individuals shown he would go to for help, he
chose the good guy over 80 per cent of the time, a result clearly
not simply chance. He had no recollection of meeting any of
these people before, although he had, but somehow the emotion
aroused in the good-guy–bad guy routine had not dissipated.[27]

Damasio needed to make a special distinction between feelings and emotion because of the nature of his neurological
research. As I am writing about meaning and not about neur-
ology, except to show how neurological research supports what

I am saying about meaning, I shall use the words emotion and feeling interchangeably.

Relationships between siblings are always very emotional affairs. Arguments between siblings are often contests in invalidating the other sibling. For example, consider that common situation where two adult siblings are reminiscing about their childhood:

> SIB 1: The Christmas I enjoyed the most was the one
> where we stayed with Auntie Jenny in Inverness.
> SIB 2: You weren't there. You had chicken-pox and
> you had to stay at home with Grandma.
> SIB 1: I *was* there. I've never forgotten how you ate
> too much Christmas pudding and threw up all over
> the dining room carpet. Poor Mother had a terrible
> time trying to clear up the mess you made.

*Invalidation by Sib 2* – Deny the other's factual truth. *Invalidation by Sib 1* – Force the other to feel shame and guilt. The invalidation by Sib 2 is disturbing to Sib 1 because part of Sib 1's meaning structure is thrown into doubt. However, the invalidation by Sib 1 is far more damaging because shame and guilt are the meanings which say that Sib 2's entire meaning structure is unacceptable. So this round of sibling argument is won by Sib 1.

*Emotions are the meanings involved in the survival or destruction of our sense of being a person.* They are the first meanings we are capable of creating. We are born with the bit of the brain that creates the simple emotions of fear and aggression. Fear and aggression have to do with both surviving physically, as a body, and surviving as a person. As our cortex develops and we are born, we meet other people and have to develop the complex emotions that arise out of our interactions with other people. We are born knowing how important it is to survive. The purpose of life is to live, and the purpose of being a person is to be a person. We want to do both, but, if we find ourselves in a situation where to be the person we know ourselves to be we have to give up our life, we do so. In acts of great heroism and in suicide the person has decided that to be the person that he knows himself to be he has to give up his life.

When congratulated for their courage, people who have risked their life to save others will often say, 'If I hadn't done that I couldn't have lived with myself.' For the 150th anniversary of the Victoria Cross in 2004 the psychologist Patrick Tissington made a psychological study of bravery by studying all the citations for this award. He said:

> If you examine all the citations, it is clear there is no one personality type that is more likely to show courage. All human life is there: from the decent, the moral and the upstanding to out-and-out scoundrels who would later end up in prison. One thing that is constant is that every VC holder appears genuinely surprised to have won it. This is not false modesty, but rather a feeling that they were just doing the right thing, doing their job. Those who cope best under fire are those with self-efficacy – the belief that you have some control over the outcome of events – and this is something that can be trained into you. There's also sometimes a hierarchy of competing fears. Many winners report that the fear of letting down their comrades – or the fear of being perceived to have let them down – was far stronger than any fear of the enemy. Faced with two poor options, the prospect of being killed in action was far more attractive than living with the knowledge that you could have done something for your comrades and didn't.[28]

People who decide to kill themselves feel that they have no self-efficacy save that of choosing when and how to die. The message that each leaves is often concerned with how he feels that there is no place for him in the society where he lives, or how he feels that the only way he can redeem himself and be the good person he wants to be is to kill himself. When Spinoza began to question his Jewish faith he knew how dangerous this was because he was well aware of the story of Uriel da Costa whom the synagogue in Amsterdam considered to have committed heresy in his book *Exemplar Vitae Humanae*. Da Costa was compelled to attend a gathering at the synagogue to recant his heresy so that all could see his repentance. There he had to confess his transgressions, and then he received 39 lashes to his bare back. Finally, he had to lie down on the threshold of the door so that every member of the congregation could step over him on their way out. He had now been forgiven and received back into the faith. He went home, finished writing his book, and shot himself.[29]

Some three centuries later and two years before he killed himself, writer and Holocaust survivor Jean Améry wrote *Hand an sich Legen,* a philosophical study of suicide. There he wrote, 'I die, therefore I am.'[30] Even though we can empathise with da Costa and with Jean Améry, we should never forget that, as the historian Lisa Lieberman writing about suicide said, 'Dying on your own terms is still dying.'[31]

Choosing death rather than being annihilated as a person can occur in far less extreme circumstances. My colleague John teaches at a university where the safety conscious authorities insist that the fire alarm be tested at frequent intervals. One morning when he was in his office trying to finish some urgent work the fire alarm sounded. John decided to stay in his office, lock his door and go on working. Some minutes later he heard the office doors along the corridor being unlocked, opened and then closed. This was likely to be the security guards checking to see that the building was empty. To avoid detection by the guards he hid behind his office door. He stood there for some minutes before it dawned on him that the unlocking and closing of doors that he had heard had been his colleagues returning to their rooms from the fire drill. He told me, 'I didn't mind being burnt to death but I wasn't going to be shamed by being found by the guards.' Shame is the feeling of being exposed as a nothing, a nobody.

Heroism and suicide involve emotional meanings which are far more complex than fear and aggression. As our brain develops and we start to interact with the world around us we develop other emotional meanings that involve moral ideas and other people, meanings such as love, shame, guilt, jealousy, and envy. Anxiety is the meaning 'My meanings may be about to be invalidated' or 'My predictions may be wrong.' Fear is the meaning 'My meanings are being invalidated.' Love is 'This person validates the most important part of my meanings.' Happiness is the meaning 'A significant part of my meanings is being validated.'

Our meaning structure operates on the principle of total self-interest. Its motivation is a kind of primitive pride which says, 'Everything and everybody must agree with me.' When everything and everybody fail to do this, primitive pride says, 'How dare they!' This is a system analogous to our body systems that serve to repair damage and ward off internal or external factors which could lead to illness or death. Like these, primitive pride can be very effective at protecting us in the short term, but these measures can work against us in the long term. An over-enthusiastic immune system can decide to kill our white blood cells while primitive pride can get us to take up a defensive position which leads to great unhappiness, yet from which we cannot escape.

Primitive pride operates very much like a doting mother who cannot hear a word said against her child and who expects the world to share her view that her child is amazingly wonderful. The world must. Primitive pride is affronted when the world fails to meet its needs. As adults we may like to think that we have outgrown primitive pride, but we have not. It is there in many of the meanings we call emotions. Anger is 'How dare you try to invalidate me or stop me from imposing my meanings on the world.' Envy is 'How dare you have something which I want.' Jealousy is 'How dare you have something which is rightly mine.'

Some emotional meanings incorporate a meaning about oneself and the consequences of one's actions. Guilt is 'I have failed to be what I should be and I shall be punished.' Shame is 'I am nothing and shall be exposed as being nothing.' An emotional meaning can incorporate a defence. Hostility is 'If you dare to try to invalidate me or stop me imposing my meanings on the world I shall attack you.' Hatred is 'You have tried to invalidate me and I shall invalidate you.' Revenge is 'You have tried to invalidate me but by attacking and invalidating you I shall be fully validated.'

Primitive pride is a way of creating meanings which are concerned solely with surviving as a person. These meanings are based on the fantasy that the person is the centre around which the rest of the world revolves. This fantasy is the opposite of realistic thinking when we know that we are but one of many millions in an infinite universe indifferent to our existence. In fantasy we see ourselves getting everything we want – in realistic thinking we know that we do not. In fantasy we can plan a revenge which will invalidate our enemy and triumphantly validate ourselves – in realistic thinking we know that revenge breeds revenge.

It is out of fantasy that primitive pride creates the defences that we use to hold our sense of being a person together. Freud regarded as very important the defence of projection where the person takes a part of himself and projects it on to something or somebody in the world around him. In one sense all of our meanings are projections. We take a meaning we have already created and see it existing in the world around us. However, there is a big difference between being aware that we have done this and not being aware. For instance, if you meet someone for the first time and think, 'This woman is just like my mother', you are well aware that you are seeing a stranger in a similar way to the way you perceived your mother. On the other hand, suppose you believe that to be envious is to be wicked and you want very much to think of yourself as being good. You learn that your brother has won a fortune on the lottery while you struggle to get by on your meagre salary. Your reaction to the news of your brother's win is 'How dare he have something which I want', but you cannot admit to yourself that you envy your brother. You tell yourself that you do not envy your brother. You take pride in the generous way you have responded to his win, and you tell yourself and others that you rejoice in his good fortune. Then you start to notice how your brother's friends and colleagues envy him. In reality they may or may not envy him, but this is how you see them. You have projected your envy on to them. You tell your brother that you have noticed that his friends and colleagues envy him and you commiserate with him because being envied can be unpleasant, even dangerous. You tell him you will do what you can to protect him from other people's envy, and with this you assure yourself that you are virtuous. Meanwhile, your own emotional truth 'How dare my brother have something which I want' has not disappeared but festers and in clandestine ways reveals itself in the sharpness of the jokes and comments you make about your brother.

This kind of projection, where we take something inside us and see it as existing outside us but deny to ourselves that we have done this, is a defence which we acquire when we are learning to be good. Babies are not born worrying about being good. They arrive in the world full of unself-conscious self-confidence, but they soon lose this as the world around tells them they must be good because as they are they are unacceptable. Learning to be good is a defence which we learn as a way of warding off the fear we feel when the adults we depend upon show us that we are not acceptable. Being good means seeing yourself as never being good enough. We are taught that only bad people see themselves as being satisfactory. Good people always strive to do better. Learning to be good may allow us to fit into society, but it also leaves us in constant need of defences. We set ourselves standards, and when we fail to live up to those standards our sense of being a person is threatened. A small child engaged in trying to reconcile his need to be good with his need to be the person he is discovering himself to be also discovers shame, feeling that he is exposed and vulnerable to annihilation, and even wanting annihilation in order to escape from the mocking, hostile eyes that are upon him. Small children often discover shame at the hands of their older siblings who laugh at them and scorn them for being unable to control their sphincter muscles and do the things they can do. Learning to be good is also learning to feel guilt. Again a small child is often judged and found wanting by his older siblings. Shame and guilt threaten our sense of being a person and so we create defences against them.

In learning to be good we develop a number of defences which we regard as sensible habits. As infants we are often overwhelmed by a succession of events which we can neither predict nor understand. We soon learn that expressing our distress by throwing ourselves down on the floor and screaming is not appreciated by adults, so we have to find ways of organising our environment or at least that bit of our environment over which we have some control. Certain toys must be kept constantly at hand and at different times arranged in a particular way. We see certain articles of clothing as being secure and manageable so we insist on wearing them despite our mother's preference for other garments. We feel we gain some control over time by insisting that certain events occur with predictable regularity and that the rituals of having a bath and going to bed should always be performed in an unvarying way. Thus we can come to feel safe because it seems to us that we have control over space and time. If our parents and siblings respect our wishes for such regularity and try to conform to them, we conclude that our methods of control are effective and so we continue to use them. Over the years they mutate into our adult habits of cleanliness and organisation.

However, if our parents and siblings fail to respect our wishes, we become more and more frightened. We can feel utterly helpless; that we are a mere thing flung this way and that by powerful people and unpredictable events. Or, the more frightened we become, the more we cling even more tightly to our strategy of obtaining control over our dangerous environment and repeat endlessly our demands and our rituals, all in the hope that these might magically work and give us safety. Even if our parents understand and respect our need for organisation and control, our siblings see our need as a weakness which they can exploit. It should not be surprising that some of the fiercest battles of childhood are fought over things and the placement and use of things.

Siblings are able to keep themselves safe and demonstrate their power when they forbid their siblings to touch their things and the other siblings obey. When I was a child my sister, who was six years older than me, absolutely forbade me even to come close to any of her possessions. If I dared to approach anything she owned she would yell at me, and woe betide me if she discovered that I had touched something of hers when she was not looking. Her proudest possession was a pair of white china dogs called Gog and Magog which stood on the hearth in the living room. They were a family heirloom given to her by her paternal grandmother whom I had never known as she died before I was born. This knowledge, and before that the fear my sister had evoked in me when I simply crawled in the direction of the dogs, led me to invest the dogs with an awe and reverence approaching that which religious people feel for their sacred objects. Many years later, after our parents had died and my sister had the task of disposing of all their possessions, she summoned me on one of my visits to Australia to the room where she stored certain things she had yet to deal with. She showed me the china dogs which were wrapped most disrespectfully in newspaper and instructed me to take them back with me to England. I was dumbfounded. I was still scared to touch these dogs, and now I had the job of transporting them safely back to England. With my friend Nan to help and advise me we packed and shipped the sacred objects and I installed them in a place in my house where I hoped they would be safe. A year later my sister changed her mind and demanded the dogs back. By then I had got used to them; their sacredness had worn off. On my next visit to Australia I packed them in my suitcase and returned them to my sister. She presented them to her granddaughter who I hope will treat them with the reverence they deserve. They had the power to create a fear that lasted some sixty-odd years.

In this account of our greatest fear and our defences against it I have tried to describe how each of us as an individual operates as a meaning-creating creature, but at every stage of the account it is necessary to talk about the presence of other people. This is the dilemma with which we have to live. We cannot help but live in our own individual world of meaning, yet we cannot create meanings which relate in any realistic way to our life and the world we share with other people unless we are in contact with them. Left to ourselves we would live solely in fantasy, completely out of touch with reality. A few of the children completely abandoned by adults have survived physically by living with animals, but even if found and introduced to a human way of life they never fully join the human race. Wars and conflicts have given us far more evidence than we ever needed that babies and infants who may be adequately fed and kept warm but never conversed with by adults will, even if they survive physically, never become fully human. To learn to speak, babies have to hear people speaking. Babies create meanings but they need other people to tell them just how accurate these meanings are. They need other people to explain the world to them. Such explanations may or may not prove useful but in the act of explaining something to a child an adult validates that child. Understanding something more of the world, the child feels more self-confident and the fact that the adult noticed the child and held him in his vision confirms the child in the reality of his own existence.

The only positive memories I have of my sister are of those occasions when she decided to instruct me on some matter. She was training to be a home science teacher and loved imparting knowledge to the ignorant. In referring to me my sister always used the word 'brainy' with the same contempt she used the word 'fat', but occasionally she appreciated that I was a quick and willing pupil. She taught me the correct way to make a bed and to lay a table. She introduced me to the theory of evolution, though perhaps it was not quite accurate. She said it all began in the land between the Tigris and the Euphrates where the Garden of Eden had once been. Our mother refused to discuss any aspect of sex so when my periods started when I was 11 it was my sister who explained to me what had happened. She made no mention of men so it was not until I went to university six years later that that part of the mystery was solved. However, I was profoundly grateful to my sister for taking the time to instruct me on all these matters.

No doubt in teaching me my sister increased her confidence in her ability to teach. For another older sibling teaching a younger meant sharing his own delight in learning. As the poet Michael Rosen told me, whatever Brian, his older brother, discovered his first thought was always, 'I must tell Mick.' He was, 'desperately interested in teaching me. Anything he learnt at school, he thought he had to come home and teach me. So he taught me to read. I can remember I was probably four and a half to five – he would have been eight or nine. I can see him sitting there with these word lists, these bloody word lists at the back of the book, getting me to read the words out. And you can multiply that times a million. Much later on, when he was getting excited about Beethoven and Mozart, he would sit there playing me Beethoven and Mozart saying, "There's the theme. See the recapitulation of the theme?" And when he was taught calculus – in his fifth year of secondary, and I was either last year primary or first year secondary – trying to teach me calculus! "Look, it's ever so easy – you just sort of rotate the curve." And sometimes I'd get these things, and sometimes I wouldn't. I benefited enormously from it, and he seemed to me to be almost multi-talented: he could do watercolours, he could sing, he could do maths, he could do science, he was quite good at sport – and it had that effect as a child that sometimes I wanted to do it, but sometimes I thought, "No, I can't do that, because that's his game." So it had a double effect.'

Most of the events in our lives have two or more effects,

particularly events which involve other people. Living with other people is extremely difficult; living without other people is impossible. We need other people to validate us; other people's actions and our emotional meanings created in response to other people's actions can invalidate us. Our parents validate and invalidate us, but even more so do our siblings. No wonder we create an attachment to them of both love and hate.

# Chapter 2

# A RELATIONSHIP LIKE NO OTHER

During the Second World War many thousands of children and babies were separated from their parents. A lucky few were rescued and brought up by caring adults but many died while others were crowded into orphanages and given food and water but no personal, individual attention. At the end of the war those who had survived the orphanages were found to be rather strange children who did not fit easily into what might be called ordinary life. Meanwhile in South America a psychiatrist called Rene Spitz was studying babies in an orphanage where they were given adequate physical care but who were deprived of human company, even of the sight of other babies in cots nearby. Spitz found that a large percentage of these babies grew grey, wasted away and died. He called this disease *anaclitic depression*. It was clear to him that there must be more to the mother and child relationship than simply mother love.

In England John Bowlby followed Spitz's work by looking at what happened to young children when they went into a hospital where parents were not encouraged to visit their children. He found that at first the children cried in protest at the separation then grew silent and fell into an apathy which the reappearance of their parents did little to change. From these studies and others that followed Bowlby developed his theory of attachment whereby the baby forms what Bowlby called 'an internal working model' of the mother based on not just what she looks, sounds and smells like but on what she does and how well she meets the baby's needs. The baby's prime need is to feel secure, so the baby who gets this from his mother soon becomes strongly and positively attached to her. A baby whose need to feel secure is met only intermittently or not at all forms a different kind of attachment. The different kinds of attachments were studied by Mary Ainsworth, and her work and that of Bowlby laid the foundation for what is now a huge area of research based on the theory of attachment. Type 'mother–child attachment' into Google and up will come many thousands of references.

The early work on attachment used the term 'mother–child', but it was soon realised that the mother to whom a baby could become attached was not necessarily the baby's biological mother. The term was changed to 'mothering figure' but it became clear that the mothering figure did not necessarily have to be female. So now the term commonly used is the unisex 'caregiver'.

The way 'caregiver' is used seems to imply that the caregiver is an adult, yet in fact the majority of children across the world are brought up by their siblings. In the developing countries a mother who has to work keeps a newborn baby with her for the first few months but once weaned the baby is handed to a sibling who may be only a few years older than the baby. Some of these siblings are quite skilled in meeting the baby's needs but others lack the skill or the concern. No doubt there are many babies who form attachments to their siblings which could in Mary Ainsworth's terms be described as 'anxious/avoidant' or 'anxious/resistant'. In both these forms of attachment the infants know that they need the caregiver but find that the caregiver fails to help them feel secure. In this situation some infants find it best to avoid the caregiver where possible while other infants want the caregiver to be around but resist the caregiver's attempts to make them feel secure.

When large families were the norm in the developed countries older siblings often became the attachment figure, the caregiver. In working-class families older children had to care for younger ones while in middle-class and upper-class families, where the parents played no direct part in the upbringing of their children who were looked after by a series of nursemaids and governesses, a younger child's closest relationship was likely to be with an older sibling. In her autobiography Diana Mosley, born in 1910, one of the famous Mitford girls, speaks with awe and admiration of her father, Lord Redesdale, who expected that everyone, family and visitors, conformed to his eccentric rules and customs. But in her account of her childhood she mentions her mother, 'Muv', only in passing as someone who just happened to be there. All of her first memories are of her nanny. She wrote:

> After tea I used to sit for a little while on her lap. She paid no attention to me but went on talking to Ida, our nurserymaid. Then she put me down in a hurry saying: 'Come along now, you children, hurry up and get dressed.' We were changed into clean frocks and taken down to the drawing room to see Muv. An hour later Nanny fetched us, it was bedtime. I said my prayer to her: God bless Mother and Father, sisters and brothers, Nanny and Ada and Ida, and make Diana a good girl amen.[1]

Just one year older than her was her brother Tom:

> With Nanny and Ida we went for walks: they only took the upright pram and often Pam was in it because she had infantile paralysis, so I had to trudge, and very hot and tired I used to get. Tom and I generally went hand in hand, and he never stopped talking. I loved to listen to him; he was the cleverest person I knew except Nancy, and she did lessons with the governess and was far too grand to bother with us.[2]

Forty years later Tom was killed in the war:

> A telegram came to say Tom was wounded. I knew instantly he had died. Near in age, we had always been more like twins than brother and sister. A day never passes when I do not think of him and mourn my loss. He was clever, wise and beautiful; he loved women, and music, and his family.[3]

Nanny may have kept Diana physically secure but it was her brother Tom who maintained her sense of being a valuable person. This was a secure attachment in which there was a great deal of mutual love. However, attachment should not be equated with love. We can love someone and still let that person go, but attachment means hanging on, not wanting to let go, yet at the same time we can be resenting the loss of our freedom. One woman described to me how the Irish village where she grew up was one where 'everyone was close'. She spoke with great warmth of the way in which everyone knew one another and helped one another, quite unlike Londoners who keep themselves to themselves. Then she said, 'Of course, when I was 16 I couldn't get out of the village fast enough. I wouldn't go back there to live.' Attachment always involves degrees of love and hate. We can be attached by bonds of hate just as strongly as we can be attached by bonds of love.

A child's attachment to his parent is always fraught with love and hate because if the parent has the power to protect him he also has the power to hurt him, and because the attachment inhibits his independence and freedom. However, a child grows up and in the ordinary course of events these issues are resolved. The child becomes an adult who takes responsibility for himself, and the parent–child attachment changes to a disinterested loving relationship between two adults. Of course this does not happen in all parent–child attachments, but what we could call the natural history of attachment gives us a baseline against which to measure each individual parent–child attachment. Attachments between siblings do not have a natural history.

As we shall see, many of the processes which bond the child to the parent are also active in creating the bond between siblings. However, there are some significant differences. In some parent–child relationships the parent and child compete for the love of the parent's partner, but in all sibling relationships the siblings compete for their parents' attention, approval and love. The sibling bond develops and the rivalry is enacted in an arena where the parents' perception of each child and the events in the life of the family all play a very significant role. Many siblings who fought with, loved and were attached to one another grow up and become adults who share a close friendship, but there are so many possible variations in this development and so many siblings who never become friends that it is impossible to describe a natural history of sibling attachment. However, sibling attachments are so important in the lives of most of us that we must try to understand them. In some attachments love prevails, in others the main theme is rivalry, and in yet others the hate and neediness destroy the two partners.

Primo Levi's biographer Carole Angier described how, when

Primo Levi's sister Anna Maria was born just 18 months after him, 'he waited impatiently for her to grow up, so that he could talk to her. .. when he was seven and she was five, he sat her down beside their cousin Giulia, who was also five, and taught them how to form the letters he had just learnt at school . . . as brother and sister grew older, they grew closer, until they seemed to be able to communicate without speaking. They invented a private language which not even their parents could understand; and thought and spoke so quickly that they were hard to follow even in Italian.'[4] Carole Angier quotes Primo Levi's first biographer, Fiora Vincenti, who wrote

> It would not be accurate to call this merely affection
> between brother and sister. The bond which grew
> between the two children, and which existed ever
> since, was certainly something more: a spiritual
> affinity, which expressed itself in solidarity and
> profound understanding. Levi does not hesitate to call
> the emotional bond between himself and his sister
> fundamental for his development as a human being:
> the bond which, in more ways than one, helped him to
> overcome the obstacles of his extreme introversion.[5]

Primo Levi's introversion was not simply shyness, though as a child he was very shy. It was reserve – what Carole Angier called 'his most characteristic and unvarying trait'.[6] A shy, reserved person needs a partner who is outgoing and can do his socialising for him. Primo found such a partner in his sister Anna Maria who, though reserved, was 'confident, outgoing, attractive . . . He was older and his intellect and knowledge superior. But if either was the leader, it was Anna Maria; if either was the protector of the other, it was not Primo of Anna Maria, but the other way around.'[7] When siblings complement one another in this way they form an attachment which can weather many storms because in such an attachment each validates the other. When Carole Angier set about the enormous task of gathering the necessary information about Primo Levi for her autobiography, Anna Maria refused to speak to her. Anna had spoken to another biographer of Primo Levi, Ian Thomson, but she told him nothing that was not already common knowledge.[8] Biographers are a scurrilous lot, well known for ferreting out the less savoury aspects of their subject's life. Anna Maria saw her task of validating her brother as going on forever.

In Hollywood in the 1940s, Joan Fontaine and Olivia de Haviland were famous not just for their acting and their romances but also for their rivalry as sisters. The family was living in Japan when Joan was born in 1917. She was just 15 months younger than her sister Olivia. Fifty-eight years later Joan decided to write her autobiography *No Bed of Roses* after their mother died and Olivia neglected to invite her to the funeral. Joan wrote: 'Only after burning the telephone wires from coast to coast were my daughter and I permitted to attend.'[9] Her autobiography tells of her career and her marriages, but the constant theme of the book is the relationship between the two sisters. Joan wrote:

> Because of eczema from a diet of goat's milk, I was
> swathed in cotton wool from head to toe until I was
> almost two. Mother was highly 'germ-conscious' and
> insisted on strict nursery procedures, a fact which kept
> the sisters apart, creating a breach we were never to
> span. Brown-eyed, olive-skinned Olivia, Mother told me,
> never toddled towards the crib of her tow-haired, hazel-
> eyed baby sister. . . . Perhaps my being a puny child had
> a great deal to do with her resentment, as I am sure
> I was a fretful infant, and in the nursery she was no
> longer pre-eminent with the servants or her parents.[10]

In comparing their lives Joan noted: 'From birth we were not encouraged by our parents or nurses to be anything but rivals, and our careers only emphasised the situation.'[11] When Joan was six the family moved to California where at Stanford University in Palo Alto, Lewis Terman needed gifted children as subjects for the Stanford-Binet Intelligence Test which he was developing. Both Joan and Olivia were tested but Olivia was ill that day and Joan scored higher than her. Joan wrote:

> Unfortunately Olivia was told of the results of both
> our tests. Joan was undeniably her enemy. Besides the
> inexcusable intrusion into her life – that of Joan's birth –
> this latest display of arrogance was the last straw
> for the older sister. I regret that I remember not one
> act of kindness from her through my childhood.[12]

In 1941 both Joan and Olivia were on the short list for a Hollywood Oscar. Joan won. She wrote:

> I froze. I stared across the table where Olivia was sitting
> directly opposite me. 'Get up there, get up there,' she
> whispered commandingly. Now what had I done! All
> the animus we'd felt towards each other as children, the
> hair-pulling, the savage wrestling matches, the time
> Olivia fractured my collarbone, all came rushing back
> in kaleidoscopic imagery. My paralysis was total. I felt
> that Olivia would spring across the table and grab me
> by the hair. I felt aged four, being confronted by my
> older sister. Damn, I'd incurred her wrath again . . .
> Actually Olivia took the situation very graciously.[13]

In 1946 Olivia won the Oscar: 'After Olivia delivered her acceptance speech and entered the wings, I, standing close by, went over to congratulate her. She took one look at me, ignored my outstretched hand, clutched her Oscar to her bosom, and wheeled away just as *Photoplay*'s photographer captured the moment with his camera.'[14] Perhaps Olivia feared that Joan might snatch the Oscar away from her!

Some siblings compete with one another simply because such competition adds excitement and interest to their lives but for others, like Joan and Olivia, the rivalry is far more important than that. As each sibling sees it, the success of the other means the invalidation of the one who lost. Every competition, be it over IQ tests or Oscars, is a fight to the death. One sibling may not want to engage in this battle, but if the other sibling sees her rival's successes as her own invalidation she will attack her rival who will then have to defend herself.

J. R. Ackerley's biographer, Peter Parker, wrote that Joe Ackerley was for a quarter of a century 'an important figure on the British literary scene. From 1935 to 1959, Ackerley was literary editor of the BBC's weekly magazine *The Listener*, where he created some of the liveliest and most authoritative arts pages to be found in any journal of that period. . . . "By common consent he was the greatest Literary Editor of his time – perhaps of all time," wrote the distinguished journalist and editor Anthony Howard.'[15] Peter Parker's biography runs to 465 pages but only 11 of those pages are devoted to Ackerley's childhood, even though the family was a most peculiar one and Ackerley himself a very unusual person, as was his sister, Nancy West.

Peter Parker tells how Ackerley's mother, Netta, an actress, disliked sexual intercourse and tried to abort two of her three children. She possessed what Peter Parker calls 'an almost terminal vagueness. Although she was unaware of the fact, Netta lived largely in a world of her own, only occasionally making contact with the lives of others. She often literally had no idea what day it was. Part of her trouble was that she never quite recovered from her early on-stage success as an *ingénue,* and it was a role she continued to play throughout her life, to increasingly macabre effect.'[16]

The father, Roger, kept a bachelor flat in central London and, unknown to his wife and children, a second family conveniently placed on Roger's route from home to his office in London. He believed that the rearing of children was 'an entirely female preserve'. 'A succession of female relations, nursemaids and housekeepers assisted Netta in bringing up the babies.'[17]

The first child, Peter, was born in 1895, Joe in 1896 and Nancy in 1899. Peter was sent away to a prep school in 1907 and Joe followed him in 1908. This meant that the three children were together at home for nine years in the care of servants and a mother, a childlike figure lost in her own fantasies. Much must have happened to the children in that time but the participants and witnesses were silent on the matter. Nancy made no record of her life. In his memoir *My Father and Myself,* Joe wrote at length about his brother Peter, but mentioned Nancy only to disparage her. Writing about his father he said:

> To what extent he directed his business I do not know; he certainly did not direct his home. Even in family quarrels, the only ones we ever had, the jealous disputes that broke out between my sister and mother, he seldom intervened, he did not take sides and put people in their places, though there were many times when he should have done so.[18]

Yet Joe and Nancy's lives were far from separate. Peter was killed in 1918 in the last weeks of the war. Nancy married in 1926 and went to Panama to live but the marriage did not last. She returned from Panama in 1932 and, according to Peter Parker, she 'threw herself and her child upon Ackerley's mercy.

This was the position she was to adopt for the rest of her brother's life.'[19] He went on: '"Rejected" by her husband, unable to cope with a young son who himself was showing signs of disturbance, and at war with her mother, Nancy saw her brother as a lifeline and she clung to him with all the tenacity of someone who is drowning.'[20]

Here Peter Parker is reflecting the view that all of Joe's friends took of Nancy, all except one, Francis King, who edited *My Sister and Myself: The Diaries of J. K. Ackerley*. When Joe died in 1967 Nancy, who had lived with Joe ever since her attempted suicide in 1949, gave Francis a large parcel which proved to be Joe's diaries from August 1948 to July 1957. Here Joe wrote about his friends who included E. M. Forster and James Kirkup, men who shared and understood Joe's situation as a homosexual man at a time when homosexuality was illegal. They understood the loneliness and yearning for love when even the public suspicion of homosexuality, much less a conviction for this crime, led to public ruin and, in the case of a conviction, a jail sentence. When homosexuality ceased to be a criminal offence many homosexual men were able to form lifelong, loving, publicly recognised attachments. However, many homosexual men have as an ideal lover a person who is impossible to find, and as a result they spend the best years of their life in a hopeless search. Had Joe devoted to writing the time and effort he devoted to risky sexual adventures he would have left behind a large body of outstanding work and not just three small books and a handful of essays. He found no sexual peace until he acquired a dog, Queenie, who became the one great passion in his life. He wrote: 'Looking at her sometimes I used to think that the Ideal Friend, whom I no longer wanted, should have been an animal-man, the mind of my bitch, for instance, in the body of my sailor, the perfect male body always at one's service through the devotion of a faithful and uncritical beast.'[21]

In October 1948 Joe went to visit Nancy who then was living in a room in Worthing. His account of this visit would remind many readers only too vividly of those visits many of us make to relatives and friends whose conversations are made up solely of complaints and excuses as to why they have done nothing to resolve their difficulties. At the end of this account he wrote:

Once she had youth, beauty, money, husband, child, a
home of her own; now, a woman nearing fifty, she lives
quite alone, absolutely friendless, in poky bedsitting
rooms at 35s. a week, cooking on a hotplate and washing
up her dishes in her bedroom in a tin basin. Once she
had the world at her feet. Now she has nothing and no
one, only me. And to me she is devoted; I get, when she is
calm, the best of her nature; yet how terrible she is.[22]

How was it that a brother and sister, so intelligent, talented,
once so lively and beautiful, could in middle age have become
so frustrated and unhappy? Why could they not live independently of one another? Joe often claimed that he wanted to get
rid of Nancy and he frequently recorded how she would berate
him for his selfishness and lack of consideration, but as much
as they wished to separate they wanted to stay together.

The reason lies in what psychologists call the Principle of
Partial Reinforcement. This principle keeps gamblers chained
to the gaming table no matter how much they lose, smokers,
alcoholics and drug addicts to their noxious substances no
matter how ill they become, abused women unable to leave
their abusive partner, my depressed clients anxiously attached
to hurtful mothers, and siblings unable to be together or apart.
It is a principle we all understand. If when we carry out a particular action we invariably get exactly what we want, we soon
come to take for granted the source of that reward. Mothers
who wait on their children hand and foot and accept whatever
the children do without criticism or correction soon find themselves relegated to the role of servant and doormat. If when we
carry out a particular action we are invariably punished, we
try never to perform that action again. As toddlers we discover
the pain that strong heat invariably gives us and so we try
never to burn ourselves again. However, when we carry out a
particular action and find that sometimes we are rewarded and
sometimes we are punished, we keep going back time and time
again, enduring the punishment in hope of the reward.

This was the nature of Joe and Nancy's attachment. Joe's
account of their life together between 1948 and 1957 reads
like a dreadful play where one scene is repeated over and over
with mounting horror. As an example, Joe recorded how when

Nancy was still living in Worthing he arranged to meet her at Haywards Heath for a walk. He wanted to get away once the walk was over but she wanted them to have tea. He agreed, but when he then tried to leave she protested, 'Oh Joe, you're *not* sending me back to that room! Oh Joe, you *can't* do it, you can't do it. O please Joe, oh don't I beg you. I can't stand it, I can't, I can't. I'm frightened! I'm frightened! I think all the time of suicide. I shall kill myself, I know. Oh Joe, *don't, don't!*' He tried to calm her with a hug and explanations about his situation in his small flat but she said, 'No, no, it's got to happen now, now. I can't wait any longer. You're just fobbing me off as you always do. You'll just go back and forget all about me.'[23] He kissed her and petted her but all he wanted to do was get his train home. He wrote in his diary:

> But I was dreadfully worried about the whole business. Besides the anger I felt against such behaviour, and the hatred I feel towards her for this sort of emotional blackmail she so constantly subjects me to, there had been a sort of frantic note the whole time that frightened and worried me. And I feel so dreadfully sorry for her, possessed by such jealousy, yet so sweet with her gifts and her pullovers and her restlessly fidgeting fingers.[24]

Next morning he sent Nancy a cheque for £50 to buy some winter clothes. She returned the cheque with a letter where she said, 'You have gone out of your way to make me feel like an exile, no welcome in the only home left to me to go to.' She ended her letter with, 'Please don't ring up any more, or try to come here. I would much rather be left alone now.' Joe responded with 'I went out directly after breakfast and sent her a wire to say that I had an invitation for her to the flat, and was writing, love Joe.'[25]

Joe and Nancy must have developed this well-practised drama in the nine years they spent together as children. As a small child Nancy was exquisite and Joe was a most beautiful boy. Nancy always said that Peter was her favourite brother but Joe must have fascinated her. Joe would have done what big brothers usually do, play with his little sister and tease her and sometimes the teasing would go too far, especially when Nancy failed to do exactly what Joe wanted. A complaint which recurs in Joe's diary about Nancy and women generally is that they do not do what Joe wants them to do. When they were children Joe would have used his teasing to punish Nancy. When she complained loudly about this their mother and the nursery maids would no doubt scold Joe. From this Joe would have learnt to feel guilty about Nancy, and to feel angry with Nancy for making him feel guilty. Nancy learned that the best way to get Joe to do what she wanted him to do was to make him feel anxious and guilty, and she could achieve this by making an enormous fuss. Noisy complaints from Nancy were an effective way of getting her mother's attention while her father would seek to quell the noise by indulging her with gifts and treats. Joe would try to escape from her but would be drawn back to her by his need to expunge his guilt. Both parents lacked the wit to see what was going on between Joe and Nancy and help them change this kind of interaction, so it persisted for the rest of their lives.

When Joe reluctantly retired from *The Listener* he had little to do. Not long before Joe's death a friend lent him his house in Brighton for a fortnight. This house was almost opposite where Francis King lived. In his introduction to *My Sister and Myself* Francis King wrote:

> Joe had now long ceased to be literary editor of *The Listener*
> and, frequently idle and bored, had taken to drinking
> heavily. Nancy, who had always shown a pathetic eagerness
> to share in all his activities, shared in this one too. Almost
> every morning of that holiday in Brighton, they would
> make their way down to our local, the Temple Bar, just
> before it opened; and, just after it had closed, one would
> see them dragging their way slowly up the hill again, back
> to the once spotless house that Nancy rarely cleaned.[26]

He went on:

> At the time of these diaries Joe's and Nancy's symbiosis
> was a ghastly caricature of the kind of marriage, devoid of
> sex, that is held together merely by feelings of obligation,
> pity and guilt. But, as in many such marriages, the
> two participants, exhausted by their own conflicts,
> eventually reached an undemanding and even mutually

helpful *modus vivendi*. Joe's friends, many of them women-haters, would often say that Nancy had ruined his life; but it could be said with no more injustice that, kind only to be cruel, he had subtly ruined hers.[27]

Victor Cicirelli, a psychologist who has carried out extensive research into sibling relationships, tried to describe these relationships in terms of three interconnected dimensions, affectional closeness, rivalry and involvement, dimensions which relate respectively to the relationships between Primo and Anna Maria, Joan and Olivia, and Joe and Nancy. He summarised research by other psychologists who had tried to create different typologies of sibling relationships and concluded: 'They share the problems common to all typologies: difficulty in classifying all cases, and use of nominal measurement which does not allow for degrees of variation within a type.'[28] That is, sibling relationships vary so much that they cannot be fitted into the neat boxes which psychologists like to create. Affection may predominate in Primo's and Anna Maria's relationship, rivalry in that of Joan and Olivia, and the hate and neediness of intense involvement in that of Joe and Nancy, but elements of affection, rivalry, hate and need are there in different measure in each of the three relationships. Such is the nature of sibling attachment.

### Sibling attachment: the younger child

Popular though attachment theory is, it is not without its critics. Judy Dunn, whose studies of sibling relationships are widely acclaimed, found that 'one limitation of the idea of the internal working model is that it is so vaguely conceived that it can be used to explain almost everything. What exactly is an internal working model? The answers range widely.'[29] Judy Dunn went on to list nine different interpretations of the internal working model. I shall spare you, dear reader, a description of what these different interpretations are because to do so I would have to resort to 'psychologese' and I try never to inflict that on anyone. It is not surprising that Judy Dunn can list nine interpretations. She could have listed ninety-nine or a million and nine. All the people who heard John Bowlby lec-

ture or who read his books created their own individual interpretation of the 'internal working model'.

In her writings Judy Dunn frequently comments on 'the
dramatically wide range of individual differences in the quality
of the relationship between siblings'.[30] She wrote that in 1984,
but by 1993 she was writing very cautiously that 'the possibility
that processes of a cognitive-attributional nature may be important'.[31] 'Cognitive-attributional' is psychologese for the way
in which we interpret, give meaning to, what we encounter. By
then she was well aware that while outside observers think
siblings grow up in the same environment, they actually grow
up in different environments because each child perceives the
environment in his or her own individual way.[32]

When psychologists write textbooks and research articles
they are writing for their colleagues. They have to be very
careful about how they do this. Slander a psychologist about
his love life and all that will cause is much enjoyable gossip
amongst his colleagues, but criticise a psychologist's beloved
theory or, worse, produce evidence that the theory is wrong and
you can be embarking on a fight unto death. Psychologists are
only human. If as a psychologist you have invested years of
your working life researching a particular theory, if all your
professional publications are based on this theory, and if your
professional reputation is built on the accuracy of this theory,
then the theory becomes part of your identity and to attack it
is to attack you as a person. Criticism of the theory threatens
you with invalidation.

From the beginnings of the academic study of psychology in
the late nineteenth century, psychologists have always taken
the stance that they are studying their subject matter, people,
objectively in the same way as geologists study rocks. They
tried to ignore the fact that, while rocks do not study geologists,
the subjects of a psychologist's study study the psychologist.
The school of psychology which dominated the profession in the
twentieth century, behaviourism, taught that what went on in
a person's mind was unimportant and all that mattered was
what the person did. When a psychiatrist and psychoanalyst
Aaron Beck showed a direct link between the ideas a person
held and the depression the person was experiencing, psychologists were forced to take notice. However, they were comforted

by the terminology Beck had chosen. A depressed person's ideas were 'dysfunctional cognitions' and the psychologists, being untroubled by dysfunctional cognitions of any sort, could put the person right. Psychologists who practise what they call 'cognitive behaviour therapy' have always been remarkably reluctant to admit that our thoughts determine our actions.

Psychologists have always wanted their study of people and animals to be a science – the equal of physics and chemistry. The fact that people think and interpret has always been an impediment to this. Physics and chemistry and the various sciences that followed in their wake study objects which are separate from the sciences themselves. Their work is based on definitions where the object being studied is defined in terms of some other things. Astronomers and geologists can define the moon as a rock which travels around the sun. Thus the moon is a rock, not a cloud, and it travels outside the earth, not inside it. In contrast, look up the words 'thought', 'idea', 'belief' and 'opinion' in any dictionary and you will find that these three words are each defined in terms of the others but basically they all mean the same thing, something that people do in the privacy of their own heads. These four words can be used interchangeably though with some fine distinctions concerning the appropriate situation where they might be used. These words cannot be defined in terms of anything outside themselves. They all refer to an activity we know so well, that is, that we are continually investing ourselves and our world with meaning.

Meaning is impossible to define clearly and unambiguously because it has no opposite with which it can be contrasted. We cannot conceive of the opposite of 'meaning'. We do use the word 'meaningless', but then we mean 'I can't quite work out what meaning best to give to this situation' or 'This situation is unacceptable', which is what people mean when they talk about 'meaningless violence'.

Whatever we encounter we invest with meaning. We live in meaning like a fish lives in water. To step out of meaning is to die.

We are meaning-creating creatures. We live to create meaning, and we create meaning in order to live.

The purpose of life is to live and human beings are remarkably efficient in adapting themselves to whatever is available that will help them stay alive. We eat whatever food our environment provides; we adapt our day-to-day habits to the climate; and we form relationships with whatever people are around us. Thus, in forming attachments, a baby does the best he can with what is on offer. No mother is perfect and siblings can help make up for her deficits.

In the literature of attachment theory the baby's development of the internal working model of his mother is so important that the other internal working models which the baby is creating are overlooked. Siblings are rarely mentioned. Neither are fathers. Judy Dunn commented: 'The great majority of parenting studies are studies of mothers' behaviour. We are still strikingly ignorant about many aspects of fathers' behaviour and relationships.'[33] What is also forgotten is that the baby is also hard at work trying to make sense of the world into which he has been born. Babies look hard and long at the world around them, and when faces swim into their view they try to make sense of the face and the context together.

At five months May is on her baby bouncer on the kitchen floor and sees Milo coming close to her and moving away. Sometimes he is quiet and sometimes he is noisy as he plays with his toy train and fights with his older brother Fred. Next day May is in her mother's car in her carrycot. She faces the back of the car. Milo close beside her is strapped into his child's seat. He cannot move away but he can make a noise until shushed by his mother who, at the wheel, is directly in front of May. Milo stretches out his arm, touches May's cheek and says, 'Baby.' He turns to me sitting beside him and again stretches out his arm to touch May's cheek and says in explanation to me, 'Baby.'

May watches all this very intently. It is not just her internal working model of Milo that she is creating. She is also learning, amongst other things, the contrasting concepts of near and far. People and objects can be near and far; sounds can be near and far. She cannot see her mother but the sound of her mother's voice tells her that her mother is not far away.

Newborn babies have been shown to prefer to watch people in movement rather than objects in movement. Research by Andrew Meltzoff and others has shown that infants gradually develop an understanding of why people do what they do, what psychologists call a 'theory of mind'. To understand why a person does what he does we need to know the context in which the person carries out his action. We cannot understand why a man strikes a match unless we know that he is in a kitchen and standing in front of a gas ring, or that he is beside some tinder-dry undergrowth which, once lit, will start a bushfire. As she stares around her a baby is creating many internal working models. She is creating many meanings which develop and change with every new experience.

A baby's first meaning for her mother is made up of sound, smell and sight. Before they are born babies know the sound of their mother's voice and very likely the sound of their siblings' voices. Even though the sounds in the mother's environment are to some degree muffled by the mother's own body and the noise made by her heart pumping and her blood flowing, recordings made from the womb show that speech sounds emerge clearly from the background noise. We usually find clear sounds more interesting than muffled sounds, and so the baby in the womb would be listening not just to his mother's voice but that of his siblings.[34] In the last weeks before Eli was born his siblings Miles and Alice became increasingly impatient for him to be born. They would put their faces close to their mother's tummy and instruct Eli to hurry up and arrive. Eli must have been born knowing that his siblings were loving but bossy.

Small children stay close to their mothers, which means that for much of the time they are close to their baby sibling. When small children take notice of a baby they put their faces close to the baby, often nose to nose, and then pull back. In *The Scientist in the Crib* the developmental psychologists Alison Gopnik, Andrew Meltzoff and Patricia Kuhl wrote:

Babies are very near sighted by adult standards, and unlike adults they have difficulty changing their focus to suit both near and far objects. What this means is that objects about a foot away are in sharp focus and objects nearer or farther are blurred. . . . The newborn's world seems to be a bit like the room full of Rembrandt portraits at the National Gallery of Art in Washington, D.C. Brightly lit faces, full of every nuance of movement, life, expression, and emotion, leap out from the background of gloomy obscurity, in startling psychological chiaroscuro.[35]

Thus a baby sees his sibling's face a foot away very clearly. Then the face moves forward, blurring and blocking the light, and then moving back and the face is well lit and distinct. Such an experience must be very memorable, especially when it is often repeated.

As the sibling faces come and go the siblings are likely to be talking. Their words are often interspersed with shouts and yells. All the time the baby interprets and remembers them in some way or other. May has had to learn the difference between Fred's shout of laughter and his shout of complaint. They are equally loud, but the first means that Fred is happy and the second is likely to be followed by screams from Milo or Alice as Fred wreaks his revenge. Through Fred, May had probably learnt many other things as well.

In the weeks before and after her birth May probably learned a great deal about Fred's enthusiasm for Australian wildlife. When I was leaving for a trip to Australia Fred told me that he wanted to learn about the dangerous animals and the creepy crawlies there. Once in Sydney I discovered there were many books about such things written for children Fred's age. These had big, close-up pictures and short pieces of text that would not overawe a lad who was not particularly interested in reading. Every two weeks or so I sent one of these books to Fred. I imagined his pleasure at getting a parcel from overseas and then reading them with his mother Isabel, but I also thought about Isabel sitting on the couch with Fred close beside her, sometimes talking quietly and sometimes shouting and whooping with joy at the sight of a crocodile's massive jaws or a sinister red-backed spider, and with May curled up inside her or feeding at her breast and listening to these dreadful words and sounds. When I returned I asked Isabel about this imagined scene and she assured me that she had interspersed the crocodiles, snakes, sharks and spiders with possums.

Isabel is very skilled at containing and moderating her children's emotions. This is one of the parent's main tasks and it begins right at the moment of the baby's birth. A newborn baby's brain is far from fully developed, but what is present at birth are the brain structures that create the meanings 'I am in danger' and 'How dare this happen to me?', that is, the emotions of fear and anger. These emotions are necessary in order to survive both physically and as a person, but the un-limited and uninhibited expression of them can itself be a danger to physical health and to a coherent sense of being a person. When a mothering person holds a distressed baby and contains his expression of fear and anger by providing food or removing the cause of some physical discomfort, the baby is restored to himself, whole and happy, which is the experience of being validated. Older siblings left in charge of their baby sibling have to learn how to do this. The siblings who are not much older than the baby cannot act in a mothering way but they can act as a distraction, and being distracted by something that engages our attention in a pleasant way can have a very calming influence that restores our sense of being whole.

Studies of newborn babies show that they 'not only distinguish and prefer faces, they also seem to recognize that those faces are like their own face. They recognize that other people are "like me"'.[36] Babies soon show that they can distinguish children from adults and find children infinitely more interesting than adults. When Isabel put May in her bouncer on the kitchen floor May had a choice. She could look to her right and watch her mother cooking and tidying with quiet efficiency or she could look to her left and watch Fred and Milo playing quietly in a sea of Lego with the occasional spat when the older brother decided that he wanted something that his younger brother had. There was no doubt which May preferred. Her unwavering gaze was centred on her brothers. A few weeks later Isabel told me, 'I've just bought May a new high chair so she can now join the others at the table – but, of course, she finds them *much* more interesting than me or the food. So now it's a real challenge to get her attention for long enough to get each spoonful into her mouth! Still, she loves being up at the table and the others love her being there too – so far!'

Newborn babies can do much more than gaze at faces. Andrew Meltzoff discovered that 'One-month-old babies imitate facial expressions. If you stick your tongue out at a baby, the baby will stick his tongue out at you; open your mouth and the baby will open hers.'[37] It seemed that this ability to imitate was innate but to prove this Andrew Meltzoff 'set up a lab next to the labour room in the local hospital and arranged with the parents to call him when the baby was about to arrive. For a year he would wake up in the middle of the night, or dash out of a lab meeting and rush to the hospital, in almost as much of a hurry as the expectant parents themselves. But this meant he could test babies less than a day old; the youngest was forty-two minutes old. The newborns imitated too.'[38]

Empathy, it seems, grows out of imitation. Andrew Meltzoff has demonstrated that as early as 18 months infants know that 'people (but not inanimate objects) are understood within a framework that includes goals and intentions'.[39] By the time children reach two they have acquired the ability to be empathetic. In *Scientist in the Crib* there is a delightful example of this. One of the authors, Alison Gopnik, had had a terrible day. A research paper she had written had been rejected by a journal, a student had criticised her teaching, and when she got home she discovered that she had failed to leave that night's dinner out of the freezer to defrost. As any 'good, strong, tough-minded professional woman' would do, she flung herself on to the sofa and wept. Whereupon her son who was not yet two got a large box of Band-Aids from the bathroom and proceeded to stick them on whatever part of her he could reach.[40]

In the same way many two-year-old children empathise with and try to comfort their older siblings. In her Cambridge study Judy Dunn found that some as young as 14 months attempted to comfort their older siblings.[41] However, understanding how another person feels also gives us the knowledge of how to upset that person. Judy Dunn told the story of Andrew, at 16 months, and his 5-year-old sister Elly. She wrote:

> The mother of Andrew and Elly is telling a visitor in the kitchen that Elly is frightened of spiders. 'There's a particular toy spider she just hates,' the mother comments. Andrew runs out of the kitchen, goes to the playroom, searches through the toy box and finds the toy spider. He runs back into the kitchen and pushes the toy spider in Elly's face – Elly cries, Andrew laughs.[42]

Research comparing older and younger siblings has shown that 'Usually older siblings do better than younger siblings on things like IQ tests. But, consistently, younger siblings do better on tests of their understanding of the mind. . . . And the more brothers and sisters they have, the better they do.'[43]

This is a very important finding because it shows that there are individual differences in how well people understand that other people have their own individual point of view. Many people do not grasp this but instead they operate on the principle that 'anyone who sees things differently from me is either mad or bad'. Amongst those who do know that other people see things differently and are not necessarily mad nor bad, there is considerable variation in the ability to make accurate guesses about how other people see their world. Just as we all like to think we have a sense of humour, so we all like to think we are good at reading other people minds, but that is not the case. If it were the case we would not make such huge errors in dealing with one another.

To read another person's mind is not to move into the realm of the supernatural. All you have to do is pay careful attention to another person. You listen to what the person says and note the intonations, the emphases, the coherence of what is said. You watch what people do, not just what they intended to do but their unintentional acts, their movements, their gestures, the fleeting expressions on their face. Most of all, you watch their eyes. One of the good things that television has done for us, though not for politicians, is to show faces clearly in close-up. Politicians have learned not to look shifty when they lie. Instead, they make their eyes go blank, devoid of the expressions that would give them away. Their simulation of sincerity is particularly blank. This blankness is often hard to spot in conversation because we shift our gaze as we talk to one another, but on television when the person's gaze is either to camera or slightly to one side of it, the camera and the lighting reveal any blankness or any other expression, clearly.

Some people find the reading of other people's minds immensely interesting, and so they polish this skill and become quite perceptive of what the other person thinks is private. Most young siblings find their older siblings immensely interesting, but to keep up with their siblings, to join in their activities and to defend themselves against their older siblings, they have to learn how their siblings think. No wonder little May on her baby bouncer is watching her siblings so closely!

Firstborns do not have to keep up with older siblings so they have no special reason to develop their skill of reading other people's minds, unless, of course, they have other reasons for doing so. It may be that they have been born into a family whose behaviour the infant finds especially hard to comprehend, or it may be that the infant has to learn to read other people's minds in order to survive.

When I used to spend a great deal of time with people in their late teens and early twenties who were going through a period of psychosis I found that they were extraordinarily perceptive of other people. It is extremely disconcerting to be with someone who has been expressing some very strange ideas and who suddenly interrupts this discourse to remark dispassionately on something which you are feeling but which you thought was well hidden.[44] I found that these young people had grown up in families where adults lied to them. Sometimes the adults had lied in order to protect the child from some awful truth. Sometimes the adults were sexually abusing the child while claiming to be the child's protector.[45] We are always engaged in trying to make sense of what is going on, but the more disparate the events are that we encounter, the harder we have to work to make sense of them. A small child who observes his mother being assaulted by her husband, and who is then told by the mother that she is not at all upset and that his father is a good man who loves his family, will have to work harder to make sense of those experiences than the child who simply observes his parents laughing and cuddling one another. The child lacks the experience of life which would enable him to resolve the conflict between what he sees and what he is told. So he finds himself with a problem he cannot solve. He watches people more and more closely and thus he develops a greater skill in reading other people's minds than the child from a happy home. If he is being told that his perceptions are wrong by adults unwilling to face the truth of the situation he can come to doubt his own perceptions, and this doubt can then become the precursor of a psychosis.

Some children are born into families where the new baby becomes the focus for conflict, anger and despair. The baby becomes aware of these emotions and knows that he is not safe. Babies are born with the ability to distinguish people from objects. They can distinguish human movements and sounds from those made by objects. Before birth babies can distinguish pleasure from pain. Thus they know safe from unsafe, good for me from bad for me. All this knowledge enables them to know that humans, not objects, create those special meanings, emotions. Babies cannot name the emotions but they can be extraordinarily perceptive of them in the people closest to them. They know when their mother is sad and they know when she is angry. If the mother directs her anger at the baby just once the baby finds the experience shocking and memorable. Many loving mothers remember with guilt how their baby reacted with enormous upset when, at a difficult time in her life, she let the loving mother face disappear to be replaced by the face of a wicked witch. If a baby is born to a mother who is often angry or into a family where the majority of the emotions expressed seem dangerous to the baby he has to learn not just how to read these emotions but to anticipate them and do whatever he can to deflect them from him.

This was my experience from birth. To survive I had to watch my family very closely and learn how to anticipate their actions. Of course I do not remember my first years. My mother would always talk about her aches and pains, and she would complain fiercely and endlessly about how the world had yet again failed to live up to her expectations, but she rarely talked about the past, and she never talked about anything even remotely connected to sex. I have often joked that my mother had resented my arrival because while she thought that people would accept one virgin birth – that is, my sister – people would not accept a second virgin birth – that is, me. I always felt that my existence shamed her, but there was more to this than the nature of my conception.

When I was 20 my father told me that he had had to work hard to love me when I was born because I was a girl and he had wanted a boy. He went on to say that the baby my mother had aborted some three years before my birth had been a boy. I already knew this. When I was about 11 my sister told me. She had ended her account with, 'You're lucky to be alive. You should be grateful.'

Abortion was illegal in the 1920s and the women and doctors who were found guilty were sent to prison. I suspect that my mother had had an abortion because she felt that she could not cope with a second child, but when a few years later she fell pregnant ('fell' as in 'fall from grace', which was how my mother saw pregnancy) my parents dared not risk another abortion. So I was born to parents who did not want me and to a sister who knew nothing of my imminent arrival. This happened on her sixth birthday. She was sitting on the birthday chair in the classroom when someone came and told her that she was very lucky. She had a special birthday present, a baby sister. Whatever she thought of this present when she saw it, lucky it was not. Soon after my arrival she was sent away to stay with an aunt. This may have been only for a few weeks but to a six year old it would have been aeons of times. I had caused her to be taken her from her mother (my sister was always as close to our mother as I was distant), her father whom she loved dearly, her bedroom (her treasured place where I was always an intruder), and her position of an only child of which she was very proud – everything that supported her sense of being a person. A vast emptiness must have opened up inside her. (Years later I discovered that this was how she experienced the fear of annihilation as a person.) However, there was one thing she could do to try to fill this emptiness. She resolved that my task in life would be to restore to her everything and more that she had lost. I have to report, dear reader, that in every aspect of that task I have failed, principally because I have never tried. Of course, the only way I could restore to her the position of only child would be to die, and I had no intention of doing that.

My sister had been sent away because my mother was not coping, and when my mother did not cope she did it ferociously, battering the people around her with her wild anger, outrageous demands, and a complete unawareness of what pain she was inflicting on others. ('Indifference' would be more accurate than 'unawareness', but it was not the indifference of the cruel but the indifference we all feel about others when we are battling for survival as a person. Simone de Beauvoir said of her mother, 'She had too much to pay back, too many wounds to salve, to put herself in another person's place.'[46]) The two people with her, her youngest sister, whom we called Auntie Doff, and my father, were always very frightened of her. Many years later, when Auntie Doff was in her nineties and living in the time past when she was a young woman, I would visit her at the nursing home. She would be pleased to see me, but within minutes she would be urging me to go home for tea 'because your mother will be waiting'. Mother had been dead for many years and the family home sold, but my aunt had not forgotten what she had learned as a very small child. She must not upset her sister Ella.

When I was born the ferocity of my mother's anger and complaints would have been all around me and very close because I had trouble feeding. Once, on a rare occasion when there were visitors to dinner, my father said something about how my mother had had breast abscesses after I was born. Mother gave him one of her fierce black looks and Dad shut up like a man shot dead, but I had gained a little more knowledge of my first year. When I was at high school I once worked out that if one day I had been dutifully riding my bike home from school, directly and not deviating to the beach for a swim, thinking only of the homework I was going to do the minute I got home, and a meteor came out of the sky and killed me, my mother would have said it was my fault. I do not doubt that she blamed me for those breast abscesses.

My mother had grown up in a family where the parents beat the children so my mother beat me. I soon learned to watch what I said because I knew that if anyone said or did anything that displeased her she was likely to retire to her bedroom and not speak to the offender for days, even weeks. Her silence was deafening, and came with a black miasma that seeped through and filled the house. On some rare but unforgettable occasions when I was alone with her, she went into a crazy rage and would beat me and declare that she was going to kill me and then kill herself. Years later when I was listening to those depressed people who reminded me so much of my mother, I came to understand why she had this rage to kill herself and me. If, to feel whole and at peace you have to know that everything is right and calm and in its proper place, you can also feel that by killing, erasing everything that mucks things up, you will restore everything to unity, completeness and calm.

I never felt that my mother loved me and indeed there was no way that she could. I always knew that I was a large part of what mucked everything up, and with this my sister concurred. My mother deplored that I grew taller and, in her and my sister's eyes, disgustingly fat, but one benefit of this growth was that I no longer feared my mother's physical strength. But I still feared her anger, and along with that came the feeling that she was killing me in a slow and subtle way. In my infancy I had developed a chronic disease, bronchiectasis, where the lungs secrete a sticky mucus which, if not coughed up, destroys the soft tissues of the lungs. I coughed and wheezed and, unable to breathe properly, was often very tired. My mother complained I was lazy and my coughing disturbed her sleep. She did not take me to a doctor but gave me boiled sweets to suck to stop me coughing. Breathing continues to this day to be a daily battle, and I loathe boiled sweets. I would like to see my ability to understand why people do what they do as a mark of some kind of special intelligence or virtue but I have to admit that it arises from a need to be vigilant and know what the danger is.

When an infant gazes intently at the world, working hard to make sense of it, the meaning the infant creates can be called a conclusion. The infant watches her siblings and perhaps draws the conclusion that one sibling is entertaining but not always reliable while another is quiet but can be trusted. Some of the conclusions we draw in our first years we modify with further experience, but other conclusions stay with us until our death, just as my aunt's fear of displeasing her sister stayed with her. Enough is now understood about the way our brains operate for us to know that when we draw a conclusion, that is, learn something, a pattern of neuronal connections is set up in the brain. These patterns can change over time with further and different experiences, but first time experiences that are then repeated can form neuronal patterns which are very strong and lasting. Also, a newborn baby's brain is not complete, but how each brain grows and changes depends on what the infant experiences in the first few years. Deprive a baby of the kind of care which validates that baby and the baby's brain will develop differently from the brain of a baby who is surrounded by acceptance and love.[47]

In all, it is not surprising that the attachments which babies make to their siblings can be as strong and as long-lasting as the attachments they can make to their parents. Michael Rosen called the bedroom he shared with his brother 'almost the cradle of my existence'. Of course, while babies are forming attachments to their siblings, the siblings are also getting to know the new arrival in their family.

## Sibling attachment: the older child

It is possible to discern a common pattern in the way most younger siblings get to know and become attached to their older siblings, but there is no common pattern in the way older siblings first meet and perhaps become attached to their younger siblings. Older siblings can range in age from ten months to twenty-odd years, while step-siblings can be well into middle age when their elderly father sires a child. Each older sibling has already established or been given a particular individual role in the family. This applies even to the youngest siblings. Robert Rose junior had established himself, at least in his father's mind, as a great sportsman by the time he was two, the year before his brother Peter was born. In Australia to be a great sportsperson is the equivalent of being a living saint in a Catholic country (though it must be said that Australian sportsmen tend not to lead saint-like lives). There is an extraordinary photograph of two-year-old Robert Rose in Peter Rose's biography *Rose Boys*. In case a reader might miss the significance of this photograph Peter Rose described it:

> The two-year-old is playing football with his father. . . . Robert is wearing dark corduroy overalls and what may be a baby tie. I like his little boots. The toes are grooved, as if he has kicked a football before. . . Dad, very attentive, props on his haunches as the little boy kicks the football. It flies off to the right, catching the sun, perfectly focussed. The expression on Robert's face is remarkable for its portent of what he would become. He grimaces, so great is his intensity. His kicking technique is flawless. His right arm shoots back out of range and his left one crosses his body and his outstretched leg. His toddler's instep is doubtless taut. Young Robert is kicking for his father, and he knows how to do it. All his later determination and obsession are printed on his face.[48]

Many sportsmen want to have a son who is a sportsman. My father longed for a son who would achieve what he had been prevented from achieving by the advent of the First World War and by family responsibilities. Robert Rose senior, the most famous of the five famous Rose brothers, all Australian Rules footballers, wanted a son who would carry on the family name. By the time he was two Robert Rose junior showed that his father had the son he wanted. Robert Rose had an heir. Peter, the second son, could only be a 'spare'. Peter Rose recorded no anecdote about how young Robert greeted his birth but he did record that, 'Mum once calmly observed that Robert and I had fought every day as children.'[49] This suggests that Robert had not greeted Peter's arrival with undiluted joy.

How an older sibling greets another sibling's birth depends so much on how the child has been prepared for it. Miles aged eight and Alice aged six had felt and conversed with their baby brother for months before he actually arrived. I was present at Eli's birth and I saw their faces when, just minutes after Eli slid gracefully into the world, they were called into their parents' bedroom. I had never seen such joyful wonder on a child's face as was on theirs. Eli saw his siblings' faces within minutes of seeing his parents' faces as Alice and Miles took turns in nursing him. There could not have been a happier welcome into the world.

Eli, Alice and Miles had been born to parents who always talked to their children about what was happening in the family. There was no such tradition of talking to children truthfully in the family into which Olive Compton-Burnett was born in 1875. In that Victorian family the children lived in the nursery and spent little time with their parents. Olive's parents went on to have another five children but in 1882 her mother Agnes Ann died. Her father James turned to Olive for comfort and companionship, but on her eighth birthday he brought home a new wife. The biographer Hilary Spurling wrote:

> Olive had come to think of herself as her father's especial companion, allowed downstairs after her brothers and sisters were in bed to dine with him on the nights when he came back from London. What must have been particularly bewildering for a small child – and made her dismissal even harder to bear, when she was abruptly banished to the nursery again – was that her father was so evidently

in love with the newcomer. . . . Olive, who remembered
her own mother clearly, never forgave this usurpation and
always bitterly resented her stepmother's presence.[50]

Katherine, the stepmother, went on to have seven children,
the eldest of whom became the novelist Ivy Compton-Burnett.
Katherine 'never cared greatly for small children, her own or
anyone else's'.[51] 'Ivy shared her mother's lack of maternal feeling and, once she had left the nursery herself, never voluntar-
ily had anything to do with small children.'[52] Yet, as Hilary
Spurling noted, 'Few other novelists have caught so sharply the
desperate emotions of very small children, or noted how quickly they acquire worldly wisdom.' Hilary gave as an example
of this worldly wisdom a conversation between Nevill Sullivan
in *Parents and Children* who 'at three years old is sufficiently
shrewd to have grave misgivings when his mother promises
him a present for tomorrow.

"No, today," said Nevill with rising feeling. "Today."

"Tomorrow will soon be here," said Luce.

"It won't," said Nevill, in a tone of experience."[53]

Those of us born into a family where the adults see no reason
to keep a promise made to a child if the keeping of the promise
would inconvenience the adult in any way know that by three
we were as wise as Nevill.

Whatever their age, all children are displaced when a new
sibling is born, and this displacement is felt immediately as the
threat of being annihilated as a person. Even those much older
siblings who no longer live at home can still feel disconcerted by
the thought that there is now another person who shares their
genes, while the thought that there may be significant changes
to their parents' will can be very disturbing. A large difference
in age can mean that an attachment is never formed, or it may
be that the older sibling assumes a parental role which requires
some kind of response from the younger sibling. Older children
who still live at home can deal with the threat to their sense
of being a person by defining their relationship with the new
sibling in a way which bolsters their self-confidence. Younger
children have not yet acquired the skill of forming self-serving
interpretations so they express their distress in jealousy and
naughtiness. Simone de Beauvoir illustrated this in the open-

ing paragraph of her autobiography. She wrote:

> Here is a photograph of Mama holding a baby in her arms
> who isn't me; I am wearing a pleated skirt and tam-o'-
> shanter; I am two and a half, and my sister has just been
> born. I was, it appears, very jealous, but not for long. As far
> back as I can remember, I was always proud of being the
> elder: of being first. Disguised as Little Red Riding Hood
> and carrying a basket of goodies, I felt myself to be much
> more interesting than an infant bundled up in a cradle.
> I had a little sister: that doll-like creature didn't have me.[54]

Simone's interpretation of her relationship to her sister Poupette worked well because, as she wrote: 'She alone endowed
me with authority; adults sometimes gave in to me; she obeyed
me.'[55] Had Simone's sibling been a boy he may have fought
her in the way that Peter Rose fought his brother Robert, but
Poupette seems always to have been overawed by her big sister.
She must have felt impelled to obey Simone because Simone
used the only power a three-year-old has to protest about the
threats that adults made to her sense of being a person. Simone
wrote:

> [Grown-ups] had the power to cast spells over me; they
> could turn me into an animal, a thing. 'What beautiful
> legs this little girl has!' enthused a lady who bent down
> to feel my calves. If I'd been able to say: 'Silly old woman!
> She thinks I'm a boiling fowl,' I'd have been all right. But
> at three years of age I had no means of redress against
> that fatuous voice, that gloating smile: all I could do was
> yell, and throw myself screaming to the pavement.[56]

The adults around Simone regarded such behaviour as naughty.
In a conflict with her mother and her nurse 'all flailing legs and
arms, I would cast myself upon the ground, resisting with all
the weight of my flesh and bones the tyranny of that insub-
stantial power; I forced it to take on material form: I would be
seized and shut away in a dark cupboard among the brooms
and feather dusters; there I could kick my feet and beat my
hands against real walls instead of battling helplessly against
the abstractions of another's will'.[57]

In her books Judy Dunn frequently comments that small

children are far more intelligent in understanding the actions and intentions of their family than standard intelligence tests would show them to be. This should not be surprising. We all have to be intelligent about those matters which to us are matters of life and death. A newborn baby studies his mother's face because this is the face which will determine his survival, not just physically but as a person. Simone de Beauvoir wrote, 'Any reproach made by my mother, and even her slightest frown was a threat to my security: without her approval, I no longer felt I had any right to live.'[58]

Every time we learn something we learn its opposite. Discover what pleases your mother and you know what will upset her. No wonder Judy Dunn's Cambridge study showed that 'It was at the moments when the mother picked up the baby to cuddle or caretake that firstborns were likely to do the one thing that their mothers had expressly forbidden, or which particularly irritated them. Tipping the baby's bathwater out, fiddling with the television, investigating the forbidden kitchen cupboards, all occurred just when the mother was most absorbed in the baby.'[59] This study showed a 93 per cent increase in naughtiness by the older sibling after the birth of the younger sibling. There was also an increase in tearfulness, clinging, anxiety and particular fears, all reactions to the threat which the child felt to his sense of being a person. Some children created rituals for bedtime, mealtimes, bathtime and saying goodnight to their parents. Such rituals are desperate defences where the child tries to impose order and control on a world which has become dangerously chaotic. An older, more self-confident child can make the discovery that the best defence against adults who threaten your sense of self is to attack. Thus a four-year-old boy could say to his mother on the birth of his sibling, 'Why have you ruined my life?'[60]

Like Simone de Beauvoir many older siblings soon discover that the younger sibling can be useful. The younger sibling is biddable and so naive that the older sibling can persuade the younger to do things which the older sibling would not dare to do. However, if you are going to boss your sibling around you need to be able to understand the younger sibling's way of communicating and you need to learn how to communicate in a way that the younger sibling understands. Perhaps solely in order to please their mother many older siblings use the same kind of baby talk to the baby that the mother uses, but then they find how pleasurable it is when the baby takes notice of them. Also, the baby has been listening to the sibling since he was in the womb and very likely finds it easier to understand his sibling than his mother because his sibling has always spoken a simpler form of the language. We all prefer to speak to someone who appears to understand us rather than to someone who does not. As the psychologist Victor Cicirelli reported, older siblings will make strenuous efforts in communicating effectively with their younger siblings. He wrote, 'Older siblings showed a great deal of accommodation to the young child's low level of language competence, including gesturing and demonstrating, speaking louder, paraphrasing, eliciting imitation, and speed. They also solicited repetitions of words or phrases by the young child, and interpreted and expanded the young child's utterances.'[61]

In some families parents come to rely on the older sibling to interpret what the younger sibling says. Karen and Laura were twins but when she was born Karen's tongue was slightly enlarged. She began to speak at the same time as her sister but not as clearly. Their parents would ask Laura what Karen had said and Laura would repeat it, perhaps not word for word and not always with exactly the meaning which Karen had intended. This left Karen feeling that she was not allowed to speak for herself, a feeling which persisted even when her tongue naturally adjusted itself to the size of her growing body.

The power that the older sibling acquires in being the senior partner in the enterprise of communication allows the older child to be bossy. This bossiness can be expressed in terms of orders about how to behave, but it also can be expressed in teaching. Both children benefit from this. The younger child gains knowledge and skills; the older child strengthens his sense of who he is. Simone de Beauvoir wrote:

Teaching my sister to read, write, and count gave me, from the age of six onwards, a sense of pride in my own efficiency. I liked scrawling phrases or pictures over sheets of paper: but in doing so I was only creating imitation objects. When I started to change ignorance into knowledge, when I started to imprint truths upon a virgin mind, I felt I was at last creating something real. I was not just imitating grown-ups: I was on their level, and my success had nothing to do with their good pleasure. It satisfied in me an aspiration that was more than mere vanity. Until then, I had contented myself with responding dutifully to the care that was lavished upon me: but now, for the first time, I, too, was being of service to someone.[62]

Much of what a young sibling learns from an older happens not in a classroom-like setting but in play, not just in board games and traditional games like hopscotch but in fantasy play. In such play the older sibling gains as much as the younger. Simone de Beauvoir wrote, 'I owe a great debt to my sister for helping me externalise many of my dreams in play: she also helped me to save my daily life from silence; through her I got into the habit of wanting to communicate with people.'[63]

Simone described two kinds of fantasy play she shared with her sister. There were the fantasy games they played when adults were around, based on banal events like 'selling hats or defying the Boche's artillery fire'. (This was during the First World War.) Then there were 'other scenarios, the ones we like the best. At that evening hour when the stillness, the dark weight, and the tedium of our middle-class domesticity began to invade the hall, I would unleash my fantasms; we would make them materialize with great gestures and copious speeches, and sometimes, spellbound in our play, we succeeded in taking off from the earth and leaving it far behind until an imperious voice suddenly brought us back to reality. Next day we would start all over again. "We'll play *you know what*," we would whisper to each other as we prepared for bed.'[64]

Not all siblings play together. My friend Fay has an older sister Paula and a younger brother Sean but she feels that they grew up as 'three only children'. Fay longed to learn from Paula 'the sensible one', but Paula shut her out. 'We didn't play together. We only kind of teamed up when there was a common enemy like our cousins. When the cousins came we had to get dressed up to such an extent we absolutely hated it, loathed and detested it, so we had that in common.'

The strongest attachment between two siblings comes about

when they both realise that they can, indeed they must, band together against the adults. The older sibling may have felt that his world was shattered when the younger sibling was born. He may resent the intruder who steals his parents' attention and love; but in a world where dangerous, unpredictable giants hold all the power and all the rewards, he at last has an ally.

## United we stand

Allied against their parents children do what the powerless always do when faced with an enemy. They form an alliance and develop a way of communicating which is kept secret from their enemy. Michael Rosen told me how his brother Brian would read him those subversive comic novels, the Molesworth books. 'I can remember him standing there in the room, reading these things out to me, hour after hour, and then us looking at the pictures and relating them to the teachers we knew, so that it then became a shared vocabulary. We have a huge shared language of gags, and language play and references and so on that once we get going it's so exclusive, excluding, that people just go, "Oh, just leave them to it." We don't see each other that often, but if we did we'd just become such insufferable bores, because there is that shared stuff.'

Sometimes children have to form an alliance because their parents are incapable of parenting them. In 1975, Rhodesia (now Zimbabwe) was a dangerous place to live. Alexandra was only six but her parents forbade her to go their bedroom during the night because they might mistake her for an intruder and shoot her. So when she wanted a pee she had to wake her big sister Vanessa who was not armed:

> Then Van has to light a candle and escort me to the
> loo, where I pee sleepily into the flickering yellow
> light and Van keeps the candle high, looking for
> snakes and scorpions and baboon spiders. . .
> I have my feet off the floor when I pee.
> 'Hurry up, man.'
> 'Okay, okay.'
> 'It's like Victoria Falls.' . .
> Then Vanessa hands me the candle – 'You can

keep boogies for me now' – and she pees.
'See, you had to go too.'
'Only 'cos you had to go.'[65]

This is how Alexandra Fuller, known to her family as Bobo or Chookies, begins her account of her childhood with her parents, whom she calls Mum and Dad, her sister Vanessa, and the three siblings who died. Although she tells her story very sparingly, letting the events speak for themselves with little mention of what these events meant to her, her book is suffused with her love for her sister Vanessa.

By beginning the book with such an intimacy Alexandra reminds us of how well siblings can know one another. A married couple over the years may get to know how each other pees, craps, farts, smells, coughs and sneezes, but even then their knowledge of one another is not as extensive, so well explored, as the knowledge that two siblings can have of one another. A marriage may dissolve in bitterness and recrimination, but though separated the couple may still feel attached by their intimate knowledge of one another's bodies. The attachment of siblings through such knowledge can be even stronger than that of couples in marriage. Children find the products of their body endlessly interesting (some never give up this interest). They talk about their products, compare them with those of their siblings, notice and comment on how they each produce such products, and find them to be the source of much humour. These products are also the means of disparaging the other sibling, a means of expressing disgust and rejection, while the acceptance of the other's products means acceptance of the other person.

Vanessa often disparaged Alexandra and her products but she also showed a degree of acceptance, which in Alexandra's eyes made her a pearl beyond price. After Zimbabwe became independent of Britain in 1980 the Fullers lost their farm to Prime Minister Mugabe's government and had to move to an area which old maps designated as 'Not Fit for White Man's Habitation'. Dad got the job of rounding up the cattle which had run wild during the war of independence. Vanessa and Alexandra went with their father on one of his trips. They made camp on the banks of the Turgwe River which in the drought was no more than 'shrinking, slime-frothed pools of water, warm and green with stagnant life'. Dad warned the girls not to drink the water from the river, but after two weeks they were running short of drinking water so they had to use the river water, but only after it had been 'boiled for ten minutes and strained to get rid of the lumps of dirt, hippo shit, the worst of the silt'. One long hot afternoon the girls became bored waiting for their father's return. Vanessa went to sleep but, restless, Alexandra made herself some tea with water that had not been properly boiled. She took only a few sips because it tasted so vile.

> By the time Dad comes into camp, Vanessa is holding me up over a fallen log, rear end hanging over one side of it, head hanging over the other. I am naked; all my clothes are in a bag in the tent, soiled with frothy yellow shit. Vanessa has a grip on my shoulders; there is shit streaming from my bum, vomit dribbling into a pool between Vanessa's feet. . . . Vanessa wipes my mouth and bum with a fistful of leaves and grass. She bathes me, running water over my burning skin from a bucket, and then wraps me in a towel. She carries me into the tent which is rank from the smell of my soiled clothes. . . . Vanessa props me up and tries to feed me some hot tea. I am so thirsty my throat seems stuck together, my tongue feels swollen and cracked. As soon as the liquid hits my belly, I vomit again. My bum and mouth are raw and begin to bleed. . . . Vanessa licks her finger and wipes the edges of my mouth with her moist fingertip. I loll back against her arm. She says, 'Hold on, Chookies.' She strokes sweat-wet hair off my forehead and rocks me. 'Hold on,' she tells me.[66]

Siblings who live together are likely to share a great deal of physical contact, in playing together, in rough and tumble, in sharing beds, bedrooms, showers and baths. In showing one another love and compassion they may kiss, hug and cuddle one another. Of course this does not happen in all families. Although my sister and I shared a bedroom and a double bed I have no recollection of ever being comforted or cuddled by her. Every family has its own style of physical contact, and the amount and kind of physical contact probably plays an important part in the degree of attachment which siblings form. In her wonderful book *Animals in Translation* Temple Grandin told how brain research on social attachment has shown that social distress is linked to thermoregulation, the regulation of bodily heat:

> Thermoregulation comes up all the time when people talk about relationships. We use the expression 'maternal warmth' and we say people are cold or warm. Warm people are loving, kind and connected, and cold people are the opposite. Also, people who are feeling lonely usually want to be touched, which comes from the fact that in the wild babies keep warm by staying close to their parents' bodies.
>
> I know this sounds strange, but researchers believe that social warmth evolved out of the brain system that handles physical warmth. That should tell you something about how important social attachment is to animals. In all mammals a baby has to have strong social attachment to its parents in order to survive. A baby wolf needs social contact to stay emotionally warm as much as it needs physical contact to stay physically warm. *Social attachment is a survival mechanism* that evolved from the survival mechanism of keeping the body warm.[67]

Animal and human siblings may comfort one another but they also fight. Fighting amongst animal siblings has been seen as the way animals, especially male animals, learn to fight to win. However, research has not supported this hypothesis. The movements in real fights are different from those in roughhousing play. In animals the brain circuits for aggression are different from those in play. (They may also be different in children and there may be some research on this but investigating what goes on in animals' brains is more ethically acceptable than doing the same kind of research on small children.) Temple Grandin wrote:

> The other piece of evidence that play fighting isn't about learning to win is the fact that all animals both win *and* lose their play fights. No young animal ever wins all his play fights; if he did, no one would play with him. When a juvenile animal is bigger, stronger, older and more dominant than the younger animal he is play fighting with,

the bigger animal will roll over on his back and lose on purpose a certain amount of the time. That's called *self-handicapping*, and all animals do it. . . Some behaviourists say that the fact that all animals self-handicap might mean that the purpose of play fighting isn't to teach animals how to win but to teach them how to win *and* lose. All animals probably need to know both the dominant and subordinate role, because no animal starts out on top, and no animal who lives to old age ends up on top.[68]

Siblings learn about hierarchy in their disputes but much, much more happens in their fights. Sometimes a sibling starts a fight with his sibling in order to distract himself from a fear aroused by the situation he is in. This is what Vanessa did one day when the war was still raging in Zimbabwe and the family's dogs had become ill:

We are not supposed to leave the valley without an armed escort because there are landmines in the road on the way to Umtali and terrorist ambushes and Dad is on patrol, so we are women-without-men which is supposed to be some weakened state of affairs. But this is an emergency. We put the dogs in the car and drive as fast as we can out of the valley, up the escarpment to the dusty wastelands of the Tribal Trust Land and round the snake-body road which clings to the mountain and spits us out again at the paper factory (which smells pungent and rotten and warm) so that when we drive past it as a family Vanessa holds her nose and sings, 'Bobo farted.'
'Did not.'
'Bo-bo fart-ed.'
Until I am in tears and then Mum says, 'Shuddup both of you or you'll both get a good hiding.'[69]

Some of the fights between siblings are far more significant matters than family hierarchy and fear. Siblings may scream insults at one another, or exchange heavy blows, or destroy each other's possessions. Some do all three. Such fights are bitter and vicious, necessarily so because each sibling is fighting for survival as a person. The cause for which each child is fighting is far greater than mere rivalry for their parents' love and attention. Each sibling knows the other so well that each knows what the other will find the most threatening. They want to turn the other into a non-person, no-thing in order to make themselves safe. Fights occur because one sibling has said or done something which the other finds a threat to his sense of being a person. He needs to assert himself as a person and so he attacks in order to deal with the terrible emotional meanings that make up his perception of the threat to the sense of being a person. These meanings include feelings of being worthless, of catastrophic loss, betrayal, abandonment, desperate hurt, torment and anguish, murderous hate, feelings of being robbed, lost and defeated.

I well remember the desperation with which I fought my big sister. Contemptuous of me, she would act with complete disregard of me and my interests in order to fulfil her own needs and wishes. I would feel that she was reducing me to being nothing but dust beneath her feet, and so I had to fight her in order to survive. On some occasions my sister deliberately instigated a fight as older children do, but on most occasions she would express great surprise that quite inexplicably I was suddenly so angry with her. To this day my sister sees me as someone who may become angry with her for no reason whatsoever. The psychoanalyst Juliet Mitchell can provide an explanation. She has pointed out that when a second child is born the first child loses his identity. He had been the mother's baby. Now there is another. For the first child this is a trauma which will diminish with time but never go away completely.

In a similar way the trauma for my sister continued to recur. I became a very pretty toddler. I learned to read without being aware that I was learning this complex skill. My sister saw me as being prettier and cleverer than she was, and every time a relative or neighbour commented favourably on me my sister saw this as a rejection. She dealt with the repeated trauma by using her preferred mode of defence, repression. She has often told me that she remembers little of her childhood and she is amazed that I remember so much. Thus, as a child and teenager she had no conscious memory of the loss of her identity when I was born and the threats to her identity which followed, but unconsciously she wanted to do to me what I had done to her. Our physical fights ceased in our teens but I came to dread having to meet my sister because I knew that without fail she would say or do something which would get under my guard and hurt me. If I protested about what she had done she would produce some rationalisation that absolved her of all responsibility and put me in the wrong.

Anyone who has a somewhat fraught relationship with a sibling knows how difficult it is to talk about these incidents which cause intense upset and frustration yet in themselves are utterly trivial. If you talk to others about them you sound petty and mean: if you try to talk to your sibling in the hope of improving your mutual understanding inevitably mutual misunderstanding increases, causing more upset and frustration. If you try to sever relations with your sibling, or simply reduce the number of times you meet, other family members will make clear their disapproval, and you will be told that 'Blood is thicker than water.' Few people seem prepared to accept that attachment between two siblings can take many forms. Most sibling attachments are composed of contradictions which allow no complete resolution.

Not all attachments are primarily loving. Some siblings are attached by a hatred that can never turn to indifference. For one or both of siblings the other looms so large, so threateningly, that it is not possible to walk away. When we see someone as being a danger to us we have to be aware all the time of where the person is and what he is doing. There is an old saying that reminds us to keep our friends close but our enemies even closer. If we see someone as having the power to destroy us our hatred becomes a defence whereby we can assure ourselves that we have the power to destroy our enemy and keep ourselves safe. Having an enemy means that you are important to at least one person, your enemy, and your enemy adds excitement to a life which otherwise may be very dull. For many people, and not just siblings, their hatred of their enemy becomes the only thing that gives them and their life significance, and they cannot give it up.

In some sibling attachments the love which one sibling gives the other is never quite enough. Sophie, only 15 months younger than her sister Ester, wanted to talk to me about her relationship with Ester but found it hard to describe. She said, 'We're very different, both in personality and appearance, and we have a relationship that is in lots of ways close, and very important, and I suspect very painful to both of us, but always difficult. There is always conflict somewhere, and I suppose I feel that there's a significant degree of competition between us.' She added, 'Although they're not very well-formed memories, I have a sense of feeling quite protected by her actually. Yet, if I look back at what my memories of childhood are, a lot of it is about competition on some level or another. I enjoyed it up to a point. But I think it's very exhausting. I've always had a sense that there was something wearing, or draining about endlessly competing.'

It seemed that Ester's protectiveness had an element of possessiveness in it. Sophie told me about an incident when she was about eight when Ester became very angry with some girls who had treated Sophie badly. 'I remember being aware, even then, that this was a sort of contrast to our interactions at other times. It was as if it was okay for us to compete – and this is my perception, I'm sure not hers – for her to be unkind to me sometimes, but it was definitely not okay for anybody else to do it.'

Sophie said, 'When we're together and getting on, it's terrific fun. I find her very funny and interesting to be with, and lively, and it's just exciting and *warm*.' Yet, 'I often feel very anxious and tense about our meeting because I think we could have a row, and we often do have a row, and I'm quite defensive and she, I think, is quite combative.' Recently they had fought over something which to an onlooker would seem utterly trivial, something that could have been sorted out with a minimum of compromise and forbearance on both sides. There could not be any compromise or forbearance on the part of Ester because as she saw the incident it posed the question, 'Do you love me more than anyone else?' Sophie said, 'I think she sets me challenges all the time. If she goes away, or if she needs something doing, it's me that she wants to do it. It feels like a test. Most of the time I'm very happy to do it, but there's a sense that I don't have a choice, because if I say no I would be rejecting her in some way, making her feel that she isn't loved. I think she wants to feel that she comes first, that she is more important to me than either anyone or anything else, and somehow if something else gets put first, then I don't love her enough.'

I asked, 'Does she come first in your affections?' Sophie replied, 'No, I don't think she does.' I commented to Sophie that people can get stuck in a situation where they want two opposite outcomes. They suspect that they are not loved as they wish to be loved and they want the object of their suspicions to prove them to be both right and wrong. Possibly Ester cannot bear to give up her hope that she is first in her sister's affections while she fears that if her suspicions were proved right then the pain of rejection would overwhelm and annihilate her. If that is the case then she will stay stuck in a circle of affection and recrimination, unable to live together peacefully or to part. Sophie said, 'We've tried when we've had a big row, we've tried not seeing one another. It's usually her that suggests it. Then that dissipates and gradually we creep back into the same kind of routine.'

Sometimes the attachment goes only one way. One sibling longs for the other to love him and take notice of him, but the other sibling does not respond in any positive way. Max was the youngest of four children. Although as a child he shared a bedroom with his brother Alec, who was nearly six years older, they were never friends. Max said, 'Alec beat me up quite hard. He meant it. My brother hated me. I had no relationship with him at all.' At school Alec had a reputation for being 'a bad boy', with the result that when Max arrived at the school the teachers expected the worst of him. Alec left home at seventeen to work as a jackeroo in the bush. Max said, 'After he left home I wrote to him for years. I worked hard to keep in touch.' When I asked him why, he said, 'I don't know. Perhaps I wanted his acceptance.'

On Max's parents' sixtieth wedding anniversary he organised an elegant garden party and spared no effort in making sure that his brother was able to attend, even though by then the two men normally avoided one another. Max had decided that as he was now 40 and had, through his work, developed all the skills of peaceful negotiation and getting along well with others, he should approach Alec in the expectation that they could now put all their past difficulties behind them. Unfortunately Alec had not reached the same point of view. He made it clear to Max that his hatred of him had not diminished in any way. Max was deeply hurt but then he had a sudden flash of understanding. He said, 'I realised that Alec was afraid of me. He thought that I had got my mother's love while he had not. I found it all very distressing, but when I chose to see his behaviour as jealousy I could let go of my anger and hurt.'

Both Sophie and Max, like most people when they talk about their relationships with their siblings, commented on how different they were from their siblings in what is usually called 'personality' or 'temperament'. This seems to be seen as the main factor in determining the nature of a sibling relationship. People often say, 'It was always a clash of personalities' or 'Our temperaments weren't compatible.' When questioned they say that what they mean is that there was something so distinctive, so individual, about the way each sibling interpreted themselves and their world that compatibility of outlook was often hard to achieve, but if achieved it was greatly valued.

In her research on sibling relationships with one another, their family and friends, Judy Dunn acknowledges that sibling attachment can take many forms. She makes occasional references to 'children's temperamental characteristics' and says: 'The personalities of both children in a friendship dyad and both children in the sibling pair probably need to be taken into account in looking for connections across the relationships.'[70] In her study with Robert Plomin of why siblings are so different she wrote: 'The term *personality* covers dozens of dimensions . . . Sibling correlations are very low for nearly all personality traits. The few exceptions reach no higher than .40 [on a range from 0 to 1] and include traits that might more properly be considered attitudes, such as masculinity–femininity, tolerance for ambiguity, and traditionalism (conformity and conservativeness).'[71]

In psychology 'personality' and 'temperament' are hugely problematic. It is a problem of the psychologists' own making. We all know that we are individuals, no two of us are the same. However, when psychologists wanted to study what they called individual variation they were certainly not going to ask people how they experienced themselves. That would be 'subjective' and 'unscientific'. Psychologists have always preferred to study fictions that can be measured and counted than real lived experience. They prefer to study what people can be seen to do rather than ask them to talk, in their own words, about their own experience. If they do ask people about their attitudes and habits psychologists prefer to use standardised interviews and questionnaires which cannot help but allow those interviewed to lie, dissemble and deny. Sometimes a questionnaire forces a person to lie because it contains questions which are not relevant to the life of the person answering the questions. Of course, none of us will reveal our private thoughts and weaknesses to someone we do not know and trust. Judy Dunn always made sure that her interviewers got to know the mothers and children they interviewed, and the mothers and children got to know the interviewers. In such interviews, differences in temperament and personality shine through what the mothers and children say about themselves, but personality questionnaires are useless in capturing this. These tests measure 'traits', little lumps of stuff that psychologists think exist inside us, lumps called 'sociability', 'moodiness', 'religiosity', 'traditionalism', and so on. What psychologists call traits are no more than abstract nouns abstracted from the attitudes, opinions, beliefs, meanings and interpretations which people create.

Making questionnaires is a profitable industry and so there are a great many personality tests. To make a questionnaire psychologists give sets of questions to large numbers of people, questions which have to be answered using a rating scale that yields numbers which can be correlated together. Then, using a statistical analysis sometimes known as factor analysis or principal component analysis, psychologists extract factors or traits. One trait which turns up in just about every questionnaire is 'extraversion'. In the largest study yet completed of extraversion in siblings a correlation of only 0.23 was found.[72] This means that in a family some but not all siblings are likely to possess the trait of extraversion. But we already know that. In any family it is likely that one child will be sociable and outgoing and another quiet and thoughtful. Sometimes these two siblings get along well together and sometimes they do not. That can be expected because each of them sees themselves and their world in such different ways.

# Chapter 3

# TWO WAYS TO EXPERIENCE EXISTENCE

Just as God or Nature decided that there would be males and females so God or Nature decided that there would be two ways that human beings experienced their existence. There would be people who looked outward to the world around them, needing always to engage with other people, and those who looked inward seeking a sense of personal achievement, clarity, organisation and control, that is, there would be extraverts and introverts. However, just as there is an infinite variety of men and of women, so there is an infinite variety of extraverts and introverts. There are as many different kinds of introvert as there are individual introverts, and as many different kinds of extravert as there are extraverts. It is possible to make some general statements about extraverts as a group and introverts as a group, just as it is possible to make some general statements about men as a group and women as a group, but beyond that the differences within the group of extraverts and within the group of introverts, and between the groups of introverts and extraverts are legion and subtle. It is relatively easy to distinguish men from women but identifying extraverts and introverts can be difficult. It is something we all know how to do but we do not always know that we know.

It is impossible to describe all the important differences between extraverts and introverts in the space of one chapter. My book *Beyond Fear*[1] is devoted to how differently extraverts and introverts deal with the extreme mental distress which psychiatrists call mental disorder, while another book, *The Successful Self*,[2] describes how introverts and extraverts deal differently with ordinary life and how wise extraverts learn to moderate their need to be liked by everyone and wise introverts learn to come to accept that there is little in the world which they can control. The need of extraverts to be liked is their defence against the fear of being annihilated as a person when they are faced with being rejected and abandoned. The need of introverts to maintain organisation and control is their defence against the fear of being annihilated as a person when they are faced with losing control and plunging into chaos. In this chapter I want to concentrate on how differently extraverts and introverts experience reality, how differently they experience themselves, and how these differences can affect family relationships.

In his book *The Pecking Order* Dalton Conley often remarks on the quite profound personality differences between siblings but he never uses the terms 'extravert' and 'introvert'. Yet when he writes about his sister Alexandra and himself he gives an excellent description of one kind of extravert and one kind of introvert:

Today, my sister and I both still live in New York. Both of us have reproduced our parents' class status, albeit in different ways. The children of artists, we both sought careers in the world of 'ideas' or 'creativity,' though both of us have forged a foundation of economic stability that would not have been possible as full-time artists. My sister manages a small, nonprofit theatre company. She has committed herself to the business side of the arts. I, meanwhile, have gone into academia which provides a level of job stability that rivals the civil service but which also offers a degree of tolerance for personal, creative expression.

For all these basic similarities, however, there are also major differences between Alexandra and myself. Even though she spent fewer years growing up in the impoverished, minority neighbourhood than I did (because she was younger when we moved), she wears the mark of the community much more prominently than I do. She uses more of the local hip-hop slang, she moves in much more ethnically and class diverse circles than I generally do (partially on account of whom our respective careers put us in contact with). Our values also diverge. She is much less career focused than I am. She is happy to do a good job behind the scenes and let others take credit for her theatre's successes. And, ultimately, what matters most to Alexandra is a comfortable home, a rich family life, financial security, and community service. I, on the other hand, hate working for other people and want to have total control over what I do or do not accomplish and put my name to – even community service. Our financial trajectories are also beginning to diverge substantially, as I work my way up the academic job ladder with complete job security (tenure) while she remains committed to a struggling arts organization where new crises crop up daily.

However, whereas l may be more stable financially, she has flourished in her personal life, while I have struggled for contentment. She is a relatively new mother, her son, Dante, having been born just over a year before this writing. Her marriage to her husband, Dan Leonardi, brings her love and happiness. Though they live in a cramped, railroad-style apartment, stress does not get the best of them; they fill their days with cute rituals like ADDs (all day dates) and kisses before all meals, and they call each other by cutesy pet names. Meanwhile, though I love my two children – ages four and five – fiercely, my marriage has been a tumultuous one that is ending as it began, with a struggle for control between my spouse and me. (The first time we ever danced, we both insisted on leading – tripping each other up in the process.) We are now muddling through the divorce process, not doing a very good job of containing our sadness and frustration in front of the kids. We both admit to having the emotional intelligence of teenagers – or perhaps two-year-olds. And of course, I worry about the impact of our tumultuous family life on our two children.[3]

Here Dalton Conley shows how, in a family where the parents valued creativity, each sibling interpreted the idea of creativity in a different way. For Alexandra, the extravert whose first priority is creating and maintaining relationships, creativity meant working creatively with other people to enable them to develop their creativity. For her, achievement means aiming at success for the groups to which she belongs, her theatre company, her family, her community. Alexandra would understand completely why Josephine Cox, an extremely successful novelist, when appearing on *Desert Island Discs,* chose as her luxury 'my family album – I wouldn't be alone then, would I?'[4] Dalton, the introvert whose top priority is individual achievement, organisation, clarity and control, creativity means setting himself the goal of making a significant contribution to science, and being fully in control while he does so. However, the success or failure of their marriages depends only in part on whether they are extraverts or introverts. There are many extraverts who make a mess of their relationships and many introverts who enjoy successful marriages.

Great writers not only know all about how extraverts and introverts behave, they also know that it is out of the different ways in which extraverts and introverts perceive their worlds that the plots of tragedies and comedies come. Whether Jane Austen had the words 'introvert' and 'extravert' in her vocabulary I do not know, but in all her books she shows how her story unfolds from the differences in the meanings which extraverts and introverts give to their experience. Her first book *Sense and Sensibility* was a picture of two sisters, the introvert Elinor and the extravert Marianne. The story is told from the point of view of Elinor:

> This eldest daughter . . . possessed a strength of
> understanding, and coolness of judgement, which
> qualified her, though only nineteen, to be the counsellor
> of her mother, and enabled her frequently to counteract,
> to the advantage of them all, that eagerness of mind
> in Mrs Dashwood which must generally have led
> to imprudence. She had an excellent heart; – her
> disposition was affectionate, and her feelings were
> strong; but she knew how to govern them; it was a
> knowledge which her mother had yet to learn and which
> one of her sisters had resolved never to be taught.

The sister who did not wish to learn how to control her emotions was Marianne: '[Her] abilities were, in many respects, quite equal to Elinor's. She was sensible and clever; but eager in everything; her sorrows, her joys, could have no moderation. She was generous, amiable, interesting: she was everything but prudent.'[5]

Dalton Conley does not describe his sister Alexandra as lacking in prudence but he does describe her as needing to express her love for her husband and child in all kinds of ways. Extraverts value action and the expression of feelings over thought and reticence. When Elinor felt drawn to Edward Ferrars she knew only too well the dangers of expressing too positive a feeling for him. 'She knew that what Marianne and her mother conjectured one moment, they believed the next – that with them to wish was to hope, and to hope was to expect.' So she said, 'I do not attempt to deny that I think very highly of him – that I greatly esteem, that I like him.' To this, 'Marianne burst forth with indignation – "Esteem him! Like him! Cold-hearted Elinor! Oh! Worse than cold-hearted! Ashamed of being otherwise. Use those words again and I shall leave the room this moment."'[6]

Marianne's outburst is typical of extraverts who become totally exasperated with what appears to be the uncaring or unwise behaviour of an introvert. However, introverts can be equally exasperated with extraverts. Dalton speaks very proudly of the work his sister Alexandra does but I am certain that he sometimes privately deplores the fact that she has not made the most of her talents, while Alexandra has observed on more than one occasion to her husband Dan that if Dalton spent more quality time with his family and thought less about his career his marriage might not have ended.

Extraverts and introverts often fall out because they cannot comprehend that they differ in what they each see as the purpose of their life, or, even if they do comprehend this, in their heart of hearts they believe that the other is stupidly mistaken. These attitudes are based on the assumption that introverts and extraverts consciously choose what they have as their top priority in life, and that extraverts *choose* to have relationships as their top priority and introverts *choose* to have achievement as their top priority. Of course extraverts and introverts like to think this about themselves. Extraverts can see their concern for others as a virtue, and introverts can feel virtuous because their achievements will make the world a better place. (Even mass murderers who are introverts think like this. I would guess that Hitler was an introvert. He certainly believed that he was making the world a better place for Germans and they were the only people who mattered.) However, acting virtuously is something we choose to do. These top priorities are not virtues because we cannot do anything other than try to reach our top priority. We cannot do anything else. They are part of what Antonio Damasio calls our 'unwitting and unconscious urge to stay alive'.[7]

Here Damasio was talking about the specifications for the survival of a single cell but he could see that such specifications could well be 'a blueprint and anchor for what will eventually become a self in the mind'.[8] We need to survive both as a collection of cells, that is, a body, and as what develops from the body, a person. When we see a threat to our survival we act immediately and later justify our actions. Often our justifications make it hard for us to see clearly just what we did and why. Our justifications usually involve the complex emotions which arise in our relations with other people.

Introverts have relationships with other people, and as part of this they have the complex emotions which come with such relationships. However, as Temple Grandin has described, autistic people like herself do not have complex emotions. She wrote:

My emotions are simpler than those of most people.
I don't know what complex emotion in a human
relationship is. I only understand simple emotions, such
as fear, anger, happiness, and sadness. I cry during sad
movies, and I sometimes cry when I see something that
really moves me. But complex emotional relationships
are beyond my comprehension. I don't understand
how a person can love someone one minute and then
want to kill him in a jealous rage the next. I don't
understand being happy and sad at the same time.[9]

There is a wide range of people to whom the word 'autistic' is applied but as Temple describes herself she seems to be an introvert who lacks the capacity to form emotional relationships with other people. Temple said, 'I could never fit in with the crowd, but I had a few friends who were interested in the same things, such as skiing and riding horses. Friendship always revolved around what I did rather than who I am.'[10] This incapacity is probably a result of some as yet unknown neuronal variation. Yet Temple has the same top priority which all introverts have. After the neurologist Oliver Sacks had visited her he wrote:

> I was struck by her rapport with, her great understanding of, cattle – the happy, loving look she wore when she was with them – and her great awkwardness, by contrast, in many human situations. I was also struck, when we walked together, by her seeming inability to feel some of the simplest emotions. 'The mountains are pretty,' she said, 'but they don't give me a special feeling, the feeling you seem to enjoy . . . you look at the brook, the flowers, I see what great pleasure you get out of it. I'm denied that.'
>
> And I was awed, as we drove to the airport before my departure, by the sudden revelation of moral and spiritual depths which I thought no autistic person would have. Temple was driving, when suddenly she faltered and wept, and said, 'I don't want my thoughts to die with me. I want to have done something . . . I want to know that my life has meaning . . . I'm talking about things at the very core of my existence.'[11]

Temple described her emotions as being 'more like the emotions of a child than an adult'. When she reached puberty 'fear became my main emotion'.[12] She lived in a state of near-annihilation. If your sensory apparatus differs from that of people around you, and they and the world make no allowances for you, you live your life in a state of near-invalidation. Yet throughout this time she achieved a great deal. To achieve one must progress, and for an introvert to live with any sense of ease there must be a feeling of making some kind of progress, even if that day's achievement is no more than doing the washing or catching up with your emails. Words that I often use to myself are, 'I must get on.' I hear myself bringing a telephone conversation to an end with 'I'll let you get on', even though I may know that the person I am talking to has all the time in the world. Not being able to get on creates a feeling of being blocked. Temple said: 'My feeling of blocked passages feels very primal, as though I were an animal that has been trapped.' Approaching a place, particularly one of the places she has designed, 'I panic, thinking I will be denied entry to my special place. . . . Will the people try to stop me? I'll find the unlocked gate even when

I'm not looking for it. I can't but help see it. And when I spot an opening, I get a rush of happy excitement . . . My fear of blocked passages is one of the few emotions that is so great that it's not fully suppressed by my antidepressant medication.'[13]

Introverts fear chaos. When at high school Temple was introduced to the second law of thermodynamics which says that in a closed thermodynamic system there will be increasing disorder, 'I found the idea of the universe becoming more and more disordered profoundly disturbing.' Some years later she discovered chaos theory and found it comforting because it says that 'order can arise out of disorder and randomness'. 'I hated the second law of thermodynamics because I believed that the universe *should* be orderly.'[14] Temple is extraordinarily honest. Whenever any of us argues ferociously and bitterly against a particular theory it is not because that theory is scientifically flawed (although it may be) but because some of the implications of the theory appear to carry the threat of annihilation. In the same way disputes between adherents to different religions are often exceedingly bitter and religious wars so destructive.

The fear of annihilation is so intense that we will cast aside all reason in order to save ourselves. For extraverts the fear of being abandoned, all relationships severed, can lead them to act against what they have always regarded as their own best interests. Even when intellectually they have no doubt that a particular person, usually a family member or erstwhile lover, has no love or interest in them, or will use and abandon them, some extraverts feel driven to expend every effort to get that person to produce the connection to them that they so desperately need; for the lover to return or the parents to say, 'I have always loved you.'

When children cannot tolerate being parted from their parents, no matter how badly they have been treated, their behaviour is usually explained in terms of the child's immaturity. The same is often said of adults who stay close to their parents, or, more charitably, they are commended for their filial devotion. However, this cannot be said of my friend Roxanne. I have known her for nearly twenty years, and over that time she has told me about her unhappy childhood and the events which followed.

The best I can say about Roxanne's father is that he was

utterly selfish and uncaring. He showed not the slightest sign
of love or concern for his wife and children whom he deserted
when Roxanne was eight. He refused to support his family but
would arrive unannounced and expect to be looked after. His
wife was frightened of him, and when Roxanne tried to stand
up to him in her early teens, he punished her by forcing her to
leave school and get a job. As soon as she could she left home,
got herself an education and entered a profession. She kept in
touch with her mother and her siblings but refused all contact
with her father.

The years passed. Her father, now old, developed cancer.
Roxanne took him in and nursed him until he died. When her
friends asked her why she had done this she would say, 'I just
had to.' Her family were as surprised at her actions as were her
friends. It was not a question of her father altering his will in
her favour because he had nothing to leave, and he took what
she was doing as his right. If her friends commended her for
her virtue she brushed them aside. She had no ambition for
martyrdom and sainthood. When I pressed her for a reason she
said, 'I couldn't not do it.'

In my conversations with individuals about their adult relationships with their siblings I found it was quite common for
an extravert to say, usually in passing, that she was the one
who kept everyone in touch with everyone else and who organised family get-togethers, or that he had rescued his brother
from bankruptcy or was putting a niece through university,
all this despite the undoubted fact that sibling relationships
in childhood had been far from good and that present sibling
relationships were difficult. If I asked why it was important to
keep in touch or to help a sibling the answer might be 'I don't
know why', or 'Can't do anything else, really'. Of course there
are many introverts who give enormous help to their not particularly loving parents and siblings, but if asked why, their
ready answer is some form of 'my conscience wouldn't let me do
otherwise', which is a very different answer from 'I don't know
why. I just have to.'

It should always be remembered that, while introverts and
extraverts are compelled to strive for their top priority, no two
introverts and no two extraverts ever do this in exactly the
same way. Each individual interprets the compulsion he or she

feels as well as interpreting his or her situation, and then decides to act in his or her individual way. In a situation similar to that of Roxanne, one extravert may decide to pay for the ailing parent to go into a nursing home while another may have long recognised and accepted that her parent was incapable of love.

## Peculiar differences

When psychologists create theories about why people behave as they do they base their theories on concepts relating to those aspects of behaviour which seemed to them to be significant. Whatever their starting point, their researches led them to introverts and extraverts, though they did not necessarily use these terms. Sigmund Freud called extraverts 'hysterics' and introverts 'obsessionals'. Carl Gustav Jung used the terms 'introvert' and 'extravert' but then went on to describe four functions, sensing, thinking, intuiting and feeling, which were used by different extraverts and introverts in different ways. However, 'Every individual is an exception to the rule,' he declared, and fitting such individuals into a rigid system is 'futile'. To 'stick labels on people at first sight' was 'nothing but a childish parlor game'.[15] Ignoring this advice, Isabel Briggs Myers turned Jung's categories into 16 types of personality. The Myers-Briggs Type Indicator became enormously popular, despite the fact that:

> While there is limited scientific support for some of Myers' basic dimensions (people do seem to differ in their relative levels of introversion and extraversion, for example) there is no evidence that her sixteen distinct types have any more validity than the twelve signs of the zodiac. And research has found little connection between Indicator types and real-life outcomes. There is scant evidence that MBTI results are useful in determining managerial effectiveness, helping to build teams, providing career counselling, enhancing insight into oneself or others, or any other of the myriad uses for which it is promoted.[16]

The Myers-Briggs Type Indicator is very popular, possibly because, unlike many psychological theories and personality tests, it is not judgemental. Freud's terms 'hysteric' and 'obsessional' belittle the person to whom they are applied, while Aaron Beck of cognitive behavioural therapy renown regards extraverts and introverts as possessing 'maladaptive forms of sociality and individuality strivings'.[17] Beck uses the terms 'sociotropy' for extravert and 'autonomy' for introvert and regards these as personality dimensions which make a person vulnerable to depression.[18] Andrew Butler, a psychologist involved in studying this phenomenon, wrote:

> Sociotropic individuals are invested in positive social interchange and in obtaining help, support, reassurance and regard. Hence, they are proposed to be particularly vulnerable to depression following life events that represent to them a loss of social support. Autonomous individuals are invested in independence and freedom from constraints. These individuals are proposed to be especially prone to depression following life events that represent to them a diminishment in their ability to operate in a self-determined manner free from significant restraints, obstacles or interference.[19]

If your top priority is your relationship with other people, it is hardly surprising that when you encounter a situation where you have lost or are about to lose all the relationships which maintain your sense of being a person, you become very frightened. Similarly, if your top priority is to have a sense of personal achievement, organisation and control, it is hardly surprising that when you find yourself in a position where you have no opportunity to achieve and over which you have no control, you feel very frightened. What to me is surprising is that Beck and his disciples have not recognised that the two ways of experiencing our sense of existence are essential parts of the human condition. Being an extravert or an introvert is neurotic insofar as being human is neurotic. When we are faced with a situation which threatens to take away the necessary conditions for our existence as a person, whether we become depressed or not depends not on these 'maladaptive forms of sociality and individuality strivings' but on what degree of confidence we have in ourselves. If we have great confidence and value ourselves too much to let us be destroyed by events, we can find the courage to say 'I'll survive this' and so ride out the storm, waiting for things to fall into place but knowing life will never be the same again. If we have little confidence and value ourselves so little that we doubt we deserve to survive, we try to create an explanation whereby things seem to fall into place, even at the cost of blaming ourselves for the disaster. 'If I had been a really good person this disaster would not have happened.' Confessing a sin may be the first step in saving our souls, but seeing ourselves as sinners unfit for any place in the world cuts us off from every aspect of life, so we find ourselves locked in the prison of depression.[20]

Most psychologists studying personality believe that it can be described in terms of traits. They have developed ways of uncovering these traits by asking many people questions about what they do and what they prefer, and then applying to their answers a statistical method called factor analysis. Raymond Cattell identified 16 factors, including one that he called 'sociable–unsociable', which seems to bear a resemblance to extraverts and introverts. Hans Eysenck also used questionnaires but applied factor analysis slightly differently and came up with only two factors, extraversion–introversion and neuroticism–stability. Thus you could be a neurotic extravert or a stable extravert, a neurotic introvert or a stable introvert. More recently researchers have conducted a great many studies to see who was right, Cattell or Eysenck. The answer seems to be that both were partly right. In all this work 'Extraversion' and 'Neuroticism' appear to be the biggest and most important of all the traits, but three others considered to be important are 'Agreeableness, the tendency to be good-natured and cooperative, Conscientiousness, the propensity to be organised and goal oriented, and Openness, the proclivity to be imaginative and curious'.[21] These traits are now known as the Big Five. When people are assessed repeatedly over a period of time it seems that they do not change much on these traits. If you're an agreeable extravert or a conscientious introvert you tend to stay that way. However, these personality assessments cannot predict what you will actually do. As an agreeable extravert you may be a wonderful parent or a successful confidence trickster. As a conscientious introvert you may be a brilliant chancellor of the exchequer or a scientist intent on designing a bigger and better bomb.

Actually, psychologists who believe in personality question-naires do not talk about people being introverts and extraverts with reasons for doing what they do but about the abstract nouns 'extraversion' and 'introversion'. These nouns stand for certain ideas which the psychologists have abstracted from the answers people have given to the questionnaires. The psycholo-gists then invest these abstract nouns with the power to force people to behave in certain ways. For instance, if you have a large amount of the trait of Extraversion you will behave in agreeable ways. Test this out on yourself. You invite friends for dinner. Are you impelled to do this by your trait of extraver-sion? Or do you do this because you enjoy spending time with your friends?

We are not puppets manipulated by entities inside us called traits. We are agents who interpret, assess, choose, make deci-sions and act on those decisions. We experience our existence vividly but, even if we are great artists or musicians, we find it impossible to convey to other people the exact qualities of our experience. I struggle to find words to describe how we experi-ence our existence. I use other people's words and hope that by giving examples, each perhaps only slightly different from the others, to arrive at some approximate description of real lived experience.

If you read the research literature in psychology you will quickly discover that many psychologists, particularly those in academia, love abstract nouns and statistics and hate real lived experience. (Judy Dunn, in her work with children and families, is an outstanding exception to this.) They use ab-stract nouns and statistics as a barrier to protect themselves from the messiness, the uncertainties, the eternal dilemmas of human existence. How do you achieve in a world which is always changing and over which you have little control? Dare you love anyone when to love is to risk loss? Psychologists must know about this because they are only human, but no one is an expert on life, so to be an expert psychologist you have to avoid investigating how we experience our existence and instead deal only with surface things, what people say they do and what people say they prefer. If we want to go beneath the surface and discover how an individual experiences his existence we have to ask of a preference, 'Why is that important to you?' and of an action, 'What were your reasons for doing that?' Two people can state the same preference or do exactly the same thing but for totally different reasons. If we don't know why someone does something, how can we predict what he will do?

Many psychologists argue that personality traits are genetic. Most of the behaviours deemed to be traits, like 'religiosity' and 'agreeableness', are ways of behaving which we learn from the people around us, but it does seem that we are born extraverts or introverts, just as we are born male or female. Eysenck certainly believed that this was so. His extensive researches found significant differences in the functioning of the nervous system of extraverts and introverts.

Nervous systems, like all systems in the body, require certain conditions which allow the system to operate at its best. Eysenck found that the nervous systems of extraverts tended to be 'sluggish' (Eysenck's word, not mine) and so needed stimulating conditions in order to operate well, while the nervous systems of introverts were naturally very active and required little external stimulation to operate at their best. On this basis it is easy to see why extraverts grow restless when little is happening, while introverts withdraw when they feel overwhelmed by a barrage of noise and activity.

Parents of more than one child have often been amazed at the differences between their offspring right from birth. Some babies are born quiet. They cry as all babies do but between cries they like peace and quiet and become fretful if there is too much going on around them. Other babies are born partygoers. They look for faces and are happiest when in the midst of family life. I saw this difference right from the start when Miles and later his sister Alice were born. As a babe in arms Miles always welcomed a new face, someone to talk to him, someone for him to entertain. Alice was born wary of people. Her mother, father and brother rapidly became the fixtures in her small universe and other faces were not welcome. She would look at a new face warily and turn away frightened if the new face came too close. It was best to smile at her from afar.

I have watched these two babies turn into young teenagers in a home which has always echoed with parental cries of 'Miles!', cries made in an attempt, often futile, to stop some impulsive act or to pull him from some fascinating, exciting activity to do something boring like getting dressed. Nowadays life is too exciting for him to go to bed at night and in the morning it is only the thought that his friends will be walking to school without him that catapults him out of bed and into a frenzied rush to get ready. Alice now has many friends and a busy life, but while she no longer turns away from strangers she watches from afar and assesses the person carefully while deciding how to act. On schooldays she comes to the breakfast table neatly dressed and waits fairly patiently while her mother brushes her long hair. (Alice may be quiet but she defends herself when necessary with vigour.) She prepares for the day ahead, has her school bag packed and leaves for school on time. Alice and Miles are hugely loyal to one another and they have monumental fights. One reason for their fights is that Alice will create a plan that has a goal which she values, and she carries out her plan with care and pleasant anticipation. Miles, coming upon the scene, sees something in it which excites and amuses him. He acts immediately and impulsively. Sometimes Alice sees and shares his joke, sometimes she does not.

We may come into the world bearing genes which determine whether we are an extravert or an introvert, but what genes carry is merely a potential. How that potential develops depends on what we encounter at birth. Miles and Alice were born to parents who knew that their babies would be different from one another. They studied their babies carefully and adapted their parenting to their individual needs. Not all babies are lucky enough to be born to parents like these.

That genial, witty extravert Mark Twain once said of himself, 'I was born excited.'[22] Suppose like Mark Twain you were born excited to an introvert mother who felt herself close to being overwhelmed by domestic responsibilities and family problems. To her you would be a difficult, demanding, naughty baby who was bringing her close to collapse. If you had been an introvert baby needing peace and quiet your mother would have seen you as a good baby and loved you for being good. On the other hand, if, as an extravert baby born ready to party you were born to an extravert mother who saw your demands for attention as proof that you loved her, then you and she would have a great time together. However, had you been born a quiet introvert baby your extravert mother may have interpreted your quietness as evidence that you did not love her.

Being an introvert or an extravert may predispose us to look for certain things in our environment, but how we do this is an entirely individual matter. Just as no two people ever see anything in exactly the same way, so no two introverts or extraverts ever interpret anything in exactly the same way. Parents interpret their babies in their own individual ways, and babies interpret their parents in their own individual ways. The possible variations on these interpretations are infinite.

In the same way there is an infinite number of ways that extravert and introvert siblings can interpret one another. Much depends on who is the older of the siblings and who the younger. The psychologist William James and his novelist brother Henry were only 16 months apart in age, but to Henry, William was so far ahead of him that there was no way he could ever be his equal. In his memoir *A Small Boy*, Henry wrote that William 'had gained such an advantage of me in his sixteen months' experience of the world before mine began that I never for all the time of childhood and youth in the least caught up with him or overtook him. [William was] always round the corner and out of sight, coming back into view but at his hours of extremest ease. We were never in the same schoolroom, in the same game, scarce even in step together or in the same phase at the same time; when our phases overlapped, that is, it was only for a moment – he was clean out before I had got well in.'[23]

As Henry saw it, the advantage William had over him was not merely his age. William was always what Leon Edel, Henry's biographer, called 'brightly communicative, full of life.'[24] He had 'an easy faculty for taking hold of an environment in a desire to demonstrate his admirably alert qualities of mind and his capacity for gregarious association with his fellows'.[25] Henry noted that William was always ready to 'help the lame dog of conversation over a stile'.[26] 'William', wrote Leon Edel, 'could be impulsive, filling each moment with imagination translated into action.' Faced with such superiority in social intercourse and in age Henry did what introverts do in such situations. He withdrew and watched. Leon Edel wrote:

> Henry, possessing an equal capacity for action, translated it into imagination; he discovered that there was a virtue

to immobility: if he could not participate in William's adventures he could actively employ his mental resources: he could observe, and his memory clung tenaciously to all that it absorbed. . . . The small boy cultivated a quiet aloofness; nothing would happen to him if he withdrew and used his eyes and his mind in that turbulent family. . . . Reduced to inexhaustible younger brotherhood, making himself small and quiet among the other Jameses, [he] turned into the depths of himself to fashion a fictional world based on the realities around him in which older brothers were vanquished, fathers were made to disappear, mothers put in their place. But it was not as easy as all that. Such day-dream accomplishments – and aggressions – had their concomitant fears and anxieties and guilts, the criss-cross of emotion within the outwardly serene little boy. Yet in this fashion, by controlling his environment, suppressing his hostilities, electing the observer's role, rather than the actor's, he was able to act in his own personal way and conquer.[27]

Reverse the relative ages of the siblings and the older intro-vert sibling can make the younger extravert sibling feel inferior. My extravert friend Fay talked to me about her relationship with her older sister Paula. 'We're very, very different. Because we are so very different, we might not have chosen each other as playmates – ever. Different interests – and I was outgoing and noisy and all these things, and my sister was quiet and tidy and good, or so I was always being told. We didn't play together. My sister, being older and wiser, I was too childish for her in terms of playing together. I remember being shut out of her life more than being included in it. Her room was private, everything she did was important, much more important than anything I could do, and private. And I had a desire, I think, to learn from her – because I was always being told, "Why can't you be more like your sister?" I felt I had to find out who she is and what she does in order to be like her. But there was no way I could do that. That information was not available. It was very frustrating.'

Both sisters are now in their fifties and live near to one another but they are not close friends, though the illness and death of their mother did bring them closer together. Paula and her partner lead very quiet lives. Fay said she was 'much more reclusive than I am'. After their mother's death when they had to share the task of disposing of her belongings, the fact that they now recognised and accepted their different outlooks on life meant that 'we were able to work together, sorting out Mum's stuff, getting it organised. Paula just wanted to complete it, get it done. I wanted to take a lot of time over it. It was a recipe for absolute disaster, yet we managed really well. I think we built up a lot of trust for each other in that period of time.'

Extraverts and introverts are opposites, so they can argue and fight, but they also complement one another so they can meet one another's needs. Michael Rosen is an extravert. He said, 'I learn my living just by hanging about and making people laugh. I can go in front of 200 kids and do a show and it doesn't involve a mass amount of nerves or stress; it's not a burden to me in any way; it's tremendous fun. For three quarters of an hour I tell them jokes and stories, and they tell me things, and I go away and I've been paid for it.' His brother Brian is an introvert. 'He would listen to the Le Mans 24 hours race. He would listen all through the night. He would keep tables. They classify cars in very different ways – index of classification – and he would keep it all through the night so he would know how well his favourite cars were doing. And then show me the lists. Some obsessives are private, but he very much wanted to share it, enjoy it with me. And also turn it into a joke. He would say, "Hey, you'll never guess what I've done. I've worked out the index classification before the guy on the radio's done it." I get a sense that I was the only person he could enjoy that with – if he tried to share it with other people they would think he was a nutter, or it would incur the disapproval of my dad in some way or another – because he was wasting his time, or not doing his French homework. I can see it's the meat and potatoes of his life, one of his strategies for survival.'

It cannot be assumed that two extravert siblings or two introvert siblings will get along well together. They may not be mystified about one another in the way that Henry James and Fay were each mystified, but the knowledge they have about themselves shows them what matters most to their sibling

– and what the sibling fears the most. What better way for one extravert sibling to torment another extravert sibling than by abandoning the sibling, leaving him all alone and unable to find his way home? Or for one introvert sibling to create chaos out of the carefully arranged possessions belonging to the other introvert sibling? When they grow out of such childish persecutions one sibling can be very impatient with or even despise the other sibling for displaying those characteristics which he hates in himself. Introverts can despise the way their sibling withdraws when social contacts become difficult or boring, or lose himself in his pet theories and ideas. Extraverts can despise the way their sibling will keep the most undesirable company rather than spend any time alone, or will respond however ineptly to any audience which presents itself. Moreover, the fact that siblings experience their existence in similar ways does not mean that they share a value system. In *Pride and Prejudice* both Elizabeth and Lydia were extraverts but Elizabeth always cast a critical eye over those she met while Lydia was overjoyed when anyone paid her attention, no matter who that person might be.

The distinctions between the physical characteristics of male and female are clear, but when it comes to their thinking and behaviour the distinctions are subtle and often hard to define. Extraverts and introverts have no defining physical characteristics, or none that have been discovered. The distinctions between their thoughts and behaviour are very subtle but very powerful. If men are from Mars and women from Venus, introverts and extraverts come from entirely different universes. Many men are wont to declare that they do not understand women, while many women tell one another that men's minds are so simple there is nothing to understand. A similar mutual incomprehension exists between extraverts and introverts. A large part of the incomprehension comes from a lack of effort in trying to imagine what it is like to be the other person, but with close observation and a lack of prejudice it is possible to imagine what it is like to be a man or a woman. With extraverts and introverts there is a point at which imagination fails. It is the point where we simply cannot translate anything from our own experience into what the other says about his experience.

I am an introvert and I have spent much of my adult life lis-

tening to people telling me about their experiences. For more
than 20 years I have thought about, discussed and written
about introverts and extraverts. I cannot help but apply this
knowledge to all the people I meet, read about, or learn about
through the media. In just about everything we say and do we
display something of how we experience our sense of existence.
Thus I have heard many extraverts describe in one way or another how they experience their sense of existence. When someone tells me about the death of their child or about their direct
experience of war I can imagine what it must have been like
to go through those experiences, but when an extraverts tells
me, 'If I'm on my own for too long I start to feel I don't exist', or
'When the disaster happened I walked and talked but inside I
felt I'd disappeared', I cannot imagine what it must be like to
experience yourself as an active body without a person inside.
I can understand the experience intellectually, but emotionally
I cannot imagine what it is like to have such an experience, or
even to be sure that such an experience is possible and to fear it.

I have come across metaphors which make the extravert's
experience real to me intellectually but I cannot translate that
intellectual understanding into my emotional understanding
in the same way that I can understand another person's grief.
However, a perceptive introvert can use a striking simile to
convey his understanding of an extravert's experience. E. Arnot
Robertson does this in her one great novel *Ordinary Families*.
From her delineation of the narrator Lallie, I would guess that
E. Arnot Robertson was an introvert because Lallie rings true
to me in every respect. At one point in the story when Lallie
is in her teens she sees her mother setting out on foot to go
shopping. She tries to stay out of her mother's sight because
she did not want to have to accompany her, but she felt guilty
about this:

> The realisation that Mother was one of those people who
> exist solely in their relationships to others forced me to
> take several steps out into the open, in order to make a
> better bargain with my conscience. But there I "froze"
> again. . . . Mother . . . if she did not think of herself as
> the wife of Arthur Rush, the producer of his children and
> the friend and customer of people in the village, could not

realise her own existence at all. Peel away from her all
her relationships and, like an onion and its skins, there
would be nothing left for her own mind to grasp, no solid
core that was unalterably Phyllis Laidler, now called Mrs
Rush for convenience. To make a person like that take
her pleasure alone seemed particularly rotten to me.[28]

Good though this description is, it still does not convey the full
quality of the extravert's experience because similes say 'It is
like . . .' and not 'It is.'

### Are extraverts taking over the world?

I know that extraverts are as limited in understanding introverts as I am in understanding the extravert's experience.
Introverts often envy an extravert's social skills, but in my
experience they never want to be an extravert. In Britain and
Australia I have encountered many extraverts who fancy being
an introvert, indeed many insist that they are introverts. If I
mention an introvert's great tolerance for being alone (introverts can feel very lonely but being left alone is not their greatest fear), these extraverts counter with 'I love being alone' and
give examples of when they are on their own, all of which prove
on enquiry to be strictly time limited and with other people
in easy reach. William James's biographer Linda Simon called
his holiday home Puttnam Camp 'his beloved retreat in the
Adirondack Mountains' where he would go for long, arduous
solitary walks. She wrote:

Puttnam Camp remained a source of physical and spiritual
renewal, a place where he could rediscover the 'real
springs' of his life. James often said that he retreated to
Puttnam Camp to escape from the irritations of too much
sociability, but he never was isolated in the balsam-scented
woods of Puttnam Camp. The camp was always filled
with families – wives, children, cousins and friends – all
of whom he knew well: Bowditches, Puttnams, various
Lowells, Cabots, Lothrops, Emersons, and Hoopers.[29]

The people that maintain an extravert's existence do not
have to be real, live people, or people whom the extravert has

actually met. They can be celebrities they admire, fantasy characters, pets, fluffy toys, or books and possessions, all of which in the extravert's imagination are people with whom he has a relationship. Years ago my friend Peter explained to me why he had many children and lived in a country cottage inhabited and surrounded by what to me were countless numbers of animals. He said that if God sent a thunderbolt it was likely that enough of these people and animals would survive so that he would not be left all alone.

If those extraverts who fancy being introverts knew what being an introvert is actually like they would choose to stay as they were born because there is an increasing social disadvantage to being an introvert. Critics of the way psychologists and psychiatrists divide people into normal and abnormal have long noted that in textbooks on psychiatry or abnormal psychology typical male characteristics are regarded as being the standard for normal while typical female characteristics are regarded as being the standard for abnormal. Now that many of the personality tests used by psychologists are thought to measure extraversion, this term has entered public discourse. The characteristics of an extravert – being sociable, talkative, outgoing – are increasingly being seen as normal and very laudable. To be accepted and admired you must be 'entertaining' if you are a man and 'bubbly' if you are woman. Entertaining and bubbly people are regarded as having 'lots of personality'. Pity the shy extravert and the introvert who has not found it necessary to learn social skills.[30] They are deemed to have 'not much of a personality'. However, shy extraverts can be very appealing, while thoughtful and reserved introverts can be criticised for being too serious, snobbish, cold and unfeeling.

From what I have read it seems that today in the USA being an introvert comes close to being un-American. My searches on the web have revealed attitudes to introverts which I find most alarming. Linda Kreger Silverman of the Gifted Development Center in Denver, Colorado, begins her paper 'On Introversion' thus:

> The American dream is to be extraverted. We want our children to be 'people who need people'. We want them to have lots of friends, to like parties, to prefer to play outside

with their buddies than retire with a good book, to make
friends easily, to greet new experiences enthusiastically,
to be good risk-takers, to be open about their feelings,
to be trusting. We regard anyone who doesn't fit into
this pattern with concern. We call them 'withdrawn',
'aloof', 'shy', 'secretive' and 'loners'. These pejorative
terms show the extent to which we misunderstand
introverts. The majority of Americans are extraverted
(about 75%). . . . Since extraversion is the dominant mode
in our society, there are no 'closet extraverts' but there
are many 'closet introverts', people who are so ashamed
of their introversion that they try to be extraverts.

Linda points out that 'the majority of gifted children appear
to be introverted (about 60%), and the percentage of introverts seems to increase with IQ. In addition to the problems
encountered with being gifted, these children are frequently
misjudged because they are introverted.' However, she reas-
sures these children and their parents that 'Introversion is a
perfectly normal personality type identified by Carl Jung. It is
actually *healthy* [her italics] to be an introvert. The only unhealthy part of it is denying your true self and trying to dis-
guise yourself as an extravert.'[31]

Jill D. Burrass and Lisa Kaenzig, in their paper 'Introversion: The Often Forgotten Factor Impacting the Gifted', state:
'Introversion is not a pathological condition; it is not an abnormal response to the world. It is simply a personality trait found
in a small percentage of the population.'[32] None of these three
psychologists seems to have wondered whether this apparent
over-abundance of extraverts in the USA might be a function
of the kind of questionnaires used to measure extraversion and
introversion. If you know that to be accepted by others you must
display the characteristics of an extravert, and if you are applying for a job or a college place and being asked whether you
prefer to work as part of a team or on your own, and whether
you prefer a team sport or an individual sport, you are not going to be such a fool as to say that you prefer working on your
own and your favourite activity is going fishing by yourself.

In her book *A Mind of Your Own: How Your Brain Distorts
and Deceives*, the psychologist Cordelia Fine reported the work

of two Princeton researchers who 'asked a group of students to read one of two (fabricated) scientific articles. The first article claimed that an extroverted personality helps people to achieve academic success. The second article, handed out to just as many students, claimed that introverts tend to be more academically successful. . . Whichever personality trait the students thought was the key to success, the more highly the students rated themselves as possessing that attribute.'[33]

It is safe to 'fake good', as we psychologists say, on these tests because you are unlikely to encounter a sneaky psychologist like me who will look at your questionnaire results and ask, 'Why is it important to you to work in a team?' If you answer, 'I like being part of a team because it's fun and I get to know people and we work well together' I will feel fairly sure that you are an extravert. If you answer, 'Because that's the way to get the best results' my next question will be, 'Why is it important to you to get the best results?' If you are an introvert trying to pass as an extravert you are now faced with having to imagine what an extravert would say and then say it convincingly. In my experience of posing the kind of question which asks about the reasons behind the reasons, everybody – extraverts and introverts – finds it impossible to lie convincingly by producing a credible answer that goes against their nature. Instead people go silent, or they keep repeating their last answer using different words. Psychoanalysts call this kind of behaviour 're-sistance', where the person does not want to reveal something about themselves.

Linda, Jill and Lisa seem never to have encountered such a situation. When they define extraverts and introverts they talk only of what they do, not why they do it. These psychologists seem not to have realised that two people can do exactly the same thing but for entirely different reasons. However, if you are an introvert and worried about being extremely gifted *and* an introvert, help is at hand. Linda gives 12 'tips on the care and feeding [sic] of introverts in your family or classroom'. (Two of these tips, 'Never embarrass them in public' and 'Don't interrupt them', I would commend to my friends with regard to me.) Jill and Lisa give eight pieces of extraordinarily patronis-ing advice to parents and siblings for supporting and protect-ing introverts, for example, 'Provide coping strategies for those times when they have to act extraverted. If some member of the family is also introverted, sharing secrets or tips to tide them through those large groups, in front of others, high noise times is very useful. If the family is extraverted, help may need to come from outside the family.' If all that fails, you can consult Marti Olsen Laney's book *The Introvert Advantage: How to Thrive in an Extrovert World*, and website.[34]

Jerome Kagan is regarded by many psychologists as one of the major thinkers in developmental psychology. His large-scale studies of how children develop from infancy to adulthood began with his observation that when 21-month-old infants were presented with 'unfamiliar people, objects, and situations in a laboratory setting'[35] some of them cried and sought safety with their mother while others did not cry and found the novelties interesting. The first group was labelled 'inhibited' and the second group 'uninhibited'. In their account of the studies which followed, Jerome Kagan and his colleague Nancy Snidman wrote:

> The central assumption behind our assessments of 4-month-old infants was that those who displayed frequent motor activity and crying when presented with unfamiliar visual, auditory and olfactory stimuli had inherited a distinct neurochemistry that rendered the amygdala excitable. These infants were biased to become inhibited children in the second year. The infants who showed minimal motor activity and little or no distress, because of a different neurochemistry, were likely to become uninhibited children.[36]

Some 237 11-year-olds, having been tested at 4 months, 2 years, 4 years and 7 years, were tested on a number of physical measures as well as being observed by researchers during the first 18 minutes of the 3.5 hour testing period and their behaviour rated in terms of being inhibited or uninhibited. Using a very highly structured measure the mothers of the children and the children themselves reported on each child's behaviour. In summing up their research Kagan and Snidman wrote: 'Carl Jung's descriptions of the introvert and extravert, written over 75 years ago, apply with uncanny accuracy to a proportion of our high- and low-reactive adolescents.'[37]

Kagan's research has led a number of psychologists to use the terms uninhibited/extravert/sociable and inhibited/introvert/shy interchangeably. However, Kagan and Snidman's results were not as clear-cut as that. Amongst the children tested there were always a significant number who showed both inhibited and uninhibited characteristics. The reason for this lies in the different ways that Kagan and Jung worked. Jung listened to his patients for many hours. He wanted to understand how each individual saw himself and his world because these interpretations became the reasons why the person did what he did. Kagan was interested only in what the children did, not why they did it. For him the 'why' was answered by the child's biological make-up and the effect that the culture in which the child lived had on his biology. Kagan simply required the children in his research to be co-operative during the physical tests and to indicate on a list of 20 statements whether each statement was 'very much like me; a little like me; not like me; definitely not like me'.[38] The child could not modify the statement to give a more accurate answer. For instance, to the statement 'I am a shy person' the child could say only to what degree the statement applied to him. He had no opportunity to say something like 'I'm not shy when I'm with other children but when adults talk down to me and ask me what I'm going to do when I grow up I can't think what to say. Then the adults always say, "Oh, he's shy!", and I feel awful.'

Shyness is not a trait. It is an emotion which we can use as a defence when we are in a social situation. We are never shy when we are alone. Extraverts who doubt their own value are very prone to using the defence of shyness. They want to be liked, and they know that people often dislike an especially confident person but will be kind to someone who is exhibiting the behaviour which denotes shyness. Introverts can also use the defence of shyness when they feel uncertain about a social situation, but often they are seen as shy when in fact they are not enjoying the company they are with. When they are with people whom they see as being interesting and amusing they can be very sociable, but if they have to be sociable with people whom they find uninteresting and dull they find being sociable nothing but hard work. As Mr Darcy said of himself, 'I certainly have not the talent which some people possess of conversing easily with those I have never seen before. I cannot catch the tone of their conversation, or appear interested in their concerns, as I often see done.' He agreed with Elizabeth that he should practise but it was clear that he had no intention of doing so.[39] Mr Darcy may have appeared shy but he certainly was not.

## Peculiar experiences

There is no doubt that being an introvert is a very strange experience, but being an extravert is also a strange experience. Feeling compelled to create and maintain relationships even when your intellect is telling you that this is not necessary is a strange experience. The extravert experience is often seen in terms of attachment, something we all understand. However, the compulsion to create and maintain relationships is different from attachment because the negation of the relationship of the kind which extraverts feel compelled to create provokes fear, whereas the loss of an attachment provokes grief. Thus the loss of someone important to an extravert provokes both fear and grief. Similarly, if an introvert experiences the loss of someone dear to him as a breakdown of control and order, then the introvert, like the extravert, will experience both grief and fear. Grief, as C. S. Lewis once observed, feels very much like fear.

What the introvert experiences in ordinary life has no near parallel like that of attachment. When you are living the experience day by day it seems to be entirely reasonable, but when you have to describe the experience to someone who is not an introvert you can see from the person's face that the experience is very odd. I have often had to describe to an audience what happens to an introvert when something significant and totally unexpected happens. I begin by pointing out that at any one time we are aware of two realities. There is the reality of what is going on around us and the reality of what is going on inside us, our thoughts and feelings. When we feel that we understand what is going on inside and around us, the realities of inside us and outside us seem to be equally real, but for introverts when something significant and unexpected happens then external reality becomes less real. When I say this I can tell who in the audience is an extravert and who an introvert. Introverts look unsurprised, though they may be very interested in hearing this familiar but private experience described. Extraverts look puzzled. How could the solid world become unreal?

Just how unreal the world becomes depends on how often the introvert has had the experience and acquired the confidence to deal with it effectively. Introverts become very quiet, even isolating themselves, after an unexpected event occurs because they are trying to put into practice the techniques they have developed to assure themselves that the world is real and they can cope with it. The qualities of the unreal world can be different for different introverts depending on which aspect of the world each individual introvert chooses to doubt.

When something unpleasant and unexpected happens to me the world takes on the appearance it has in my dreams. When I am asleep and dreaming I am moving through a landscape or cityscape where items such as houses, rooms, furniture, water, mountains and roads are clear and distinct but the relationship between them is entirely plastic. Cartoonists using animation often depict a kind of world where the rules of depth, distance and solidity are suspended but the cartoons look like cartoons, whereas all the things in my dream look real while they behave in relationship to their own qualities and to one another in ways which are unreal. In the dream this does not surprise me. When I am awake and shocked by the unexpected I see the world as I do in my dreams, except that my dreams are rarely unpleasant while the strangeness of the world when I am awake is very disturbing. I know that there is another way of seeing it but I do not know which way is correct. I stay quite still and silent until the world around me goes back to being as I see it when I am awake. For me as an adult this massive doubt about the world lasts only a moment, but when I was a child and teenager this experience happened often and lasted for longer.

The best description of external reality becoming unreal that I have come across is in the novel *Ordinary Families*. Lallie, the introvert narrator, was obsessed with time. She spoke of 'Time, my shadow' and 'my old friend-enemy' Time. She was always aware of 'an anxious sense of the racing of time as it slid by maliciously faster than usual, trying to outstrip my vigilance'.[40] But when the disastrously unexpected happened, Time stopped.

Lallie fell in love with Gordon, an archaeologist who from her adolescence onward had been an occasional visitor to her family home beside the Orwell River. One afternoon Lallie with her sisters Dru and Margaret and their friend Basil accompanied Gordon to his car before he left on a long trip to Orkney. Lallie silently begged Time 'be kind for once, move gently when there is purpose in your slowness; stop for a little while, because his voice, and the way in which his eyes wrinkle up, have become more important than anything else in the world.' Then, 'Timelessly, as I looked back from the river to other people in the group around the car, I saw Margaret glance from Basil to Gordon; not for once idly as she usually looked at people, but appraisingly; a woman comparing two men who might serve her need. The need was not imperative, being satisfied for the moment; the comparison was instinctive. And of the two men whose desire she held at the moment, Gordon – older, harder, more experienced – was better in her eyes. Margaret did not want Gordon as much as he wanted her in that moment, when something flamed up between them, but she was experienced with men – I knew that for certain now – and already this looking on men as potential lovers had become a habit now.' The conversation in the group went on, Gordon was farewelled and drove away, and 'Time poured back into the gap that had opened in it.[41]

Lallie had always known that Margaret was strikingly beautiful but it took her longer to realise that Margaret was casually, cruelly promiscuous. She was also becoming aware that whenever Margaret perceived something was important to Lallie she carelessly destroyed it. This Time-stopping moment about which no one other than Lallie would know laid the foundation for the quietly sad ending of the story. Lallie married Gordon and was happy. Margaret married and went with her husband to India, but three years later returned on a visit. Lallie invited her to stay a day or two with her and Gordon in London. Lallie met her and brought her to their flat. Gordon welcomed Margaret and 'fussed over getting both of us some tea':

I went into the bedroom to take off my things.

They had not moved when I came back. Margaret was in
our worn armchair, and he was bending over the gas-ring
by the fire, but they were tense and still –
unnaturally stilled for me by the stopping of Time as I
stood in the doorway – and looking at one another with
the expression I knew, having seen it once before.

Even this she must have, in all but face at least. Even
this. Gordon was fond of me: actually nothing would
happen. For me, Time would start again, sooner or later,
would fling tortured seconds into the gulf that had opened
in it once more, would flow and obliterate it at last. One
day I should find that I could not remember just how
they had looked. Only a tie of allegiance had broken.
Even this she must have: all I really had. Even this.

Time. Time was starting now slowly, agonisingly,
gathering way. Time, flow on.[42]

In telling her readers about Lallie's experience of Time stopping, E. Arnot Robinson did not use a simile. It was not 'as if
Time stopped': it was 'Time stopped'. The familiar reality of the
external world becomes unreal. Lallie could tell no one about
what happened. On most occasions when we tell someone about
the way we have been hurt and betrayed by a sibling, in the
telling the event itself seems to be petty and trivial. Because
we do not talk about our great fear of being annihilated as a
person when the reality around us or inside us becomes unreal,
we have no way of explaining why one action by a sibling we
can see as slightly annoying while another seemingly trivial
action by the same sibling becomes the greatest hurt, the unforgivable betrayal.

My experiences of the world becoming unreal and Lallie's
experience of Time stopping (I suspect E. Arnot Robinson was
describing her own experiences) are hard to describe because
under stress introverts can lose those sophisticated ways of
organising the initial meanings that the human brain creates
about what is going on. For instance, when we look around,
all that our brain registers is a series of disconnected images.
We/our brain then connects these disconnected images to form
a continuous sequence, analogous to the way in which we see a

moving film when a series of still photographs is shown to us at speed. In effect we take on trust that one event has led to another. When external reality becomes strange to me I have lost this trust. Similarly, all that our brain registers is a series of present moments. To make sense of this series of present moments we learn to see events in terms of time passing. In effect we take on trust that time passes. When Time stood still for Lallie she lost this trust.

In contrast, under great stress extraverts lose their trust in internal reality. Our sense of being a person is an act of trust. Our meaning structure is constantly changing, yet we take on trust that, despite this constant change, something essential in our meaning structure remains the same. When we wake in the morning we are the same person who went to sleep the previous evening. Introverts never lose this trust. Even when they feel that they are shattering, crumbling to dust, the shards and the dust of themselves still exist. Extraverts often lose or doubt their trust in their internal reality. *The Catcher in the Rye* is a brilliant account of an extravert who finds himself alone and friendless except for his dead brother and his kid sister, neither of whom can save him except in his fantasies. Holden begged his brother, 'Allie, don't let me disappear.' In her study of hysteria, *Madmen and Medusas*, Juliet Mitchell does not use the word 'extravert' but her description of an hysteric is of an extravert who lacks self-confidence and a belief in his self-worth. She describes how, when such a person suffers a trauma, that person 'is suddenly no one, annihilated, in danger of psychic death'.[43] She wrote: 'This state is one in which the person has felt in danger of their non-existence' and 'The dread of the death-like experience of trauma . . . is the equivalent of an absence of subject or ego.'[44]

In the place of 'subject or ego' I would put 'meaning structure'. We experience the greatest threat to our meaning structure when we have experienced an event which shows us that our meaning structure is not an accurate picture of what is going on. More frequently we become aware of the possibility that we have got things wrong. Fear says, 'I have got things wrong.' Anxiety says, 'I might have got things wrong.' To stop ourselves from being overwhelmed and annihilated by our anxiety we turn to our preferred reality. Extraverts become busy and introverts withdraw into themselves. Often this withdrawal makes it difficult for introverts to pay proper attention to what is going on around them. I am very well aware that I do this, and when my introvert friend Matthew behaved in a way so unlike himself I asked him if this was what had happened to him.

Matthew understands how things work. He can plumb a bathroom, rewire a house, set up a computer. So when he asked if he could stay overnight in my home while I was away I had no doubt that he would be able to deal with the new alarm I had had fitted. It was not markedly different from the old, just a slightly different keyboard layout. However, when I returned home I found that when he let himself in he could not work out that a small cover had to be lifted to reveal the keypad. He dithered and the alarm went off. He managed to silence it but then forgot to phone the security control to tell them not to contact the police. They arrived when Matthew had gone out and were not at all pleased to find no one there. Ordinarily I would have been greatly irritated by this turn of events but I knew that Matthew had come to London for the funeral of one of his closest friends. When he and I talked over what had happened I asked him if, when he reached my place, he had been so perturbed by the events of that day that he had gone into that place of retreat and was operating in external reality on a kind of automatic pilot. He agreed that it had been so, not only because of his friend's death, but because the setting of his funeral was part of London where Matthew spent his early childhood. My home is near where Matthew lived as a schoolboy. Every time he had visited me he talked about his memories of that part of London.

The death of anyone close to us makes us think about our own death and our life, how we have lived our life and how strange life and death are. Such a meditation may cast doubt on some of our ideas, often ideas which are central to our meaning structure. Just as removing a retaining wall in a house is a very risky business, so rethinking ideas central to our meaning structure is risky. We cannot predict what changes will follow. So in defence introverts retreat into themselves while extraverts rush into external reality and become very busy. However, if their external reality offers no means of defensive activity, extraverts can resort to fantasies of activity, fantasies which can become to them as real as real experience.

Like *The Catcher in the Rye,* Heinrich Böll's novel *The Clown* is a brilliant study of an extravert who found himself alone and friendless, but here the setting is post-war Germany and the protagonist, Hans Schnier, a gentle and loving man who worked as a clown. He was the 28-year-old son of a wealthy industrialist Protestant family who, as his mother had said, had 'cast him out' when he married a Catholic girl. Older and more experienced than Holden, Hans saw and despised the hypocrisy of the Nazi lovers like his mother who after the war declared themselves to be anti-racist and champions of democracy. He also saw and despised the hypocrisy of Christians, both Catholic and Protestant, who prided themselves on the Christian virtues and ignored the sufferings of others. He was wounded, first, when his brother Leo joined the Catholic Church and studied for the priesthood, and, second, when his beloved Marie left him and married a Catholic. While waiting for Leo to visit him Hans thought about Marie:

> Marie was doing all right, she was in Rome now, in the bosom of her church, and wondering what to wear for an audience with the Pope. . . . I made up my mind to go to Rome and request an audience with the Pope. There was something of a wise old clown about him too, and after all the figure of Harlequin originated in Bergamo.[45] . . . I would do a few turns for him, nice light little things like Going to School and Returning from School, but not the one called Cardinal; that would hurt his feelings because he had been a cardinal after all – and he was the last person I would want to hurt.
>
> Time and time again I become prey to my imagination: I pictured my audience with the Pope so minutely, saw myself kneel down and as an unbeliever ask his blessing, I saw the Swiss guards at the door and some benevolent, only slightly disgusted Monsignore in attendance – that I almost believed that I had already been to see the Pope. I would be tempted to tell Leo that I had been to see the Pope and had been granted an audience. During those minutes I *was* with the Pope, saw his smile and heard

his wonderful peasant's voice, told him how the local
buffoon of Bergamo had become Harlequin. Leo is very
strict in these matters. He is always calling me a liar.[46]

Leo was an introvert and, like all introverts, he was passionate
about truth. Introverts care about the truth, not because they
are virtuous, though many of them like to think that they are,
but because they need to be as certain as possible about what
is going on in their external reality. Introverts are likely to
declare that it is much better to know the truth no matter how
painful it may be, while many extraverts prefer uncomfortable
truths to be wrapped in a few comforting lies.

Fortunately there are also many extraverts who view the
world with a clear, discerning eye. Holden and Hans are rep-
resentations of such people. The best comedians are those who
observe human foibles and juxtapose them with sharp irony.
Of course not all comedians are extraverts but many are, particularly those comedians who draw on the extravert's skill of
mimicry to become the person whose foibles, and sometimes
lies and hypocrisy, need to be exposed to the public view.

In such ironic comedy the extravert is saying, 'This is what
this person does.' The question 'Why does he do this?' is not
asked. 'Why?' is the introvert's question. Introverts seek answers to the question 'Why?', but unfortunately many of the
answers they find are neither wise nor clever. The introvert's
need for certainty can lead some introverts to claim that the
answers they have found contain a higher, greater truth than
that known by mere mortals or the proletariat. In Stalin's Great
Terror when millions died many people were forced to confess
to crimes they had not committed: '[Stalin] knew that some or
all of the confessions were not necessarily true in the pedes-
trian meaning of the term in which statements corresponded
to observable facts. For him, this distinction made no difference. If certain "facts" were not empirically true, they became
functionally true to suit political purposes that, in Stalin's universe, represented a higher reality.[47]

On the other hand, the search for the answer to the question
'Why?' has led many introverts into science or into literature.
Virginia Woolf's early life was marked by many deaths in her
family. Her biographer Hermione Lee wrote:

During the years of these family deaths, Virginia Stephen
evolved a dark but coherent idea of existence which allowed
her an almost *proud* sense (inspired by her reading of
Greek) of having been singled out for tragedy: 'the Gods (as
I used to phrase it) were taking us seriously.' She began
to think of life as a narrow strip which had to be ridden,
a small space of 'extreme reality' threatened by hostile
forces – an 'invisible giant' or 'two great grindstones'.
She would give these views to her characters. . . . Mrs
Ramsay thinks of life as a 'little strip of time', and of
herself as carrying out 'a sort of transaction' with it.
Sometimes she got the better of it; but for the most part
'she felt that this thing she called life terrible, hostile,
and quick to pounce on you if you gave it a chance'.

Out of this image of a narrow, perilous strip of existence,
Virginia Woolf developed her sense of herself as a writer.
She had already, as a small child, experienced moments
of profound horror or desolation. Now these deaths
intensified her anticipation of a hidden enemy waiting
to deliver a 'sledgehammer blow', and the need for some
form of fight or resistance. When she came to explain to
herself in her late memoir what made her a writer, she
described it as a process of *welcoming* or finding valuable
these shocks: 'And so I go on to suppose that the shock-
receiving capacity is what makes me a writer.' The shock
is followed by an immediate desire to explain it. The
'blow' is to become 'a revelation of some order'; 'it is a
token of some real thing behind appearances; and I make
it real by putting it into words'. This making of 'order'
or 'wholeness' out of 'shocks' is, she says, 'the strongest
pleasure known to me'. This 'pleasure' leads her to the
philosophy of life which she was beginning to evolve in
her 1903 notebook: that there is a pattern behind the
'cotton wool' of daily life and that all individuals, and
all individual works of art, are part of that pattern.[48]

Virginia Woolf's extravert sister Vanessa Bell was as passionate about painting as Virginia was about writing, but Vanessa
was not interested in the question 'Why?' Her daughter
Angelica Garnett wrote:

The whole cast of her mind, unenquiring and passive, was opposed to analysis: unlike Virginia, she never learnt to project the light of self-questioning onto her own behaviour. Instead she clung to a hope that all problems could be solved by rationalising them, and that there was somewhere a perfect system that would do away with threatening or painful situations.[49] From Vanessa's conversation it soon became apparent that she still believed, as she always had, that subject and even motivation in art had no importance. Crucifixions and entombments, people being impaled or burnt alive, could be looked at for their abstract qualities alone, a blind eye turned to the human content, as well as to the stimulus derived from it that may have affected the artist. . . . With Madonnas and children, or Susannah in the bath, she could see them as contemporary nursery or domestic subjects, while happily divesting them of their religion; though she didn't deny that this was at the root of their inspiration, she still didn't believe that it had any 'real' importance. She was unmoved by the fact that a lot of Bach's music is literally figurative – that descending intervals describe the Virgin's tears, or arpeggios the Sea of Galilee. Had one told her, she would have dismissed it as irrelevant. There was a split in her mind as to why things were done, and how; it did not occur to her that the one cannot exist without the other.[50]

The introverts' search for 'why?' and the extraverts' lack of interest in 'why?' is present in how they regard the emotional meanings which they create. Extraverts value emotion so much that many of them resist any kind of analysis of what they feel. They fear that if they seek to find out why they feel this or that emotion, their inquiry will dissipate the emotion and leave their life flat and stale. They value the highs and lows of life and do not want to live it on an even keel. Extraverts who have lost all self-confidence and fear that they are about to be annihilated as a person can swing from the heights of mania to the depths of depression. However, even when the highs cause chaos in their lives and the lows are the worst torments of depression, they do not want the treatment they receive to eradicate the highs and lows altogether. The drug lithium may limit the extremes of their experience, but many people who take it find that it renders their life colourless and without feeling. They exist but they do not live.[51] Self-confident, sensible extraverts place some limits on expression of their emotions, but they do not reject the expression of all emotion as some introverts do.

Introverts find emotions dangerous because they threaten chaos and annihilation, and so they try to organise their feelings and bring them under control. Introverts are adept at separating their thoughts from their feelings. Tsitsi Dangarembga described this way of thinking in her novel *Nervous Conditions*. The central character, Tamba, was a Shona girl living with her family in a village in Rhodesia in the late 1960s. She led a very different life from that of Alexandra Fuller and her sister Vanessa. They lived a rackety life while Tamba's life was dominated by Shona rules and customs. Tamba's family was very poor and she had to help her mother in the fields and in their home. Tamba longed for an education and studied as best she could, but only her elder brother Nhamo was considered by the men in her family to merit an education. Nhamo attended the mission school where their uncle Babamukura was headmaster. When Nhamo became ill and died Tamba was allowed to take his place at the school. She was to live with her uncle and his family in much more comfortable and European surroundings than that of her family.

On her first evening there her uncle 'summoned me to make sure that I knew how lucky I was to have been given this opportunity for mental and eventually, through it, material emancipation. . . . He concluded by defining for me my immediate tasks: "to be good, listen to what we, your parents, tell you to do, to study your books diligently and not let your mind be distracted by other things."[52] Tamba resolved to do this, but when she retired to bed she felt overwhelmed by her new situation. Like all introverts, she tried to get her thoughts in order and, like many introverts, she used 'ought' and 'must' to do this:

> The smug determination that Babamukura's talk had
> instilled in me evaporated. I began to feel inferior
> again. I was a bit masochistic at that age, wallowing
> in my imagined inadequacy until I was in real danger
> of feeling sorry for myself. Then I reprimanded myself

for this self-indulgence by thinking of my mother, who suffered from being female and poor and uneducated and black so stoically that I was ashamed of my weakness in succumbing so flabbily to the strangeness of my new circumstances. This gave me the fine lash of guilt to whip myself with. I reaffirmed my vow to use the opportunity my uncle had given me to the maximum advantage.

A lot of my reactions were of this complicated sort in those days, requiring a lot of thought to sort them out into organised parts. But the activity and excitement of the day's events had exhausted me: I fell asleep before I could order my thoughts neatly.[53]

In ordering her thoughts Tamba was stripping them of the emotions which otherwise would threaten to overwhelm her. This process is the introvert's favourite defence. Freud called it isolation, where the introvert separates his perception of an event from its emotional meaning. 'I am in a strange place and I am afraid' becomes simply 'I am in a strange place' and the 'I am afraid' is pushed from consciousness. Wise introverts know that they do this. They wait until they are alone and private to express their feelings. When introverts weep they usually weep alone. Unwise introverts bury their emotions and if asked about a disturbing event will acknowledge that it happened but deny that they were upset in any way. Unacknowledged emotion cannot be resolved but will find expression at some time, perhaps years later, in sudden fear, rage or weeping. Extraverts' favourite defence is repression when they simply forget that anything unpleasant occurred. However, while it may be relatively easy to forget that something occurred, it is a good deal harder to forget the warning of danger given by anger and fear. In general it is a good idea to remember where danger lies. So an extravert can find that the warnings of danger keep breaking through no matter how deeply buried the memory of the event may be. Rather than search his memory for the dangerous event an extravert is likely to attach the emotion to some current event. A comment Henri Matisse made about himself that, 'I get worked up too easily'[54] is one which many extraverts make about themselves.

## Understanding one another?

The difference in the way they appreciate and deal with emotions is at the root of the prejudices that extraverts and introverts can have about one another. Introverts can see extraverts as being all display and no substance, while extraverts can see introverts as being cold and unfeeling. Listen to siblings of whatever age criticising one another and it will be very much about feeling, feeling too much or too little.

My extravert sister was always convinced that, apart from occasionally becoming unexpectedly and unjustifiably angry, I had no feelings. She was greatly surprised one day when I was at home during my university holidays and let out a cry of disappointment when the postman on his bicycle sailed past our letterbox. I was in love and waiting for a precious letter. She approved of this brief show of feeling, but soon forgot it and reverted to her old comfortable belief that I had no feelings and therefore anything could be done to me because, 'Dorothy won't mind'. I guess I hid my feelings more carefully than many introverts because I had learned in early childhood that if I revealed my feelings to my mother and sister I would invite criticism and mockery, not their sympathy.

I always knew that my sister had feelings and I never doubted the sincerity of her anger, envy and sheer wanting of anything that might fill the empty space inside her which opened up when our parents appeared to reject her after my birth. It seems that this empty space continued to exist even after she had been restored to her home. She had lost her absolute, unquestioned certainty of their love and her position in the family and so, no matter how many of her wants were met, there was never enough to make her feel whole again. Focusing on her own feelings, she had no time or inclination to try to understand mine.

However, extraverts who try to understand an introvert's situation and who accept that introverts deal with emotion differently from extraverts can become aware of the nature and depth of an introvert's feelings. Liam and Joe were brothers born to parents so taken up with one another that they had little time for their children. The parents could not live with or without one another. There were passionate fights and part-ings, and equally passionate reconciliations, all accompanied by many moves from place to place. The boys' only security was with one another. When they were children Liam looked after his younger brother. As they reached their late teens Liam seemed to lose his way and Joe began to look after Liam, but with increasing difficulty as Liam gradually withdrew into himself and became strange and unreachable. He would disappear for days, then weeks. Joe would go looking for him, finding him wandering or living in a squat, and bring him home, feed him, give him a bath and change of clothes. Picked up by the police on suspicion of stealing, Liam was sent to a psychiatric hospital. Joe found him there, and with that each of them entered into a new career – Liam as a psychiatric patient and Joe his advocate who battled the psychiatric system on Liam's behalf. Finally, after ten years, Liam reached a kind of steady state where he managed to live in a bedsit with a simple daily routine. This way of living was far below what Liam's ability should have allowed him to achieve but it was a kind of peace.

Throughout that time Liam never showed Joe how he appreciated all that he did for him. Joe could not help feeling that an expression of gratitude or brotherly love was his due. The only indication Liam gave that Joe mattered to him was the interest he took in where Joe was going whenever he went on a business trip abroad. Joe was an engineer and visited many out-of-the-way places. Liam was not interested in the purpose of Joe's trip, just its destination. Joe would get out a map and show him exactly where he would be, and then write the information down along with the dates of his departure and return.

Joe said to me, 'I came to realise that Liam saw me as a fixed point in the world, perhaps the only fixed point. Liam always seemed to me to be sort of self-sufficient. He doesn't seem to need people to be thinking of him. I need to know that people are thinking of me. When I go away I tell everyone where I'm going and what I'll be doing. I like to think that people are thinking of me wherever I am.'

The story of Joe and Liam illustrates the different way in which extraverts and introverts need other people. Joe perhaps did not understand that, as well as being the only fixed point in Liam's life, he was the person against whom Liam measured himself. Both extraverts and introverts need other people but in very different ways. Extraverts need to be liked. Some extraverts want to be liked by everyone in the world. Other extraverts can get by with just a few who love them – provided they never leave. To fulfil their need to achieve, introverts have to have some standard against which to measure themselves. From all the people they have met or learned about they select a small group whose opinions they value. Jane Dunn said of Virginia Woolf, 'Her work had to be admired, had to be publicly declared by those people whose opinions she valued to be worthwhile, for if she was not a writer she was nothing.' However, above all these people was her sister Vanessa. 'Vanessa was also her audience: it was for her she wrote and her approval which mattered the most. "I always feel I'm writing for you more than for anybody".'[55]

Throughout their lives Virginia and Vanessa wrote to one another every day. Virginia's letters were full of endearments, statements about how important Vanessa was to her, while Vanessa's letters were more prosaic. She found it hard to put her love and need for other people into words. She gathered people around her – sister, husband, lovers, children – and could not bear to let them go. Her daughter Angelica wrote:

> Vanessa clung to Roger, Duncan, myself and Julian, and perhaps to a lesser degree Quentin – who had his own system of self-protection – like a limpet. An apparently strong, even self-sufficient character, when it came to love, she bent like a flower under the weight of a humble bee. It was her way of loving, actuated by as great a need to be loved as to love. When the moment came to separate either from children or lover, in spite of all her good intentions, she was unable to recognise it; the stream of desire continued to be transmitted – like the messages of animals and insects – irresistibly. When someone she loved died, she was so disorientated that she fastened onto the nearest person who seemed to offer both safety and an echo of the one lost. Even when she ceased to be 'in love', she needed evidence of her power over the loved one. Clive and Roger both hovered nearby, compelled by her need, as later did Duncan.[56]

The lives of Virginia and Vanessa are well documented by their own writings and by those of people who knew them.

Thus it is possible to say that Virginia's periods of insanity and finally suicide followed crises which showed her that she had no control over her life, whereas Vanessa's periods of depression followed loss. Moreover, it was not a chance coincidence that two years after Virginia died in 1941 Vanessa was diagnosed with breast cancer. The profound destabilising effect that loss of control has for introverts and rejection and loss have for extraverts is well documented in a wide range of biographical texts, even ones where the writer is unaware that the subject of the biography is an introvert or an extravert.[57] Just how profoundly loss of control and rejection and loss affect the body is now being shown in the multitude of studies of the relationship between psychological stress and the efficient functioning of the immune system.

'Stress' is now divided into different kinds of 'stressors', events which challenge our ability to cope, and a number of different measures of the functioning of the immune system are now used. Sally Dickerson and Margaret Kemeny reviewed 208 laboratory studies of acute psychological stressors and their effect on cortisol levels which can inhibit many aspects of immune system functioning:

> Psychological stressors affect physiology by activating
> specific cognitive and affective processes and their central
> nervous underpinnings. The thalamus and frontal
> lobes (e.g., prefrontal cortex) first integrate sensory
> information and evaluate or appraise the significance
> or meaning of environmental stimuli. These cognitive
> appraisals can lead to the generation of emotional
> responses via extensive connections from the prefrontal
> cortex to the limbic system (e.g., the amygdala and
> hippocampus). The limbic structures, which connect
> to the hypothalamus, serve as a primary pathway for
> activating the hypothalamic-pituitary-adrenocortical
> (HPA) [which regulates the release of cortisol].[58]

The research reviewed studied healthy adults who were given tasks to perform under laboratory conditions. These studies showed that the tasks which produced the most marked changes in cortisol levels were those which either presented the person with a situation over which he had no control or where the person's efforts were disparaged by an onlooker. The biggest effect came from tasks which combined lack of control with criticism. This research made no attempt to distinguish extraverts from introverts, and how the subjects interpreted the tasks was not reported, but it is possible that the introverts were most affected by the loss of control and the extraverts by criticism. When these features were combined the introverts could have thought, 'I've lost control of this: the people whose opinions I value will despise me', while the extraverts could have thought, 'I've made a mess of this: everyone will hate me.'

Where do these ideas come from – 'the people I value will despise me', 'everyone will hate me'? Have they not evolved from two ideas we each created even before we had language in which to express them: the ideas that, 'My parents don't approve of me' and 'My parents don't love me'? These are ideas that we created when we were learning to be good.

# Chapter 4

# COMPETING TO BE GOOD

Our lives are dominated by the need to be good. We think about being good. We worry about being good. We think about being good so much that we do not have to think about it in words and sentences. Years of practice allow us to run through the permutations and combinations of the exhortations we give ourselves – be good/you ought/you must/try harder/do better/you're not good enough/not as good as him/a failure/what will they think/ they won't like me/they'll despise me/I've failed others/I've failed myself – that we can go through a long, complex argument of criticism/fear/defence/guilt/shame/self-punishment/ reparation in a split second. The fear of not being good enough slides easily into the fear of being annihilated as a person. If we are not good enough people will reject us and everything will fall into chaos. Such fear can dominate our thoughts, making living a torture, or it can simmer away at the back of our minds, leaching the colour and sparkle from our lives, while every so often we hear the tolling of the bell of dread.

By 'good' I do not mean the standard list of virtues, truthfulness, loyalty and the like, but the attributes which are valued by you and the community in which you have to live. This is the *virtutis* of Spinoza, the virtue required to survive as a person. If your community is Pol Pot or drug dealers, 'good' would include a capacity to be ruthless in killing your enemy, or to be effective in deceiving the gullible. Being 'good' and thus a credit to your parents could mean getting your PhD or becoming a suicide bomber. Being 'good' and thus your parents' favourite child could mean becoming a priest or a television celebrity. You may never use the word 'good' in relation to yourself, but all of us know the uncomfortable feeling that arises when we become aware of discrepancies between who we are, what we are doing, what our community expects of us and what we expect of ourselves. We have to keep thinking about being good because being so is never easy and simple.

Being good in the way our community expects allows us to make some kind of resolution of the dilemma which every human being faces. Our physiological make-up condemns each of us to live in our individual world of meaning, yet to survive we have to find a way of living in a group that can both validate and annihilate us as a person. Once born, we gradually become conscious of being a person amongst other people. We begin by expecting that we shall get our own way in everything, but gradually other people force us to relinquish that idea. In its place we develop the idea of justice. Long before they can articulate its meaning children understand the concept of fair shares.

Justice has to be dispensed by someone who has the power to do so. First, this is our parents; then we discover the justice of some transcendental power such as God or Allah or Jehovah; and then we discover the justice of the state. Provided we can manage to understand and obey the laws of the state this kind of justice is usually not a problem. The justice dispensed by our parents and by a transcendental power is always a problem to us, often a problem which we cannot solve.

## Parental Justice

In his memoir *Almost a Childhood: Growing Up Among the Nazis*, Hans-Georg Behr calls his central character 'the child' and later 'the boy'. He began his memoir with: 'The child had been cured early of any notion that he was the centre of the world, and had learned that it is less painful to be inconspicuous.' The child was learning to be good. He went on:

A house was big, so big that everything must have a proper place if it was to be found again. That was called tidiness, and anyway there was a war on. For the moment both these ideas were foreign to the child, but he learned quickly, for he was trying to avoid the ever-reproachful tone in which the necessity for tidiness was drummed into him, and if he didn't instantly recognize the warning in that tone there was usually a spanking. Spanking hurt the bottom, slapping hurt the face, and the two together were known as a good hiding. There wasn't quite so much of that at Grandmother's, although she lived in an even bigger house. 'You must be neat and tidy,' the child was always told, but he neither knew nor understood the fundamental principle of the making of a human being whereby all imagination, desire and dreams must be pruned away, or else held tightly until they dropped off like lambs' tails, and what was left would pass as a useful member of society. 'A jewel must be cut and polished,' they said. Such had always been the case, and anyway there was a war on.[1]

The child's brother and sister from his mother's first marriage were away at school and he had to negotiate his relationships with his cold, punitive mother, his high ranking Nazi father, his kindly, aristocratic grandparents, the 'uncles' and 'aunts' of the Nazi elite, the servants, and prisoners of war working on his grandfather's property. He was curious about these grown-ups but he knew they were dangerous. To some greater or lesser degree this is the experience of all children as they try to negotiate their relationships with the adults around them.

Some parents do love their children but some parents merely tolerate them as best they can, and some parents wish to be rid of their children whom they see as useless objects. Just how many parents fall into the last category has little to do with a parent's capacity to love and much to do with economics. The anthropologist Robin Dunbar has pointed out that 'bubbling under the otherwise calm exterior of society' is the fact of infanticide. He explained how in tribal societies the men 'simply cannot afford to rear another man's offspring when they take over his former spouse.'[2] In all societies:

The costs of rearing children are so high in humans that it is difficult for a single parent to provide sufficient care. Orphans and the offspring of single parents bear a heavy cost in terms of higher-than-average mortality even in our more enlightened and economically better-off societies. In earlier societies, the costs of single-handedly rearing children commonly led to high levels of abandonment and infanticide. During the eighteenth century, for example, the frequency of infant abandonment in the city of Limoges in France correlated with the level of hardship (as indexed by the price of barley) in any given year. The frequency of infanticide and abandonment of children by the poor (especially among single women, widows and women living alone) in Victorian England reached such levels that it came to occupy a great deal of parliamentary time, and eventually culminated in the 1922 Infanticide Act.[3]

The Act did not prevent the murder of infants and children. Each year some 80 children in the UK die at the hands of adults, usually their parents or step-parents.

Babies may not be born knowing that they might die at the hands of their parents or step-parents but they are born with the ability to be aware of the feelings of those caring for them. Video studies of the interactions between a mother and a new-born baby show the baby responding very differently to the depressed or distracted mother than to the happy, loving mother. Angry or frightened people handle a baby differently from the way happy, loving people do. Babies sense danger when they sense an adult's anger or fear. Babies just a few days old can distinguish their mother's smell from that of other mothers. They would know when their mother's smell changed as she became angry or frightened.

Parents who would never think of harming their baby still have high expectations. No pregnant mother says simply, 'I don't care what my baby's like.' There is always the proviso 'as long as he or she is healthy'. This proviso sounds loving and accepting, but it also carries the message that 'an unhealthy baby is unacceptable to me'. This point is often made by those physically handicapped people who intervene in any debate over abortion where the participants assume that any foetus with physical handicap should be aborted.

Parents want their child to be more than healthy. They will readily admit that they want their child to have all the virtues and talents they themselves value, and that they want their child to come to share their passions and interests. There will be many more things they want and do not want, but they may not realise that they have these desires. Then the child arrives. The parent may discover that the child has just the kind of beauty the parent admires, but equally the child can bear a startling resemblance to a hated relative or a faithless spouse. The small child will know whether his appearance pleases or displeases his parent, but why is a mystery he has to unravel.

All children have to discover just what it is their parents want. 'Eat up your dinner' and 'Don't go near the gas fire' are fairly straightforward commands, provided the child finds the food he is given palatable and understands the words 'gas fire', but often what a parent wants is not clearly stated. A child may know that somehow he is not what his parent wants yet have no idea what exactly is wrong with him. Anthony Fingleton was one of the Fingleton brothers who were champion swimmers in Australia in the 1960s. In his autobiography *Swimming Upstream* he told how, right from the beginning, his father treated him harshly. Anthony wrote, 'I never felt a great wave of love or affection from Dad, the way I felt it from Mum.' His father's favourite was the oldest child, Harold, who had modelled himself on his father and, in the way that the children in a family each acquire a role, he became the 'hard' one while Anthony was the 'soft' one. When Harold was worsted in a fight with some boys which he himself had started, Anthony, obeying his mother's instructions, did not go to his aid. When his father found out he said to Anthony, 'You little poofter! Hide behind your mother's skirt, that's right. You were always a little dingo bastard. Get out of my sight!' The full significance of that insult did not become clear to Anthony until he was 14 and his father, who had sworn off drink, came home very drunk and sorry for himself. When Anthony went to commiserate with him for the hard life his father had led, his father said angrily, 'What would you know? Why don't you come over here and sit on me?' His mother hustled Anthony from the room but he had understood what his father meant. Next day his mother explained to him that when his father had been without any family to care for him during the Great Depression he 'did some awful things to survive. I think he was trying to lash out and hurt someone. It's usually me.'[4] Many parents take their bad feelings out on their children. Some parents later feel guilty about this and try to make amends, but some ignore the fact that their children take their insults to heart and believe that they are as wicked and unacceptable as their parent says they are.

A child cannot afford to ignore what his parents say. Small

children know that they need their parents to look after them. They need their parents to accept them, but to be accepted they have to be good in the way in which their parents define good. But being good is very difficult if you cannot work out exactly what it is your parent wants or, even if you do know what your parent wants, you do not have the skills and maturity to do it. Learning to be good is a painful process.

Children learn to be good by giving up something of who they are. Giving up part of who you are can go on all through our life as we try to fit into society, but the first and most important time this occurs is before the child has language in which to describe it. The child finds himself in a situation from which he cannot escape and in which his parent is punishing him for something he has not done, or done by mistake, or cannot do. It may be that the child has not eaten his food or emptied his bowels as his parent required, or that his parent has disappeared and the adults around the child seem to imply by their words and deeds that the disappearance is his fault, or that the parent is physically or sexually assaulting him and he is confused, hurt and frightened. The child's interpretation of the situation is, 'I am being unjustly punished by my bad parent.' However, he soon realises that this bad parent is the person on whom he depends. This state of utter helplessness threatens him with both death and annihilation of his sense of being a person. To reclaim some control of the situation he reinterprets it. Now it becomes, 'I am bad and am being justly punished by my good parent.' In blaming himself he gives up acceptance of himself. From then on he sees himself as unacceptable and having to work hard to be accepted by being good. Thus he becomes a good person. Good people believe that they are not good enough and that they have to work hard to be good. The defence of being good, like all defences, does not work perfectly.

Although the child does not remember when he first became a good person, this first experience is repeated many times in different ways, and many of these experiences are well remembered. In his study of memory Douwe Draaisma wrote:

Ask someone if he can call to mind a moment in which
he felt humiliated and you are likely to get an answer

so detailed, so graphic, that it is as if his memory had
kept a special account of it. Insults are described in
indelible ink. They never fade with age. As we grow
older they travel with us in time so that hardly a day
seems to have passed between the event and its recall.[5]

From such humiliations and from his transgressions of
parental rules a child draws conclusions about himself and
how he should live his life. These conclusions affect the way he
interprets himself and his world for many years after. Just how
difficult the struggle to be good can be is shown in the life of
Neil, one of the subjects in Tim Hewat's television series *7 UP*.
In 1963 Tim Hewat began filming this series which followed
the lives of a group of children who had been born in 1956.
Every seven years Tim Hewat returned to see what had happened to each member of the group. Over the years some of the
group members left the series but the others continued to have
their lives recorded in this way.

The latest film in the series, *49 UP*, revisited Neil who had
been born into what appears to be a conventional middle-class
family. At seven Neil was an enchanting, lively, imaginative
little boy. His face sparkled with wonder and delight as he discovered the extraordinary world around him. At 49 his face
was lined and he looked much older than his years. He had an
air of sadness and of wisdom earned by harsh experience. At
seven he had wanted to be an astronaut or a coach driver; at 14
his enthusiasm for adventures was outweighed by his sense of
responsibility for others, something he thought he could pursue
through politics. He had wanted to go to Oxford but missed
out and went to Aberdeen University instead. There just one
year, he dropped out and by 21 he was working on a building
site and living in a squat. At 28 he was homeless and living in
Scotland. Something then changed for him, for at 35 he was
living on a council estate in the Shetlands and was a Liberal
Democrat councillor. At 42 he was back in London and a councillor on Hackney Council, and at forty-nine he was in Cumbria
and a member of the district council. A hint as to why his life
had taken this course lies in his answer as a seven year old
to a question about whether he wanted to have children when
he grew up. He said, 'When I get married I don't want to have

any children because they're always doing naughty things and making the house untidy.'

This naive answer revealed more about his family life than his parents perhaps would want strangers to know. The conclusion that Neil had drawn from his family's view of him was that all children are naughty and, as he was a child, he was naughty, incorrigibly so. As he became a man the feeling that he was unacceptable had become the conviction that he was in essence bad. In answer to the question about having children he said, 'Children inherit something from their parents, and even if my wife was the most high spirited, ordinary and normal person, the child would stand a fair chance of being not totally full of happiness because of what he or she would have inherited from me.'

In his forties he could talk about his parents, how at first he had got on well with his father, but when he entered his teens he was unable to please his father. They remained distant in their relationship with one another until they had one good conversation shortly before his father died. His relationship with his mother improved somewhat after his father's death but he said, 'It's never been an easy relationship and I'm not claiming that everything has healed.' There was only one mention of his brother who, when Neil was a councillor, gave him his wife's old car when she was replacing it with a new one. From this we can perhaps deduce that his parents would have seen his brother as being more acceptable than Neil. His brother had married and was doing well enough not to need to sell an old car before buying a new one.

In the series of interviews Neil showed himself to be struggling with the question, 'How ought I to live my life?' He took as given that he was in essence bad and had to work hard to be good. Although he described his religious education as being merely conventional, he tried to find the path to goodness through faith. However, by the time he was 49 his life in one way had come full circle. He had learned to be good simply because it pleased him to be so. He lived a simple, modest life as a councillor and volunteer for Oxfam. He had learned that, as he said, 'Life comes once and it's quite short. Perhaps there can't be anything more to life than being what you are.' Just as he had been at seven, he was good at being what he was.[6]

The series of interviews with Neil does not say explicitly that Neil's parents had ensured that he had to compete with his brother over which of them was the 'goodest', but Orhan Pamuk in his memoir *Istanbul* showed that this was what had happened to him and his brother Şevket. At first he spoke of competing for his mother's love:

> If evil encroached, if boredom loomed, my father's response was to turn his back on it and remain silent. My mother, who set the rules, was the one to raise her eyebrows and instruct us in life's darker side. If she was less fun to be with, I was still very dependent on her love and affection, for she gave us more time than our father, who seized every opportunity to escape from the house. My harshest lesson in life was to learn I was in competition with my brother for her affections.
>
> It was, perhaps, because my father exerted so little authority that my rivalry with my brother took on the significance it did: he was the rival for my mother's love. As we knew nothing of psychology, the war with my brother was initially dressed up as a game, and in the game we would both pretend to be other people. It was not Orhan and Şevket in combat, but my favourite hero or football player versus my brother's. Convinced we had become heroes, we gave the game all we had; and when it ended in blood and tears, the anger and jealousy was to make us forget we were brothers.[7]

Later he wrote:

> These early fights were sparked by defeat, excessive teasing and cheating, but it was rivalry which fuelled them. They were fought not to establish who was in the right but which of us was the stronger, more skilful, more knowledgeable or clever. And they expressed an anxiety we felt about having to learn the rules of the game, and, indirectly, the rules of the world where, in an instant, we would be called upon to prove our agility and our mental prowess.
>
> My mother may have had her hand in it too, because, perhaps to make her daily life easier, she turned everything she could into a contest. 'Whoever puts on his pyjamas and is in bed first gets a kiss,' my

mother would say. 'Whoever gets through the whole
winter without catching cold or falling ill, I'll buy him
a present.' 'Whoever can finish supper first without
spilling anything on his shirt, I'll love him the most.'
These motherly provocations were designed to make
the two sons more 'virtuous', quiet and cooperative.[8]

Trying to be good is a never-ending quest. A person's degree of
goodness is measured against the standard of perfection, but
even if a good person reached perfection he could not recognise that this was so because to claim perfection is itself an
imperfection. To assure themselves that they are good enough
to be permitted to exist, good people have to compare themselves with other people and try to comfort themselves with, 'I
might not be perfect but I am better than . . .' In adult life such
comparisons may be made with a wide variety of people, but
for children the comparison most readily at hand is with one's
siblings. The great advantage of having siblings is that the
force of parental justice is likely to be spread across all the siblings, while an only child receives it in full measure. The disadvantage of having siblings is that they provide the standard
against which you can fail. Parents, other family members and
teachers are prone to compare one sibling with another. Even
when the adults do not do so, the siblings compare themselves
with one another.

   Douwe Draaisma tells the story of Willem van den Hull who
wrote 'a voluminous autobiography' of his life in the Netherlands from 1778 to 1858. 'What Willem remembered of his first
years were mere snatches. He would, for instance, greet his
mother as politely as possible in the mornings: "Good morning,
Mama; how are you today? Very well, too, Mama, I would say
then, imagining myself far superior to my brother and sister
in manners".'[9] Human nature does not change. When people
talk to me about their siblings the commonest theme is 'the
good one and the bad one'. Often 'the good one' sides with the
parents in criticising 'the bad one' and marks up a win in the
competition to be good. 'The good one' can take pride in his or
her 'good' role, but often it is clear that this is a kind of desperate pride because 'the good one' sees 'the bad one' as being indulged by the parents and able 'to get away with murder'. Such

a phrase is not an empty cliché for 'the good one' has sacrificed so much to create his defence of being good, only to find that his sacrifice is unappreciated by the parents to whom the sacrifice was made.

Helen talked to me about her brother James who was two years older than her. 'We always used to fight a lot. It was a very volatile relationship. I felt that James broke more rules than me, and he could get away with more than me and would be forgiven. He would do terrible things that would upset my mum – like he crashed her car once, and it was basically his own fault for not being careful: he was driving his friends – and she was really upset, and I thought that was something I'd never have done. I've always been really sensible driving the car. And I would resent the fact that he could do things like that and be forgiven, whereas I wouldn't get extra credit for not having done them!' Later she added, 'I don't think my parents really did favour James – certainly he didn't get special treatment – it was just that I felt the injustice of not being more loved when I had tried so hard to be good.'

'The bad one' may not have got away with murder but he or she is annihilating 'the good one' by showing that the defence of being good has not worked. No matter how good you are your parents will give 'the bad one' more than they give to you. No wonder the Prodigal Son was so hated by his brothers! Children have to develop the concept of fair shares early in their life. When food is in short supply fair shares is a matter of life or death, and when food is plentiful getting the smaller slice of cake or the smaller amount of pocket money can mean the threat of annihilation as a person. It is abundantly obvious that life is not fair but we all believe that it ought to be. Not that many of us care about other people's fair shares, but we all care about our own fair share, our own validation. If we lived in a perfect world we would enjoy the sense of perfection which is complete validation as a person, an oceanic feeling of complete bliss, 'God's in His heaven, all's right with the world.' But imperfection exists, so the perfection of complete validation can only be the exact balance between good and bad. Nothing bad happens that is not balanced by something good. There is no more pervasive belief amongst human beings than the belief in the supernatural justice in the form of the Just World.

## The just world

Long before scientists had devised ways of discovering how the universe operates, human beings had decided that the world they inhabited was governed by some overarching grand design that controlled events and dispensed justice. Just what this grand design was exactly is the subject of the mythologies which developed in different cultures. Various though these mythologies are, all have a common core, that of a kind of Just World which ensures that ultimately bad people are punished and good people rewarded. All people believe that everybody *ought* to get their just desserts. The Just World ensures that they do – or so we hope. Even when we cast aside every scrap of religious indoctrination we have received and scorn the notion of a grand design of justice, we continue to harbour some kind of belief in just desserts, and still feel aggrieved when they fail to materialise. For siblings not getting what you believe you deserve can be a lifelong memory. My Auntie Doff was an unwanted sixth child, born four years after her brother Jack. She had always been devoted to her mother. When she was 95 and her memory for events almost non-existent, she would talk about her mother as if she were still alive but an old woman. Once when visiting her I asked what her mother had been like when my aunt was a child. She shook her head to show that she remembered nothing of that time and smiled apologetically. She sat silent for a moment and then suddenly said, 'Mother always favoured Jack.'

If we could see the world without having first learnt how to see it, we would see an ever-changing, ever-moving chaos. For us to survive in it we have to learn how to turn the chaos into patterns. Then we can look at random splashes of colour and see a shape; we can hear random noises and say it is the wind blowing through the trees; we can see people walking by and say that a football match has ended. The patterns we create are guesses about what is going on, but the patterns comfort us by assuring us that we know what is going on and can predict what will happen.

Babies are born with the ability and desire to see patterns. They then discover that there are connections – patterns – between what they do and how part of their environment responds. Wave a hand and a bell tinkles; smile and Mummy smiles back. The patterns baby sees in the chaos become more complex. Gradually one very important pattern emerges: I do this and something pleasant happens; I do that and something unpleasant happens. 'Pleasant' becomes a reward and 'unpleasant' a punishment. Now the pattern is clear. *If I'm good I get rewarded. If I'm bad I get punished.*

Punishments might be painful and dramatically memorable, but the simple patterns of reward and punishment make life predictable. The baby gets a glimmer of an idea, 'If I'm good I'll be safe.' Not that rewards and punishments are always predictable. Small children do not always know what they are being punished for. Recently I saw a boy of about five cowering in a shop doorway while a woman, presumably his mother, dragged his arm upwards and shouted, 'Get up! Get up!' He struggled to his feet, whereupon she dragged him on to the footpath and screamed at him, 'Sit down! Sit down!' As he must have seen it, he was being punished if he stood and if he sat. He did not understand, though I did from the way she spoke, that his mother wanted his instant and unquestioning obedience. He was unlikely to produce this, but he was likely to conclude from this episode that he lived in a world where he could be punished for sins he did not know he had committed.

No doubt he had already reached this conclusion. Long before a child has full grasp of language he can know he is being punished but not know the reason why. My friend Stephen, a middle child with an older sister Margaret and a younger sister Julia, told me about his earliest memories. He said, 'My first memories are of being in the playpen. A nanny had been taken on. My mother, I think, was ill – she actually had a miscarriage between me and Julia – not a miscarriage, a blue baby, heart defect, something that's curable now – and so she was pretty traumatised by that. I was consigned to the playpen while the nanny looked after Julia. To the best of my recollection she didn't look after me at all, I was just kept in the playpen, pretty well all the time. I can describe that playpen in great detail, including the number of balls it did or didn't have. Probably why I'm bad at maths – because it had a number that didn't add up to ten. I discovered that I could get out of the playpen, so then I was tied in it. There was a hook on the wall and the string was tied to that and tied round my waist, so I was tied in the playpen. That was probably less worrying than the fact I could collapse the playpen – it would concertina in – and I could concertina it in but I wasn't actually very good at putting it back out again.'

At least as Stephen got older he knew what he was being punished for, even though he may have questioned the justice of it. I asked Stephen if he had been beaten as a child. He said, 'It probably made up in quality what it lost in quantity. If my father said do something and you didn't do it – he was logical, he was consistent. "If you don't do this, I will beat you." And yes he would. But I don't remember many. I remember one where I'd eaten too much cream, as it turned out, and I was sick and kept on being sick and my father said, "If you're sick again, I'll beat you," and I was and he did. The only other beating I can particularly remember – he just sort of grabbed me and walloped me. I don't remember him using an instrument. I remember being chased up the stairs, and he grabbed me and ripped my shirt – my mother was cross because he ripped my shirt.'

Stephen had no memory of his sisters being beaten by his father and he doubted that his mother would have beaten them. His wife Fay said that in her family it was the two daughters who were beaten while the youngest, a boy, was not. Fay said, 'My father, like Stephen's father, was a strict disciplinarian. There was the line and if you crossed it, you'd had it. My parents had both come out of the services. Dad had been in the Navy from the age of 14, something like that. He beat me with a Mason Pearson hairbrush.' (A Mason Pearson hairbrush is oval with a handle, somewhat like a paddle.)

Extreme punishments by parents lead children to create extreme definitions of goodness as they try to live up to what they see as parental expectations. Stephen showed that he defined being good as not just being truthful, kind and reliable but as working very hard and always seeing something more to be done, while Fay defined being good as doing everything perfectly. She berated herself cruelly when she failed to reach perfection. By becoming aware of the ridiculously high standards they set themselves they eventually managed to modify these definitions. Now Stephen does take some time off work, and Fay no longer aims at perfection, merely at 'reasonableness'.

However, their sense of duty and loyalty to their siblings has not lessened. If anything, it has become stronger.

Like most children, Stephen and Fay were taught about goodness and badness, rewards and punishments, in a religious context. In some families the parents give their children a very simple message that relates only to the family, 'Behave yourself and everything will go along fine: misbehave and you're in trouble.' However, most parents expect their children to generalise the simple formula of good and bad, rewards and punishments to the world in general. In such families children are expected to believe that, while the world may appear to be random, it is in fact governed by a Grand Design of Justice. The world is a Just World where good people are rewarded and bad people are punished. All religions teach that we live in a Just World, though they differ on definitions of good and bad, rewards and punishments. In countries where a religion wields great political power the belief in a Just World becomes the very basis on which society functions. In less religious countries parents may still seek out religious teaching for their children on the grounds that a religious belief will keep the child on the straight and narrow path of virtue. Even if parents go to some efforts to protect their children from any religious teaching their children will still encounter it at school in one form or other.

In most societies, particularly in those where one religion is very powerful, children learn to see the functioning of the Just World all around them in their everyday life, defining their existence and identity. In her autobiography the Egyptian writer Nawal El Saadawi wrote about her father's mother, a poor woman from a village:

> When I was a child I didn't know whether my grandmother was laughing or crying. She was probably laughing, for after she had wiped the tears away her eyes shone with a sudden light, and she would begin to laugh again, almost choking as she held the black shawl over her nose and mouth and muttered, 'Allah, let it lead to something good'.

In a footnote Nawal explained: 'Accustomed to tragedy in their lives, village people are afraid to laugh, as though God may punish them for laughing, as though they had no right to laugh, so that when they do, they pray God that it might bring them something good and not evil to them.'[10] As a child Nawal discovered how religion defined her value. She wrote:

> At night [my father] would sit on the balcony and look out over the city at the stars. My mother would be in the kitchen preparing the evening meal. My brother sat next to my father gazing at the stars with him. My father spoke to my brother but said nothing to me. He read out of the Qur'an to him, told him about God. . . . The world of the Qur'an was like the world of my father, the affair of men only.[11]

On the first day of Eid, when the butcher came to slaughter a sacrificial lamb, her father would tell the story of Abraham and Isaac and how God tested Abraham by ordering him to sacrifice his son to God. Nawal felt that she was always being tested by God and, no matter how hard she worked to be good, she was always being found wanting. After Ramadan came the Eid Al-Sagheer (small feast) with relatives and visitors. Her grandmother would come with presents for the children:

> She began with the boys, with my three brothers. She gave two millimes to each of them. But to the girls she gave only one millime. Angry, I threw the millime back into her lap. 'God has told us that a girl is worth half a boy, the light of your mother's eye,' she would say to me.
>
> My elder brother, Tala'at, would stare at me, a gleam of arrogant pride in his eyes. I did better than him at school, and the only thing that soothed his feelings of frustration was the verse from the Qur'an echoing in my father's voice which said: To the male a share equal to two females.
>
> I retreated to my room, lay on my bed, buried my face in the pillow and wept. Could God be unjust? My brother played all the year round, and kept failing his examinations. I worked at school and at home and never had a holiday, and yet what was the result of all my efforts? I was given one millime and he was given two.[12]

When we are small children certain people feature very large in our life. They may be real people – our parents and siblings – or people that the adults around us talk about all the time. These may be absent relatives or friends, people who are dead, or people from certain myths, legends and holy books. When people feature large in our life we take them inside us and they become, in the language of psychotherapy, internal objects. Thus we can have as internal objects people whom we have never met. For instance, my paternal grandfather died long before I was born, but my father talked about him with such love that I came to love him too and often thought about him. In families where the adults not only talk about God but use Him in their negotiations with one another ('If you do that God will never forgive you') God can become a very real person to the child growing up in that family. Nawal felt that God was always nearby, watching her:

> God hid in the dark behind the coat-stand, or in the cupboard. Lying in bed I felt His presence, wondered whether I should hide my head under the covers or just keep still. Then I would hear His footsteps on the floor, jump out of bed in a fright, rush off to do my ablutions, and prostrate myself on the prayer mat, repeating again and again, 'I ask Almighty God for His forgiveness for every mighty sin', until my throat went dry.[13]

The photographer Don McCullin, famous for his photographs of most of the conflicts from the 1960s onwards, described his experience of being wounded in Vietnam, 'I must have seen thousands of wounded on battlefields since I first started going to the wars. Why them and not me?'[14] War after war, and he began to wonder why it was that 'while I was away in some dreadful hell-hole I yearned to be back with my family; when I was at home, tinkering around the outhouses attached to my farm in Hertfordshire, I itched to be again in foreign parts'.[15] He asked David Cornwell (John le Carré) for advice and received something that told him more about himself than he perhaps was prepared to learn. David Cornwell wrote of him:

> He has known all forms of fear, he's an expert in it. He has come back from God knows how many brinks, all different. His experiences in a Ugandan prison alone would be enough to unhinge another man – like myself,

as a matter of fact – for good. He has been forfeit for
more times than he can remember, he says. But he is
not bragging. Talking this way about death and risk, he
seems to be implying quite consciously that by testing
his luck each time, he's testing his Maker's indulgence.
To survive is to be condoned and blessed again.[16]

From his autobiography Don McCullin appears not to have
grown up in a religious family but he could still make a bar-
gain with some kind of internal object called God. However, a
child may grow up in a religious family but still not acquire an
internal object called God and thus a belief in the existence of
God. My friend Ann told me about her experience of growing
up in a strict Methodist family. Even though every Sunday the
whole family attended church and the children Sunday school,
and her parents were very active in church affairs, God hardly featured in what made an impression on her. Her parents
rarely mentioned God, so busy were they in setting out all their
rules for proper conduct and seeing that Ann and her siblings
obeyed them. Ann felt that she did not need God to supervise
her. Her mother, who brooked no objection or complaint from
her children, did that. However, Ann did learn the Methodist
rules of morality and as a child she regarded them as absolute
and unquestionable. In adult life Ann may have left the Methodist Church but its rules about honesty, integrity and doing
one's best in everything never left her.

Years ago I worked with a psychiatrist who always encouraged her patients to hold a strong Christian belief. In case
conferences she would remark to her colleagues that without
religious belief a person would have no morals. Whenever she
said this I would check the distance between me and the door.
I was concerned that my colleague might suddenly suffer a loss
of her faith whereupon she would immediately fall to murder,
rape and plunder. Although she was a mother of several children she had not observed that children learn to be good long
before they acquire a religious belief. Children may be taught
the tenets of a religion from their earliest days but it is not until they have a fairly clear understanding of their religion that
they can turn a teaching into a belief. Small children believe in
many things – Santa Claus, fairies and that their parents know

everything – but by the time they go to school such beliefs are likely to have faded. Young children may acquire an internal object called Jesus who is like a kindly uncle or older brother and another called God, a grandfather of uncertain temper, but they do not gain some understanding of concepts such as submitting one's will to the will of God or of Jesus sacrificing himself to save us all until they are much older. These concepts are part of a structure of beliefs that give an explanation of why things are as they are and which demand a loyalty based on faith not reason. As a schoolchild I puzzled over the significance of what Jesus had done. The minister at St Andrew's Church which I attended preached many sermons about Jesus' sacrifice, but having no understanding of the concept of sacrifice in Christianity, Judaism and Islam, I could only disapprove of a father who let his son suffer in this way. Similarly, as I was growing up in a family who believed that to praise a child was to spoil her, and to expect praise was utterly reprehensible, I was shocked that God expected His people to sing those endless hymns of praise to Him. Certainly 'Praise God from Whom All Blessings Flow' was my favourite hymn, but that was because, when the organist played its opening chords, I knew that the service was coming to an end and I could escape.

The belief in the Just World is bound up with learning to be good, and acquiring a religious belief merely reinforces belief in the Just World. Thus, when in adult life people abandon their religious belief, they may discover that their belief in the Just World has not been abandoned, merely tucked away in implicit memory where it continues to exert as powerful an influence. Many people abandon a belief in God but not in the belief that if you are good nothing bad can happen to you. Vanessa Bell was profoundly affected by the death of her son Julian. Her daughter Angelica Garnett wrote: 'Nothing could restore her previous confidence in life which had been born of a feeling that, doing no harm, we should not suffer much.'[17]

Having made the discovery that no amount of goodness prevents disaster, many people search for the sin they did not know they had committed but for which they are now being punished. The journalist Dea Birkett described what happened to her:

When my daughter was about three months old, queries arose about her development. Why wasn't she doing the same things as other babies her age? Slowly, over a period of many months, it emerged that something wasn't quite right. I've been to that dark place where we search and search for what we have done wrong. But I wasn't trying to remember the odd sneaked glass of wine or covert cigarette. I was searching for past sins, believing, although I was no longer a believer, that they must now be being visited upon my offspring. Good girls don't have disabled babies. Bad girls get punished by having bad babies.

So deeply entrenched is this idea that, when my daughter was facing her diagnostic tests, I started trying to prove that I really was a good person after all. That way, the tests would all come out fine, wouldn't they? And everyone's concerns would be proved unfounded. I started stopping at every zebra crossing I drove up to, waving children and old ladies across. I tried very hard not to get annoyed with my mother for no reason; I'd judged this as the very worst thing I did. I even tipped excessively; a waiter's judgement on my level of goodness could even weigh the balance in my favour. If only I could reform, my baby would be fine.[18]

In a Just World good parents have healthy babies, and good children make their parents happy. Many children feel that if their parent is unhappy it is because they are bad. If they can be truly good they can make their mother happy, and then their reward will be that they themselves will be happy. Virginia Ironside had a mother whom no one could make happy. As a child Virginia could not know this. All she knew was that her mother was unhappy and it was her duty to make her mother happy. In her biography of her mother Virginia wrote:

This feeling of responsibility for everyone else's miseries, the endlessly caring role that I was forced into, must certainly have contributed to my sense of fulfilment in becoming an agony aunt later on. I must have felt at some unconscious level, that constantly striving to make others feel better, happier and less erratic, would result in my feeling less guilty for whatever nameless sin I must have committed to make my mother so unhappy, and if my caring worked, it might result in being better cared for myself. I have learned that almost everyone in 'altruistic' professions, from doctors to nurses, is also prompted by the same fundamentally selfish urge – if I can cure this person, they may look after me; if I provide help and comfort for this person, I shall get off on some of my own kindness and, like lighting a fire for a freezing man, I may find that some of the warmth may come my way as well.[19]

Many people spend their whole lives doing penance for a name-less act in childhood which in some way hurt their parent. Virginia's mother Janey, an extremely talented and beautiful woman, was to a considerable extent the author of her own misery but, as the recipient of her mother's frequent rebukes, Virginia blamed herself for her mother's unhappiness. In her adult life Virginia had the good sense to work out that this was what she was doing but many people do not manage this. Over the last two decades I have seen two friends of mine, both men, living in different countries and with very different back-grounds, form very close but ultimately very unhappy relation-ships with a series of women. Both are what I call 'lovely men', entertaining, thoughtful, gentle, reliable, conscientious, the kind of men most women would seek as a partner. Both these men are well aware that there are many splendid women who would be loving, supportive, sensible (in the best meaning of that term) wives and mothers, yet they seem not to see the significance of the fact that the women they fall passionately in love with may be beautiful but they are without exception totally self-absorbed, needy and insatiably demanding. I know the family history of each man and how each history contains an unhappy mother who felt trapped in her misery.

Freud wrote about the necessity of mastering events. If we put mastery in terms of meaning, we can say to master an event we need to create an interpretation of that event which will fit into our meaning structure without disrupting it. How-ever, some events conflict with our meaning structure and so we have to make some kind of adaptation to our meaning struc-ture before we can master the event. For instance, Virginia Ironside's mother expected Virginia to do and be exactly what she wanted, and she took no account of Virginia's needs and wishes. Even as a small child Virginia would have seen that her mother was behaving selfishly. In the language of learning to be good Virginia would have seen the situation as 'I am being unjustly punished by my bad mother.' Seeing the person she depended on as bad was far too frightening so Virginia reinterpreted the situation as 'I am bad and am being justly punished by my good mother.' Her badness consisted of being the cause of her mother's unhappiness. The only way she could avoid the inevitable punishment for making her mother unhappy was to make her mother happy. There was no way that Virginia could master this situation, first because she could not make her mother happy, and second because a reinterpretation does not destroy the original interpretation. It lurks below consciousness ready to come into consciousness.

Freud said that we do not forget an emotional trauma: we simply repress it into our unconscious. Research in how and what we learn has shown him to be right. Animal scientist Temple Grandin wrote:

> All intensely emotional learning is permanent. That's why you can forget everything you learned in trigonometry, but no one born before 1958 is ever going to forget where they were when Kennedy was shot, and no one born before 1996 is ever going to forget where they were on September 11. You couldn't forget where you were even if you wanted to, and even if you tried to.[20]

Behaviourist psychologists showed that they could teach an animal to be afraid when it heard a particular sound, but then, over time, the animal appeared to forget his fear. Psychologists called this process 'extinction'. Temple Grandin explained:

> It turns out that extinction doesn't actually wipe out the fear from your brain. It's still there. If you teach an animal to fear a tone that precedes an air puff to the eye, and then teach him not to fear the tone because there's no more air puff, he hasn't forgotten. He stops blinking reflexively every time he hears the tone, but all you have to do to get him blinking again is to pair the tone with the air puff just *once* and the animal is right back where he started. He *knows* that tone means air puff. He

hasn't forgotten. Both animals and people can 'get over' a
learned fear. But today we understand that getting over
a fear isn't the same as forgetting a fear. Extinction isn't
forgetting; it's new learning that contradicts old learning.[21]

You might think you have forgotten all the terrible things your
siblings did to you, but something quite tiny can remind you
and suddenly you are as angry as you were when you were a
child.

Thus Virginia's meaning structure contained both the meanings 'my mother is bad' and 'my mother is good'. If her mother
had been less extreme in what she did and if she had not
pushed Virginia into extreme situations, Virginia would have
been able to arrive at the meaning by which most people reconcile themselves to their parents. This meaning is 'my parents
are merely fallible human beings, a mixture of good and bad'.
But there was nothing 'mere' about Janey and so, in the way
that old rich men turn to philanthropy, scattering their wealth
amongst the needy in the hope of foiling their nemesis which is
fast approaching, Virginia plunged into saving needy people in
the way she had tried and failed to save her mother. She was
trapped in this frantic, often futile, endeavour and it was not
until she looked at what she was doing with eyes undimmed
by her need to be good that she could see its futility and thus
bring her concern and care for others within the natural limits
imposed by what our life and our skills will allow.

Unfortunately, neither of my friends who kept falling in love
with demanding women was brave enough or wise enough to
step back and look at what he was doing. It is impossible to
measure the perilousness of one person's situation with that of
another person but it may be that, terrible though Virginia's
situation was, she was an only child and her issues were
directly with her mother. Both my friends had siblings. Even
the most loving and attentive mother cannot satisfy her children's demands that each has his fair share (i.e. more than anyone else) of her love and approving attention. When a mother
is completely self-absorbed all her children will fight over what
scraps of attention she does give them. If she defines 'good' as
'looking after me' then the children can either compete for being 'the best at looking after Mother' or they can refuse to join

the competition and in effect leave the family. Without realising it, both my friends want to prove that they are best at looking after Mother, and to show that this is so they are expert in finding women who need to be looked after.

Neither of these men would say that he believed in the Just World, and that, in trying to make their mother or their lover happy he was trying to assure himself that there was a Just World, yet it seems that this belief, though unrecognised by both of them, is impelling them to repeat actions which, without this belief, they would readily see as being utterly fruitless. They are not alone in seeing the Just World in this way. Indeed, most people do. Believing in the Just World leads us into self-delusion, denial and acts of cruelty against ourselves and others.

In 1980 Melvin Lerner published an account of his research in a book entitled *The Belief in a Just World: A Fundamental Delusion*.[22] Lerner and his fellow researchers argued that people need to believe that they live in a Just World where people get what they deserve. This belief determines many of the interpretations we make and thus determines many of our actions. In 2005 Carolyn Haber and Laurent Bègue reviewed the extensive research that has been done on the Just World belief and found it 'unsystematic', which in one way is hardly surprising since the Just World belief has implications in perhaps all aspects of human life. The importance of the study of the Just World belief has been recognised by many researchers in the social sciences and the law but, sadly, very few researchers in clinical psychology and psychotherapy. The belief in the Just World is a philosophical, metaphysical or religious belief, and many psychologists and psychiatrists prefer to ignore how much metaphysical, philosophical and religious beliefs influence what people do.[23]

Some metaphysical beliefs are simple statements such as 'There is a God', 'Allah is merciful'. Some are stories such as 'Through meditation the sense of self drops away and we become one with everything that exists.' The belief in the Just World is a story, and stories are supremely important to us. We are meaning-creating creatures and we are storytellers. Anything new or unexpected we encounter has to be fitted into a story with a beginning, a middle and an end before it becomes fully meaningful to us. Suppose you come home to a locked house where no one else could have been and find a parcel sitting on your kitchen table. You know it is a parcel, but until you have discovered how it got there and you decide what you are going to do with it the parcel is not completely meaningful to you. Until you can put this event into a story you have to struggle with uncertainty.[24] We have to find out where the new or unexpected came from and what will happen because all stories have to have (or so we feel) a beginning, a middle and an end. Stories mean so much to us. It is our passion for stories which maintains all forms of media and the arts. Instructions about how to do something come in the form of a story. In conversation we tell one another stories. What is gossip but the telling of stories?

We prefer stories which are in some way complete because they give us some sense of satisfaction, a sense of completion, a sense that the world, or at least some part of it, is back in balance again, and the balance is that of the Just World. The good people have been rewarded and the bad people punished. In comedies the balance is restored within the story. In tragedies we focus on the suffering and death of people who do not deserve such a fate but, as the story comes to an end, we know that out of their suffering and death good will come and the balance will be restored.

Melvin Lerner argued that, in learning to be good, children make a contract with the world wherein they promise to give up those aspects of themselves which are unacceptable to their parents and in return for such a sacrifice they will be rewarded, if not now then when they grow up. For the contract to be fulfilled the world must be a Just World. Thus we grow up needing to see the world as a Just World, and our need often blinds us to reality.

However, the belief in the Just World and the child's contract with the world gives the child a framework for negotiating relationships with their siblings. Thus the phrase 'It's not fair' comes early to a child's lips. The conduits between the child and the Just World are the parents, and so the child goes as a supplicant to the parents. When the parents fail to deliver the required justice, the children battle it out between themselves. Like all human beings, children judge their deserved rewards as being greater than outside observers might judge them and again, like all human beings, if the opportunity arises children will take a little more than they deserve. However, siblings watch one another like a hawk watches its prey. What a recipient may see as a deserved reward can be seen by the other siblings as an undeserved and unforgettable act of favouritism by a representative of the Just World. Unless a child comes to understand that justice is a meaning created by human beings and not an everlasting attribute of all that exists, that child can never free himself from battles of one kind of another with his siblings. This is why sibling rivalry can last a lifetime.

When a parent decides upon a certain distribution of, say, pocket money he or she takes into account that the oldest child has school expenses to meet while the youngest will spend all her money on sweets and adjust the sums accordingly, but the children take other matters into account. The younger children are likely to resent that older children have privileges which they lack; the girls may resent the fact that the boys have greater freedom than they do; one child may be resented by the others for being the parents' favourite; one child may be resented for having a particular talent which the others lack; one child may have a physical disability or chronic illness and feel hard done by. All these matters and more the children put into the scales of justice and when the balance goes against them they cry, sometimes aloud, sometimes just to themselves, 'It's not fair.'

The belief in the Just World helps the child make his way in a manifestly unfair world. His sense of being a person can survive many disasters and humiliations because he can assure himself that in the future he will be rewarded. If born into a rich or at least comfortably off family he can see his rewards as being the position, power and wealth that will come with adulthood. If born into a poor family with no avenue of escape he can take to heart his religion's teaching that his rewards will come in the afterlife. Children dream of fame, fortune and love, not just because they see these things as being pleasant in themselves; they see them as the rewards which will show that they are good, and because they are good they are safe.

People continue to hold fast to the religion of their childhood sometimes because it gives them the courage to live, sometimes because to give up their religious belief would mean leaving the community to which they belong. Some people perform a kind of cherrypicking of their religion, keeping the nice and comforting parts and discarding the harsh and punitive parts. The current fashion in 'spirituality' is an example of this. Dr Giles Fraser, vicar of Putney and lecturer in philosophy at Wadham College, commented: 'The idea that spirituality represents some innate human aspiration to the ultimate is a piece of modern candyfloss that neatly accords with the desire to participate in religion without any of the demands it makes on you.'[25] There is a tendency amongst those who lay claim to being 'spiritual' and those evangelicals who say they have been saved to exude the happiness of those believers in the Just World who are certain that, as they are good, their rewards will follow as night the day. The economist J. K. Galbraith has often commented on the tendency for rich people to take their riches as proof of their superior virtue.

Then there are the people who, though still espousing the Just World belief, have discarded the religion they were taught in childhood yet continue to see the Church as the most appropriate place for the ceremonies of birth, death and marriage. Such ceremonies are themselves based on the belief in the Just World. Some people go further than this and abandon all forms of religion. They describe themselves as being non-religious but very few of them actually give up their belief in a Just World, for to do so means living in a world without certainty. So it is that people may not see the hand of God dispensing justice but they still feel that somehow, in the end, the good are rewarded and the bad are punished.

The Just World research shows how people will adjust their interpretations of events in order to preserve their belief in the Just World. An undeserved reward leads some people to see themselves as being a much better person than they had previously thought, while others in this position fear that they will suffer some terrible blow so that their suffering matches their reward. One great advantage of the Just World belief comes when people observe the manifest unfairness of the world and, rather than be troubled by the pain of pity, they blame the victim or tell themselves that the person is 'poor but happy'. (Curiously, those who believe that the poor are happy never give up what they have got so that they can be happy.) The poor of the world are said to enjoy 'simple pleasures', presumably the pleasures of starving and dying young. Our tabloid newspapers joyfully report the ill-fortune that the rich suffer and the abject failure of lottery winners to enjoy their riches. However, all but the most strictly brought up children discover that wicked pleasures can be taken secretly and an ordinary pleasure can have the added thrill of being naughty and undeserved. Thus cream cakes and chocolates are advertised as 'naughty but nice' while an advertisement for some luxury can assure the potential customer that 'you deserve it'.

In a Just World nothing happens by chance, so the word 'luck' loses its meaning of random chance and instead becomes a kind of commodity which a person possesses. In the way that the law of 'three strikes and you're out' operates a run of good or bad fortune can be seen to use up all your luck. A client was referred to me because he had become exceedingly anxious after surviving unscathed a particularly dangerous accident. He told me that this was the last in a series of serious accidents he had survived. He was convinced that he had used up all his luck and it was only a matter of time before something as simple as crossing the road would kill him. In contrast, Jim and Mary Smith in one day won £30 on the Grand National, £12 on a bingo game and then their 21-member lottery syndicate won £9.4 million. Mary said, 'I think we have used up all our luck.'[26] Luck can also be a lady, a mythical figure who can smile on you and reward you for some smidgen of virtue which you might not know you had. Such a belief keeps many gamblers playing and losing.

The belief in the Just World lies behind an idea often held by political and military leaders that 'My enemy's enemy is my friend.' Franklin D. Roosevelt, President of the United States during the Second World War, believed that Joseph Stalin must be his, and America's, friend because Stalin and Roosevelt had a common enemy in Hitler. Roosevelt did not live long enough to see how wrong he was. Children may acquire the belief in the friendship of my enemy's enemy as they form and break alliances with their siblings, and not realise that there is no golden rule that your enemy's enemy must be your friend.

Even intellectuals who have no religious beliefs can be

seduced by the comforts of the belief in a Just World. Francis Wheen in his book *How Mumbo-Jumbo Conquered the World* does not mention the Just World but he writes of those 'secular liberals' who are unable to see that what is good can also be bad, what is bad can also be good, and that the bad can far outweigh the good. He writes of their 'political version of double entry book keeping' where they try to balance the good with the bad, how they assessed the Soviet Union by 'offsetting the Gulag against, say, Moscow's backing for anti-colonial movements in Africa or its distaste for the profit motive'.[27] A 'master of double entry maths' is the most frequently quoted living intellectual Noam Chomsky who 'after 11 September 2001 decided that al-Qaeda's murder of 3,000 people was less appalling than President Clinton's missile strike three years earlier on a pharmaceutical plant in the Sudan (wrongly identified as a chemical weapons factory), which claimed the life of a lone security guard'.[28] By concentrating on what American governments get wrong through their ignorance, stupidity or greed, many people, including left-wing intellectuals, try to make a Just World balance rather than have the courage to face unflinchingly the vastness of the cruelty perpetrated by people, often people in power, who have no concern for those whom they see as valueless because they are different from themselves. There can be no goodness that can balance the evil deeds of Pol Pot, Stalin, Hitler, the murderers in Rwanda and the Congo, in Sudan, Chechnya, Bosnia and so on. The list is endless. These are tragedies where there can be no recompense, no reward.

This brief overview of how widely and subtly the belief in the Just World permeates our lives can only give a glimpse of how powerful it is. It can be difficult to distinguish natural justice – that people ought to get what they deserve – from the Just World – people get what they deserve. From birth to death sibling relationships are fraught with expressed and secret resentment, jealousy, envy, competition, hatred, love and longing. To survive as a person and to feel safe siblings have to feel that they are good and that their parents appreciate them for being good. But being good is actually a state of uncertainty. Being good is being not good enough. We can tell ourselves that we have reached a satisfactory level of goodness but then an event can jolt us out of our complacency. Michael Rosen said, 'We all have this idea that disasters happen to other people, and very often the disaster that devastates us is the one that teaches us that nobody's spared.'

The stories which people tell about their life leading up to when they became depressed always have two common features. The first is that in childhood the person learned to think of himself as being unacceptable and having to work hard to be good. The second feature is that immediately before the person became depressed there was some kind of disaster which showed the person that there was a serious discrepancy between what he thought his life was and what it actually is. Discovering that you will not be spared, that one day you will die, can be the disaster that reveals this discrepancy. Often the discovery the person makes is simply that no amount of goodness prevents disaster. The world is not a Just World.

Everybody at least once in their life discovers that they have made a major error of judgement and that their life is not what they thought it was. People who can tolerate the uncertainty involved in going through a period where they have to change their ideas about themselves and their world do not become depressed. However, tolerating uncertainty is difficult and so many people in this situation refuse to change. Instead, they try to force the world to be what they want it to be. If the world is not a Just World then it *ought* to be and they *will* get their deserved rewards, even if that means they become depressed. Some of these people then learn from their depression that they cannot force reality to be what it is not, and they give up being depressed, but others feel that they have made such an investment in being good that they cannot afford to change, and so they go on being depressed. The feeling of having wasted time and effort is horrible, and we all experience it when we try and fail to live up to our family's expectations.

### Being what your family wants you to be

Every family has a particular morality and a particular style, and every child born into that family is expected to follow the morality and learn the style. Some families allow more leeway in this than others, but all families regard the children who do well in following the morality and learning the style as being good. However, the morality of the family might not be appropriate to the life each child has to live, and the style might not fit each child's ability. So in each family some children are better than others at meeting the family's requirements. In addition, the parents might not actually agree upon the morality and style, or the child might find that what the parents present as a morality and style is no more than a façade to show outsiders. The reality of family life might be quite different. In such unknown and sometimes dangerous territory each child has to find his or her own way. One advantage of being an only child is not having to compete with siblings who are trying to achieve the same goal. Fortunately, no child ever manages to fit every family requirement, for to do so would be to lose every aspect of being an individual and thus become a non-person.

The common term 'sibling rivalry' has been turned into 'sibling revelry' by the Levitt siblings, Jo Ann, Marjory and Joel, who conduct workshops to teach siblings how to 'enhance their adult sibling relationships'. They wrote:

Family legends often contain a built-in moral. The moral might be that we are smart, or that we might not be rich but we're 'good' people, unlike most of those rich people. The legend or the actual story that family members tell will show the moral as the only logical conclusion to the story. These legends are internalized and help us know who we are in the world. When we act contrary to the legends, we feel like we are betraying the family (even if they are all a thousand miles away, or long dead and buried.)[29]

The Levitts described the moral of the family they had been born into:

In our extended Jewish family, there was a larger, cultural and religious legend, based on grim reality, that we had to stick together. You could trust other Jews, but never, ever trust a Gentile. World War II and the Holocaust were close enough to be an object lesson that allowed for little contradiction. Our maternal line, except for our grandmother and a few of her husband's kin, were killed in concentration camps. For the generation which preceded ours, hostility towards Jews was not merely a legend but a cruel fact of life. The same kind of bitter legends have shaped the lives of African-American, Latino, and Asian-American families. Yet, our generation has not lived in fear as our parents did. Gradually, we've re-written that part of the legend and our lives have expanded accordingly.[30]

The moral of the Levitt family was that they had to stick together to be safe and that the danger lay outside the family. In some families the danger is seen to lie within.

For her book *Long Shadows: Lies, Truth and History*, Erna Paris interviewed a therapist, Hanni Lewerenz, who ran psychotherapy workshops for young Germans and some children of Jewish survivors of the Holocaust in Berlin. Hanni said, 'We ask everyone why they have come. The Germans do not express their motives clearly; they say they are students of this or that, but they do not say what always comes out sooner or later – that what they want to know is how their grandfather influenced their father, and how their father has influenced them. Deep down they fear they may have criminal tendencies. We still have this blood thing in Germany. We call it *Abstammung*, meaning from which stem you come. So people come here with a conscious, or subconscious, idea of genetic culpability. It's pure fantasy, but it can be powerful and disabling.'[31]

Many families have a moral legend that is based on a family secret of, perhaps, a mad uncle or a grandmother who brought disgrace upon the family. The standard of 'good' that the children in such a family have to live up to might have as its top priority the opposite of the vice contained in the secret. The family with the mad uncle can have as its prime virtue not showing a nervous disposition, while the family with the disgraceful grandmother must always behave with the utmost propriety in sexual matters.

Some families take an inordinate pride in what they see as their superior virtue, and do not notice that such pride is likely to reveal itself in undesirable ways. Edie, the youngest of the Macdonald siblings, at 73 wrote a little book of family memoirs where she commented:

If there was a flaw common to all their characters it

could be said, and doubtless was said in the broader-minded world that acknowledged their enchanting virtues, that, while they were seldom slow to bless, they were incontinently swift to chide. Forbearance of others' conduct which they deemed below their own moral standards was not among the social graces successfully learned in chapel or at home; and as they fared abroad they found no lack of occasion for disapproval that was prone to find expression in immediate and telling form.[32]

In many families the more dominant of the parents determines the legend of the family and therefore its style. In the Rush family this was the father, the centre of whose life was boats and sailing. The Rush children were allowed on their eleventh birthday to choose what their treat would be. Lallie would have loved to see a pantomime, but she felt compelled 'to do the Rush thing' and ask for a sailing trip. So family and friends set off in two boats to sail south from the River Orwell:

I was in the *Wanderer*. Her sails flapped . . . Most sailing people loathe that sound, connecting it in memory with hours of helpless rolling, becalmed in Channel or North Sea swells: but we made a point of liking it, being proud of our hard-won detachment from our stomachs. 'Lord, yes,' Father would say to anyone who inquired about any of our worst passages, 'all my troupe were as sick as dogs. Doesn't affect them though. They carry on all right.' And we glowed. Dru positively gloried in cutting to the minimum the necessary pause in her work. As the eldest of us she had even more experience, and a well-timed turn of the head was all that was now required. I envied her; this was so awfully Rush. I think she enjoyed sea-sickness as a means of earning Father's commendation.[33]

But it was not until she was a young woman and on a sailing trip to Belgium with her parents that Lallie had her moment of apostasy and she lost her faith in the family legend. Her father had insisted that they smuggled some alcohol into England:

This successful end to the whole childish business, about which Father did not seem in the least uncomfortable,

finally discovered in me, in a flash of awed delight, my
loathing for small boats and everything connected with
sailing; more, that I had unconsciously hated them for
years! I was amazed at the realization. It brought nearly
as much upheaval of mind as my former discovery that I
must relinquish God and all the heavenly etceteras; but
jettisoning my family religion like this was a mental act
that required nearly two years' more preparation than
the other apostasy. With a pleasant, mounting sense
of blasphemy, I recalled, one by one, all the occasions
which I had believed to be red-letter sailing days,
and decided that I had not enjoyed any of them.[34]

Children are presented with the family morality, myth and
style when they are very young. It tells them, in part, how 'good'
is defined in their family, and they have a choice whether or not
they will accept it. Some children know right from the start
that they can never fit what is expected of them, while others
try to fit it and fail. Some of the ones who fail forever blame
themselves for failing, while others, like Lallie, find recognition of their failure the opportunity to outgrow their family and
become an adult. Some children see themselves as the keeper of
the family flame, and are hurt if another sibling criticises their
parents. Such differing interpretations inevitably lead to major
misunderstandings and disagreements among the siblings.

A family's morality, myth and style are never simply a matter
for the family alone. The family is part of society, and many
families see themselves as having to follow their society's traditions, no matter what this may cost the children in the family.
Nawal El Saadawi wrote:

In 1937, at a time when I had just reached the age
of six, all girls were circumcised before they started
menstruating. Not a single girl, whether from the city
or the village, from a rich or poor family, escaped.
Grandmother Amna, the wife of Soukri Bey, and my
mother Zaynab Hanem were both circumcised. My mother
did not rescue me from this operation, nor did she rescue
any of her other daughters, but I was able to protect
my daughter, and many other girls, from undergoing
it, when I started writing over forty years ago.

At the age of six I could not save myself from it.
Four women, as hefty as Um Muhammad, cornered me
and pinned me down by the hands and feet. . . Since I
was a child the deep wound left in my body has never
healed. But the deeper wound has been the one left in
my spirit, in my soul. I cannot forget that day in the
summer of 1937. . . I could not bear to see my body
naked in the mirror, the forbidden parts steeped in
shame and guilt. I did not know what other parts of my
body might need to be cut off in the same way. So at
night I lay in bed, my eyes wide open in the dark.[35]

The meaning of a girl's circumcision is very different from that
of a boy. For a boy being circumcised means that he will take
his place in the company of men and be respected because he
is a male. For a girl circumcision means that she is an incomplete,
lesser being whose duty is to serve men. Thus, no matter
how much Nawal excelled in her studies (she became a doctor
and renowned writer) her older brother would treat her with
contempt.

Nawal saw that in her family all the women had accepted
their humiliation as inevitable because this was the only way
they could see themselves as being good. They suffered greatly
but, so that they would not be overwhelmed by the pain of
their helplessness, they did what most humiliated and helpless
people do. They asserted what little power they did have to do
to those weaker than themselves what had been done to them.
'Why shouldn't they suffer in the way I suffered?' is a rhetorical
question used by those who do not have the courage to confront
their own pain and helplessness.

It is a common pattern in families that parents bring up
their first and perhaps second child more strictly than their
subsequent children. When older children see their young siblings
being treated more leniently they can feel jealousy and
rage against the younger siblings made all the more ferocious
because they dare not show how angry they are with their
parents. They might attack the younger sibling physically, or
complain about their siblings very loudly and bitterly, or parade
their superior virtue and age in such a way as to humiliate
their younger siblings. If the parents do not recognise and

resolve this situation, the younger siblings can suffer injuries which they find impossible to forgive, while the older siblings can bear a grudge until the end of their days. Nawal chose not to treat her younger sisters in this way:

My paternal aunt, Rokaya, said the Prophet had ordained that the *bazar* of girls be cut off. Yet I could not imagine that Prophet Muhammad, or Jesus, or any other prophet could ordain that such a thing be done. Could any prophet be like that? How could the prophets carry such a hatred of the *bazars* of young girls, and if they did, why was it so? The word 'why' stayed with me through my life.[36]

Nawal's memoirs are part of that vast body of literature, written in the nineteenth and twentieth centuries, which charts the effects of the authoritarian family on the children, and the children's attempts to resist the power which threatened to turn them into nothing but obedient automatons.

The Second World War destroyed many authoritarian structures or showed them to be hollow shams. In those places where authoritarian religion has lost its supremacy, the authoritarian father became an object of scorn and derision. However, every organisation has to create some means of keeping the members of the group in order. Those families that lacked an authoritarian parent turned to criticism and teasing to achieve this. Lallie explained:

Robust humour was a speciality in our family, and being laughed at considered a tonic automatically wholesome for anyone at any time, with the exception of God, who alone was not supposed to be improved with having His corners rubbed off (Mother's favourite expression) with this strong mental abrasive: the Old Testament contained too many records of His inability to take a joke in good part; but save on sacred subjects one was always safe in being funny with a Rush; it was part of the home-made tradition.[37]

Different styles in criticism and teasing have different outcomes. The contrast could not be greater between two families I have known for many years. The first family does not have conversations with one another. They are far from silent people, but if any discussion on one topic goes on for more than a few minutes it is cut across by another family member who will change the subject abruptly or start talking to one of the two discussants and thus exclude the other. Conversation mainly consists of a question requiring a brief answer, or a criticism of the person which is often presented as a tease intended to diminish the person teased. Sometimes an individual will start to tell a story which turns into a monologue, and the others feel free to wander away if bored. The children in the family know that certain topics are absolutely forbidden, and they know only too well that doing anything their parents have forbidden results only in painful punishments. The one topic which can be discussed at any length is sport, and this is confined to asking a question such as 'What's the score?' or giving an opinion about the game and the players.

Family life in the second family is all about conversations. The parents have always listened to their children and taken their concerns seriously. Everything is discussed, from the most intimate personal matters to world politics, science and the arts, and anything that is important to one of them is important to them all. There is much humour and gentle teasing of the kind which leaves the object of the teasing feeling valued and important.

If the task of parenting is measured in the amount of time the parents spend on child-related matters, then it would be clear that the parents in the first family had by far the easier time. Frightening children into obedience takes up little of a parent's time. It is also clear, now that the children have grown up, that the children in the first family lead lives fraught with difficulties and pain, while the children in the second family are at ease with themselves. The siblings in the second family are good friends, whereas the children in the first family still live like disparate passengers in a lifeboat who know that they have to stick together if they are to survive.

Children learn the family style and use their interpretation of it in making sense of the adult experience. Whatever Michael Rosen's politics might be now, his style in company and in his work is completely egalitarian. His parents, who had known poverty in their childhood, were Communists in the 1930s. In those years many people saw Communism as the means of ending injustice and poverty in the world. I asked Michael, 'Was it important to your parents that you and your brother got on together?' Michael replied, 'Yes, it was. As they saw it, the family was a microcosm of the Soviet Union, and the family was the collective farm. You had to produce things together, whether it was a meal, a camping holiday, or O Levels – the whole family was involved in everything. There was utter engagement with everything. If Mum was applying for a job, everybody knew about it and everybody was talking about it. So the idea that me and my brother didn't get on would be like the collective farm breaking down, wouldn't it?'

Michael's brother Brian, alas, was an introvert and this caused family problems. 'There was a sense that Brian wasn't somehow fitting in or at various times, he wasn't playing by the rules of the collective farm. I remember disputes like he hadn't come back for something, or if he had come back he was late. If he formed any strong relationships or attachments, it was always seen as a bit of a threat, unless that person or subject could be brought into the family. Brian got totally absorbed in things my dad knew absolutely nothing at all about, like palaeontology and model railways and that didn't please Dad.'

Richard is a very successful businessman. He had been born some 15 years after Michael's parents and so knew the 1930s as a child. The Great Depression of that time had left many families penniless, but Richard's father was determined to provide for his family. He thought in terms of business, just different small business enterprises, and the whole family itself in effect became a business. He expected his three sons to work, Richard the youngest included. Richard told me that when his father had a butcher's shop he, not yet five, 'had a sharp knife and used to cut up the cat's meat'. Later his father used to buy poultry and kill, clean and sell it. Richard said, 'I can pluck a chicken in four seconds flat. My father was a pretty bossy guy. He was a good worker. We all had a job to do, either in the house or helping him. No, we didn't get pocket money. It was the family. Everyone contributed. He was a good influence on us. He made us work.' The principle which his father followed and which Richard made his own was, 'If you did nothing, nothing happened, but if you did something, something happened. That's a pretty good principle in life.'

In his family money may have been scarce but Richard felt

secure. When I asked Richard what feeling he had for his brothers he said, 'Brotherly love. They were just big brothers. They were there like my mother and father were there. That's what life's supposed to be. I felt we were all treated the same. My mother and father were pretty up and down people. They were good, solid citizens. Father would say do it and you did it. There was no argument. Sometimes he got the strap out but it never landed on you. If he said something he meant it. I think he did a good job. I think they both did a good job. They taught us the value of work and they taught us be to be good honest citizens, and if parents can teach you that they've taught you a lot.'

Step-siblings joining a new family must feel somewhat like a prospective bride or groom meeting the future in-laws for the first time. The family styles of the two families, if markedly different, can cause problems. Richard's wife Sarah told me that when she made her first visit to Richard's family Richard, his brothers and their mother began a spirited argument. Sarah became very anxious because in her family any argument resulted in raised voices, slammed doors and her mother retiring to her bedroom, her feelings deeply hurt. In Richard's family the argument came to an end, the family members went on with whatever they had been doing and conversation went back to being ordinary. This style of conducting a family argument must have contributed greatly to the success of the business which Richard and his brothers set up together. Their style of argument and the loyalty they had to one another allowed them to separate the important decisions from the unimportant. Richard said, 'If we wanted to paint the toilet pink instead of blue there would be an argument for three hours or four days. If we wanted to buy a block of land the decision was made within a minute. We all agreed on major decisions.' He summed up his philosophy with, 'If you are a decent, honest, hard-working conscientious individual you will have a reasonably successful life. But if you expect people to do things for you and expect to get handouts from other people you will fail.'

Richard interpreted the family style very much in the way his parents hoped he would. Other parents might envy them because what makes being a parent so impossibly difficult is that what determines a child's behaviour is not what the parent does but how the child interprets what the parent does. Thus even the most well-intentioned actions by parents can have unfortunate results. This is what happened to Sophie. She described how her family kept together as a family. 'Certainly the event which pulled the family together was eating. From way back into my childhood, all of the family get-togethers, which included my grandparents, my father's parents, were all linked round food. These were very warm and sociable events.'

As a child Sophie was closer to her father than her mother while her sister Ester was closer to her mother than her father. When Sophie was 13 her father developed Parkinson's disease. She said, 'I think both he and my mother became understandably very preoccupied with what was happening to him. It was a progressive deterioration until in the last five years of his life when he was unable to do anything at all, and was completely bed-bound. I think – and I'm very uncomfortable about saying this – that I rejected my father on some level because he was sick, and so moved away from him.' Sophie had something else to contend with. 'I went to a boys' grammar which took girls in the senior forms, having been at a girls' school. I was very shy, and found it very strange and threatening.'

Sophie wanted to get closer to her mother but Ester saw this as her rightful place. Moreover, Ester 'was very slim at that stage, and tall, and I think elegant'. Sophie had put on weight after she had broken her leg when she was 11. She said, 'I can remember my father saying to me that I was very Rubenesque, which is not the thing you want to hear as a girl of that age. But on the other hand, I can remember my mother saying, "Oh, you've got a lovely figure." I can remember us having this huge battle when we were on holiday because she wanted me to wear a bikini and I didn't want to wear a bikini.'

If you were a very unhappy girl in a family where the parents were too busy to notice your unhappiness, and this was a family which regarded eating together as very important, how could you make sure that your family would take notice of you and not complain that you were a nuisance? By stopping eating, of course. Sophie became anorexic.

Whenever we need to construct a desperate defence to hold ourselves together in the face of massive invalidation, the materials we need for our defence are so much part of us that we do not have to think consciously about how to put them together. The necessary meanings have been learnt long ago. All small children find it hard to adapt to the parents' standards of 'being good' in respect to eating. Whether the mother is giving the child nourishing food or the only meagre scraps available, she wants the child to eat. The child may not want to eat there and then, or not eat that particular food. The child soon learns that not to eat means either 'you are bad' or 'you are ill'. 'Bad' means punishment; 'ill' means being looked after. Bad children scream and disobey; ill children are wan and listless. Hence, do not eat, look wan and listless, and your mother will notice you and look after you. There is no need to rehearse this line of thought consciously, anymore than it is necessary to think consciously about putting one foot in front of the other in order to walk. As an adult Sophie had reviewed her childhood and now she could say, 'Looking at it critically, that was a very attention-seeking response. It's very uncomfortable stuff to look at because at the time I think you're thinking "poor me", but actually, when you look at it analytically afterwards, it's really destructive, unpleasant, attention-seeking behaviour.'

Anorexia does not always result from wanting attention. Sometimes it comes from just plain fear. Pat told me, 'I had a real eating disorder until I was about ten. There was always a struggle – hiding the food, not wanting to eat, being sick, being punished for not eating. I remember eating as being a real horrible experience. My analyst connected the birth of my sister with me not eating. I don't know. Maybe it was, maybe it wasn't. I don't know. My sister used to have stomach aches and she used to vomit a lot.'

I asked her what the attitude to food was in her family. She said, 'There was a lot of the violence about food. If the potatoes were cold, they would end up on the ceiling and my mother was in trouble. The food had to be hot. There was a lot of what I now see as baby-like behaviour by my father. As well as getting angry he would also not be able to eat because he had stomach disorders. He was always vomiting, being sick. My mother always had stomach aches because of her nerves, because she was upset and worried. It was her rage, probably, her fear. There was a lot of fear around food, I think.'

I often read in the popular press how families should gather around the dining table for their meals, but it seems to me that in some families eating separately prevents murder, if not physical murder then the 'soul murder' that a child can suffer when the family gets together and the child is required to be good. Often it is no more than a simple statement or an apparently unimportant act by a parent that shows a child that he is not good enough and his place in the family is not secure.

My friend Clara was the second of eight siblings. One day when we were reminiscing about our childhoods she recalled an incident from the early childhood of her youngest sister Edith. Each evening, after dinner, their father would sit in his armchair beside the fire. He was a slim man and so there was space in the armchair for a small child to sit beside him. Settled in his chair he would pat the space and little Edith would climb up and sit close beside him as he stroked her hair. Then Harry was born. Edith's trauma of being supplanted by the baby did not end there. Soon Harry was big enough to climb up on to his father's chair. Edith was banished from her special place, never to return. 'My parents never thought about what that meant to Edith,' Clara said. 'They didn't do that in those days.' I knew Edith well, and she was a wonderful woman, very talented and seemingly very strong, but inside her was a little worm that nibbled away at her self-confidence until there was none left. This little worm was her belief that anything she had which she valued would be taken away from her. Edith did not want to lose her place in her family, even though it had long ceased to be the most favoured place. Other children can doubt that they have a place in the family at all.

Just before the Second World War, Don McCullin was born in London where his parents lived in poverty. He wrote:

My most painful memory of the war was born of the attempt to get me away from it. When I was five, [my sister] Marie and I were faced with evacuation. . . As soon as we arrived in Norton St Philip in Somerset, Marie and I were separated. My mother had been promised that we would not be split up but we were. My sister was taken to the wealthiest house in the village. . I was sent to a council house. My sister's existence and mine in that same village was from then on quite separate. Where she lived they had a maid with a black and white uniform who used to serve my sister tea. I would go around and peep through her window. Although I was her brother, I was looked upon as one of those scruffy council house children and not allowed in. Looking back, I think it may be the beginning of something you can see in my pictures – an attempt to get as close to my subject while remaining invisible myself.

His experiences as an evacuee led to more than his style of photography. He said:

You soon became aware of, and resigned to, the position you have in society: the fact that I lived in a council house meant that, somehow, the die was cast. My sister was leaving us through the privilege she enjoyed in that house. My mother took the amazing decision of allowing her to stay on after the war as a permanent foster child of that rich family . . . I felt cast out, unchosen, rather as if I was the wrong breed of dog. I remember running after my father when he set off home after a visit and begging him to take me with him.

His third evacuation was the worst, with a chicken farmer who put him in a room without furniture or lino and clouted him in the way Don was clouted at school. The whole experience of evacuation, he said, 'gave me a lifelong affinity with persecuted peoples. I know what it is like to be branded uncivilised and unclean. Except that I was ostracised and ill-treated by my own people, and not by an alien race.'[38]

Don learned in an unmistakeable way that the world is a terrible place and to survive he needed to be an outsider. I became an outsider in a much more subtle way. We all have had the experience of a situation where, on the surface, all seems fine. However, we start to suspect that all is not as it seems. One small event follows another, and our suspicions grow. Then one day there is an event, perhaps of no more significance than all the previous events which aroused our suspicions, but this event brings together all our past suspicions into one absolute certainty. Small children can have this kind of experience. Later in life a therapist might tell you that some tiny event led you to become this or that, but in fact that tiny event was simply the one that confirmed all your suspicions. In adulthood it may seem that just one tiny event had a profound effect, but in fact that event was just the tip of an iceberg of suspicion. This is what happened to me.

By the time I was five I had had enough unhappy encounters with my mother and sister to suspect that I was not wanted in the family, but I hoped I was wrong and one day my mother and sister would show me that I was wanted. The event which confirmed for me that I was right in my suspicions that I was not wanted was my grandmother's seventy-fifth birthday party. I was very excited about this because I had never been to a family party. In my family such events were extremely rare. There was to be a supper in my grandparents' small cottage and all the family, grandparents, their children and their spouses, and all their children plus some neighbours and friends were to be there. I spent all day helping my mother and my aunts with the preparations. I fetched and carried, and it should have been obvious to any adult that the party was very important to me. It was a hot evening and the front door was open when we began to take our places at the table. A figure loomed in the doorway, someone I did not know. He was welcomed, but then there was consternation. There was no room at the table for another person. My mother said, 'He can have Dot's place. She doesn't need to sit at the table.'

My heart stood still. I could not breathe. I had to get away, to hide. I ran down the hall, out the front gate and into the night. The closest hiding place was the back seat of my father's car. A long time passed. No one came to search for me. Eventually my father appeared at the side of the car. He leaned on the half-opened window and asked me if I would like to come in and have something to eat. I guessed that dinner was over and people had moved away from the table. I could not expose myself to all those eyes and the clucking about how I had got over my little upset. I shook my head, shrank back in the corner, and Dad went away. I was asleep by the time my family got in the car to drive home. No mention was ever made of this event but I did not forget. That night I began my journey away from my family. Years later, when my marriage was breaking up, I heard Nina Simone singing, 'You've got to learn to leave the table when love's no longer being served'. I had learned what that meant when I was five.

Every family has its own legend, morality and style, and each child in that family interprets the legend, morality and style in his or her own way. Those siblings whose interpretations produce the kind of behaviour which the parents approve of are seen by the parents as 'being good'. Those children whose interpretations produce the kind of behaviour which the parents do not approve of are seen as 'being bad'. This does not mean that the 'goodest' sibling has won the contest. The 'good one' can find herself weighed down by parental expectations and scorned by her siblings, while the 'bad one' may be the scamp whom his mother indulges. The 'good one' may feel that the reward for being so good should be power, while the oldest, biggest or cleverest may feel that power is their right. Whatever their status in the family, all siblings want to be powerful because power validates the person as a person. So the siblings fight not just over who is the 'goodest' but over who will have the power.

# Chapter 5

# POWER STRUGGLES

Power, like beauty, is in the eye of the beholder. To be powerful you have to convince other people that you are. Prime ministers and presidents have publicists who devise all kinds of stratagems aimed at making the leader appear powerful, but siblings have to fight it out among themselves. Each one tries to force the others to see him or her as being powerful. Children are quick to determine who has power amongst the adults around them and to identify with the most powerful person, or at least envy that person his power. Ordinarily children see their parents as the most powerful, but during wars and conflicts the parents may be shown to be helpless, so the children look beyond the family to see who has the power. The people they see as the most powerful are revealed in the children's games. In his study of children's lives under the Nazis the historian Nicholas Stargardt wrote:

> During occupation, children feared and hated their enemies, but also profoundly envied them. Polish boys had acted the 'Gestapo', and children in the Vilna ghetto and the Birkenau camps had played at being the SS searching for contraband, or carrying out round-ups and selections [for the gas ovens]. Defeat and occupation altered German children's games too. Before they even emerged from their Berlin cellars, children had started playing at being Russian soldiers. Waving make-believe pistols, they had relieved each other of imaginary watches, crying, *'Bangbang, pistolet, uri!'* As they assimilated the real and terrifying power of their enemies and masters into their games, children were also enacting their own impotence in all its startling contrasting emotions, from shame and guilt, to rage and envy.[1]

Parents are often startled, and sometimes shamed, when they hear their own words of instruction, criticism and complaint coming out of the mouths of their children as they order other children around.

In a democracy power is supposed to be intimately linked with responsibility. Most parents try to teach this to their children along the lines of, 'You can boss your young brother around provided you look after him.' Parents and teachers constantly urge children to 'be responsible', while the children are well aware that what adults actually mean by this is 'Do what I want you to do even though I'm not there to see that you do.' Children also discover that there are adults who have power without assuming any responsibility, and that people can have responsibility without power.

It is often the oldest sibling whom the parents expect to be responsible. One man told me how his big brother turned responsibility for his younger siblings into bullying them into obedience and punishing them when they failed to live up to the standards he set. Some older siblings take their responsibilities very seriously but find the power which their parents have invested in them too delicious to relinquish once the siblings have grown up. Cynthia told me that when she had been a three year old her sister Rosemary 'was immensely important to me'. Later she followed her sister to boarding school where 'Rosemary made it clear to me that she wanted to have little to do with me. When she became a prefect and then head girl she would stop me in the school corridor to lecture me about my bad behaviour. When I needed her she ignored me, and that hurt.' Cynthia left school, went to university, and then into business with her husband. She felt she managed her life quite well but Rosemary still felt she had to supervise her. 'Rosemary believes that now our parents are dead she's head of the family. She and her husband visit us about once a month. It's not so much a visit as an inspection. They ask us questions about what we're doing that verge on the impertinent.'

Many parents find that trying to understand the subtle differences between one child and another is far too difficult. Instead they slot each child into a role – 'the happy one', 'the lazy one', and so on. Each role comes with certain implications. The happy one must not be sad; the lazy one must not be seen to make an effort. In Australia perhaps the most popular role for a boy is 'the larrikin', where the outstanding characteristics are boyish charm entailing the power to get others to do what you want along with almost total irresponsibility. It is a role that blends well with that of a sportsman. Peter Rose described his brother Robert as a larrikin, 'impish, vexing and endearing',[2] 'vexing because, as the larrikin role requires, the only subject that must be taken seriously is sport, something which is, as a football commentator once remarked, 'more important than life and death'. Taking sport seriously shows that you are a man that other men admire: taking anything else seriously shows that you are not. The larrikin is at ease with himself only when he is with his mates, but because he secretly lacks self-confidence and is frightened of everything other than what he is already familiar with, he depends on his womenfolk to look after him. However, his womenfolk must be seen to be subservient to him and to demonstrate that this is so he interprets any request from them as an order and, as a larrikin must, he disobeys. Robert was 'an erratic driver',[3] but if his wife Terry complained that he was driving too fast he drove faster. He was at the wheel of his car with two mates as passengers when he rolled it, and thus he left an active sporting life for that of quadriplegia.

In his biography of his brother, Peter Rose tried to be very fair in everything he said about Robert, but he refers to him as 'my eternal adversary'.[4] Even when they had given up their physical tussles they competed endlessly in games like table tennis. Relations did not improve until Robert married and left home. Peter stressed that their father treated them equally, but it seems that Peter did not see himself as Robert's equal. He wrote: 'At fourteen I decided I would always be alone, a sort of outcast . . . By the time I went to university – absurdly unready, at seventeen, for the adventure – I was killingly shy. During my first year at Monash, the year before Robert's accident, I spoke to no one and eschewed clubs and activities. I seem to have been chronically and suicidally depressed.'[5]

The elder of two girls, Pat had great responsibility and little power. She said, 'My role seemed to be always the caretaker, in various ways, and I got very good at it, but I never was really a caretaker to my sister. I have a cousin the same age as I am, and as a grown-up she would verify, in a very indignant voice, that my mother always wanted the pair of us to take care of Helen. I know I resented that. I felt that I just couldn't manage that as well. I know how distorted that sounds – because I was a five year old and my sister was a baby – but I just couldn't take on having a baby because I already had two babies, my mother and my father. I seemed to have figured out, from a very young age, that they were not functioning. I also knew fairly early that I had to develop almost that false persona, so acutely that I knew that it was important to play the child so they could feel that they were parents. But I had this detached part of myself that was somehow aware of that. It was very curious. Somehow, for my sister, there just wasn't enough of me left over to take care of her.'

Pat's way of dealing with her unhappy family was to assume responsibility while her sister Helen refused to acknowledge that there was a problem. Pat said, 'When I was a teenager and there were domestic rows – which were a constant feature in our lives – my experience was to not miss a word. If I was in my room, my ear would be against the wall because I couldn't miss any clues. It seemed like my job was to figure out how to make it better between my mother and father. I couldn't miss any important information; otherwise I wouldn't have been able to sort it! My sister – I remember once there was this huge row going on and my sister went to the television and turned it up as loud as she could. Or she was with her animals – she loved her dogs. Or she'd go out. She didn't want to hear it, she didn't want to know about it and she certainly didn't want to talk about it.' In some unhappy families two siblings become close in order to support and protect one another, but Pat found herself struggling on alone.

## Complex emotions

Power struggles between siblings are never simple. In politics or business an ambitious man may have no compunction in using or injuring others in pursuit of his goal, but such simple but ruthless competition is comparatively rare amongst siblings. A sibling may struggle to have power over another in order to validate and protect himself from the siblings who might invalidate him, but at the same time he can need the sibling against whom he struggles because his sibling is the only member of his family on whom he can rely.

This is the kind of relationship portrayed by L. P. Hartley in his trilogy *Eustace and Hilda*. Hilda, the older of the two, sought to dominate Eustace. He sometimes longed to be free, but he had learned young to be very good:

> The effort to qualify for his sister's approval was the ruling force in Eustace's interior life: he had to live up to her idea of him, to fulfil the ambitions she entertained on his behalf. And though he chafed under her domination it was necessary for him; whenever, after one of their quarrels, she temporarily withdrew her jealous supervision, saying she didn't care now, he could get his feet wet and be as silly and lazy and naughty as he liked, she would never bother about him again, he felt as though the bottom had dropped out of his life, as though the magnetic north had suddenly repudiated the needle.[6]

The opening chapters of the first of the trilogy, *The Shrimp and the Anemone*, reveal how cleverly Hilda had made Eustace dependent on her and obedient to her orders, but as the story progresses we learn why she had done this. Hilda had once been the only child of her beloved mother. Then she had been displaced, first by Eustace and then by baby Barbara whose birth brought the death of her mother. Neither her father, aunt nor nurse could give Hilda the relationship which secured her sense of being a person. Only Eustace could do that because she was the most important person in his life, but she feared that she might lose him in the way she had lost her mother, or that he would grow up and leave her. To keep herself secure she had to make him subservient to her.

The trilogy begins with Eustace as a child discovering in a rock pool an anemone eating a shrimp, 'sucking it in'. The trilogy ends with Eustace, now a man and dying, dreaming that he is back beside the rock pool. The same anemone is there but there is no shrimp in its mouth. Fearing that it would die of hunger, 'he waded into the water. The water was bitterly cold; but colder still were the lips of the anemone as they closed around his finger. "I shall wake up now," thought Eustace, who had wakened from many dreams. But the cold crept onwards and he did not wake.'[7]

This may seem to be a rather melodramatic way of describing a power-dependency relationship between two siblings but such relationships are not uncommon. There are those siblings who may marry and have families but each still sees the other as the most important person in their life. Where one sibling clearly dominates the other the submissive sibling may complain endlessly to other people about her sister's constant interference in her life, but when urged to reject her sister's control she demurs, saying that she does not want to hurt her feelings.

Power validates us: impotence invalidates us. Impotence is painful, often unendurable, so we turn it into another emotion which gives us the illusion of power. Jealousy means 'That person has what is rightly mine,' that is, 'I demand the return of my power', which is a stronger statement than 'I am powerless'. Contempt means 'I despise you', that is, 'From my superior point I look down on you.' From the superior position of jealousy and contempt the person can seek to avenge the injury he has suffered.

Nancy Mitford, the eldest of the Mitford sisters, was the prettiest of little girls. According to their biographer Mary Lovell, after her sister Pam was born, she 'engaged in a series of jealous rages'. Years later she admitted 'to being "vile"' to her sisters and brother in those early years. It seems that while she loved her siblings in one sense, she never recovered from the halcyon period when, as an only child, she had the undiluted attention of her parents and nanny. Pam became the main target for Nancy's retribution and temper tantrums, and barbed teasing became second nature to Nancy and the ethos of the Mitford nursery. Nancy 'was the Queen of teasers – a "cosmic teaser"', Decca would write. She seemed to know what would irritate her victims most, fastening on any insecurities with devastatingly accurate effect. 'She once upset us,' Debo recalled, 'by saying to Unity, Decca and me, "Do you realise the middle of your names are nit, sick and bore?"' One friend likened her humour to the barbed hook hidden beneath a riot of colourful feathers in a fishing fly. And barbed is an accurate word, for there was often a cruel element to her teasing, which caused real distress. For example, while Nancy longed to go to school, Diana could not stand the thought of it: she became physically ill at the idea and was therefore an easy victim of Nancy's tease that she had heard their parents discussing to which school they might send Diana. That this might cause her sister to lie awake at night worrying did not concern Nancy. It was 'a good tease' and that made it all right. Pam recalled that when they were debs Nancy would find out the name of the young man Pam most fancied and tell her that she had seen him out with another girl.[8]

When I was a child I could understand, though not enjoy, why my sister found me to be a great nuisance, but what puzzled and hurt me was the way she treated me with great contempt. I could understand her jealousy of me because I was jealous of her, but I could not understand her contempt without having to assume that there was something intrinsically contemptible about me. My sister made it very clear to me that there was. I longed for her to take favourable notice of me and be interested in me, but she either ignored me or used me for her own ends. She could get me to do anything by telling me that if I did not my father would be inconvenienced and upset. Sometimes something I had said or done caught her attention and she would look at me curiously and comment with the fascinated disgust of someone who had inadvertently kicked over a stone and found a particularly strange and loathsome slug hiding there. I was in my fifties before I discovered that my sister had developed this attitude from something she had learned when she was six.

My sister and her husband were visiting London and I took them to lunch at Fortnum and Mason. In the baroque splendour of the restaurant my sister chatted on about family matters. There was something about her daughter-in-law getting a kitten as a pet and having to toilet train it. She said, 'The kitten piddled on the floor and she picked it up and rubbed its nose in it. I suddenly remembered when you were a baby. You were propped up in your high chair and you wet and it went all over the seat and dripped on to the floor. Mother rubbed your nose in it.'

My sister told this story in the 'fancy that' tone of voice much used in my family to drain the significance out of any unusual event and to forestall any speculation about the event or search for causes. She was apparently unaware of the effect her story had on me.

It had always been tremendously important to my sister to preserve her picture of her mother as being good. She did this in two ways. First, she wiped her conscious memory of all the events of her childhood which had led to her intense fear of her mother, a fear which did not abate until after Mother's death. The memories had vanished but not her fear. Second, since she did not dare blame her mother for her unhappiness after I was born, she blamed me. All siblings in a position similar to mine, and there are a great number of us, find ourselves in a power struggle where we are in double jeopardy: first, the ordinary power struggle between two siblings; second, the undeserved revenge for something which we had been powerless to prevent. In contrast, some siblings are able to apportion blame among the parents and the competitor siblings in a far more just way. Charles Dickens was one of these.

Dickens had already established a loving bond with his older sister Fanny when his improvident parents sent him, aged just 12, to work in a blacking factory while Fanny continued her studies at the Royal Academy of Music. Though desperately wounded by this betrayal, Dickens was able to see that Fanny was not the sole cause of his downfall. Later he was able to take the writer's revenge on his parents. They appear in his books in various guises. Dickens' biographer Fred Kaplan wrote that in *Hard Times*, for instance: 'The unredeemed father who put him to work in the blacking factory appears in aspects of Mr Bounderby, the mother who insisted on him remaining in the portrait of Mrs Sparsit.' However, even when having suffered an injury we try to separate the knife which wounded us from the hand that wielded the knife, in our emotional meanings the two can become conflated. Fred Kaplan told how in his stories Fanny became 'the woman who is the nurturer-protector but who also has the potential to be the vehicle of deprivation'.[9]

Power struggles between siblings began, so the Bible tells us, with Cain and Abel. When I told my friend Kevin Sullivan that I was proposing to write a book on siblings he told me a story:

The Holy Brother was greatly renowned for his purity of thoughts. The evil emotions of anger, hate, jealousy, greed, resentment, envy, gluttony and bitterness were unknown to him. When he went into the desert to spend the rest of his life in solitary prayer the Devil called his newest group of imps and demons to him and instructed them to set upon the Holy Brother and tempt him into evil thoughts. This they set about doing. They showed the monk cool streams and gentle waterfalls which banished thirst forever; they put him before a sumptuous feast where he could satisfy his hunger a thousand times over; they offered him wealth and power beyond his imagination; they surrounded him with languorous young women and men offering him all the known and unknown sexual pleasures. When all these failed to tempt him from his path of righteousness the imps and demons taunted him, telling him he was old, ugly and forsaken by God. Throughout the Holy Brother remained unmoved and steadfast in his prayer. The imps and demons, defeated, returned to the Devil and reported their failure.

The Devil chided them. 'All those temptations to evil thoughts are as nothing to someone who is truly holy. You must tempt him with the greatest temptation of all.'

The trainee imps and demons crowded around him. 'Tell us, please, what is the greatest temptation of them all?'

The Devil spoke. 'Tell him that his brother has been made Bishop of Antioch.'

Not long after Cardinal Ratzinger became Pope the columnist Richard Ingram reported:

When the new Pope was elected, the tributes and congratulations flooded in – the Queen, George Bush, the Archbishop of Canterbury, the Chief Rabbi all expressed their unqualified delight at the elevation of Cardinal Ratzinger, 78. Only one sour note was heard amid the general rejoicing. The cardinal's elder brother, Georg, also a priest, expressed his disappointment, not to say his fears, for the future. Cardinal Ratzinger was too old for the job, he said. His health was none too good and the strain of his new post might well hasten his death. He went on to compare his brother with a doddery, absent-minded old university lecturer who was always losing his spectacles.[10]

Human nature does not change.

## Sexual politics

The close physical intimacy in which most siblings live can easily allow for the mutual exploration of bodies and sexual feelings. It can also allow for the wielding of sexual power. To see what psychologists have been saying about this I typed the words 'sibling incest' into Google. Some 372,000 references appeared. However, this did not mean that I had an enormous amount of reading to do. Few of these references related to reports by psychologists. The rest were pornographic websites apparently devoted to sexual practices of siblings of all ages. This number of websites suggests that there is a huge number of people interested in the sexual practices of siblings, or of people purporting to be siblings. Why is this so?

An asexual alien observing the sexual activities of human beings would be puzzled as to why these activities are so important to people. Through literature and art the alien could come to understand the nature of a passionate sexual attachment between two individuals. By observing his own curiosity he could understand the curiosity that children and young adults have about sex. However, he would also observe that the number of permutations and combinations between two or several people, with or without the use of objects and animals, is quite limited, so a reasonably sexually active person could satisfy his or her curiosity about sex fairly quickly. If he observed the sexual activity of couples who believed that they needed to introduce some novelty into their sexual practice in order to create some sexual passion, he might well conclude that the couples had satisfied their curiosity and outgrown their passion, and that they now should take up a hobby such as gardening or kite flying.

What an alien might not understand is our need for validation as a person and the need to be touched and held close. Sex can meet these needs. Under the guise of sexual passion, even simulated sexual passion, an unhappy, lonely person can feel their fragmented self come together again, however momentarily, and the warmth and closeness of another person's body comfort them. This can apply to children as adults, and explain why so many of us engage in and submit ourselves to sexual practices that, were we brimful of the confidence which can come from the accepting, uncritical love and comfort of those around us, would seem crude, ridiculous, even disgusting. Since such love is in short supply, many people will turn to pornography and less than perfect sexual practices in the way that starving people will devour anything at all which might sustain them.

However, for many people pornography is more than the thin gruel of simulated passion. Pornography is not about just sexual passion, or even simple curiosity. For a great many people it is concerned with a desperate and inevitably fruitless attempt to master an unmasterable memory.

The acts of sexual passion that each person involved finds absorbing, enjoyable, amusing and fulfilling are those where each person gives and receives freely without coercion. Acts where the more powerful person forces the less powerful person to accept and obey cause the weaker person pain, revulsion and humiliation. If the physical stimulation involved in the act produces an automatic response of physical arousal in the weaker person, that person is likely to be left feeling confused and guilty. In short, the weaker person has been invalidated.

Whenever we are invalidated we are impelled to carry out some act or reinterpretation of the event that in some way will serve to validate ourselves. Sometimes sexually abused people murder their abuser, and sometimes they seek redress through the courts. Prostitutes usually despise their clients. Children who are sexually abused by older children or adults are rarely able to carry out an act of revenge which in itself does not bring further punishment. If they lack the confidence to despise their abuser they can either tell themselves that they deserved what was done to them, or they can lie to themselves and say that they have suffered no harm. Neither method results in a reconstruction of meaning that secures their sense of being validated as a person. Their anger continues to assert itself: the truth keeps breaking through to consciousness. Thus the event or some simulation of the event has to be gone over and over again and again in a doomed attempt at mastering the trauma. Pornography appears to offer a means of mastering the event, but it can never achieve this because it does not enable the person to face his own truth, namely, that he has suffered harm.

Probably there are more websites devoted to sibling incest

than Google revealed to me, but whatever the exact figure it is huge. This suggests that the number of people who have been the victim of sibling incest could be very large indeed. However, this is a very difficult subject for psychologists to research because any conjunction between the words 'child' and 'sex' always creates an immense furore amongst adults in which the child's voice is drowned out completely.

In his memoir *Almost a Childhood* Hans-Georg Behr lets the child speak. In what he says we can see that, provided it does not involve physical injury, what harms the child is not the sexual act itself but the adults' interpretation of the sexual act. The child, as Behr calls his protagonist, was living on his grandfather's estate in the early part of the war when a number of Russian and Polish prisoners were sent there to work. One May night the child peered out of his bedroom window and saw one of the kitchen maids with a bare behind and 'there was another figure there too, also with a bare behind, and the two of them were whispering close together. The girl was holding tight to the bean poles, and the other figure, which looked like the young Russian who was always digging in the nursery garden, came close to her behind, and then the whole thing reminded the child of what the bull had been doing with the cow on the farm the other day, which he hadn't really been allowed to watch. But what was going on down there lasted longer and was much more exciting, so exciting that the child had to put his hand on what he called his little bunny and play with it until it felt itchy. The child couldn't remember when he discovered this game, but it must have been back in Mother's house, because once she caught him at it, and then she behaved very strangely. The child remembered that perfectly: Mother was sitting at the sewing machine making something that looked like a sack out of stout white cotton, and then she said, 'You're not to play with your little willy or it will turn black one day, and then it will fall off.'[11] Thus he learnt that sex means destruction.

One day the child was in the garden engaged in what he saw as an act of mercy killing. He was smashing to smithereens those of his toy soldiers which were already broken. He then buried the remains in a grave while at the same time playing with his bunny. Then he saw two legs in coarse blue twill in front of him. It was the young Russian prisoner. The man was smiling 'but his smile made the child suspicious, because he had a hand inside his trousers and they were swelling as if he had a stick hidden in there. The child asked cautiously, "What's your name?" – "Ivan," said the Russian, crouching down in front of the child, but then his trousers flapped open and out jumped a bunny such as the child had never seen before, enormous, with a big purple knob on top, dark-skinned and with a lot of black hair at its root. The child could see that Ivan was smiling, but most of the time he was staring at the bunny, which was much more interesting than Ivan . . . "You like that, eh? Want to see it?" whispered Ivan after a while. "Yes," breathed the child.' So Ivan led him into the tool shed. There he showed the child what to do. Afterwards Ivan went away. 'As for the child, he sat down on the sacks and stayed there for a little longer, because it had been even more exciting than the way his own bunny had itched during the mercy killings.'[12]

The child thought of his encounters with Ivan as adventures, but when the kitchmaid became pregnant and Ivan was taken away and hanged, his association of sex with death became stronger. When his half-brother Stefan returned home from Napola, the school for the sons of the Nazi elite, the child, now a boy, discovered that sex could also be part of the power struggle. Stefan was 16 and 'had been shaving for three months, wore a smart Hitler Youth uniform and had a dagger of honour by his side because, he said, he had proved his worth at the Napola School. He was very condescending to the boy, who was still so small, and the most annoying thing was the way he called him Hasi. It had always infuriated the boy, because they called him that in his grandparents' village. His brother could still remember it, even if the child couldn't remember his brother, so he used the name only because the boy hated it.'[13] 'When it was bedtime the boy looked through Stefan's door, which was ajar, and saw him kneeling beside his bed. But he wasn't saying his prayers, he was playing with his bunny. It was much bigger than the boy's, and had black hair around it. Then you heard Mother coming and went quickly and quietly back to your room. After that you heard Mother being cross with Stefan. Good.'[14]

The war ended and the boy was sent to a Catholic boarding school run by monks. Life at home was boring but 'it was even more boring in the monastery, and not just because of the Fathers and their rules but because of the boys too. What interested them most was what the Fathers called "unchastity" or "unnatural practices", except when they were playing or scuffling, but even then they liked to grab at each other's trousers and say "Ow!" and giggle. . . .You often heard a lot of whispering in the dormitory too, or saw a boy steal into another boy's bed, but it was boring.'[15]

One evening 'you were in your pyjamas and were just putting your toilet things away in your cupboard, when Father Anselm came along and told the boy to come with him. . . . Then you were with him in his room . . . Father Anselm . . . wanted to talk to the boy, he said, and you had to sit on the sofa beside him. He asked questions and said a few things, laughing, and he began to tickle the boy. You were very ticklish and laughed too, and suddenly Father Anselm was tickling you in the pyjama trousers. He asked the boy if he liked that, but he couldn't reply, he was confused and afraid of stammering, and he also knew he had to obey the Fathers, but Father Anselm picked him up and carried him into the bedroom. He put him down there on an armchair which was very uncomfortable. Then the Father pushed the front flap of his habit aside, and his soutane was open underneath it. He took out his prick. "Put it in your mouth," he said, breathing heavily. You didn't want to, but you couldn't say no. He slapped the boy's face, and then slapped it again, and pushed his prick into his mouth. It was disgusting and hurt. . . . It went on for ages and the boy was still crying when the Father buttoned up his soutane again. . . . Father Anselm . . . told the boy not to cry. He had only wanted to find out if he had been doing anything wrong . . . and now he knew he hadn't and the boy wasn't as bad as he had thought. . . . The Father said . . . you were not to talk to anyone about it because it was a secret of the confessional, and he forgave the boy, who was to go now.'[16]

The next morning the boy went to see Father Coelestin before Mass. 'You said, "Father Anselm hurt me in the mouth." "What is he talking about?" Father Coelestin asked Father Anselm, who had come up and was looking sharply at the boy. "I've no idea what he's talking about," said Father Anselm. . . . Father

Coelestin looked angrily at the boy. "You are a slanderer! A stammerer and a slanderer!" And he said you were unworthy of the monastery, you were nothing but a little criminal, and you were to beg Father Anselm to forgive you on your knees, this minute, and as this was Saturday you would get detention after school for the weekend, and the next two weekends as well. . . . Father Anselm's face wore a smug smile, and he said he forgave the boy, and then he went into the chapel to robe himself for Mass. The other boys went into the chapel too and sat down, but you had to stand at the back by the harmonium yourself, because you were a sinner.'

The memoir ends when the boy turned 14 and ran away from school. When God failed to send a thunderbolt to punish Father Anselm who was reading Mass in a state of sin the boy decided that he was no longer afraid of going to hell because 'You knew there was no God.'[17] Other than this the reader is not told what effect these events had on the boy. However, we can wonder what happens to a boy who has been abused in this way and who continues to believe in a God who punishes sinners.

What this memoir shows is how a child's interest in sex is about curiosity, not passion. Children are curious about bodies, their own and other people's, and what other people do with their bodies. What harms a child is being used sexually by people who are more powerful than the child; being told that sex is wicked and means sin and death; and being lied to and betrayed.

If all child sexual abuse was committed by adults who are strangers to the child the people who are responsible for the welfare of children would have no reason to lie to children. But because nearly all child sexual abuse is committed by people known to the child, children are lied to in order to protect those responsible for the child, including the perpetrator himself or herself. The perpetrator can be the child's sibling.

When Vernon Wiehe investigated physical, sexual and emotional abuse amongst siblings he discovered that, of his subjects, 71 per cent of the survivors of physical abuse and 69 per cent of survivors of emotional abuse felt that their parents were aware of the abuse but only 18 per cent of survivors of sexual abuse felt that their parents were aware. The sexual abuse usually occurred when the parents were absent, and often the victims could not tell their parents about the abuse because of the perpetrator's threats if the survivor did so. From his extensive research of the effects that physical, sexual and emotional abuse has on its victims Vernon Wiehe concluded that the victims learn not to value themselves, they blame themselves for what has happened, they find it hard to form relationships with members of the opposite sex, they can never be at ease in a sexual relationship, and they can easily find themselves in the victim's role in other relationships. Living like this, the victims often become intensely frightened of being annihilated as a person and they resort to the desperate defences of depression, anorexia and agoraphobia.[18] Vernon Wiehe also found that where the victim's parents did in fact know about the abuse they often did nothing about it. They did not believe that it was happening and they blamed the victim.[19]

This and other research shows that the extent of sibling sexual abuse is not generally recognised. Children whose power struggles with their siblings go beyond a few physical tussles and some teases and taunts are unlikely to write in their memoirs about the abuse they themselves inflicted, while the victims of the abuse are equally unlikely to reveal their shame. Biographers who believe that a person's childhood has no effect on their adult life simply give a passing nod to their subject's 'happy childhood' and 'loving family'. The biographers of the artist brother and sister Augustus and Gwen John have sometimes wondered about the nature of the closeness of the two siblings, while Eric Gill's sexual relationships with many women, including his sisters and daughters, are now well known,[20] but all this is usually regarded as the peculiarities of artists. Other people would not do such things. However, biographers, like the rest of us, often can find little more than what they are looking for. If they do not know to look for or at least be aware of sibling incest and other forms of abuse they are unlikely to find it.

Even when some kind of abuse becomes too blatant to be ignored, biographers often minimise it by saying that children are not affected by it, or if as adults they complain about it, they are exaggerating. Rudyard Kipling wrote a short story, *Baa, Baa Black Sheep,* about a very young brother and sister whose parents, without explaining what was to happen to them, left the children with a couple living in an English seaside town and returned to India. The boy was then subjected to prolonged mental and physical abuse. Rudyard and his sister Trix spent the first years of their lives in India with their parents. When Rudyard was nearly six and Trix three their parents brought them back to England, took them to Southsea to visit a husband and wife, the Holloways, and without warning to the children left them there. The biographer Judith Flanders wrote:

> The standard account of this period says that Mrs Holloway terrorized Rudyard; her son viciously persecuted him; they made his home life unbearable, and his school life too. He was beaten, isolated, made to appear in school wearing a placard marked 'Liar'. Trix was petted but, young and powerless, was unable to help her brother. Some of this was undoubtedly the case, but just how brutal the Holloway regime was is difficult to assess.[21]

She noted that later in life Trix had said that Rudyard had exaggerated what had happened to him, although in another document Trix did seem to suggest that 'terror was part of her life as a child'.[22] Nevertheless, Judith Flanders apparently did not see that this terror very likely played a major part in the psychosis Trix suffered when she was 30 and from which she never recovered. Judith Flanders wrote: 'Child-rearing is one of those areas that has changed so radically in the last one hundred years that it is almost impossible to look back, with our values now, without feeling that much of what happened then verged on the criminal.'[23] She seems not to realise that if a child feels that he has been abused he has been, and that cruelty is cruelty whether fashionable or not.

The lack of acknowledgement or only partial acknowledgement of the suffering which can be inflicted on children has meant that biographers often fail to question the implications of the events they record. J. R. Ackerley's biographer Peter Parker (Chapter 2) spent little time describing the childhood of Joe Ackerley and his sister Nancy West and saw no reason to question what their childhood meant to them. Francis King, the editor of Joe's diaries, believed that Joe would have approved of the publication of his diaries after the death of Nancy. He wrote, 'So intense was this hunger for truth-telling that considerations of libel would not persuade him to make the kinds of alterations deemed expedient by lawyers.'[24] When we write frankly about our lives we write about what we deem to be important. Some events are indeed unimportant, but equally we can deem as unimportant events which are so painful, so frightening and guilt-ridden that we cannot bear to remember them, much less talk about them to others.

Joe wrote about how he had felt about his brother's 'abnormally long dark cock'[25] but he did not mention any sexual exploration he and Peter might have engaged in with their pretty little sister. Their mother lived in her own world of fantasy, their father was frequently away from home, nursemaids and other servants came and went and the children must have been little supervised. In such a situation Nancy would have had to seek affirmation of herself from her brothers. In adult life she was always pathetically eager to join in Joe's pursuits and very likely did as a child. In retirement Joe turned to drink and Nancy joined him there. Might not she as a little girl have allowed him to draw her into his sexual activities and, in her intense desire to please him, let him do what he wanted? His attention and physical contact would have comforted her, but he would have been acting out of curiosity and the need for physical relief, not loving passion and, when satisfied, he would have had no further use or interest in her until he next felt a pressing sexual urge. Nancy would not have been able to reject him for his cruelty because without her brothers she was alone. As an adolescent and young woman she had major rows with her mother. When Peter was killed in the war there was only Joe for her to cling to. It was to him she returned when her marriage failed.

In his diaries Joe was observant but not perceptive. It did not occur to him that Nancy had become agoraphobic. Francis King wrote, 'Nancy did not mind being with familiars in a familiar place; but she had a terror of being with strangers in a strange environment.'[26] As I read Joe's diaries I became aware that Joe, unknowingly, had drawn a picture of a woman whom nowadays psychiatrists would diagnose as having borderline personality disorder. One striking feature of the women who are given this diagnosis is that they are very likely to have suffered sexual abuse in childhood. But there is more to Joe and Nancy's story than this. Francis King wrote:

> Clearly, Nancy loved Joe; and, when I once said that to E. M. Forster, he gently corrected me, "Nancy is in love with Joe." No less clearly, Joe loved Nancy, and was, to some measure, in love with her; but since that love and being in love both frightened him, they were transformed, in the years when I first knew him, into what often seemed to be cruelty near to hatred.[27]

After I had written this I was concerned that there could be some facts of which I was ignorant and which would show that my speculations about Joe and Nancy were wrong. Through a mutual friend I was able to send what I had written to Francis King. In reply he said that psychiatrists and others 'often ascribe a man's homosexuality as caused, in part at least, by an excessive dependence on – and closeness to – his mother. I suspect that that kind of relationship with my widowed mother, a woman of remarkable courage and kindness, may have profoundly influenced my own sexual development. I think that an intense brother/sister relationship may have the same effect – as in the case of Joe and Nancy and of L. P. Hartley (a close friend of mine) and his sister (with whom he was strangely determined never to let me become a friend). When I once asked Hartley why he did not openly acknowledge his homosexuality, he replied that he could not embarrass his sister by doing so.'[28] So L. P. Hartley hid his homosexuality from his sister in order to protect her from unkind gossip, yet he wrote a huge novel, *Eustace and Hilda*, a trilogy, describing their relationship and how she had always dominated him.

Compared to this the Biblical story of Amnon and his sister Tamar is straightforward and simple. 'And it came to pass after this, that Absalom the son of David had a fair sister, whose name was Tamar; and Amnon the son of David loved her.' Amnon plotted with a friend to entice Tamar into his chamber. He pretended to be ill and asked David to instruct Tamar to look after him:

> And Amnon said unto Tamar, Bring meat into the chamber, that I may eat of thy hand. And Tamar took the cakes

which she had made and brought them into the chamber
to Amnon her brother.

And when she brought them unto him to eat, he took
hold of her, and said unto her, Come lie with me, my sister.

And she answered him, Nay, my brother, do not force me;
for no such thing ought to be done in Israel: do not thou
this folly.

And I, whither shall I cause my shame to go? And as
for thee, thou shalt be as one of the fools in Israel. Now
therefore, I pray thee, speak unto the king; for he will not
withhold me from thee.

Howbeit he would not hearken unto her voice: but, being
stronger than she, forced her, and lay with her.

Then Amnon hated her exceedingly; so that the hatred
wherewith he hated her was greater than the love
wherewith he had loved her. And Amnon said unto her,
Arise, be gone.

And she said unto him, There is no cause: this evil in
sending me away is greater than the other thou didst unto
me. But he would not hearken unto her.[29]

At one very unhappy point in my life my then boss, Bill, was
an ex-serviceman who had had a long and weary war. He was
kind but he had no time for sentimentality or half-truths. I
told him about my troubles and he said, 'Dorothy, a standing
cock has no conscience.' This was a piece of information that
later I often had occasion to pass on to women friends and clients. Some men have no conscience, irrespective of the state of
their penis, but most do have a conscience which can punish
them ferociously following the acts of their conscienceless cock.
Some men are brave and truthful enough to see themselves as
the author of their own actions, but many men are not. They
plead, 'She made me do it', and hate the woman rather than
hate themselves. Joe hated women because, he said, they did
not do what he wanted them to do. Behind this we get a glimpse
of the pretty little girl who cried and made a fuss, got him into
trouble, and made him hate himself.

When adults lie to children about sex and teach them to
associate sex with guilt, destruction and death, all they create
is pain, confusion and misery. What adults should teach

children about sex has been stated very simply by the philosopher Avishai Margarlit. 'Nobody has the right to impose himself or herself on another as a sexual partner, but everyone has the right not to be rejected by others as a human being.'[30]

### 'You're nothing but a pack of cards!'

In the courtroom scene at the end of *Alice's Adventures in Wonderland* the Queen ordered Alice to hold her tongue but Alice refused. Purple with rage, the Queen ordered, 'Off with her head!' but nobody moved. 'Who cares for you?' said Alice (she had grown to her full size by this time). 'You're nothing but a pack of cards!'[31]

*Alice's Adventures in Wonderland* is full of subversive messages but this is the most subversive message of all. Lewis Carroll knew that the children who would read his book lived in a rigid hierarchical society where they were subjected to a very strict discipline. They were expected to honour their parents without question and respect everyone in authority over them. But in the court Alice saw those in authority for what they are, nothing but a pack of cards, or, in real life, ordinary, fallible human beings pretending to be wise, omniscient and powerful.

To get his book past the censors, that is, the adults who might read it, Carroll immediately reasserted the power of the grownups. Alice woke, and her big sister kissed her and then ordered her to run home and have her tea. But Carroll's message was plain. If you see people as being powerful, they are; if you don't see them as being powerful, they aren't. Of course people who claim to be powerful can use the tools of their power – their laws, their henchmen, their weapons, their superior physical strength – against you. If you see the person as being within himself no more powerful than any other person, then it is only against the tools of his power that you have to struggle. But if you see the person as being intrinsically powerful, different from and superior to you, you have made yourself powerless.

Many people never learn Alice's lesson. They continue to regard those in authority as being intrinsically powerful, and thus they render themselves helpless and frustrated. The sibling they saw in childhood as being powerful continues to be so in adult life. Of course, there is one great benefit to maintaining this point of view. You are not to blame for your misery. God, the Church, the government, politicians, the rich, the council, strangers of all hues and beliefs, your father, your mother, your big brother, your bossy sister, they are all to blame.

Many people do learn Alice's lesson. The general scepticism directed at politicians is evidence of that. Moreover, as we move from childhood to adulthood the age differences between siblings become less significant, and younger siblings cease to be intimidated by their older ones. Events can change relationships. One woman told me, 'All my life my big sister treated me as her kid sister. She looked after me. Then her husband died suddenly. It was a terrible blow to her, and now I look after her.'

Some power struggles between siblings never die away completely. The scene might shift to business rivalry or competition to see who has the most successful children. One woman laughed as she told me that her brother still 'gives me the occasional Chinese burn'. Two brothers may have long given up their physical tussles but they have only exchanged them for verbal jousting. The august pages of the *Guardian Education* carried the following paragraph:

Andrew Thomson, the Learning and Skills Development Agency boss, may well be a big cheese – certainly a tall cheese – as he towers over its summer conference this week, but he can't persuade his brother, Channel 4 News chief correspondent Alex Thomson, of this. 'Whenever we meet for a drink I can never get past the first sentence explaining to him what I do,' Andrew complains. 'I get as far as saying my job contributes to the delivery of learning and he says, "That's bollocks! Midwives deliver. Milkmen deliver. But you don't deliver anything!" And we leave it at that.'[32]

When as children siblings struggle over who is the goodest and who has the power it seems to them that their struggle is a matter of life and death. Then one of them dies and nothing is ever the same again.

# Chapter 6

# THE DEATH OF A SIBLING

Michael Rosen told me, 'My brother's four years older than me – I'm fifty-seven, he's sixty-one. When I was about ten, I was going through old photos – we used to have a big box of old photos – and there was a picture of my mum with a baby on her knee, and I said to my dad – my mum was down the road – "Is that me or Brian?" He looked at me and said, "That isn't either of you. That's Alan, the boy who died." And that was the first time we'd heard about him; he'd never been mentioned. So there was this kind of awful moment. I can remember my brother and I looking at each other and looking at this picture and then we said, "Well, how did he die?" And he said, "It was a kind of mixture of whooping cough and pneumonia." I said, "When?" And he said, "It was between you. We had Brian and we had this baby when Brian was about two." So really he would be two years older than me, and two years younger than Brian. And I remember looking at this child – and do you know, we've never had a conversation with our mother about it. She never ever mentioned it. My dad, out of earshot, mentioned it two or three times, would sort of allude to it, would mention his name. Mum never ever mentioned it, and I assume he'd told her that he'd told us. But it was never ever mentioned.'

Michael's brother Brian does not remember Alan. 'He does remember a baby, but he's confused as to whether the baby is me or this other baby. He was less than two and maybe three and a half. It was confusing. The state of bereavement around the house must have been enormous. This is all during the war, and they were evacuated to Leicester and then Nottingham and then came back again. And then, lo and behold, I turned up when Brian was four, so he was dethroned a couple of times and then, at the same time, in the trauma of bereavement people do withdraw, no matter how hard they try not to, so there must have been a sense of all that. He must have experienced all that.'

Michael went on, 'Now, as you know, I lost Eddie, my son, in 1999 and it took till then, if you think how many years that is, and it's pathetic – over thirty years – for me to realise that my parents had brought me up in a state of bereavement. They were bereaved parents, so I was the one after the bereavement. I'd always thought that I was very lucky to be the younger son for a variety of reasons – you're the witness, the observer as the younger one, and you get all the benefits of the fact that they've been through some rough times with the first one, but I'd never seen myself as the sort of consequence, the outcome of a bereavement. And now I've got a little two year old. And it maybe didn't really occur to me until she was born, and then I suddenly realised I am bringing up a child in the state of mind of having lost one. We all have this idea that disasters happen to other people, and very often the disaster that devastates us is the one that teaches us that nobody's spared. Parents could think of other people's children dying and say to themselves, "Well, I look after my children very well, so mine will be safe," and then their child dies, and the parent discovers that if that child could die, then the next child could die. They see their young children as vulnerable.'

Michael's parents may have seen him as vulnerable but they must have known that to cosset him would not have been in his best interests. 'I look back and see that they never treated me as vulnerable. I was travelling on buses on my own aged about nine and ten. My dad was reminding me the other day that we were on holiday in East Germany in 1957 – so I was eleven, my brother was fifteen – and we were getting bored on one occasion in this teachers' delegation, and they shifted us off to two separate families. Me not speaking German, only eleven, people they'd never met, on two farms in Turingen Forest, and they just said goodbye to us. So, I suppose all I can say is they had an attitude to me and my brother that fought with their feelings of bereavement. They fought hard to give us lack of fear, a lack of feeling claustrophobic.'

The fact that a child does not know that he once had a brother or a sister does not mean that he is unaffected by the death of that sibling. How the parents have interpreted that death, whether it was caused by illness or accident, miscarriage or abortion, greatly affects the child. When the child does learn of the dead sibling he cannot treat it lightly. The fact that there was once someone like me but not me is something to puzzle over and take into account. From all the accounts I have been given about the death of a sibling it is clear that the death of a sibling is a very different experience from the death of a parent.

While it is well recognised that the death of a parent has a great impact, people often fail to see that a child can be equally but differently affected by the death of a sibling. Shelley Bovey recalled that she had been 20 years old when her 17-year-old brother died in a car accident:

> My brother and I had just become friends. Like many siblings, we had spent much of our lives locked in conflict over the sort of pettinesses that acquire their true perspective only with the dawning of adulthood. When he died, we were both aware that we stood on the threshold of a new relationship in which we would be partners, not opponents.
>
> There was no chance to grieve. Almost immediately I was surrounded by my parents' friends telling me that my parents had experienced the most terrible loss. Part of me wanted to cry out that I, too, had suffered a devastating loss, but I was only twenty and the prospect of my parents falling apart was terrifying. Besides, these older, surely wiser, people seemed not to acknowledge that I might be affected.
>
> I did what was required of me. I was strong for my parents, and buried my own grief in some remote, inaccessible place. I emerged strangely unscathed. Or so I thought.
>
> A sudden devastating, disabling panic attack on the Underground one day ended with me being hospitalized, then reassured. I'd lost a brother recently, they said, so this was reaction, nothing to worry about. The panic attacks continued, but it was 'only stress'. The notion of suppressed grief was not proposed. No one suggested bereavement

counselling. The loss of a brother, it appeared, did not
occupy a noteworthy place in the hierarchy of tragedy.[1]

In Victorian England genteel society had made it very clear
that the death of a sibling did not occupy a noteworthy place in
the hierarchy of tragedy. Much was made of outward displays
of grief and self-imposed social exile, and these should last for
a specified period of mourning. A wife should mourn her husband for at least two to three years but a husband need mourn
a wife for only three months. A parent should mourn a child
and a child a parent for a year, but siblings need mourn one of
their number for merely six weeks.[2]

To the Victorians Shelley's reaction to her brother's death
would have been a social faux pas. However, the words 'a panic
attack' is psychiatric jargon for experiencing the terror of being annihilated as a person. Not being able to grieve for her
brother meant that Shelley had not been able to go through
the lengthy process of accepting that her brother had died and
constructing a meaning for this which her meaning structure
could accommodate. The death of someone can bring home to
us the fact that we too shall die, and this thought alone can
provoke the fear of annihilation, even in a person who believes
in an afterlife. We go into the valley of death on our own, and
we have no control over the process that takes us there, that
is, death presents us with the situations which extraverts
and introverts fear the most. I do not know whether Shelley
believed in the Just World, but if she did her brother's death
would mean that either she and her brother had deserved this
disaster or that the Just World belief was wrong and the adults
who had taught her that belief had been mistaken or had lied
to her. Such a discovery would be a major threat to the core of
her meaning structure, and so she would feel that she was falling apart, shattering, even disappearing.

The grieving process is hard work and people, including
children, need support and understanding while they are going through it. After interviewing 159 older adolescents and
adults who had lost a sibling in childhood or adolescence, the
psychologist H. Rosen concluded that 'significant prohibitions
exist against adequate mourning and working through the
loss',[3] and these can occur at the level of the child himself, in

the family, or in society. Some of those questioned had denied themselves the time and space to grieve, perhaps feeling that they were not allowed to do so. As Shelley Bovey wrote:

> Throughout the next twenty or so years, my brother was rarely mentioned. My parents had banished all reminders of him: photographs were put away, his possessions had been disposed of, his name was not spoken. I did not know how to answer the standard question: 'Have you any brothers or sisters?' Sometimes, perhaps to avoid the pain I had not touched, I said I was an only child; sometimes I told the truth. 'How dreadful,' came the sympathetic response. 'How terrible for your parents.[4]

As a young adult Shelley was deeply affected by her parents' reluctance to talk about her brother. At least she was old enough to understand the nature of her brother's death in a way that a six-year-old child could not possibly do. The Bush family with its two Presidents is famous for their disdain for any acknowledgement of personal feelings. Thus many events in the life of George W. Bush are known but not what the participants in these events made of them. George W. was born in 1946 while his father was still immersed in his student life at Yale. On graduating his father immediately became involved in the oil boom in West Texas and was rarely at home, leaving the care of the children to his wife Barbara. In his book *Bush on the Couch* the psychiatrist Justin Frank wrote, 'Referred to by her children as "The Enforcer", Barbara Bush has by her own admission always been the family disciplinarian. She was, from most accounts, a cold disciplinarian, and she spanked the children readily.'[5]

A daughter, Robin, was born in 1949 and a second son, Jeb, in 1953. George W. was six when, 'in the spring of 1953, young Robin was diagnosed with leukaemia, which set in motion a series of extended East Coast trips by parents and child in the ultimately fruitless pursuit of treatment. Critically, however, young George W. was never informed of the reason for the sudden absences; unaware that his sister was ill, he was simply told not to play with the girl, to whom he had grown quite close, on her occasional visits home. Robin died in New York in October 1953; her parents spent the next day golfing in Rye, attending a small memorial service the following day before flying back to Texas, where the family remained while the child's body was buried in a Connecticut family plot. There was no funeral.'[6]

If as a child we insist to ourselves that our parents are good and would not harm us in any way at all, despite all the evidence we are presented with to the contrary, as adults we are likely to repeat our parents' actions in some form. This is an attempt to continue to hold in place the lie that we told ourselves about our parents' goodness. This may be one of the reasons why George W. did not require the American forces to count how many Iraqis died in the Iraq War. He also ordered that the bodies of American soldiers killed in the war should be returned to their homes without fanfare, photographs and media attention. He explained that he wished to respect the privacy of the family of each soldier, but in doing so he denied each man and woman the recognition and significance which their sacrifice demanded. Everyone is someone's child, including Iraqis, every child has a parent, and most children have siblings. By his actions George W. is saying that a child's death is unimportant and that parents and siblings do not grieve.

George W. is not the only person who tries to deny his own grief and the grief of others, particularly the grief which children feel. Many of the people in Rosen's study reported how adults had urged them to 'be strong', that is, not to show any grief. In a study by Clare Jenkins and Judy Merry, Corrin Abbott told how she had been four when her older sister Lisa died. Their parents had separated when Corrin was 18 months old:

> I feel the family put a lot of responsibility on to me, especially my mum's family. 'You must look after your mum. You must watch out for her. You be good.' If a four-year-old hears five times in one day, 'You must look after your mum', it's a big thing. It's worrying and frightening. I'm now a single parent and, if I'm not so well, friends will pop round to help and I notice they'll say to my son, 'Now look after your mum, won't you.'[7]

Adults prefer to believe that children's feelings are shallow and brief, and that they readily forget. Recognising the reality of a child's grief leaves the adult feeling helpless, unable to give to a child any explanation that would make the child feel secure. No one knows what death is. All we can know is that a living being grows strangely still. We create many fantasies of what death means but all of these can be but variations on two basic meanings. Death is either the end of my identity or a doorway to another life. Neither of these meanings gives us complete comfort and security. Losing our sense of being a person is our greatest fear and, whatever kind of afterlife we imagine, it will have some distinct drawbacks if we take with us the desires, needs, interests, opinions and attitudes that make us who we are. Yet, if these all disappear, who will we be?

Being assured that a loved one has gone to heaven merely puzzles small children. Karen Rea's sister Elaine died when she was ten and Karen six. Karen said:

> That evening the vicar came round and he told me that
> Elaine had gone to heaven to live with Jesus. Because
> I was only six I didn't really understand what he meant.
> Our family went to church and it seemed an OK thing at
> the time to be told that my sister had gone to live with
> this person that I vaguely knew and I thought he was
> a good person so she would be OK. But what I couldn't
> understand was that every time I went into our house,
> all these people were there when I just wanted mum
> and dad to myself. I found that very frustrating.[8]

When I was a child the most popular book for children in Australia was Ethel Turner's *Seven Little Australians*[9] which was first published in 1894. It concerns seven siblings living with their father, called The Captain, and their stepmother Esther. I read the book when I was about eight and developed a strong dislike for The Captain who, in my eyes, treated his children most brutally. Ethel Turner seems to have regarded his behaviour as quite ordinary. The liveliest, brightest and most interesting of the children was Judy, but she often incurred her father's wrath because she insisted on being herself. Her father punished her severely. The book ends with a tragedy. The children were enjoying a picnic in a paddock where there were several old trees which had been ring-barked to kill them. Such trees might stand for years and then without warning crash to the ground. Judy was entertaining Esther's baby whom they called The General. He had toddled a little distance away from her when a gust of wind brought down one of the ring-barked trees. Judy flung herself across the baby. The baby survived but Judy was killed. When my sister saw that I had finished reading the book and was upset she said, 'It's not really sad. Judy had tuberculosis. She would have died anyway.' I puzzled over this explanation for a long time. It seemed to me that the fact that Judy had an ultimately fatal illness did not make any difference. My sister's attitude that as Judy was going to die anyway she may as well get it over with did not appeal to me because, on those grounds, all of us may as well be dead. I could not have put that argument into words but I knew her argument was wrong. For me Judy's death was a tragedy, and the fact that she had died in an accident rather than from an illness made no difference. I failed completely to see that Ethel Turner had meant that Judy's sacrificial death redeemed her, a disobedient child, in the way that a sacrifice is seen to restore the balance of the Just World.

Judy's death became one of the ingredients of my fantasises in which 'You'll be sorry when I'm dead/gone/famous' was a well-worked theme. I do not remember re-enacting Judy's death in the way my friends and I re-enacted our favourite radio serials and the traumas of school, perhaps because death to us then was something that occurred only to fictional characters and the old (this changed after September 1939) but in Victorian times the death of children was common and children were not sheltered from it. In her biography of Ivy Compton-Burnett, Hilary Spurling told how, when Ivy's father died, her mother put the whole family into black, even the baby in her pram.[10] Judith Flanders, in her book *A Circle of Sisters*, a study of four sisters in the Macdonald family, wrote:

Louise was particularly delicate and nervous. Once, when feverish, she was found warming her hands in front of a door, thinking it a fire, saying, 'I am going to a little child's funeral.' Louise was not unusual; children's funerals loomed large, and it was not at all uncommon for small children to play 'Funerals' instead of 'Mummies and Daddies'.[11]

Re-enacting a death can help a child not only deal with the loss but also with guilt, often a bigger problem in the death of a sibling than the death of a parent. Victor Cicirelli reported:

> In Rosen's study about half of Rosen's respondents reported experiencing guilt at the sibling's death, ranging from guilt at being alive when the sibling had died to having negative feelings toward the sibling or wishing the sibling dead at some time in their relationship, and so on. They reported grief reactions of feeling sad, lonely, frightened, or angry following the loss, but 76% did not share their feelings with anyone. About a third reported feeling a responsibility to comfort their parents, and a third felt a responsibility to make up to their parents for the loss.[12]

Ivy Compton-Burnett's father had six children by his first wife Agnes and on her death married Katherine Stace who went on to bear him seven children. Ivy was the eldest. In families where the parents lack the time, interest or aptitude to parent the children, the children have to band together in different ways to parent themselves. Closest to Ivy in age was her brother Guy. Their sister Juliet once commented, 'Guy and Ivy were everything to each other when they were young.'[13] When their father died their mother 'was inconsolable and her despair took the form of open lamentation. . . . She gave way to terrifying storms of crying which lasted sometimes all night and, though the younger ones would lie awake in bed and hear her, the older ones lived in her presence under what became an almost intolerable strain.'[14] For the next four years Guy, not quite 16 when his father died, took on responsibility not only for his mother's exorbitant emotional needs but also for the comfort and security of his small sisters.[15] Four years later Guy died of pneumonia. Guy had been his mother's favourite but 'it was Noel, still young for his age at seventeen, who grew up to take the place of his father and Guy. . . . Noel became his mother's "darling boy", though he could not respond to her as heroically as Guy had done. . . . Noel from this time became Ivy's inseparable companion. Both bore their grief with resolute courage in silence; and both must have suffered from their mother's emotional collapse.'[16]

'Noel had been a poor student but at Cambridge he took a double first. He explained, "I cannot forget the bitter disappointment caused to my mother by the death of my elder brother. Any small worldly success which I might gain would be to her perhaps the only recompense that would be still possible".'[17] His recompense did not last long. Shortly after the outbreak of the First World War Noel joined the army. He was killed on 14 July 1916 at Bazentin-Petit. 'Some six hundred yards of ground were gained on 14 July at the cost of nine thousand British casualties – "as brilliant a success as British arms have ever gained," according to that day's despatch in *The Times*.'[18] '"Them both dying like that," Ivy said many times, "quite smashed my life up." The violence of phrase was most uncharacteristic, but she never varied it.'[19]

Of course not all people mourn the death of their sibling. Tsitsi Dangarembga began her novel *Nervous Conditions* about the young Shona girl Tambu: 'I was not sorry when my brother died. Nor am I apologising for my callousness, as you may define it, my lack of feeling. For it is not that at all. I feel many things these days, much more than I was able to feel in the days when my brother died, and there are reasons for this more than the mere consequence of age.'[20]

In Shona society women were regarded by the men as being no more than a man's chattel. Tambu's brother Nhamo was lazy, would not help with the hard labour needed on their farm, and expected her and her young sister Netsai to wait on him and always obey his orders. Tambu, almost as big as Nhamo, could sometimes refuse to do this but if she did 'Netsai compensated for whatever I got away with. Nhamo enjoyed taking a stick to her at the slightest excuse.'[21] Tambu grew a crop of maize to make some money so she could go to school but once the cobs were ripe for eating Nhamo began stealing them to prevent her from going to school. When Nhamo died suddenly from an illness and Tambu took his place at the school she did not pretend to herself that she grieved for her brother.

Another time, another culture, and the Macdonald sisters did not mourn the death of their brother Harry. He was the eldest, their parents' favourite. Harry 'had learned that he was cock of the walk and could cajole his mother into almost anything. Harry always got the best of what was going.'[22] He was a bully and a prig. He won a scholarship to Oxford but failed to sit his finals. He dithered about taking a job, and then suddenly announced that he was leaving for New York. The sisters' biographer Judith Flanders wrote:

> The family needed to explain this incident to others, and to themselves, and they approached it in various ways over the years. The eldest and youngest sisters took similar routes: they ignored their brother's existence as much as possible. Edie published a family memoir in 1923 in which she managed to include one solitary sentence about Harry, blandly saying that he moved to America when she was young and she saw him only once thereafter. Alice too blocked him out of her mind. When her son [Rudyard Kipling] was preparing to go to America for the first time she 'recalled' that she had a brother in New York.[23]

After Harry left, his mother Hannah wrote to him regularly, his sisters practically never. At Christmas 1858, only six weeks after he sailed, Hannah wrote that 'Poor Harry's absence was sorely felt by some of us.' Clearly not his sisters.[24] When Hannah died it took the sisters 16 days to write to Harry to tell him of her death. When only 55 Harry became desperately ill and wrote to his younger brother Fred to say that he wished to die among his family but his doctor had told him he was too ill to travel. Fred decided to go to New York to see Harry. Alice decided that 'the sea voyage would be good for Rudyard in his present state of health, and so he and Fred set off at once for New York' but Harry died two days before they landed.[25]

The opposite of love is not hatred but indifference. In a family I have known for many years the eldest boy of six siblings was always greatly disliked by the others. They gradually ceased to have anything to do with him because he was impossibly difficult. When he was old and dying, two of his sisters, unable to bear the thought of him dying alone, looked after him but the youngest brother, who lived not far away, said he was unable to visit his dying brother because 'he had to mind the dog'.

### A lifelong grief

Children live their lives at a tangent from their parents. Children want to know that their parents are available when needed but they have a child's perspective on the world which only other children can share. Fortunate is the child who can live all his childhood like this and then come slowly into the adult world in stages with which he can cope. But sometimes the adults' world does more than impinge on the child's world. It can overwhelm it. In the television programme *My Life as a Child*[26] three children were given cameras to record their day-to-day lives. One of them, Mary, was nine years old:

Her dad lives in Portugal with his new girlfriend, while Mary lives at home with her mum. 'The thing I don't like is that my mum has depression,' says Mary. 'She cries and it makes me feel upset, cos when my mum's upset I'm upset, when she's angry I'm angry, when she's happy I'm happy.' Mary's mum doesn't seem to be happy very often. One of the problems, Mary realises, is that her mum hasn't come to terms with the fact that her dad doesn't love her any more, and they'll never get back together again. She's going to have to learn that. Of the two of them – Mary and her mum – it's the daughter who is the most mature and holds things together. 'My mum's is so a big kid. She's a child trapped in an adult's body. I'm an adult trapped in a child's body. It's really annoying because I really still want to be the kid.'[27]

When children are dragged into situations involving adult dramas and crises they can thereafter show little inclination to grow up. This may be because they now see adult life as one of pain and heavy responsibility which they have not the strength to bear, or it may be that there is something in childhood which they are not prepared to give up. J. M. Barrie, the creator of Peter Pan, had the task of trying to preserve his brother David, a boy who would never grow up. Barrie had first tried to be his brother, and then, when he himself became a man, he turned David into the boy who passionately declared, 'I don't want to go to school and learn solemn things. No one's going to catch me, lady, and make me a man. I want always to be a little boy and to have fun.'[28]

In 1896 Barrie wrote a biography of his mother Margaret Ogilvy of whom he said: 'She had a son who was far away at school. I remember very little about him, only that he was a merry-faced little boy who ran like a squirrel up a tree and shook cherries into my lap. When he was thirteen and I half his age the terrible news came.'[29] David had been killed in a skating accident in January 1867. After that Margaret Ogilvy 'was always delicate from that hour and for many months she was very ill . . . . the first thing she expressed a wish to see was the christening robe, and she looked at it long and hard and then turned her face to the wall.' Barrie continues:

> My mother lay in bed with the christening robe beside
> her, and I peeped in many times at the door and then went
> to stair and sobbed. I know not if it was that first day, or
> many days afterwards, that there came to me my sister
> . . . who was then passing out of her teens, with a very
> anxious face and wringing her hands, and she told to go
> ben to my mother and say to her that she still had another
> boy. I went ben excitedly, but the room was dark and when
> I heard the door shut and no sound came from the bed
> I was afraid and stood still. I suppose I was breathing
> hard, or perhaps I was crying, for after a time I heard a
> listless voice that had never been listless before say, 'Is that
> you?' I think the tone hurt me, for I made no answer, and
> then the voice said more anxiously, 'Is that you?' again.
> I thought it was the dead boy she was speaking to, and I
> said in a little lonely voice, 'No, it's no him, it's just me.'
> Then I heard a cry, and my mother turned in her bed, and
> though it was dark I knew she was holding out her arms.

After that Barrie 'sat a great deal in her bed trying to make her forget him'.He also tried to make his mother laugh:

> I suppose I was an odd little figure; I have been told that
> my anxiety to brighten her gave my face a strained look and
> put a tremor into the joke (I would stand on my head in the
> bed, my feet against the wall, and then cry excitedly, 'Are
> you laughing, mother?') – and perhaps what made her laugh
> was something I was unconscious of, but she did laugh now
> and then, whereupon I screamed excitedly to that dear
> sister, who was ever in waiting, to come and see the sight,
> but by the time she came the soft face was wet again.

Barrie kept a record of every time she laughed and would

proudly show this to the doctor each morning. Then his sister told him:

> not to sulk when my mother lay thinking of him, but to
> try instead to get her to talk about him. I did not see how
> this could make her the merry mother she used to be, but
> I was told that if I could not do this nobody could, and this
> made me eager to begin. At first, as they say, I was jealous,
> stopping her fond memories with the cry, 'Do you mind
> nothing of me?' but that did not last; its place was taken
> by an intense desire (again, I think my sister must have
> breathed it into life) to become so like him that even my
> mother could not see the difference, and many and artful
> were the questions I put to that end. Then I practised in
> secret, but after a whole week had passed I was still rather
> like myself. He had such a cheery way of whistling, she
> told me, it had always brightened her at her work to hear
> him whistling, and when he whistled he stood with his legs
> apart, and his hands in the pockets of his knickerbockers.
> I decided to trust to this, so one day after I had learned
> his whistle (every boy of enterprise invents his own) from
> boys who had been his comrades, I secretly put on a suit of
> his clothes, dark grey they were, with little spots, and they
> fitted me for many years afterwards, and thus disguised
> I slipped, unknown to others, into my mother's room.
> Quaking, I doubt not, yet so pleased, I stood still until
> she saw me, and then – how much it must have hurt her!
> 'Listen!' I cried in a glow of triumph, and I stretched my
> legs wide apart and plunged my hands into the pockets of
> my knickerbockers, and began to whistle.[30]

The death of a sibling creates for the surviving child a whole complex of conflicting emotions. There is the loss of a loved companion, or protector, or simply a solid figure in the child's world. There is the confusion which arises from the way the adults fail to explain exactly what has happened. There is the guilt that comes with remembering things done that should not have been done and things that should have been done but were not. There is the loneliness of being closed out of other people's mourning, particularly that of the mother. There is the exultation at having won the competition to be good, rapidly followed by the guilt at having thought such a wicked thing. There is the realisation that the competition goes on still with the dead child who is being idolised by the parents, while the living child continues to err and fail to please. In the competition with a sainted dead sibling the living sibling is bound to lose. There are the efforts to make up to the parents what has been lost, and the weariness and bitterness of the failure of such efforts. There are the efforts, often lifelong, to preserve the dead sibling in some way, and the efforts to save others in the way the living sibling should have saved the dead sibling. For many children in this situation the only solution is to become especially good. Karen Rea said:

> The main thing that I've now realised is that I felt I couldn't upset my mum and dad, because every time I looked at them they were crying. I got it into my head – being six – that I couldn't do anything now to upset them. They'd been through enough. So I turned into what you probably would call a bit of a 'goody two shoes'. Everything they asked me to do, I did, even if I didn't want to. And I did it with a smile.
>
> I used to be a little rebel, but Elaine wasn't and when she died I felt I had to be good all the time and live my life the way Elaine would have lived it. From the age of six until now, I've done everything – absolutely everything – with this one thought in my mind: 'I mustn't do anything wrong and I mustn't be a rebel.'
>
> Also, every time my parents asked me how I was, I told them I was fine although I wasn't. I was really missing Elaine, but I thought, 'I don't want to burden them with that.' They're burdened enough, so if I keep telling them I'm fine, then that's something less for them to worry about.' Little did I know that they were upset because I wasn't talking about it. I bottled it up for so long. Consequently I've gone through the whole of my life until recently covering up, telling everybody I'm fine about all sorts of things, when I'm not.[31]

Karen's sister Elaine was four years older than she was. Helen's sister Miranda was six years younger than Helen. Miranda was just three when she died unexpectedly after a brief illness. Nineteen years later Helen asked if she could talk to me. All that she told me and more she had already talked over with counsellors when she had been at university but Miranda's death was still very much part of her life. Helen said, 'I did realise this summer that next year it will be twenty years. It really shocked me that it's such a long time, but there isn't really that comfort. Yes, time does heal and I don't feel the same now as I did ten years ago, or even fifteen years ago, but there are times when the way I feel is the same as I did then. My emotions are slightly more muted now, not as raw – but it's the same feeling. I still don't have any answers. It shocks me that twenty years later I still feel the same. Not every day, but occasionally I still feel the same.'

Helen had two brothers, James two years older than she was, and Daniel, three years younger. She said, 'I was always terrified of breaking rules, at home and at school, and I really tried very hard to be good all the time.' I asked her why it was so important to her to be good. She replied, 'I'm not really sure. It was very important for me to do well at school, and I worked really, really hard to do well and be the best. I worked very hard for my exams in a way my brothers couldn't comprehend – neither of them worked very hard at all! I think that was partly in a bid to kind of be noticed more. I was always very quiet as a child. And I think also partly – I don't really remember but I can look back and think – after Miranda died my mum and dad were quite caught up in their own grief and their own relationship and they probably didn't have as much time for the three of us as they did before. That was probably when I really started. It was that kind of age as well – I was nine, and it was when things at school started to get more serious, whereas before it had just been fun. It meant a lot to me to do well, and be good. If I got into trouble at school I felt really terrified of the teachers and what they would do to me. I'd feel very guilty, as well, if I'd done something wrong.'

I asked, 'Did you think that by being good and doing well you were in some small way offering some kind of recompense to your parents?'

'I'm not sure. I think it was more that I would make myself a better person and then I would be more worthy of being loved.

So, indirectly, it was a justification for still being alive, being around. Earning the right to be loved.'

'Do you still believe that you can't just exist, you have to earn the right to exist?'

'I think less so, but I still have that feeling. I had a strong sense throughout my childhood of not really being good enough. I have very high standards, and I think both my parents have very high standards as well, and I never measure up to my own standards. So I think that, combined with losing my sister, was a pretty terrible combination really. Because I was always feeling I had to be as good as her, and comparing myself to her, and it took me a long time to realise that I was very jealous of her. I would always be thinking that my brothers had got on much better with her than they did with me. It took me a long time to realise that it was ridiculous to be jealous of a two year old because she was at the peak of being a lovely, lovely child and she was very bubbly and outgoing and people really responded to her, and had a real connection to her. I'd be very hard on myself if I was being shy and wasn't able to make friends the way I wanted to do.'

Miranda had developed croup and was not responding to the care she was getting at home. In the hospital she got worse and an attempt to help her breathing stopped her heart. She became brain dead and her parents made the decision for the machine that was supporting her to be turned off. I asked Helen how she had explained this disaster to herself.

She said, 'I wrestled with it for a long time, and still struggle with now. Not so much now but I remember as a child just kind of believing in God in the way we just did. We had Assembly at school, and we went to church with the Brownies, and we never really questioned what happened. When she was ill, I remember praying that she would be all right, and she wasn't, and so that immediately made me stop believing in God, because that just didn't connect in my mind at all. If I'd asked something as important as that, it should have happened, and what kind of God would let a little girl die? So I immediately stopped believing and thought that all this stuff I had been told was rubbish. I still have that attitude really; that hasn't really changed at all. That was my way of dealing with it – there isn't an answer to the why, it's completely unfair, and completely random. And I just have to come to terms with these things happening.'

I asked her how James explained their sister's death. She said, 'I don't know really. We don't discuss it that much. With both my brothers, they can't really talk about it without getting very upset, and crying. It was something we didn't really talk about, because it was too painful, and I wouldn't want to bring it up and upset anyone, and one of us would invariably get very upset. They're really still like that now. I can talk about it with my mum, in quite a detached way, without getting upset. We can talk about things like something funny she did once, or just an anecdote about when we were children, and there was a long time when we couldn't do that, but I don't think either of my brothers would be able to do that. I know that my older brother's attitude to it has affected him in the opposite way to the way it affected me – because it made me feel very insecure, that at any moment everything can go wrong. You think everything's fine and then something like that can happen and the world is turned upside down. I was always waiting for the next bad thing to happen. Whereas for James, he said the worst thing that could happen has already happened, so for the rest of his life he's an optimist – nothing that bad can ever happen again, so why worry? So in some ways our personalities have been opposite – he's been very outgoing and an optimist, and I've been pessimistic.'

Helen had not forgotten the circumstances of Miranda's death. She said, 'There's obviously something going on at the back of my mind and comes to the forefront when I'm ill, or someone I know is ill, and I suddenly get very, very scared that they're going to die, even if it's something quite minor. I have a small panic – but it wouldn't always be in my mind. It's not a logical connection to make at all that if you get a chest infection you're going to die. But it's there, and it's quite raw, that feeling. It always surprises me when it comes up, because I'm not expecting it at all. When I was in Cambodia, I had to go into hospital and they put an IV tube in then, and this horrible raw emotion came up from nowhere. So that connection's definitely there for me still.'

Barrie immortalised his brother David in Peter Pan but he also created many female characters that were based on his mother. Remembering a dead sibling and the circumstances of that sibling's death is a way of somehow keeping the person alive. If no one remembers us we have well and truly disappeared. Writers often try to immortalise their loved ones in the characters they create. However, the dead stay fixed at the point where they died. Jonathan Franzen ended his memoir of his father with the words: 'There would be no new memories of him. The only stories we could tell now were the ones we already had.'[32]

Virginia Woolf tried to overcome this limitation and to learn more about her dear dead brother Thoby by turning him into a fictional character. Her biographer Hermione Lee wrote: 'The brother she lost was the brother she was always trying to get to know better. Thoby haunted her: she perpetually remembered and re-imagined him. She wrote three versions of him over twenty years, as Jacob in *Jacob's Room*, as Percival in *The Waves*, and as himself in her *Sketch of the Past*.' In *Sketch* she 'describes him as having an obscure and depressive side, and a reserve which she cannot penetrate'. 'Virginia recalled how they never kissed Thoby, as much as they loved him, rarely touched him, and never talked about personal matters.' They would talk about literature but 'with his sisters, sex and death were taboo subjects. He never talked to them about how he felt about women, and he never mentioned the family's losses'. 'Both Jacob and Percival are, ultimately, absent, obscure and silent, fictionally embodying not just Thoby's absence in death, but his aloofness in life.'[33]

When we suffer greatly as a child often we later find ourselves drawn to protect those people or animals who seem to be suffering in the way that we suffered. We can feel that we have special knowledge of such suffering and as a result we can empathise accurately with those who suffer. Thus people who in childhood felt trapped and helpless in the hands of powerful people who intended them harm may be drawn into the animal liberation movement, while people who felt that as a foetus or infant they could have been destroyed by parents who did not want them may be drawn into the anti-abortion movement. Such people may not be consciously aware that this is what drew them into this particular charitable work rather than another. The extreme acts of self-sacrifice or persecution and

destruction carried out by some members of the animal liberation movement and the murders and destruction carried out by
some members of the anti-abortion movement reveal a fierce,
angry and vengeful desire to protect and save the innocent and
punish those who would harm them which goes far beyond a
strong and realistic concern for the weak and the vulnerable.
The weak and vulnerable whom the person is trying to save
and avenge may be himself as a child or it may be a sibling or
an animal which had been the perfect sibling, a true and loving friend.

A person may not see it as necessary to join a movement in
order to save a sibling who has died. Such can be the strength
of the attachment between two siblings that, in trying to save
a sibling, the person is also trying to save himself, both physically and as a person. As children we want to hold on to our
initial vision of the world as a wonderful place, full of delights,
and of other people as universally kind, loving and protective
of us. Then events can conspire to take that vision from us.
These events can seem to involve horrible, frightening things,
people can be cruel and neglectful, and the sense of evil darkness, the darkness which invades us when we blame ourselves
for what has happened and thus learn to see ourselves as being
irredeemably flawed, spills out over our surroundings until
they, we and everything seem to be sinister, wretched, loathsome, odious, despicable and malignant. We could be swallowed
up and annihilated by this vileness, or else have to live out our
days in a morass that offers no hope, no delight.

To save ourselves we have to save a small fragment of all
that was a beautiful delight, something to inspire us and give
us hope, and what could be better than a person who is pure,
innocent and perfect. Only such a person can save us from despair and annihilation. Thus we might come to idolise a god, a
saint, or some famous figure. If our first clear vision of the all-
encompassing evil of the world comes with the death of someone
we loved then that person can become the innocent perfection
that must be preserved, provided, of course, that the person's
imperfections can be forgotten, or that the person can be seen
as being too young to have been tarnished by the world.

With or without this kind of transcendent experience a sibling's death illuminates our own physical fragility and the thin

membrane that separates us from death. When his brother
Allie died Holden Caulfield saw that he too could die: Hans
Schnier knew that, if the need arose, his mother would sacri-
fice him just as she had sacrificed his sister Henrietta.

*The Catcher in the Rye* and *The Clown* are about that aching void of love, longing and pity which presses itself against
the heart and stretches out to the weak, vulnerable beloved, a
void which cannot be filled by anything other than the presence of the beloved held tightly against the heart. Why do parents hug their children and lovers embrace? When the beloved
is no longer there to be held close, the aching void becomes a
constant companion who ceaselessly draws attention to the
beloved's live doppelgangers, all weak and vulnerable people
needing to be saved and avenged. Parents whose beloved child
has died know this aching void only too well, and some try to
deal with it in practical ways, perhaps by establishing a char-
ity or endowing a hospital which will help children in the way
that their beloved child had not been helped. Siblings may not
be able to redress the balance of justice in this way. For Hold-
en and Hans the hurt went too deep, the injustice burned too
fiercely. The death of their sibling tore them and their world
into fragments, and only by saving everyone like their beloved
sibling and administering justice to those who brought about
this death can they and their world be whole again. They were
unable to lay down the burden of this impossible task.

In the last months of the Second World War young German
teenagers dutifully went to defend their Fatherland against the
advancing Allied armies. Hans did not know, when he waved
goodbye to Henrietta as she sat in a streetcar, that this was
the last time he would see her. He thought she was going on
some outing:

> I waved once more in the direction of the streetcar which
> bore Henrietta away, and walked through the grounds to
> our house where my parents were already having dinner
> with Leo. We had thin soup, potatoes and gravy for our
> main course, and an apple for dessert. Not until I got to my
> dessert did I ask my mother where Henrietta's school outing
> was going to. She gave a little laugh and said, 'Outing?
> Nonsense. She has gone to Bonn to volunteer for the Flak.

Don't peel your apple so thick. Look, son, watch me,' and she actually took the peel from my plate, snipped away at it, and put the results of her frugality, paper-thin slices of apple, into her mouth. I looked at Father. He was staring at his plate and said nothing. Leo was silent too, but when I turned to my mother again she said in her soft voice, 'You do see, don't you, that everyone must do his bit to drive the Jewish Yankees from our sacred German soil.' She looked across at me, I had a strange feeling, then she looked at Leo in the same way, and it seemed to me she was on the verge of sending us both off to the front to fight the Jewish Yankees. 'Our sacred German soil,' she said, 'and they have already advanced far into the Eifel mountains.' I felt like laughing, but I burst into tears, threw down my fruit knife and ran upstairs to my room. I was afraid, I knew why too, but I couldn't have put it into words, and it enraged me to think of that damned apple peel. I looked down at the German soil in our garden covered with dirty snow, I looked towards the Rhine, across the weeping willows to the mountains on the other side and the whole landscape seemed crazy to me. I had seen a few of those 'Jewish Yankees': they were brought down by truck to an assembly point in Bonn: they looked frozen, scared, and young. If the word Jew conveyed anything to me at all, then it was someone more like the Italians, who looked even more frozen than the Americans, much too tired to be scared. I kicked the chair beside my bed, and when it didn't fall over I kicked it again. It finally toppled over and shattered the glass top of my bedside table. Henrietta with her navy-blue hat and rucksack. She never came back, and today we don't know where she is buried. When the war was over someone came and told us she had 'fallen near Leverkusen'.

This concern for the sacred German soil is somehow comical when you realize that a good proportion of brown-coal mining shares had been in the hands of our family for two generations. For seventy years the Schniers have been making money out of the scooping and digging the sacred German soil has had to submit to; villages, forests, castles fall in the path of dredgers like the wall of Jericho.[34]

Holden had agreed to write a composition for a fellow student Stradlater who had suggested that he write 'something descriptive' about a house he had lived in. This did not appeal to Holden so he wrote about his brother Allie's baseball mitt:

Allie had written poems on the mitt so he'd have something to read while he was in the field and nobody was up to bat. He's dead now. He got leukaemia and died when we were up in Maine, on July 18, 1946. You'd have liked him. He was terrifically intelligent. He was two years younger than I was, but he was about fifty times as intelligent. His teachers were always writing to my mother, telling her what a pleasure it was to have a boy like Allie in their class. And they weren't just shooting the crap. They really meant it. But it just wasn't that he was the most intelligent member in the family. He was also the nicest, in lots of ways. He never got mad at anybody. People with red hair are supposed to get mad easily, but Allie never did and he had very red hair.[35]

When Allie died:

I was only thirteen, and they were going to have me psychoanalysed and all, because I broke all the windows in the garage. I don't blame them, I really don't. I slept in the garage the night he died, and I broke all the goddam windows with my fist, just for the hell of it. I even tried to break all the windows on the station wagon we had that summer, but my hand was already broken and everything by that time, and I couldn't do it. It was a very stupid thing to do, I'll admit, but I hardly didn't even know I was doing it, and you didn't know Allie.[36]

When we are young and love someone greatly it is very easy to idolise that person to the extent that, as we get older, we fall in love only with those people who seem to have the characteristics we loved so much in our first love. Thus Hans sees in Marie what he loves in Henrietta, her particular beauty, her gentle generosity. He said of Henrietta:

She had a surprisingly dark voice and light laughter. . . .
I would have liked to have phoned Henrietta but the

theologians have not invented this kind of dialling. . . .
I would have liked to hear Henrietta's voice so much, even if
she only said 'nothing' or for that matter 'Oh shit'. From her
lips it didn't sound vulgar at all. . . . Sometimes she used to
help me with my homework, and it always made us laugh
how good she was with other people's homework and so bad
at her own.[37]

He said of Maria: 'I was twenty-one, she was nineteen, when
one evening I simply went to her room to do the things that
men and women do with one another.'[38] Afterwards:

Quite suddenly she started to cry, and I asked her what she
was crying for now, and she whispered: 'For Heavens sake,
I'm a Catholic, you know I am –' and I said that any girl,
Protestant or Catholic, would probably cry too, and I knew
why; she looked at me questioningly, and I said: 'Because
such a thing as innocence does exist'[39] . . . A lot of things
went through my mind as I watched Marie dress. It made
me glad and at the same time unhappy to see how she took
her body for granted. Later on, when we moved together
from hotel to hotel, I always stayed in bed so I could watch
her wash and dress, and when the bathroom was placed so
I couldn't watch her from the bed, I lay in the bathtub.[40]

Holden loved all his siblings, his older brother D.B. who was
'my favourite author', and his young sister Phoebe:

Old Phoebe. I swear to God you'll like her. She was smart
even when she was a very tiny little kid. When she was a
very tiny little kid, I and Allie used to take her to the park
with us, especially on Sundays. Allie had this sailboat
he used to fool around with on Sundays, and we used to
take old Phoebe with us. She'd wear white gloves and
walk between us, like a lady and all. And when Allie and
I were having some conversation about things in general,
old Phoebe'd be listening. Sometimes you'd forget she was
around, because she was such a little kid, but *she'd* let
you know. She'd give Allie or I a push or something, and
say, '*Who?* Who said that? Bobby or the lady?' and we'd
tell her who said it, and she'd say, 'Oh' and go right on

listening. She killed Allie. I mean he liked her, too. She's ten now, and not such a tiny kid any more, but she still kills everybody – everybody with any sense, anyway.[41]

When we are children we know that children are a tribe apart from and very different from adults. Most children leave their tribe as soon as they can pass themselves off as young adults. After that they do good to children, they patronise them, and complain about them, and they try to forget what it was to be a child. They do not want to remember how they suffered as a child and how they saw other children suffer. Some children never forget, no matter how old they become. They remember what happened to them, and they see what happens to the children around them. Neither Hans nor Holden had forgotten what it was to be a child.

In his five days in New York Holden had a series of conversations with children. He talked about the girl of Phoebe's age, at the ice rink, who 'was having a hellava time tightening her skate. She didn't have gloves or anything and her hands were all red and cold. I gave her a hand with it.'[42] At the museum 'these two little kids came up to me and asked if I knew where the mummies were. The one little kid, the one that asked me, had his pants open. I told him about it. So he buttoned them up right where he was standing talking to me – he didn't even bother to go behind a post or anything. He killed me.'[43] He remembered James Castle, a boy at school, who, when he was attacked by six bullies, jumped out of a window and was killed. He was wearing a sweater Holden had lent him.

Holden was walking over to Broadway when he saw a family, father and mother and a boy of about six. 'He was making out that he was walking a very straight line, the way kids do, and the whole time he kept singing and humming. I got up closer so I could hear what he was singing. He was singing that song, "If a body catch a body coming through the rye" . . . It made me feel better. It made me feel not depressed any more.'[44] Later Holden snuck into his family's apartment and talked to Phoebe in her bedroom. He asked her if she knew the song 'If a body catch a body coming through the rye'. Phoebe told him it was a poem by Robert Burns and the correct line was 'If a body meet a body coming through the rye'.

I thought it was 'If a body catch a body', I said. Anyway,
I keep picturing all these little kids, and nobody's around
– nobody big, I mean – except me. And I'm standing on the
edge of some crazy cliff – I mean if they're running and
they don't look where they're going I have to come out of
somewhere and *catch* them. That's all I do all day. I'd just
be the catcher in the rye and all. I know it's crazy but that's
the only thing I'd really like to be. I know it's crazy.[45]

As much as Hans loved children and wanted to protect them,
his relationship with Marie showed how, if saving someone else
becomes the means by which we try to save ourselves, we can
become blind to what is actually happening to those we try
to save. This can be clearly seen in the activities of the animal liberation extremists. They released mink in mink farms
into the wild but neglected to protect the animals in the wild
on which the mink prey. Those who attack the scientists who
use chimpanzees in their research into the causes and cures
for cancer fail to understand that apes die of cancer just as
humans do. Hans may have taken Marie with him in order to
save her in the way he should have saved Henrietta, but it was
not until Marie became ill that he discovered that 'the things
that men and women do with one another' can have deleterious
effects on a woman's body. He was hurt when she left him for
Züpfer and blamed this on the Catholics who enticed her away
from him, but he was quite unaware that when a woman is
totally economically dependent on a man she can find the helplessness of that state unendurable, especially if the man cares
little for work or money.

There is one major difference between Hans and Holden.
Hans blamed his parents for what had happened but Holden
did not blame his parents. Indeed, he tried to protect them.
Right at the outset he said, 'My parents would have two haem-
orrhages apiece if I told anything pretty personal about them.
They're quite touchy about anything like that, especially my
father. They're *nice* and all – I'm not saying that – but they're
also touchy as hell.'[46] Yet, as his story unfolds, we get glimpses of an angry father who had not made any attempt to understand Holden and a concerned but distant mother. Holden
reminds me of those clients who in their first session with me

would tell me how good their parents were ('Mum's not happy with me having another baby but she'd do anything for me', 'Dad's gets a bit grumpy but he's got a heart of gold'), and then over the following weeks tell a story of themselves as a child whose suffering followed from the actions of these parents. If I asked about a particular event, 'How did you feel about that?' the clients would give an excuse seen from adult eyes, 'Mum wasn't well at the time', 'Dad was worried about his job', rather than anything, however truthful, which might reflect badly on their parents. The so-called symptoms of a mental disorder – depression, anxiety, panic attacks, obsessions and compulsions, psychosis, anorexia – the client sees as being preferable to admitting that the sacrifice of seeing himself as bad in order to see his parents as good was nothing but a futile gesture. A great many people prefer to suffer in order to hold on to their belief that their parents always loved and cared for them because that way they can feel that their parents, alive or dead, are still with them and they are not alone in the world

Holden always longed for his parents' love and could not give up the hope of that. Hans had given up all hope of his parents' love long ago. He once loved his parents as all small children love their parents, but unrequited love eventually dies and nothing but a blankness, a kind of deadness, remains. Hans felt some sorrow for his parents in their old age, but this was nothing more than what he would have felt for any old person. However, by hanging on to a sibling or a sibling substitute, Hans, like those people who stay close to their siblings no matter what suffering that entails, could try to believe that he was not alone in the world.

When parents die many adult children find that, even though they had sensibly prepared themselves for the death of their aged parents, they are shocked by the discovery that in facing the world they are on their own. Some people stay close to their siblings, even though they may not particularly like them, because they feel that the connection to their siblings keeps them connected to their dead parents who, somehow, continue to act as a buffer between them and the infinite. In her old age my sister one day expressed concern for my physical well-being. Somewhat sentimentally she explained, 'You're my only family.' I was astounded. My sister has within her call (and no one in her family would dare disobey) a husband, three sons, a very kind and attentive daughter-in-law, four grandchildren and innumerable cousins to the nth degree. When I recovered from my shock I understood. Through me she was still connected to her parents. She could tell me how much she missed being able to tell Mother about what she was doing, something she had done all her life. She could get my approval for the way she had gathered up Dad's war memorabilia and seen that it was properly stored and catalogued at the Australian War Museum. However, she did not want me to reminisce about our childhood because my memory of that conflicted with her desire to believe that we both had a happy childhood. Of all the areas over which siblings can fight, as siblings get older, the bitterest and most passionate fights are about their memories of the past.

# Chapter 7

# A QUESTION OF MEMORY

In his memoir of his school days in Nazi Germany *What's to Become of the Boy?* Heinrich Böll warned that he has 'a justifiable mistrust of my memory. All this happened forty-eight to forty-four years ago, and I have no notes or jottings to resort to; they were burned or blown to bits in an attic of 17 Karolinger-Ring in Cologne. Moreover, I am no longer sure of how some of my personal experiences synchronize with historical events.' He noted: 'It is somewhat warily that I now enter upon the "realistic", the chronologically confused path, wary of my own and other people's autobiographical pronouncements. The mood and situation I can vouch for, also the facts bound up with moods and situations; but, confronted by verifiable historical facts, I cannot vouch for the synchronization.'

Memory is a constant theme in Böll's work. He knew – though he did not express it in this way – that we create memories that support our sense of being a person. Thus many people will create memories that deny, or overlook, what actually happened in order that they can think well of themselves, while others who want to maintain the standards for truth and compassion which they have set for themselves will strive to be accurate in their memories. Böll had seen how many Germans conveniently 'forgot' their support for the Nazis and their own activities in furthering the Nazi aims. He believed that the events in Germany in the first half of the twentieth century should be remembered, but he also knew that our memories of our emotions – the meanings that concern the validation and invalidation of our self – do not always coincide with 'verifiable historical facts'. Although many people lie to themselves about their emotions, Böll could see that our memory of our emotions is more likely to be true than our memory of 'verifiable historical facts'. However, our memories of emotions can easily attach themselves to memories of events where in fact these emotions were not involved. Thus Böll wrote:

My memory doesn't betray me when I recall that one morning a schoolmate of mine, a member of the black-uniformed S.S., exhausted yet with the hectic light of the chase still in his eyes, told me they had spent the night scouring the villas of Godesberg for the former cabinet minister Treviranus. Thank God (as I, not he, thought) without success. But when, to quite make sure, I proceed to look it up, I find that Treviranus had already emigrated in 1933; in 1933, the minimum age for membership in the S.S. was eighteen, though we were only sixteen then; thus, this memory cannot be placed earlier than 1935 or 1936. In other words, either Treviranus must have re-entered the German Reich illegally in 1935 or 1936, or the S.S. men must have been fed the wrong information. The story itself – that strange blend of exhaustion and eyes shining with the light of the chase – I can vouch for, but I cannot place it.[1]

Emotions have traditionally been seen to be the opposite of calm, rational thought. They have always been considered to be wild, wilful, selfish, inconsiderate, preventing us from seeing reality as it actually is, and, since they are so, they can be disregarded. Despite this, some people pride themselves on their ability to feel emotion and see this ability as making them more humane, more caring than those people who keep their emotions under tight control. This is the territory over which extraverts and introverts can fight most fiercely. However, both sides know that emotions are dangerous because they can destroy the structures that hold society together. We can fall in love with unsuitable people; we can take offence where none was intended.

Though much has been said and written about emotion, language always fails to capture just what it is that we experience when we experience an emotion. Different languages do not agree on how many emotions there actually are. For instance, English lacks a word for that delicious feeling which German names as Schadenfreude, and lumps together a vast range of extraordinary feelings under one word love, with affection being a lesser kind of love. Different individuals can consider different experiences to be emotions. In describing his seaside holidays with his nanny, the philosopher Richard Wollheim wrote: 'The first two or three weeks of the holiday were divided between long periods of routine and brief moments of terror, with, I am sure, some pleasure in the middle. I call these parts "pleasure", "terror", and "routine" to mark the fact that for me in those years routine too was a kind of emotion.'[2] A thesaurus of emotions can be only the crudest attempt to classify the emotions because emotions, being the meanings we create in terms of the degree of safety or danger we feel, are as infinite in their variety as are all the meanings that we can create.

Memories of emotions can bedevil those discussions amongst siblings when they reminisce. When individual memories coincide, the joy of remembering past happinesses increases enormously, and even the memories of past sadnesses create mutual comfort, but when memories differ there is pain and a feeling of isolation. Why can't my sibling remember as I do?

## Memories are made of this

Siblings can disagree on the simplest facts of their childhood. Dalton Conley wrote:

> You may grow up in the same house – even the same room – as your brother and sister and yet have very different memories of those who raised you. Fifty-three percent of sibling pairs do not remember their father's education similarly; 46 percent remember their mother's education differently. Twenty-one percent of siblings differ on whether their mother worked for a year or more during their childhood. Twenty-five percent even disagree on how old their parents are.[3]

Moreover, our memory of an event is not a once-and-for-all construction. Every time we bring a memory into consciousness we create a somewhat different construction. Knowledge acquired later may alter the memory of an earlier event, or the memory of the earlier event may arouse emotions different from those aroused by the original event.[4] A child who was tricked and humiliated by an older sibling and felt frightened and hurt at the time may in adulthood remember the event with considerable anger.

The ferocity of sibling arguments about past events is often based on the belief that there is one true account of the past. Rose, someone I met occasionally at mental health conferences, offered to show me the account she had written of her period of psychosis, and of what she felt had led up to the psychosis. She told me that she thought I might be interested in the different ways she and her sister remembered these events. Rose knew that writing an account of our experiences is an excellent way of understanding them, and of diminishing the frequency of unhappy memories coming unbidden into our mind. However, she wanted to do more than that. She wanted to understand exactly what happened to her and why it had happened. This made her memoir infinitely more valuable than most of the 'misery memoirs' that make it to the bestseller lists, which add nothing to our understanding of ourselves and merely turn the reader into a voyeur of someone else's suffering. Moreover, Rose wanted to make sure that in her account she was as even-handed as possible. She contrasted her memories with those of her sister Elaine, but while Rose admitted that she had doubts about the accuracy of some of her memories, Elaine had absolutely no doubts about the correctness of hers. She alone had the one true account of their past. Rose gave me permission to quote directly from her memoir, but, when Elaine read what I had written, she insisted that all direct references to Rose's memoir were to be deleted and that I should give Rose and herself complete anonymity. For me to do otherwise would bring shame on the family. Rose felt compelled to acquiesce. I felt that the difficulty Elaine had was not so much with Rose as with me and my belief that there are as many histories as there are participants in those histories to recount them.

Those who believe that there is only one true account of events overlook the fact that different people cannot help but see things from different points of view. Where siblings are concerned this may be literally so. Two year olds live in a world of giants, while a healthy twelve year old may be able to look adults in the eye. But when it comes to interpreting events, no two people ever see anything in exactly the same way. Two people can be involved in the same event but only one of them feels invalidated by the event. When the journalist Lucy Mangan wrote about the fears that assailed her when as a child she went to bed, and about her mother's attempts to reassure her that there were no bad men hiding in her wardrobe and that none of her family were going to die of cancer during the night, she concluded her account with, 'Dad, it must be observed, never woke up [while all this was going on] but this was only marginally less comforting than having him conscious as he was wont to make suggestions such as leaving me on a hillside while they concentrated their energies on raising my sister.'[5] No doubt her father had interpreted his remark as being no more than a loving tease, while Lucy's sister could pride herself on her parent-pleasing goodness, but for Lucy the remark only added to her suspicions that her parents, or at least her father, wanted to abandon her.

When adult siblings compare notes about their childhoods one sibling may have no recollection of an event that the other sibling remembers well. Sometimes one sibling will remember the event but not the feelings that were aroused in the other sibling. A remark like 'I didn't think you were upset' can be extremely hurtful. Equally hurtful can be 'I know you always felt that Dad didn't love you but he really cared for you a lot', because it implies that the other sibling has misinterpreted certain events and has no right to feel unloved.

In his book *How the Mind Forgets and Remembers: The Seven Sins of Memory*, Daniel Schacter summarised the research which shows that we remember facts and events relating to ourselves better than we remember facts and events that do not. He wrote: 'Numerous experiments have shown that when we encode new information by relating it to the self, subsequent memory for that information improves compared to other types of encoding.'[6] Moreover, 'Everyday experience and laboratory studies reveal that emotionally charged incidents are better remembered than non-emotional events.'[7] Thus one sibling may remember his great disappointment at not getting a much longed for Christmas present, while another sibling, whose presents were just what she wanted, may in adult life not remember that particular Christmas at all.

Not only are we likely to remember emotionally charged events but very likely we remember them in pictures and not in words. The incidents from childhood that I have described in this book unfold before my mind's eye as clearly as the actual events did at the time. It is as Richard Wollheim described it in his autobiography: 'This book, and my manner of writing it, should make one thing about my life clear: that everything I have lived through either has been completely forgotten or it is as yesterday. There is no blue to the horizon of Time.'[8] Much of Richard Wollheim's work as a philosopher was concerned with issues that are central to the visual arts. Recalling his suburban childhood in London before the Second World War he wrote:

> To this day I remember every inch of the Black Fence, every path, every bend in every path, every patch where the roots of trees erupted, every stretch where the trees grew together and blocked out the light, every mound and bank of sand, every silver birch, and every small oak tree, and every likely source of blackberries, and this knowledge has been kept fresh in my mind because of the way in which images retained from many walks have formed an involuntary backcloth to much thinking in my mind, particularly of an abstract kind.[9]

Of course, many of our memories are acquired before we acquire language and therefore must have been recorded in pictures, the contents of which we may not be able to recognise once our body grows bigger and its relationship to its surroundings change markedly. Some autistic people, like Temple Grandin, continue to record all their memories in pictures while the rest of us learn to encode many of our memories in words, but it seems that whenever we encounter a startlingly unusual or dangerous event we are likely to record our memory of that event in pictures.

After a disaster the participants may be able to deal with their memories in the usual way by spending some time thinking about the events, telling the story to those who were not there, perhaps getting angry, crying, or puzzling over how the events fitted into the great scheme of things, or even wondering if there actually is a great scheme of things. But sometimes doing all of these fails to create a memory with which the person can live. Instead, they relive the events with an immediacy that is greater than the actual present. Pictures of the events constantly force themselves upon their mind's eye, and the emotions which the event aroused do not diminish with time. Psychiatrists call this inability to assimilate experience post traumatic stress disorder (PTSD) and fail to understand that we are compelled to go over and over an event until we can construct a meaning which will fit fairly easily into our meaning structure. Believers in the existence of a Just World are likely to find it impossible to assimilate an event which allows of no reward and no recompense, while those who believe that we live in a world where bad things can happen through chance or plain human stupidity may still experience fear and anger after an event which does nothing but lay waste to people and places, but they have the satisfaction of knowing that their theory about the world has been confirmed.

Being able to create a memory of a disaster that fits into our meaning structure allows us to turn our picture of that event into a verbal description when we recall it. However, a verbal description is likely to be less accurate than a picture. Daniel Schacter noted: 'A strong sense of familiarity, together with an absence of specific recollections, adds up to a lethal recipe for misattribution.'[10] Thus a sibling whose memory of a certain event in childhood was easily translated into words can differ markedly in his recollection of an event from that of his sibling who is still troubled by what happened and remembers the event in pictures. Temple Grandin described the research where brain scans of people with PTSD who had suffered sexual abuse, assault, or had been involved in car crashes were compared with scans of people who had suffered the same experiences but did not develop PTSD. The first group remembered their experience visually, the second verbally, as a 'verbal narrative'. Their scans backed this up. She wrote:

Somehow words are associated with lower fear. This is one of the meanings of the saying, 'A picture is worth a thousand words.' A picture of a scary thing is a lot more frightening than a verbal description of a scary thing. By the same token, a visual memory of a scary thing is more frightening than a verbal memory.[11]

Memories in pictures allow us to identify specific details. A memory of an event recorded in words such as, 'My mother disliked going to the beach' has an easy familiarity, but my mental picture of my mother grudgingly taking me to the beach, then insisting that we leave long before I was ready to do so, and of how ungraciously she scraped the sand off me with a thin towel reawakens my misery and puzzlement as to why she always turned a happy event into a torment for her family, or at least for me. My verbal memory of my mother's attitude to one of my favourite occupations can in no way convey the full truth of my memory.

For the full truth of a memory to be conveyed the description must include the memory of the emotional meanings. The same applies when someone tells a story. If my little story of my grandmother's party had excluded every emotional meaning then all that could be said was that a group of people were sitting down to a meal when someone came to the door and a child ran out of the house and climbed into a car. In his study *The Ethics of Memory* Avishai Margalit considered how acts of great cruelty inflicted on people are remembered, and he distinguished between a moral witness and a political witness to that event. He wrote: 'Both are engaged in uncovering what evil tries to cover up. The political witness may be more effective in uncovering the factual truth, in telling it like it was. But the moral witness is more valuable at telling it like it felt, that is, telling what it was like to be subjected to such evil. The first-person accounts of moral witnesses are essential to what they report, whereas political witnesses can testify from a third-person perspective without much loss.'[12] The television critic Nancy Banks-Smith was often asked why she persisted in watching the news and documentary programmes that gave accounts in shocking pictures of the sufferings of so many people. She would always reply that we all need to have a witness to our lives who will say, 'Yes, that happened.' 'That' for her was not just the event but the emotions of the people caught up in that event.

The problem with moral witnesses reporting emotional meanings is that emotional meanings are difficult to define unambiguously in words and always raise difficult questions of right and wrong. When Elaine refused to accept the emotional meanings which her sister Rose related to a possible sexual

assault by her father when Rose was a small child, she rested
her case on the moral imperative of the Fifth Commandment,
'Honour thy father and mother so that thy days be long in
the land.' Elaine remembered her father as being an upright,
honourable man, and she did not want his reputation tarnished
in any way. The moral imperative of the Fifth Commandment clashes with a moral rule that many people regard as
an imperative, that children should not be sexually assaulted
by adults. However, there is also the question of diminished
responsibility. The family had been living in Hong Kong where
the father was a much respected civil servant, but with the
threat of war in the Far East he sent his wife and their two
little girls back to England. He remained in Hong Kong, was
captured by the Japanese Army and had to endure four years'
internment in a prisoner-of-war camp. When he returned home
he could not summon up the patience and emotional restraint
that parents of small children need. He physically chastised
his daughters, Rose much more than Elaine. Should he be
held morally responsible for this and for the intense fear his
behaviour aroused in Rose?

One way of avoiding such moral questions is to relegate emotional meanings to the dustbin of subjectivity. Emotions are
irrational and unreliable and should be ignored. Children's emotions, indeed all their memories, can be ignored because they
are children, incapable of distinguishing fantasy from reality.
Certainly children can be persuaded to produce 'memories'
that an adult may wish them to have. Children know that to
survive physically and as a person they have to try to discover
what it is that adults want and then give them what they want.
However, as Daniel Schacter wrote: 'New research has shown
that children's spontaneous recollections tend to be accurate,
whereas their responses to specific questions are more likely to
include distortions.'[13] Children can remember certain events,
usually isolated events, from a remarkably early age. In his
memoir of his first five years John Simpson, political editor for
the BBC, wrote:

> I am fourteen months old: this is October 1945. I accept
> that it is unusual for children to be able to remember
> things at such an early age, but not impossible. My younger

daughter, Eleanor, has memories of lying in a creaky little cot on a holiday we took in the West of Ireland a year and a month after she was born. Perhaps our memory is a brain function which, if left to itself, will switch on at around the age of two or two and a half, but in cases of particularly strong events can start earlier. For most of my life I assumed that this scene with the mirror took place when I was older than eighteen months; but having gone through all the available documents, it is now clear to me that it happened even earlier. And I now assume that none of this would have stayed with me, if something of such major, incomprehensible importance had not been taking place in front of me. . . . What I was observing was the start of the break-up of my parents' marriage. . . .

[My mother] goes up on tiptoe once more, staring into the mirror as though it can tell her something; for years afterwards, when I think about the fairy story where the wicked stepmother says, 'Mirror, mirror on the wall,' I will remember that mirror, with its inch-wide scalloped edges and its strange curves, hanging heavily forward with a kind of menace.

It must, I assume, contain some sort of secret: the secret of why my mother is crying with such abandon. Yet I can't see the reason. I shift my position on the floor. Perhaps I am frustrated at not being able to speak properly and ask her what is happening. I doubt it, though; at this age I have not entirely appreciated that I will soon be able to talk and communicate like adults do. I accept that I am altogether separate from my parents, a different species altogether.

My mother is talking to me now, but I have no understanding of what she is saying. I do not recognize any of the words she uses; she is talking to express herself, not to communicate with me in the limited terms of love or annoyance which parents mostly use towards babies. All I can see when she turns her head away from the mirror is that she is still crying as much as ever. The tears make marks on the front of her camel coat. She puts her lipstick away in her small dark brown handbag – could it perhaps be crocodile? – and sits down with me on the floor.

This is usually the start of a game of some sort, and

perhaps I grin in the middle of my perplexity. It makes no difference to her mood. There is more talk, another flow of undecipherable words. All I can understand is that we seem to be about to go somewhere: I too am being prepared for the outside world. I am turned and bundled into a coat whose colour I cannot any longer remember: perhaps pale blue, though that may be a conflicting memory from a later time. My mother isn't rough with me, because she never is; but there is an urgency about her movements which I find somehow painful. And all the time those terrible, puzzling tears, as her face comes close to mine and she holds me closely in her arms. Have I done something bad? What is wrong? The entire world seems to have been turned upside down.[14]

Perhaps if John Simpson's parents had subsequently learned to live together happily this early memory might have faded. The events that followed, when, just six years old, John was forced by his mother to choose between his parents and he chose his father, are likely to have pinned this early memory into place.

## Memories that defend us

John Simpson is renowned for his detailed, accurate, well-analysed reporting of major events. This would seem to be his habitual style of thinking. To understand the events of his childhood he had to remember clearly and accurately. Ever the good journalist, he checked his memories against the records. Only by working in this way could he validate his image of himself and create a story of his childhood with which he could live. Although he records his emotional memories of the events, he is more of a political witness than a moral witness to his life. In contrast, the Turkish writer Orhan Pamuk, no less concerned with recording the truth of his childhood, sought the emotional truth. He wrote:

Between the ages of six and ten, I fought with my older brother incessantly and as time went on the beatings to which he subjected me grew more and more violent. There were only eighteen months between us, but he was considerably bigger and stronger, and because it was (and perhaps still is) considered normal, even healthy for two brothers to fight and come to blows, no one saw the need to stop us. I saw the beatings as personal failures and blamed them on my weakness and lack of coordination; during the first few years, when my brother angered or belittled me, I was often the first to strike, and, half believing that I deserved the beatings, of course I wasn't going to challenge violence in principle. If one of our fights ended with broken glass and windowpanes and me bruised and bleeding, my mother's complaint when she finally intervened was not that we had hit each other and not that I'd been beaten up, but that we'd messed up the house – and that, because we'd been unable to settle our differences peaceably, the neighbours would complain yet again about the noise.

Later, when reminded of those brawls, my mother and my brother claimed no recollection of them, saying that, as usual, I'd invented them, just for the sake of something to write about, just to give myself a colourful and melodramatic past. They were so sincere that I was finally forced to agree, concluding that, as always, I'd been swayed more by my imagination than by real life. So anyone reading these pages should bear in mind that I am prone to exaggeration. But what is important for a painter is not a thing's reality but its shape, and what is important for a novelist is not the course of events but their ordering, and what is important for a memoirist is not the factual accuracy of the account but its symmetry.[15]

When we recall an event we can do so truthfully. 'This is what I remember' and it was so. Or we can lie to ourselves. We can construct a fantasy and tell ourselves that it is the truth. Similarly, when we recall an event, we can do so truthfully and then give as accurate an account of that memory as we possibly can to another person. Or we can recall an event truthfully, and in our account to another person we can lie. Or we can lie to ourselves and to another person. When we try to be as truthful as we can in our recall of an event, we are still constrained by the habitual patterns which we use to interpret the world. It is these patterns that Orhan Pamuk calls their 'symmetry'. Every story has the symmetry of a beginning, a middle and an end. Human beings see the world in the patterns that they each have learned.

One pattern that dominates our thinking is the pattern we call 'my life'. It has an overall shape – a past, a present and a future – and within that shape there is a complex of meanings that aim at keeping the concepts 'my life' and 'myself' unfragmented and a source of personal pride. Thus, when we recall our past, our memories come to us in the shape of 'my life' and 'myself'. We prefer not to remember events that suggest that our life is not what we thought it was, and that we are not what we thought we were. Perhaps Orhan Pamuk's recall of the fights he had with his brother had to be rejected by his brother and mother because his brother wanted to think of himself as a kindly, loving person, and his mother wanted to see herself as a good parent.

Our habitual patterns of thinking are all aimed at defending our sense of being a person. The habitual patterns of introverts relate in one way or another to keeping things in order and having some sense of achievement, while those of extraverts relate to creating and maintaining good relationships. Thus extravert and introvert siblings growing up in the same circumstances not only deal with these circumstances very differently but they remember what happened differently. An extraordinary example of this is given in the shared autobiography of Gregg and Gina Hill, children of the notorious gangster turned federal witness Harry Hill. Their mother Karen Hill was one of those women who fall in love with an exciting rogue who has no conscience and prefers to lie, cheat and be abusive, even in situations where he could be honest. Such women find excuses for all the man's failings until finally certain extremely horrendous events become too terrible to be ignored any longer. Karen Hill married Harry knowing that he could be violent but expecting that he would never use his violence against her or her children. She was wrong.

In the 1970s Harry Hill lived in New York and worked for the Mob. When federal agents persuaded him to give evidence against the Mob the whole family had to go into the federal witness protection program because Harry's former colleagues were trying to kill him and his family. Harry, a loud, brash man who always wanted to be the centre of attention, could not

manage to live quietly and inconspicuously, and so the family
was forced to make sudden moves from Queens to Nebraska to
Kentucky to Washington State, with each move necessitating
a change of identities for all the family.

Even before these forced migrations, family life in the Hill
household was chaotic, despite the mother's attempts to maintain a semblance of family and child care. Harry came and
went as he pleased and demanded that his family fit in with
whatever he wanted. If they failed to do so Harry's retribution was swift and brutal. Gregg, the introvert, said of himself, 'I was a particular kid, the kind who kept his room neat
and organized, probably because it was one of the few things
in life I could control.' 'I was much more serious, much more
independent [than my sister].' 'The only lesson my father ever
taught me, the only one that really mattered, even when I was
just a boy, was not to depend on anyone else.' 'From the outside, I probably looked like a normal kid: I played stickball and
roller hockey with my friends, I had clean clothes and enough
to eat, I did well in school, I kept my room neat and organized.
But it felt I was raising myself most of the time, that I was the
adult.'[16] When the first order to move was given, their mother's
mother and other relatives came to the house. Gregg wrote:

All the hysteria was making a terrible situation worse.
I knew if I stopped, even for an instant, I'd lose it too.
I couldn't let myself cry. Crying would make me one of
them, the same as my compliant mother or my powerless
relatives who were weeping and wailing, but unable to just
say no, to say, *Wait, let's think this through*. And that was
the last thing I wanted to be at that moment. I ground
my teeth together hard, and it made me squint like I was
watching a gory scene in a movie. I followed an agent out
to the car, and another opened the door for me. I got in
the backseat and waited. The crying and screaming had
spilled out onto the street. 'Kaaaarren!' my grandmother
howled as the agents pried her away, literally tore her
from my grandmother's arms. I stared straight at the
seat in front of me, my vision blurred by the water in my
eyes. I didn't say anything. I didn't even say goodbye.[17]

Gregg might not have cried on this and later occasions but he was well aware that his father's every act of monumental self-ishness, foolhardiness and cruelty increased his anger with his father. One night when Gregg was 16 his father came home drunk and drugged and attacked his wife. Hearing his father's shouts and his mother's cries, Gregg seized a homemade mace and headed for his parents' bedroom. His thoughts raced:

> My fuse was burning
> We'd had to move three times because people wanted to kill my father.
> I'd had to say goodbye to my best friend in a two-minute phone call.
> I'd had to change my name, abandon my past, dissolve my roots.
> My father was going to get us all killed.[18]

He did not kill his father but he kicked him very hard in the stomach, breaking a rib. His father yelled and cursed him but for the first time he became afraid of Gregg. 'He limped out of the room, then out of the house, cursing over his shoulder, promising he'd kill me. After a moment I heard the car start and pull away down our driveway.' His mother said, 'I hope you didn't hurt him. Gregg, you've got to control yourself.'[19]

Gina was her father's Princess. She said, 'My dad was always buying me dolls. He'd say "Whaddya want, Princess?" and I'd say, "Barbie's swimming pool" or something like that, and the next day or the day after he'd bring it home. That's who my dad was to me then, a wonderful man who brought me dolls and called me Princess.'[20] When he went to prison her grandmother would say to her mother, '"Why are you taking them to see that gangster? That's no place for children. Children don't belong in prison. Let him rot in hell."'

> Those were terrible words for a little girl to hear about her dad. As far as I was concerned, my grandma didn't understand him. My mom had built him up pretty well in my mind, probably more than she had to because when you're six years old it doesn't take much to believe that your dad is the best man in the world. To me, he was smarter than everyone else, which meant that everyone else – prison guards, police, my grandma – was wrong. I knew he got into

trouble for doing things he shouldn't be doing, and that's why he had to go away, but I never thought of him as a criminal. Never in a million years could Dad hurt someone or steal or kill someone. He had a weak stomach and loved everybody.[21]

When she described herself Gina said, 'I guess I had my dad's charm.' Despite all that was happening, 'I was never depressed – just the opposite; I was the bubbly one in the family.'[22] Wherever she went she made friends. Her father would say, 'Trust me, it'll be great.' She said, 'I did trust him. I always believed him.'[23]

However, she was growing up and she realised that by now all of her father's friends were junkies. He bought her the horse she had dreamed of, but at a barbeque with his friends he became wildly angry and hit her with a large plank of wood. Although 'a small crack in my faith started to open up' she decided that, 'the time he'd tried to beat me with the two-by-four was just a terrible mistake, one of those freak episodes that everyone has once in a while.'[24] Then something terrible happened:

*My father beat me up. My father kicked the living shit out of me.*

The bastard. I believed in him. All those years, I believed in him. I'd always forced myself to hold two different images of him in my mind, the good man I knew he was and the bad man the drugs and alcohol made him. I kept the good image alive, too, when no one else did, when the bad one was suffocating it.

*He tried to kill me. He tried to run me down.*[25]

Gregg said of Gina, 'My father had never been able to buy me off like Gina.' Gina said of Gregg, 'I'd always loved Gregg, even when he was so serious. I'd never understood why he was so negative about everything. Now I wondered if he was just being realistic, if I was being naïve, blind to how bad things were and always would be.'[26]

Gina said of herself, 'I'd wasted my whole life being proud of my father.'[27] Yet, when her parents finally divorced and her father married his girlfriend Dawn and they had a son, Justin, Gina went to see them. As they were both drug addicts Justin was sent to foster parents. Gina worked hard to get custody of him. She married and when Harry and Dawn rehabilitated themselves, Gina gave Justin back but kept in close touch with the three of them. Gregg and Gina now live in different parts of the country under aliases. Gregg concluded his account of his life with:

> In 1985 I flew off to a faraway city with nothing but my made up name and a fictionalized past. I started off as Gregg Scott, alone and broke, and built a respectable life for myself, a good life. It was an act of will, of sheer determination. I went back to school and graduated with honours, and then I went on to law school. I'm a practising attorney. I've never broken the law. I've never pulled a scam. I've never told anyone who my father is. Only my wife knows, and we don't talk much about it.[28]

Gregg and Gina each gave the events of their childhood a particular shape and meaning which served to defend their individual sense of being a person. However, events can all too often show us that the meanings we have created in order to defend ourselves are not an accurate representation of what is actually going on. If, like Gregg, we have tried to be truthful with ourselves and accept that the world is not always what we want it to be, we are likely to be in a good position to discard old ideas and create new ones, painful though that may be. Gregg did not say so but I suspect that, despite his unsentimental assessment of his father, he still held a hope that one day his mother would show that she valued her children more than her husband by leaving him, but her reaction to his defence of her showed that he was deluding himself. Abandoning this hope, he was free of any tie he had to his family and could leave home.

In contrast, Gina lied to herself throughout her childhood and adolescence. Only a brutal beating from her father could force her to face the truth. Even then she could not relinquish her longing to belong to an ordinary family. When her father quietened down, as psychopaths usually do as they get older, she felt she could try again to fulfil her longing, although in a much modified form.

In their book there is no record of how easily they each

accepted their differing memories of their childhood. Despite their different ways of dealing with their experiences, very likely in childhood they had developed that kind of particular loyalty to one another that often, but not always, grows out of the siblings' mutual recognition that there is no one to care for them except themselves.

The salvation of Gregg and Gina depended on each of them realising the perilousness of their situation. While they still lived with their parents, their mother might have deplored Gregg's criticisms of his father and later Gregg's attack on him, but she did not forbid Gregg and Gina to speak about what had happened. Thus, they did not have to deny their memories but simply modify them in ways that allowed them to get on with their lives instead of being caught in a tangle of unacknowledged memories and lies. If we deny our memories, if we tell ourselves that something did not happen when it did, one way or another the denied memories will keep breaking through, forcing themselves upon our consciousness. If other people deny our memories, particularly if these are people who can punish us for remembering, then we have no way of understanding what has happened and of constructing a memory with which we can live.

## Memories denied

We like to think of our memories being our own private property, and so they should be, but other people like to believe that they have the right to tell us what our memories should be. Orhan Pamuk was charged with 'insulting Turkish identity' in some remarks he made to a Swiss magazine. He said, 'Thirty thousand Kurds and one million Armenians were killed in Turkey and no one dares talk about it.' He was referring to the Turkish army's brutal suppression of a Kurdish separatist movement and the mass slaughter of Armenians between 1915 and 1917, matters that are forbidden by the state to be mentioned in Turkey. There are many writers and journalists in prison in Turkey because they have challenged the government's version of Turkey's past. Orhan Pamuk would have joined them had there not been a worldwide outcry about his arrest and trial, an outcry which put in jeopardy the Turkish government's application to join the European Union.

All states, not just Turkey, try to control what their people remember. Since it is the victors who write the history, not the vanquished, the state decides which past events are to be remembered and which forgotten. The degree of freedom of speech within a particular state relates directly to what people are allowed to remember and what sanctions are applied when someone speaks about matters the state (and sometimes the Church) has deemed not to have happened. The family is a small state and those in charge, usually the parents, decide what the official history of the family is. Unhappy events in the family are allowed to be remembered if they can be presented as victories or examples of the courage and moral rectitude of certain family members. Events which show the family in a bad light should not be remembered. Any family member who insists on remembering and talking about these events will be punished, just as Orhan Pamuk was being punished. If one child in the family insists on remembering what the family want forgotten, that child may be supported by the other siblings or punished by them, as the stories of Karen and Rose show.

I have known Karen for over 30 years. I first met her when she was 14 going on 15 and had been admitted to the clinic where I worked. She had been diagnosed as manic depressive, but what I found was a child so terrified she could barely speak. Why she was so frightened did not interest the psychiatrists who had diagnosed her, but the cause of her terror was not hard to find. I visited her home and met her parents. As they lived a considerable distance from the clinic I stayed overnight and so I learned much more about the family than I would have learnt in an interview in my office. I have told Karen's story in the third edition of *Beyond Fear*,[29] but here I want to comment on one part of the story.

It was clear to me that there was something seriously amiss in Karen's family. There were secrets, and some of them at least had to do with Karen's father. He was friendly to me and helpful, driving me to and from the train. He drove a van with a sliding door on one side. Preparing for the drive one morning, he opened the sliding door. I got in, sat down and he closed the door – nothing remarkable in that except that as he slowly closed the door he looked at me. There are looks and looks. I knew the difference between a man's long, warm, mischievous look that promises affection and joy, and the cold, penetrating stare that signals danger. His was the second kind of look. It told me a great deal about him.

There was no point in telling my psychiatrist colleagues about this. They were completely convinced that the problem resided solely in Karen – she had a mental illness – and the family were an ordinary family struggling to care for a mad child. In my conversations with Karen I would try to create openings where she could, if she wished, tell me more about her family, but I came to realise that she was operating under four internalised injunctions: don't remember; don't ask questions; be afraid; know that you can never be good enough.

Gradually Karen came to be more able to cope with her life and she returned home. We kept in touch over the years by letters, phone calls and the occasional social visit. Karen worked, brought up two children very successfully and had a good marriage, but she endured bouts of depression and far too frequent migraines, both the kind of miseries often suffered by those people who never get angry, which Karen never did.

Thirty years had gone by when Karen rang me, told me that her father had died, and asked if she could come and talk to me. She told me that she had been with her mother in the hospital when her father died. As she took her mother home, her mother said, 'He was always a good father to you all.' Suddenly Karen felt very angry. In the days that followed she began to recall some long-forgotten events from childhood. She had always remembered her father's physical assaults, but now other more disturbing memories were breaking through as if some sanction which had kept them hidden had disappeared.

When Karen and I were making our arrangements to meet I suggested that she and her husband come to my home for lunch one Saturday. This caused them consternation because they then had to explain to me that Karen ate such a limited range of food that they did not want to put me to the trouble of trying to create a meal she would feel able to eat. In all the years Karen had been writing to me, long newsy letters about every member of her family, including her parents, her brother, two sisters and their families, their schooling, jobs, marriages, children, illnesses, holidays, birthdays and Christmases, she had never mentioned her habits about food. She was not keeping this a secret. It was simply her regular habit, begun in childhood and, unremarkably, it had not occurred to her to mention it to me.

Children are not born finicky eaters. In a family where food and eating are never associated with angry, frightening scenes, or when children have a bad experience with certain food they are comforted, not punished in any way, once their palates have adapted to the range of tastes and textures their parents give them, children have no complete and lasting aversions to any kind of food, though they will have preferences which change over time. However, once a child learns to associate a particular food with fear, the child cannot manage to eat the food. It has become repulsive and dangerous. The child may forget the event that gave rise to the fear but the fear remains.

In an interview about his autobiography *Toast*, Nigel Slater, the cookery expert, told how he had dealt with his fear of certain foods by making cooking his profession. 'As a boy he would not drink milk or eat eggs, though he could cook with both. This refusal angered his father whose family had run a dairy. At the time, he said, it was the taste [that put him off], but now the fact that he can't face a poached egg is down to "all the crap that went with it".' His dad would hold him down, hold his mouth open and force egg into it. If Nigel still refused he risked his father's vicious temper. '"If ever he hit me, he could not stop."'[30]

The three matters around which a small child can suffer violence at the hands of their parents are toilet training, food and sex. This violence is based on the parents' beliefs that toilet training must be completed in a certain space of time, irrespective of the child's stage of development and with little inconvenience to the parent; that the child must eat what the parent wants the child to eat; and that the parent owns the child and can do whatever the parent wants to the child. Nowadays there are many parents who do not hold these beliefs, but alas there are many parents who still do.

Those of us born before the 1950s were expected to become toilet trained long before our sphincter muscles had developed to the stage where we could have voluntary control over them, and we were taught that to be dirty was one of the greatest sins. For many of us being toilet trained was the arena in which we learned to think of ourselves as being bad and having to work hard to be good. Many sibling bonds and enmities were forged in this same arena. When six-year-old Alice came without fuss to fetch me because her small brother Milo needed his bottom wiping, I was reminded of situations in my life when, at Milo's age, I was 'told on' for making a mess and then punished and humiliated for it. In the 1950s I was overjoyed to encounter the writings of Dr Benjamin Spock and know that I was not going to be expected to inflict on my baby son what had been inflicted on me. However, the shelves of constipation remedies that can be found nowadays in pharmacies suggest that some of the generations since the 1950s have been toilet trained in emotional circumstances. Equally the number of nurseries which will not accept toddlers who are not toilet trained suggests that there may be many toddlers whose toilet training at the hands of parents who need to work may not be the kind of tolerant, patient training which Dr Spock advised.

I have reached an age where people over 60 see me as one of their generation and assume that I will join them in deploring the way children these days are spoilt by their parents. On a crowded train I was sitting beside such a woman who was becoming increasingly annoyed by a group of young children who were noisy and fractious after what I took to be a Christmas shopping expedition with their mothers. As the children rejected the food that one of the mothers put in front of them and demanded something else, the woman beside me said with considerable self-satisfaction, 'In my day we ate what was put in front of us.' I agreed and privately remembered what would have happened to me if I had refused to eat the food my mother had prepared. Then, as the noise level of the children rose, she added, 'What those kids need is a good hiding.' For many children food and punishment go together.

Sweden was the first country to ban parents from using physical punishment, and in more recent years a number of countries have followed suit. In each case the particular government has had to force the law through despite considerable resistance or had to use a certain advantage to outwit an Opposition which held firmly to the beliefs that, 'I was beaten as a child and it didn't do me any harm' and 'Spare the rod and spoil the child'. The latter belief is usually quoted by certain Christian churches who see inflicting suffering on children as their God-given right. In the UK children do not enjoy the same protection from physical assault that adults enjoy. Parents have the right to inflict 'reasonable chastisement' on their children. The precise level of pain which can be defined as 'reasonable' cannot be defined by law, yet no doubt parents who justify their use of physical punishment as an effective means of discipline would claim that whatever level of pain they inflicted on their child was reasonable.

No doubt Karen's father would have claimed that what he did to his children was reasonable. Karen said, 'He was very strict. He needed to be in control.' She recalled one occasion when the whole family was having a meal in a hotel owned by an uncle. She said, 'Even there I got sent to my room for not eating a meal. It was a battle of wills, because he'd be sitting there as good as saying "You're not going to win", and I'd refuse to eat so, in the end he'd just have to send me away He knew I wasn't going to eat it.' At least in the public dining room she was spared the trauma of having the food forced upon her in the way Nigel Slater's father forced food on him, which was what happened to Karen at home.

Many parents and children enjoy a teasing relationship, but when teasing becomes a cover for the parent's aggression there is no joy in it for the child. Karen had not forgotten the pet tortoise. She said, 'We had a pet tortoise and I used to hate the claws on it, I used to be frightened of it, and he used to say, "Oh just pick it up. It won't hurt you. Pick it up", and I wouldn't. And one day he just picked it up and chased me down the garden path, and there was a coal bunker near the kitchen door and I bashed all my hip going past it, and I ran upstairs and locked myself in the bathroom. He knew I didn't like it but he'd still do that. Looking back now, I think my Mum must have known but she let him do it. Where the food was concerned, I suppose she was too scared to say, "Don't make her."'

Karen learned to associate food, not with the voluptuous pleasure of swallowing something satisfying and delicious, but with the gagging response where the throat goes into spasm and the food is forced out. She said, 'I think that's why I'm not adventurous with food. Rather than try something, my big fear is if I don't like it I'll be heaving. I'd rather just say, "No, thank you." I'm past embarrassment now. I'd rather say no thanks, no gravy, no this or that than sit there struggling to eat it. I think if I start heaving, it will be worse, because that's my biggest fear.'

In her account of her childhood Rose described how, almost immediately on returning home after the war ended, her father took charge of the way his daughters were disciplined. Rose was a very lively six year old, incapable of being the quiet, instantly obedient child her father wanted her to be. His punishment was smacking. His was not a one-smack-and-it's-all-over kind of smack. If in an attempt to avoid the resounding thwack a grown man can inflict on a small child Rose ran away, her father would follow her and administer his punishment. Running away from an angry parent only serves to make the parent angrier, and the punishment when caught much worse. Rose remembered climbing out of an upstairs window to escape her father. Years later, when she had been psychotic, she would hide under her hospital bed and refuse to come out. Rose wondered if this was a re-enactment of something she did in childhood to escape from her father. It probably was. People who have looked for the meaning of their delusions and strange actions when they were psychotic have usually found that they were re-enacting memories from childhood that they saw in their mind's eye, not from an adult's perspective but from that of a child. Members of the Hearing Voices Network have found that by discovering the particular memories that became the auditory hallucinations the person experienced while psychotic, they could significantly diminish the power their voices had over them.[31]

Some children manage to survive relatively well when a parent flies into violent rages and beats them because between such terrifying events the parent is very loving and may even express regret for being so cruel. This was not the case for Rose. She would try to please her father, but she found that to be impossible. If she tried to sit on his lap or kiss him to show that she loved him, he would push her away.

Why did two men from very different backgrounds believe

that they were entitled to beat their children? It is very likely that as children they too were beaten and had dealt with the pain and humiliation by telling themselves that they were being beaten for their own good by their parents and teachers. By denying what they actually felt, they could then justify beating other children as they had been beaten. However, there are many men who suffered beatings as children yet refuse to inflict what they suffered on their own offspring, or if they do resort to hitting their children, they feel guilty afterwards and try to make amends. They certainly do not resort to methods that suggest that they have lost control over themselves, or are so concerned with imposing their will that they lose all reason.

Both men here did have one thing in common. They had both been involved in a long war. When Karen's father was only in his late teens he was going on bombing raids over Germany and knowing that each time he set off the chances were that he would not return. No man left a Japanese prisoner-of-war camp unscathed by his experiences. When the war ended and the prisoners were released, the British and Australian army officers responsible for their welfare instructed these men, traumatised by the brutality of the camp and pitifully thin from years of near starvation, that they were not to speak of their experiences to friends and relatives back home. Such advice, being the general view at the time of the best way to treat trauma, was given to soldiers and civilians alike. So Rose's father said nothing about his experiences and no one explained to Rose what had happened to her father. Rose's mother had talked to her daughters about their absent father and shown them his photograph, but this photograph bore no resemblance to the gaunt, emaciated man who returned home. Rose found him very frightening.

Karen had always been a quiet child but when she was 14 her behaviour changed and she became what psychiatrists call 'high', that is, talkative but unable to engage in conversation, very active but rarely to a sensible purpose, easily distracted, unable to concentrate, revealing a stream of ideas which ranged from the over-optimistic to the grandiose. She was admitted to a large psychiatric hospital and given drugs to quieten her. Then she was transferred many miles away to a clinic where I met her. She did not know why she behaved in this way until her father died and she could allow herself to remember.

Karen told me, 'I can't remember how I got in the situation but I can remember him doing it, and pushing him away when he was going to try to get on top of me, and I can remember the look on his face. It was really frightening. But I don't really remember after that, whether I just ran out, whether we were at home on our own – I don't really remember that. But even if you don't really realise what it is, then years later you can see, looking back, what exactly it was, although at the time – because of the age you are, you're that innocent you don't know quite what's going on. I think I blanked it all out, put it to the back of my mind, then I realised when I got married something was making me sort of fight my husband off even though I wanted a good sexual relationship, but I didn't quite know what was making me do this. I think I must have then remembered something of it, enough to talk to my husband about it. It wasn't really until I suddenly started to have sort of flashbacks that everything became clear and I could connect one thing with another. Not very clearly though. I remember there may have been one occasion when he was messing around, fondled my breasts, but I can't remember if that was before or after I went into hospital. I think I remember it was at a weekend – I used to go home at weekends from hospital, and some weeks I might be on drugs and a bit high. I reckon probably it was a time when I was a bit vulnerable and a bit high, but I imagine it might just have been him and me at home. I can't remember what happened after. I think he would have had full sex if I hadn't pushed him off. He was getting me aroused – although I was enjoying it, I knew it was wrong, and when he overpowered me I really pushed him off. I suppose I must have run out and gone to the bathroom. It frightens me even now to think what could have happened. I just can't believe it really. I suppose partly you don't want to believe it. When I was in hospital they gave me different tablets and I was all over the place. That would probably be when it happened. I can't remember anything before then, not when I was a lot younger. I obviously didn't say anything to anyone. I felt a bit ashamed and shocked. I never told anybody until my husband years after. Anyway, Dad would have said I was mad. I know that for certain. I wouldn't have been believed. He'd have said I imagined it because I was on my tablets, I know that's what would have been his reaction.'

A child who is physically abused by her parent is presented with two views of her world that are impossible to reconcile, namely that the person who should love her and care for her inflicts pain on her and frightens her. Self-confidence is built on a clear, consistent view of the world. Karen had little self-confidence. A particular physical or sexual assault may have been the event that destroyed her fragile picture of herself and her world, forcing her to resort to mania as a desperate defence against the annihilation of her sense of being a person.[32] Once she had been labelled as mad she had little defence against her father's sexual assaults except her own awareness that what he was doing was wrong. But there was no one she could turn to for help. No one protected her from his physical assaults, so no one would protect her from his sexual assaults. The best she could do was to try to forget what had happened.

Rose had no conscious memory of sexual abuse until she became psychotically hypomanic. There is nothing mysterious about psychosis if we think about how we experience ourselves and the world. We operate in what seems to us to be two realities, the reality of our thoughts, feelings, dreams and fantasies, and the reality of the world around us. One of the tasks that confronts us when we are born is to learn to distinguish these two realities. It takes a long time for us to do this. Small children can be confused about whether something was a dream, a fantasy, or a memory of a real event. We never learn this distinction perfectly. In adult life we can wonder whether something actually happened or whether we dreamt it. We need to be confident in our ability to make this distinction. When events conspire against us and we lose all confidence in ourselves we can lose the skill of making the distinction between our internal and external realities. Then the world around us and our inner world flow into one another, and we produce interpretations which other people call hallucinations and delusions. All our interpretations, whether objective and logical or totally fantastic, can come from only one source, our past experience. We have nothing else on which to draw. Whether we produce the correct answer to the solution of an equation or an account of an hallucinatory experience, both have the same source, our past experience. Hallucinations are not random and meaning-less but are themselves meanings which relate to the person's past experiences.

Around the time that the psychiatric staff were finding Rose hiding under her bed, reliving the fear which her father had inspired in her from his beatings, she remembered other things that she had forgotten. It was a powerful memory but hard to define exactly. It seemed to be a dark room, someone else in the room, something pressing on her, something being forced into her mouth. She could not tell whether it was something that had happened several times or only once but it was so terrible it could not be forgotten. Yet she had forgotten and now it was coming back. Later, when she remembered this hallucinatory experience, she interpreted it through her adult experience, that of a mental health professional whose training had in-cluded studies of the effect that childhood sexual abuse had in adult life. She could see how she would have had to repress any knowledge of this – if that was what she was remember-ing – because through her childhood, spent mainly in boarding schools, she had needed to idolise her parents as being wise and loving, even though the evidence to support this belief was very slim. As a child she knew she could not survive without her parents, and so she had to see them as being good. She was not able to create with Elaine the close, supportive relationship of two siblings who know that the only way they can survive with dangerous or neglectful parents is to look after one another. Rose maintained this view of her parents until well into adult life. Then a series of events challenged her view of her parents and her life and she began to feel herself falling apart.

Her defence was to create a fantasy that she had an ex-traordinary power to save her family from some terrible but unidentified danger by sacrificing herself for them. This is a popular fantasy with children who feel themselves to be misun-derstood, unappreciated and unloved by their family. As an or-dinary daydream it can be very satisfactory, but it is a difficult one to act out unless circumstances allow you to become a Joan of Arc, a Christian saint, or a martyr in a jihad. Acting out a compensatory fantasy as a defence against annihilation can never be successful. What we experience as falling apart in the process of being annihilated as a person is actually the falling

apart of those ideas that no longer form a reasonably accurate
picture of our situation. We have discovered that our life is not
what we thought it was. Amongst the ideas that crumble can
be those which enabled us to keep certain memories hidden by
the lies we tell ourselves. In her memoir Rose did not describe
the series of events which showed her that her life was not what
she thought it was, but as her family was central to her life the
events must have thrown doubt on what she had been telling
herself, that she was part of a close, loving family. Those of us
who use fantasising as a form of solace know only too well how
a fantasy can have a life of its own, and what we began as a
pleasant daydream can turn into a nightmare as our own truth
shows us the folly of our dream. If we are engaged in acting out
our fantasy, we can find ourselves acting out the truth that we
had hidden. We enact what we would not say.

There is a Helen Reddy song called 'Angie Baby' with the
line, 'It's so nice to be insane no one asks you to explain.' In a
psychotic state people say things that they had been unable to
say when they were sane. However, telling other people about
the memories that have surfaced during a psychotic period
may allow us to avoid the responsibility of telling other people
quite straightforwardly something that they are likely to find
unpalatable, but these same people can dismiss what we say
as the product of madness. Psychiatrists have always defined
such disclosures as hallucinations and delusions that are
symptoms of a mental illness and have no intrinsic meaning
in themselves.

From reading Rose's memoir I gained the strong impression
that she had grown up in a family where it was impossible to
speak openly about what was happening. In her madness Rose
was able to say what in ordinary life she had felt forbidden to
say. Very early in life Rose was given the role of 'the bad child'.
Elaine felt that this role was justly deserved. Elaine was the
good child and Rose the bad. Straitlaced relatives also agreed.
No child should be so energetic and talkative. Some parents
take great delight in having a lively, energetic, confident, talkative child. However, when parents are beset by anxiety and
suppressed anger, a child's confident and energetic behaviour
can be defined by them as rebelliousness, liveliness as wilfulness. Parents may not be aware that children usually express

their own anxiety and distress in behaviour which they define as 'bad'. Rose was certainly one of those people who dealt with anxiety by keeping busy. As adults people like Rose can put this defence against anxiety to productive use, but as children they are seen as overactive and unable to settle. The other children in the family are likely to accept and use the parents' definition of their sibling as 'the bad child' because that means that they are winning the competition to be the 'goodest' of them all.

In a family where very important things must not be mentioned, a talkative child has to be kept quiet. Parents who are filled with suppressed rage over what has been done to them often take their anger out on their child and blame the child for things which were not the child's responsibility, or for simply behaving as a child. From Rose's descriptions of her reactions to her father's beatings it would seem that she would not have dared to complain about her treatment. She would have to keep her fear and resentment to herself.

Karen's brother Keith and her younger sister Shirley, like Karen, had no difficulty in remembering their father's physical assaults on them. Rose described the terrifying physical punishments she received from her father, and Elaine did not contradict her. Neither of them condemned their father's cruelty. Rose described being smacked as normal. However, when Rose remembered something from her childhood which may or may not have been a sexual assault on her by her father, Elaine was horrified and rejected Rose's interpretation with such vehemence that their close relationship was threatened. Why is sexual assault on a child so much worse than physical assault? Is there something intrinsically terrible about a sexual assault that is absent in physical assault?

Consider this: a child may be sitting in her bath being bathed by her father. His hands are moving all over her body, gently probing in the cracks and crevices of her ears and nose and between her thighs. She is enjoying his devoted attention to her, one person to another. Then, as his hand goes between her thighs she realises that something has changed. He might be still talking to her but he has withdrawn from seeing her as a person. His attention is directed at himself, what he is doing and feeling. She has become an object that he is using for his own personal benefit. It seems to her that her kind, loving father has disappeared and a frightening stranger has taken his place. The stranger is using her body to express his sexual and aggressive needs. She is helpless in his power.

Another scene where a child is sitting in her bath being bathed by her father: his hands are moving all over her body and they are talking to one another, person to person. As his hands go to probe her ears and nose she pulls away and protests. He places one large hand on her head and forces her to be still. She resists, pulls away, screams and cries. He stops trying to reason with her, and with this her kind, loving father disappears to be replaced by a terrifying giant who hits her hard, lifts her out of the bath, puts her across his knee and spanks her. She is now an object that this strange giant can use to express his rage and aggression. In both sexual and physical assault the adult turns the child into an object that he can use for his own purposes. The child feels helpless, totally vulnerable and completely in her assailant's power. Being reduced to such a state damages every human being, adult or child.

Physical assault takes more forms than beatings. Forcing a child to eat by pushing food into the child's mouth is a physical assault. Every parent is familiar with the drama of a child refusing to eat the food that the parents regard as nourishing and necessary. Parents who are not gripped by the desire to force their child to obey every order are usually able to walk away from a confrontation which would achieve nothing but distress on both sides, but a parent who fears being seen as weak cannot accept that sometimes it is best to let a child win. So eating becomes a battlefield and physical assault the means by which the parents can win. In this case the child who refuses to eat finds herself being gripped and rendered helpless by an angry giant. The giant's weapon is something large and horrible that the giant is forcing into her mouth. Her tiny throat closes against this intrusion. Her nose blocks with snot and tears. She is in danger of choking and suffocating.

Part of Elaine's evidence that Rose could not have suffered an act of fellatio by her father was that neither of them had ever seen their father naked. A child ignorant of the appearance of a man's penis would be equally frightened by a large penis or a large spoon piled high with food that the child found inedible – a mass of baked beans or Brussels sprouts or cold potato –

being forced into her mouth by a giant who was pressing back her shoulders and blotting out the light. If we could recognise that physical abuse can create in the child the same degree of terror and helplessness as sexual abuse, we would be able to see that both kinds of abuse are wrong and that the first kind of abuse should not be seen as normal and the second so shocking that it cannot be remembered and talked about openly.

Children can suffer another kind of abuse that involves no physical contact. It is the abuse of being rejected and abandoned by those whose role is to care for you. Karen was not as close to her sister Marjorie, who was nearest to her in age, as she was to her younger sister Shirley. It was on Shirley's twelfth birthday that Karen was taken by her parents to the large psychiatric hospital. She said, 'Going to hospital it was bad enough at my age but being sent away, not knowing what was going on. It took me ages to get over the fact they hadn't told me. For days they just left me there. When we set out that morning I was just told I was seeing a doctor. That was it. I didn't know that my suitcase was under the seat in the van. That really annoys me. Years after Mum said, "We were frightened you'd perhaps lock yourself in the bathroom", but it might have been easier if I'd been prepared. We've talked about it a couple of times. She said she didn't know what to do for the best. She was being told, "We've got to find out what's wrong with her", but I think it could perhaps have been done a bit easier. It was Shirley's birthday – that's why I always remember it. It was her twelfth birthday and that made it all the worse.'

Shortly after Rose's father returned home, her mother sent the children to stay with a relative, just as my mother sent my sister away after I was born. As an adult, intellectually, Rose could understand why her parents needed to be together to get to know one another again, but emotional memories are keener than intellectual ones. Elaine felt that Rose was quite wrong to see being sent away as a rejection. Elaine was sure that what their mother had done was entirely sensible and told Rose so. Here the older sister is telling the younger one that she, Elaine, knows her better than she knows herself. Even if Elaine knew nothing of extraverts and introverts, it is perhaps surprising that Elaine had not noticed how important, indeed essential, relationships were to her extravert sister.

After the war the parents returned to Hong Kong and the two girls were sent to a boarding school in England. Elaine described this as simply what the British who represented the Empire in the colonies did. School rules meant that Rose saw little of her sister, though in the way that bad news travels fast, Elaine always seemed to know when Rose was in trouble for misbehaving. She would speak to Rose most sharply about her shameful behaviour. Rose did not remember her schooldays with great affection.

If your parents send you away from home without any explanation other than that this is the right thing to do, you could not help but suspect your parents did not want you. Similarly, if your father treats you cruelly and your mother does nothing to protect you, you cannot help but suspect that your parents do not love you. How well you can live with such suspicions may depend on what kind of relationships you have with your siblings.

Karen said, 'Even now I can't say I love Mum. There's nothing there. It worries me a bit. I think she probably does love me, but I can't feel the same thing back. I don't remember ever having been cuddled or anything. I think she probably did love me but she just didn't show it. I just accept it. She's my Mum and that's it. She'll always be my Mum.' However, if she became estranged from Shirley, 'I would be gutted. It's the same with my brother Keith. We don't live in the same country but I still feel close to him.' Karen and Keith visited one another frequently, and Karen always described these visits to me as being very happy.

Karen did not tell her sister Marjorie about her memories of her father's sexual assaults, nor did she tell her mother. Marjorie had had her own problems in maintaining her mental stability. Even though she suspected that their father may have had something to do with this, Karen thought that her revelations could upset the balance Marjorie had achieved. Her mother was old and deaf and relied on Karen and Shirley. Karen saw no point in reawakening her mother's memories of what must have been an unhappy marriage. However, she did have long discussions with Shirley and Keith who did not reject Karen's account of how certain memories had returned. They pooled their memories and speculated upon why these things had happened. Karen felt supported and loved.

Rose did not want to fall out with her sister, and she did not want to cause any member of her family distress. Perhaps her situation was similar to that of Orhan Pamuk when he spoke about his memories of his fights with his brother. He wrote: 'When reminded of those brawls, my mother and my brother claimed no recollection of them, saying that, as usual, I'd invented them, just for the sake of something to write about, just to give myself a colourful and melodramatic past. They were so sincere that I was finally forced to agree, concluding that, as always, I'd been swayed more by my imagination than by real life.'[33] But is not our imagination part of our real life? And do we not need to tell our own story in our own way in order to know that we exist?

Terrible though they both are, there is one major difference between physical and sexual assaults by parents on children. Parents know that in a family of more than one child you only have to assault physically one of the children to keep the others in order. Many people have told me that seeing their sibling beaten was more traumatic for them than being beaten themselves. Children in this position often lose all self-confidence and become exceedingly good. Some siblings protect themselves from the horror by joining with their parents in believing that the child who was beaten was bad and deserved the beating. Whether or not the siblings feel sympathetic to the beaten child, they never think of that child as being the parent's favourite.

Paedophiles select their children carefully. Karen told me that her father would never have approached Shirley because Shirley was a great talker, whereas she Karen was very quiet. It is common for paedophiles to tell the children they assault that they are their favourites. Neither Karen nor Rose was ever given the impression that they were their father's favourite, but in a family where there is persistent abuse those siblings who were not abused can be aware that one child is special to the parent in a way that none of the others is. The other children will know that the abused child receives more gifts and privileges than they do, or they may wonder what is wrong with them that they have never been singled out in this way. Quite early in their lives children become aware that in our society sexual attractiveness is regarded as a highly desirable attribute. Part of Elaine's evidence against Rose was that her father had never made any kind of sexual gesture towards her, the older sister. Elaine overlooked the fact that she was older than Rose and better able to describe her father's action to another person. However, when in this situation a sibling asks, 'Why did you prefer my sibling to me?' the question has echoes of a common sibling complaint, 'Why does my parent prefer my sibling to me when I'm prettier/cleverer/gooder than my sibling?' A sibling who asks, 'Why you rather than me?' does not realise that incest, like rape, is more to do with hate, rage, power and revenge than it has to do with desire. Nevertheless, in families where incest occurs, the parent's sexual choice raises all the issues involved in the competition to be the goodest. This can be clearly seen in the family portrayed in Debbie Tucker Green's play *Born Bad*.[34]

Writing about a real live family is always difficult. In Rose's memoir there are references to some unidentified people who may have contributed to the stress that Rose was under before her breakdown. When I wrote about Karen I did not use her real name and I omitted a great deal of what I knew about her life. I included only what I saw as essential to her story. The only way to tell a story completely is to turn it into fiction, but this has the same disadvantage as turning a truth into an hallucination. Other people can say, 'You made that up.' Nevertheless, we can see in fiction truths that might be hidden from us in the reality of our lives.

In presentation, Debbie Tucker Green's play *Born Bad* is very simple. The characters are Dad, Mum, Dawta, Sister 1, Sister 2 and Brother, a blood-related black family where Dawta is also sister to Sister 1 and Sister 2 and to Brother, and all these are 'dawtas' and son to Mum and Dad. The stage is bare except for a few chairs. Once on stage the characters never leave. The text of the play contains virtually no stage directions. All the meaning of the play is in the dialogue.

The following account of the conflicting interpretations of events by the characters is flat and unemotional, and conveys nothing of the drama of the play where people lacerate and are lacerated by the words of their nearest blood relatives, words spoken in the private code which every family develops for itself and which outsiders have to decode. Just as a close family –

close because they have secrets to hide – excludes strangers, so the audience is excluded, being like passer-bys on a pavement that runs past the veranda of the family home where the family conduct their impassioned conversations. We cannot help but stop, curious, wondering, and gradually comprehending what is happening, we are appalled by the cruelty and moved by the loneliness and helplessness of these fellow human beings, and in them see ourselves and the universality of human tragedy.

The plot of the play is very simple. All the action takes place within one day. Dawta has returned to the family home to confront the family with the fact that, as a teenager, she had been sexually abused by Dad. The play is not about whether or not Dawta is telling the truth but about how each member of the family interprets the past, and what effect these interpretations have on the present.

We speak of two people having a relationship, say, Alison and Bob, but there are really two relationships, say, Alison's relationship to her brother Bob and Bob's relationship to Alison. Thus, in a relationship there are two interpretations, as each person interprets the other. Alison may interpret Bob as, 'He's a good, reliable person whom I can trust,' while Bob interprets Alison as, 'I'm very fond of her but she can be clingy.' If Bob and Alison are two of the siblings in a family of four siblings and two parents, and each person interprets the other five, this makes a total of 30 interpretations. But Alison also interprets Bob's interpretation of her, and Bob interprets Alison's interpretation of Bob. Alison suspects that Bob thinks she's clingy and she feels that he is wrong, while Bob feels that Alison has overestimated just how reliable he is. (If you're interested you can do the arithmetic to work out how many interpretations so far.) However, Alison also interprets the other family members' interpretations of other family members, and so does every other member of the family. Thus Alison can create the interpretation, 'Bob thinks that Colin loves Dad but actually Colin's never forgiven Dad for not being sympathetic to Edith when Mum was making so many demands on Edith.' Judy Dunn has shown that children as young as 18 months can have the ability to interpret other family members (Chapter 2) so the number of interpretations of interpretations that can be made in a family over time is infinite. Yet family life is largely made up of such interpretations. No play, novel, biography, psychological description or theory can take account of every interpretation created by a family, yet every interpretation created can affect in one way or other the life of each family member.

There is a multitude of plays and novels about family life and these usually concern many aspects of that family's life – aspects to do with politics, money, religion, class and race, and with people outside the family. In *Born Bad* all these aspects are missing, except for the religious beliefs of Mum and Sister 1. By excluding everything extraneous to the immediate story the playwright presents us with the family's conflicting interpretations of one stage of the family's history. Such interpretations are not chosen randomly by each individual. Each person chooses an interpretation that will both validate and defend the individual's sense of being a person. Such interpretations might require the individual to deny certain of their own memories and/or the memories of other family members.

Debbie Tucker Green writes about a black family because that is the background she knows well, but what she portrays are universal experiences. When they want to use their child for their own purposes many parents give the child to understand that he is special to them. It may be that the parent wants the child to be untroublesome and obedient, or to take responsibility for the parent, or to fulfil the parent's sexual urges. The child interprets 'special' as meaning that the parent loves the child, when all that the parent means is that the child is special in the same way as we regard a particularly useful object as being special. Both my computers are special to me, as is one of my potato peelers.

Dawta had felt that she was special to her father and so she had performed what he demanded, but as she got older she sometimes doubts his love. She needs to have him confirm that to him she is special because without that she would feel degraded. At the same time she wants her mother to admit that she had allowed her husband to use Dawta so that she, the mother, no longer had to fulfil her marital duties. Thus Dawta had not been 'born bad' as the mother always insists. Dawta also wants her sisters to acknowledge that the sexual abuse had happened and Dawta was not to blame. Dawta dreams of her family recognising her martyrdom and the part they played in it and so humbly begging her forgiveness. However, Dawta cannot be content with fantasy. She wants the real thing.

Being special to her father had always supported Dawta's sense of being a person, while being rejected by her mother and sisters has threatened her sense of being a person. Dawta wants confirmation of her worth from all her family so badly that she is blind to the fact that, if her mother and sisters admit that Dawta has been the victim of the father, she can no longer feel proud that she was special to her father. If her father was a villain how can she draw comfort from being special to a villain?

Dawta has returned to her family home with the aim of having her interpretations confirmed. Her mother would admit her guilt and say that she was sorry, and her sisters would confirm that they had known about the abuse and were wrong to blame her for it. The one confirmation Dawta feels sure of receiving is from her brother whom she loves and feels she knows well. The tragedy of the play is that all her interpretations are disconfirmed. This is a tragedy worse than death, because in death pain and conflict come to an end, while in disconfirmation pain and conflict overwhelm and defeat.

We can suffer two kinds of disconfirmation. The first is where the other people persist in their view that they are right and we are wrong. The second is where we discover that we had failed to observe something important in our situation. Dawta suffers both kinds of disconfirmation. All her family insist that they are right. She discovers from Brother something that Sister 1 confirms, that Dad also abused Brother. Brother knew that Dad was abusing Dawta but he believes that he was special to Dad because, 'All the things you wouldn't do I guess, I got.' To which Dawta replies, 'There was nothing I wouldn't do. Brother. There was no choice.' So concerned with her own situation had she been that she had failed to notice what was happening to Brother. Sister 1 points out to her that, at breakfast, 'You never wondered why he weren't down there the mornings you was? There wasn't a science to it.' Dawta can no longer see herself as being special and as being a martyr sacrificed by Mum.

The other members of the family cannot change their interpretations because they maintain their sense of being a person. To be able to live with herself Mum needs to see herself as a good mother, and she wants Dawta to admit that she recognises this. However, the only way she can see herself as a good person is to see Dawta as bad. If Dawta was not bad then she, her mother, has failed in her duty to care for her child. Dawta did not become bad because of her upbringing but she was 'born bad'. She tells Dawta, 'I knew you were born bad right from the beginning.' Such a view of her daughter is in line with her Christian religion which sees children as being 'born in sin'. No amount of goodness on her part could have prevented Dawta from doing what she did.

When Dawta confronts Sister 1, Sister 1 admits that, as much as she does not want to think about the past, fragmentary memories keep breaking through. As the play progresses it becomes clear that Sister 1 remembers far more than fragments. Sister 1 cares about Dawta and does not see her as being born bad. She tells Dawta, 'And it was me who'd pack your school bag knowing that you'd never have time. And it was me laid out your school clothes knowin you wouldn't have time.' Sister 1 knows that Mum chose to see Dawta as born bad and that Mum chose Dawta to take her place in the marital bed. 'She chose you because she wouldn't let him. She chose you. Deliberate. Decisive.' Sister 1 takes pride in the fact that she sees things as they are, and, because she does not lie to herself, she can love her siblings. However, she needs to protect herself from the pain of the pity she would feel for Dawta if she could not comfort herself with the belief that Dawta was strong and well able to bear the burden of what she had been chosen to do. She says, 'You got the gift, the gift of strength, you did. Give thanks for that. God made you like that – made you strong like that. Mum saw that strength, seeing that made her choice – made her choice easy. You made her choice easy, God gifting you how you are – that you could take it like that and I pray for you.' She tells herself that her prayers were answered. She envies Dawta for the strength God gave her. 'You got gifted that and, I never got gifted by God nuthin.' She was not strong, she was not special.

Sister 2 hates Dawta. She sees her as bad – lying and manipulating. She says, 'Move away from mi cos I know you're lying – I know you're lying – I was there.' Dawta asks her to tell her how she knows she's lying. Sister 2 says, 'Cos he never. Yeh?

He never. Not a once. Not a once – yeh. Not my cute little head plait wide eye's home made fresh face, nothing.' However, such proof is not uncomplicated. Sister 2 is jealous that she had not been special in any way to her parents. Her father had not seen her as sufficiently attractive to engage his attention, while her mother, 'She liked you – yeh – and you know it, you come out first – first born and adored – yeh, it was you, then it was her Jesus – you was even ahead a him – then her, then him – then the next one me – yeh, me somewhere down the ass end of the family tree.'

By blaming Dawta, Sister 2 could try to keep from herself the devastating thought that she was the unwanted, unloved runt of the family. That way she did not have to blame her parents for her unhappy childhood. She needs to be loved by Dad but he ignores her. She is jealous that Sister 1 loves Dawta and watched over her and she wants Sister 1 on her side, but by blaming Dawta she prevents herself from being close to Sister 1. She rejects Brother's advice that she should sort out her issues, and thus, in defending herself as a person, she maintains her isolation in the family.

Each person is alone, locked in their own private world of meaning, but perhaps Brother is the loneliest of all. We can guess that he has no lover to comfort him because he shrinks away from human touch. People who cannot bear to be touched often take pride in their ability to keep themselves to themselves, being self-sufficient and asking nothing of other people, but such pride is a defence against the wretchedness of feeling unloved and unlovable. They fear too that if other people get too close to them they will see that in essence the person is vile and evil, and retreat in disgust. Brother needs his parents to love him. He values himself so little in order that he can value his parents more. He chides Dawta for the way she turned on her mother, calling her a bitch. He says, 'She's our mum she borned us out and I ent sayin shit. I ent saying niche.' He protects his mother because 'she didn't have a clue' about his father abusing him, and he protects his father because 'he chose me', and 'He told me I was the only –' to which Dawta replies, 'So he said the same shit to me.' This leaves Brother in agony, 'Which makes me what – which makes me what? Which makes me more nuthin then.'

All through the play Dad sits silently. Silence is his power. Dawta, Sister 2 and Brother have asked him to confirm his love for them and he has not responded. The last scenes of the play reveal that Mum also needs his confirmation. Sister 1 may have transferred her need for confirmation from Dad to Jesus, but none of them has the strength to accept that Dad does not love his family but needs them as objects that confirm his sense of who he is. He prides himself in his power over them. Dad needs them to confirm that he is powerful and, like all tyrants, he has to hurt to demonstrate his power. At the end of the play his victim is Mum. He orders his children to tell her how she failed to protect her son, and he administers the last blow by stripping her of her protective belief that Dawta was born bad. He says, 'You made the wrong choice.'

The play ends with stalemate, the greatest tragedy of all. No one can move, no one can change. Like the trio in Sartre's play *No Exit*, they are all trapped in hell forever.

Were Debbie Tucker Green a romantic writer she would have written a second act where all the family members come together to confront and resolve their differences and declare their love for one another. To do so they would each have to be suffused with courage and a love of truth that would hold them together while the ideas that sustained each of them crumbled away to be replaced with a new conception of themselves. None of the characters has such strength and honesty. They are simply ordinary, fallible human beings, just as we all are.

There are many families like this one, tied together by the bond of family relationships, yet each person is alone, unable to communicate openly and truthfully with other family members. Some families are united only by the pretence that they are a close, loving family. Others come together only to bicker and disagree. Some siblings sever their relationships with one another, but they then find that the severance has become a wound that does not heal. The secrets that divide families may be no more than various fallings-out over petty matters, but they are matters that relate to the siblings' image of themselves, and so they find that they cannot move from the positions they have taken in the family. Even if they want to change their self-image, they can find that the other family members will not let them. One woman told me, 'I run my own

successful business, but when I go home for the family Christmas they reduce me to the little girl who can't even tie her own
shoelaces.'

In my conversations with siblings who were in this situation
I usually gained the impression that they wanted, perhaps only
vaguely, to resolve this situation but they did not know how. No
one wanted to make the first move because that would make
them vulnerable to attack by the other siblings. Perhaps the
point to start would be to understand what memory is.

## Memories matter

As a reader of the *New Scientist* I have come to the conclusion that there are many scientists who believe that it is only a
matter of time before they and their colleagues make the dis-
coveries that will ensure that we have a pain-free existence.
We shall feel neither the physical pain that tells us there is
something wrong with our bodies nor the mental pain that
tells us there is something amiss in the way we live our lives.
A recent report concerned the work of some scientists who believe that, now it has been shown that memories are formed by
certain neurones in the brain linking together, all they have
to do is find the drug which would stop this happening when
the memory to be formed would be painful.[35] These scientists
do not seem to have realised that we learn more from our pain
and our failures than from our pleasure and success. The latter
pass easily from our minds: the former we have to think about,
and in so doing we can increase our understanding of what life
is about.

When I first met Karen I was shocked by what had happened
to her, but years later she said to me, 'I think it was a good
thing that I went away from home to the clinic. It meant I had
to make a life for myself. It made me more independent and
stronger. So probably it was a good thing. I think that what I've
gone through has helped me as a person.'

We have to create a story of our life that is coherent, otherwise we feel incomplete and confused. Wipe out our bad memories and our story can never be coherent. We are our memories
and our memories are us. When someone denies our memories
that person denies us. If siblings are to get along together – and

not merely pretend to do so – they have to discard the notion that there is One True History and accept that, while events do occur, every participant and observer of that event has their own individual interpretation of it. If a sibling's interpretation of an event makes you feel uncomfortable, your task should not be to deny this alternative interpretation but to discover why that interpretation makes you feel uncomfortable. Not that this is easy. In this chapter I have written about being betrayed by parents, but what happens when one sibling betrays another sibling, or one sibling shows outstanding loyalty to the other?

# Chapter 8

# LOYALTY AND BETRAYAL

Some years ago I was betrayed by a person I thought was a good friend. I shall call him George. I had known George for nearly 20 years and I had always thought that he had my interests at heart. However, a situation arose which he saw as one where he had a choice of playing safe and protecting his own interests or taking a small risk to protect mine. He chose to protect his own interests. I learned of this through a third party. Had my erstwhile friend talked to me about his decision before he acted on it I would have been sad, but at least prepared for what was to follow. However, he did not. I was hurt and angry and despised him for his cowardice in not warning, and still do.

I always ponder for a long time about significant events in my life, trying to bring into clear consciousness what such events actually mean to me. I saw George's action as a betrayal, but I also came to see that I was not interpreting this betrayal in terms of the multitude of petty but hurtful betrayals my sister had inflicted on me. People betray one another for many different reasons, but all such betrayals fall into one of two categories. There are betrayals where the betrayer is acting in his own interests, knowing or hoping, even self-deludingly hoping, that the person he has betrayed will survive. This was the kind of betrayal George had effected. In the second kind of betrayal, the betrayer may not even be acting in his own interests. The aim of his treachery is to injure, even destroy the person he has betrayed. This is the nature of sibling betrayal.

In childhood when siblings fight, in that moment of intense anger one sibling wants the other sibling dead, annihilated, vanished forever into non-existence, expunged from memory. It is death of the body and annihilation of the person. Only then can the betrayer feel vindicated. When the moment of anger passes the child who would betray his sibling in such a fashion is forced to recognise that this person is a fixity not so easily removed. The child who at the height of his anger wished his sibling dead may find that his anger has turned to the coldness of the desire for revenge. He now looks for some method of subtle but devastating vengeance. E. Arnot Robertson's novel *Ordinary Families* is the story of a revenge conceived in childhood by the younger sister Margaret and inflicted in instalments on her sister Lallie. Margaret did not want to destroy Lallie entirely in one onslaught. She wanted to attack Lallie when she least expected it, and thus remind Lallie of her power.[1]

After his anger cools, another child might then remember that the existence of his sibling is important to him because his sibling gives him a sense of security that no one else can. This is where sibling loyalty is different from the loyalty we can give to those people we see as giving us something in return for our loyalty. They might give us financial security, or a certain status in society, or the love that assures us that we are loved and needed, that we are an altogether worthwhile person. Young children have nothing like this to exchange for loyalty. They have only themselves, their own existence, and by continuing to exist young children give each other a point of fixity in an ever changing world which the children can neither understand nor control. In sibling loyalty all that matters is that the other exists.

Betrayals and loyalties feature in the lives of all siblings. One may dominate over the other, depending on how the siblings interpret the circumstances in which they find themselves. Whether a sibling chooses to be loyal or to betray depends on how each sibling deals with any threat to his sense of being a person. Maintaining and defending the sense of being a person is our prime need. A loyal sibling will lay down their life for their sibling provided they know that they will die as themselves. Faced with the choice of being annihilated as a person or betraying our sibling, we can feel that we are being forced into an act of betrayal. We have to do this, for to act as we are not, to give up everything in our life which sustains us, is to consign ourselves to a living death. We breathe but we do not live.

Sometimes one person betrays another because not to do so

would mean that the person had to take responsibility for his action, and that would mean recognising that he is not the person he wants to think he is. My friend Charles told me about a squabble he had with his older brother Martin when he was eight and Martin was ten. He said that he had forgotten what the squabble was about but it was over something that mattered very much to him at the time. When Martin, using his superior size, placed some stinging blows, Charles, was very upset. Their mother intervened to protect Charles. She told Martin that he was being cruel to Charles and to make amends he should go to the shop and buy Charles a Kit-Kat chocolate bar. Martin went, but came back with a tin of Kitekat pet food which he insisted his mother had told him to buy. At the age of ten Martin must already have constructed a picture of the very moral man he is now. Rather than admit he had been cruel to his brother, he denied responsibility for what he had done and thus took revenge on his brother while preserving his picture of himself as being good.

## Childhood betrayals and loyalties

As an adult it is always difficult to talk about events like Martin's betrayal of Charles without sounding petty. Do so and others, particularly your siblings, are likely to say reprovingly, 'You should be over that by now.' That does not make your pain any less keen because small though the actual event was it revealed something about your position in the family. Max was the youngest in a family of four siblings. When he was five he was given a scooter which became his prize possession. By the time he was eight he had outgrown it but he loved it still. One day he came home and found that his big sister had given the scooter to a child in a neighbouring family. He told me, 'Thirty-five years later it still hurts.'

After I had listened to the recording of our discussion I emailed Max to ask if he had ever talked to his sister about the incident. He replied, 'I raised it the next day because I was very upset. However, it was in a blaming context of "how could you be so mean?". The response was, as always, a diatribe about what a nasty, selfish prat I was and how I didn't need the scooter and how I should get over it. The Scooter Incident is now part of our family lore, but I have never calmly asked my sister about it or told her how it made me feel. I feel I wouldn't get very far with that discussion even if I approached it calmly. However, I have subsequently learned that the boy my sister had given the scooter to was the son of a woman whose husband had left her with four children and no money. I realise now that I can focus on how much pleasure that scooter would have given that little boy. While I can still feel cross about the treatment I got, it's lovely to have a positive thing to think about instead of letting myself be angry about it. Looking back, I think that I probably would have given the scooter to him myself if only I'd been asked.'

Most of us can tell stories from our childhood which end with, 'I wouldn't have minded if only I'd been asked.' Being asked means being treated as a person: not being asked means being treated as an object.

In our experience of betrayals in childhood so much depends on how our parents dealt with the arguments we have with our siblings. Charles's mother stepped in to protect him. I remember an incident where my mother protected me from my sister when I was four and my sister ten. I think I remember this incident for the same reason that Diana Mosley remembered her father (Farve) travelling on the train with the whole family. She wrote: 'When we were small we took our pony in the carriage with us; Muv, Farve, Nanny, Ada, Nancy, Tom, me, Dicky, Brownie and Luncheon Tom, all in a third class carriage. Brownie was an extremely small Shetland pony. I think it was saintly of Farve to travel with us children; possibly it only happened once, and that is why we never forgot it.'[2]

When I was four autograph books were all the rage. My sister had one. I must have been intrigued by the way she studied it, reading and re-reading the verses friends had written and commenting on the signatures. One day when my sister was out I had the idea to write my name in her autograph book. This I did in big capital letters, filling the whole of one page with the name everyone called me, DOT. When my sister discovered what I had done she was incandescent with rage. I should not have even dared touch her book, much less write in it. She showed the offending page to Mother and in tragic, angry tones cried, 'She's ruined it. I'll have to throw it away.'

Mother looked at the page where the word DOT reached the very edges and did not seem angry. She told my sister not to make a fuss. I was astounded. Mercifully, I have forgotten the revenge my sister wreaked on me in the privacy of our bedroom, something more easily forgotten in comparison to the unique event of my mother being loyal to me instead of my sister. When I was writing this it occurred to me that perhaps the reason my mother never defended me from my sister's assaults (although, like Orhan Pamuk's mother, she would stop us fighting if the noise disturbed her) was that she was trying to make up to my sister for what had happened to her when I was born. The autograph book was an exception to this rule because my mother, like many Australians of her generation, valued education and she was pleased with my progress. However, if she had been trying to right the balance, she failed. My sister's sense of injustice in no way diminished, while I became increasingly certain that I was an unloved and unwanted child, allowed to remain in the family only on sufferance. I cannot help envying the Australian writer Elizabeth Jolley who wrote: 'Once, years ago, my sister wanted to sell me her bicycle. "Sisters do not buy and sell with each other," my mother said, "sisters share."'[3]

There is no greater story of sisters sharing than that of Molly, aged 14, Daisy, 8 and Gracie, 11, who were amongst the stolen generation of aboriginal children. Led by Molly, the three girls escaped from the Moore River Native Settlement, where they had been confined after being taken against their will from their home, and walked 1600 kilometres back to their family at Jigalong on the edge of the Little Sandy Desert in northern Western Australia. They followed the rabbit-proof fence that ran north to south, living off the land and avoiding the police and trackers who were searching for them. Their story was told by Molly's daughter, Doris Pilkington,[4] and made into a most beautiful film of the same name. The degree of loyalty which the girls showed to one another suggests that the idea of loyalty to one's siblings had been presented to each girl by the adults in their family as an absolute and unquestionable rule of life. Siblings look after one another. They might deplore what one another did, just as Molly and Daisy deplored Gracie's decision to leave them in the forlorn hope of finding her mother in Wiluna, but they accepted it without rancour, just as Molly accepted that she would have to carry Daisy when the terrain was very difficult and Daisy was tired and her feet very sore.

Richard's parents had presented him and his two older brothers with the same kind of absolute, unquestionable rule, that siblings looked after one another and are loyal to one another. When I asked Richard what kind of feelings he had for his brothers he replied, 'Brotherly love. I know my brothers as well as I could know anyone. If I picked up the phone and asked them for anything it would be done. They could do the same, ask me for anything and I'd do it.' Richard's wife Sarah told me that when she first met Richard's brothers she saw that they treated Richard as their kid brother, but what amazed her was how well they looked after him.

Blaming and betraying a sibling can be useful weapons in the intense rivalry over who is the 'goodest' in the family. My sister expected that my mother would see my use of her autograph book as an act of wickedness, but she did not, while Max's mother agreed with his sister that he was wickedly selfish. When parents accept the word of the betrayer rather than that of the betrayed, the betrayer is rewarded for his treachery. Telling on and being told on are events in most siblings' lives, but there are exceptions. Simone de Beauvoir and her sister Poupette had worked out that it was better to stick together against the adults. Simone wrote: 'We stood staunchly by one another whenever it was a question of facing grown-up music; if one of us upset a bottle of ink, we both took the blame and claimed common responsibility for what had happened.'[5]

Michael Rosen and his brother Brian had also worked out a way of supporting one another in the face of their father's anger. Michael said, 'My brother had a difficult relationship with my dad, but not with my mum. All in all, my dad was just crazily demanding. Brian could never be good enough, and I was often good enough, but when I wasn't I could laugh it off. This is something my brother taught me to do, and I will always be grateful to him for that. I would see my dad having a go at him. Then Brian would come back to our room and act it out, imitating my dad going on, "What do you think you're doing?" and all the rest of it, and we'd be laughing. We'd just turn it into a joke, bat it away, so that it lost all its sting. Brian had de-stung Dad. But of course Brian was stung.'

Throughout history children have recognised that, in the absence of adult care, they have to band together to protect themselves. In his history *Witnesses of War: Children's Lives Under the Nazis*, Nicholas Stargardt showed how some children in the Warsaw ghetto and the concentration camps formed groups bonded by loyalty and mutual need. In another place and time the mutual need might not be food and shelter but to be recognised as a person and all which that entails. Tim Guest was one of those children who had no choice but to follow their parents into the ashrams of Bhagwan Shree Rajneesh. There the adults were totally absorbed in themselves and their worship of the Bhagwan. According to the Bhagwan's teachings, children needed to be free to grow. Thus Tim and his friends were free of all adult supervision. Tim has described his childhood in his memoir *My Life in Orange,*[6] where he told how his mother joined the Bhagwan and became an Orange Person. Tim could visit his mother from time to time but it was up to him to get himself to communal meals and to find clean clothes in the communal laundry. Left to themselves, the children of the Orange People banded together and created their own games.

The children were free to wander in and out of some of the adults' group activities, so very likely they had seen the adults playing the game Lifeboat which is used in encounter groups where the participants are supposed to discover (encounter) their true selves. In this game the participants make a lifeboat out of cushions, get in it, and pretend that they are survivors of a shipwreck floating in an empty ocean. How they deal with this situation is supposed to reveal the innermost secrets of their personality. In the course of the game some participants are thrown from the lifeboat by the others, and some choose to fling themselves into the sea where they will perish. My friend Peter told me that when he played this game he had no sooner entered the lifeboat than he threw himself out of it. He had expected the other participants to reject him, so he got his rejection in first. The game ends when only one participant is left in the lifeboat or the boat is entirely empty. The children built their own lifeboat out of pillows and duvets. However, they created a different version of the game. They all wanted to stay together in the lifeboat. If an adult attempted to join in the game the children would not let them get in the boat. If by chance one of the children fell in the water, the other children would cry 'Shark' and haul him back in. The adults' Lifeboat game was a self-regarding pretence: the children's lifeboat was an accurate picture of their real situation.

These children showed very clearly that they did not trust adults, and well they might. Children may betray one another, but the scale of their perfidy is minute compared to that of adults who betray children. Adults who sexually abuse children are betraying them, and throughout history children have been sexually abused.[7] Reports of child sexual abuse always provoke shock and horror in adults, but the shock and horror response of adults to those who betray children by physically abusing them is quite limited. Many adults excuse any physical punishment of children on the grounds that they were punished in this way when they were children and it had done them no harm. They fail to see that the harm it did them was that it enabled them to betray children in the way that they were betrayed. Toddlers may be able to understand their siblings' thoughts and feelings well enough to know what would upset their sibling and then carry out this act, but they have no idea of the complexities of an adult betrayal until an adult does betray them. Betrayal by an adult is painful, frightening and very confusing. No toddler is capable of preparing an act of betrayal over days or even months, nor can a toddler understand that a betrayer can choose a victim simply because that person is weak and ignorant.

The mistaken belief that 'children forget' is used by adults as an excuse to cover not only sexual and physical abuse but that multitude of small acts of betrayal which adults perpetrate against children. Often these acts of betrayal spring from the curious pleasure that some adults take in fooling a naive child. I could understand, though not enjoy, my sister's acts of betrayal but there was one act of betrayal by my mother which puzzled me when it happened and puzzles me still.

My maternal grandparents and their unmarried son Jack lived on a small property 13 miles from where I lived. Every Saturday Dad would drive Mother and me to my grandparents' home and collect us in the evening. My grandmother kept chickens and from time to time my uncle kept an animal or two. When I was about nine Uncle Jack bought two pigs and put them in a pen in the paddock. I was very interested in these pigs and spent much time in their company. I knew that the pigs were being fattened for slaughter. I accepted this but announced that when it happened I would not eat any of the meat. I could not do that to my friends.

I was not there when the pigs were slaughtered and on our next weekly visit nothing was said about the pigs. When I found they had disappeared from their pen I assumed that they had been sold. On our Saturday visits Mother usually cooked a midday dinner which was always the typical Australian meal in those days, roast meat, vegetables and gravy. I ate the plate of food my mother put in front of me and then my mother, with a little smile, told me that I had eaten my pet pig.

Why had she done this to me? It was not that I was anorexic and needed to be tricked into eating. Quite the reverse, I ate too much. There was no need for my mother to tell me what I had eaten. I had not asked, and there was no crackling or apple sauce, just two slices of some bland meat. (My mother was what was known then as 'a good, plain cook', and a good, plain cook could make beef, lamb, pork and chicken quite indistinguishable.) What she had done was not intended as a joke. My mother had no sense of humour. She did not understand jokes so she never made one. Now, years later, I can only surmise that as my mother had grown up in a family of six siblings in which she was the fourth she was well acquainted with the tricks older children play on the younger ones. She probably would have known what it was like to have tricks played on her, and to expunge her humiliation she probably played tricks on her younger brother and sister. At some point early in their lives my two uncles had fallen out with one another and, following in the family tradition of not speaking, they never spoke to one another again. While the four sisters kept in contact with one another, the siblings could not be described as loving and close. My mother was fond of her youngest sister, my Auntie Doff, but she never spared any of her siblings her criticism of them. Perhaps my mother had found those childhood betrayals of one another very painful and she had much left-over hurt which she could expend on me, a trusting, gullible child. Perhaps the same could be said of a woman whose interaction with her children I had the opportunity to watch.

On the lower deck of London buses there is a space for wheel-chairs, prams and pushchairs. Sometimes this space becomes a stage where all kinds of dramas are acted out. I was in the audience for one of these dramas when I was sitting facing this space and two women, locked in an intense conversation got on the bus. They had with them a baby in a pushchair and three children, boys aged about eight, seven and six. Whatever these children did, they couldn't interrupt the women's conversation for more than a moment. The baby became restless and cried, and one woman, whom I took to be the mother, extracted a bottle from her bag and pushed it into the baby's mouth, all without ceasing to talk to her friend. However, the baby did get more of her attention than the oldest boy who pressed himself against her and tried to interrupt her conversation with a re-peated question, but she ignored him and several times pushed him away.

The bus was crowded and the three boys had to cram them-selves into small spaces in order to stay near the women. They quickly tired of this and as soon as there was room they started to climb up and stand on the handrails. The woman sitting beside me and I watched anxiously, fearing that the bus might suddenly stop and the boys crash to the floor, but the mother and her friend paid no notice at all. The smaller boys soon found this climbing too difficult, but the oldest boy was proud of his skill and tried to get his mother to look at what he was doing. She did not look but she paused in her talking long enough to give the seven-year-old boy a fifty-pence piece. This only increased the oldest boy's entreaties. When she ignored him he moved to the side of the bus and kicked it several times as hard as he could. She did not notice, so he returned to press-ing himself against her and asking her for his money. This time she tried to silence him by picking him up as if he were a toddler and putting him on her lap. At first he tried to comply, hoping that this might lead her to actually talk to him, but he was far too big for her lap and had to wriggle free. With this the mother looked at the woman sitting beside me and said, 'I don't know what's wrong with him. He's a terrible trouble to me.'

Shamed at being brought to a stranger's notice, the boy moved away from her and stood silently for a while, but no doubt the thought that his brother had been given some money forced him to try again to get his mother to talk to him. He became more insistent and finally she looked at him and began to explain in a 'trust me, I'm your mother' tone of voice that she could not give him any money because she needed what she had for their train fares. He was unconvinced, so then she told him that on Saturday, if he was good, she would give him some money. He said, 'No you won't. You'll trick me and you won't give me any.' His mother did not deny this. I left the bus wondering if, when this boy grew up, he would vent his anger with his mother on other women in his life. Would he also feel that he could betray his siblings and other people in the way his mother had betrayed him?

When adults are teaching children to be good in the way that adults define 'good' they often betray the children by telling them lies. Some of these adults would say that they cannot tell the child the truth because the child is too young to understand it. Some adults defend themselves by arguing that if children are not taught that 'If you're good nothing bad will happen to you' as part of a religious belief they will have no morals and go completely out of control. Some adults are themselves so in thrall to a lie that they are unaware that it is a lie. It was adults like these who perpetrated what is perhaps the greatest mass betrayal of children the world has ever seen, that by the Nazis on my generation of German children.

The television documentary *Hitler's Children*[8] told the story of the Hitler Youth. In Germany in the 1920s there were a variety of movements similar to the Boy Scouts and Girl Guides but when Hitler came to power all of these except the Hitler Youth were abolished. When they were ten, boys were required to join the *Deutsches Jungvolk* (German Young People) and at 13 they transferred to the *Hitler Jungvolk* (Hitler Youth) where they stayed until they were 18. Girls at ten joined the *Jungmädelbund* (League of Young Girls) and at 14 transferred to the *Bund Deutscher Mädel* (League of German Girls). The boys were trained to be soldiers and the girls to be mothers. They were taught that there was nothing nobler they could do than lay down their lives for their Führer. The children were presented with a very simple view of the world. Nicholas Stargardt wrote: 'With their dichotomy between good and evil, their appeal to feeling and their demand for moral commitment, Nazi values could have been designed for adolescents.'[9]

In his memoir *A Hitler Youth,* Henry Metelmann described how he was drawn to the Hitler Youth and all it taught despite the fact that his parents did not share his admiration for Hitler. As a Hitler Youth he had holidays the like of which his parents could have never afforded, and he could make many friends. Young Henry was a boy who was interested in action, not in critical thought. He described his reaction when a neighbour was arrested:

> I personally liked Herr Eyken. He had always been
> friendly to me, had gone out of his way when he saw me
> in the street to say something funny to make me laugh.
> Deep down I could not accept that he could be a traitor
> or whatever. On the other hand, having been taught in
> the Hitler Youth that it was necessary to take people
> into custody for security reasons, I could and would
> not believe, as my parents did, that our government
> would do something wrong, something illegal.[10]

Even when he joined the army and was sent to the Russian front he did not question what he had been taught:

> To my shame, up to Stalingrad I had still been full of
> the Hitler Youth 'ideals'. Only after that battle and the
> retreat did they begin to crumble. The very nature of
> the battle in the east was that we often stayed in one
> place for a period, and, during one of these periods,
> I fell in love with a Russian girl, Anna. I learned to
> appreciate her great human quality, which at the same
> time was a recognition that my conviction of German
> racial superiority was nothing more than a nonsense.[11]

When the German army was in full retreat before the Russian army and the Allies were advancing from the west, the Nazi Party Gauleiter was entrusted with raising a final levy of teenage boys and late middle-aged men called the Volkssturm to be a last ditch defence. As far as Goebbels and Hitler were concerned: 'It was morally preferable that the whole nation should be annihilated than that it should capitulate.'[12] The inexperienced youths in the Volkssturm were no match for the Russian tanks. A great many of them died or were wounded. Once it was clear that Hitler was not going to save Germany from the Russians, German adults realised that they needed to pretend to the Russians that they had had no connection with the Nazis. The Russians advanced:

As adults burned their old uniforms, Party badges and many of their own books, including their children's, they ritually rid themselves of many things their children had been brought up to prize. For children and teenagers, the moment when they had to tear off their Hitler Youth badges and throw away their daggers was often bitter, and undermined all they had ever been taught about duty, obedience and honour. Some boys secretly noted where the weapons had been thrown, so they could retrieve them later.[13]

Because it is always so difficult and yet so necessary for us to feel that our understanding of what is going on is reasonably accurate, being lied to is a betrayal. At the end of the war German children discovered that the adults they depended on had lied to them twice, first about the virtue and truth of Nazism, and second about how they, the adults, had never supported the Nazis. When we, as children, discover that we have been lied to by our parents or by our older siblings, we feel enormous pain. Later, through our adult eyes, we might understand why these people thought it necessary to lie to us, but that does not lessen the sense of being betrayed when we were naive children. In *Hitler's Children* several members of the *Hitler Jungvolk* and the *Jungmädelbund*, now in their seventies and eighties, were interviewed. What was very striking was the pain in their eyes as they told their stories. The pain of betrayal had not diminished in any way.

Heinrich Böll tried to convey this pain in his novel *The Clown*. In telling his story Hans kept returning to the memory of Herbert Kalick who at 14 ran the local Boys' Brigade: 'My mother had generously put our grounds at his disposal so we could all be trained in the use of bazookas. My eight-year-old brother Leo was along, I saw him marching past the tennis court with a practice-bazooka on his shoulder, his face as serious as only a child's can be.' Hans went along with his brother but, in an argument with Kalick, Hans, only 11 years old, called him a 'Nazi swine'. Kalick arrested him, locked him in the shed and then, having organised a group of adults to try him, took him into the drawing room of Hans' parents' house for a hearing. Hans tried to explain that he had not heard these words said but had seen them written on a railway barrier. '"The boy doesn't know what he's saying," my father said, putting his hand on my shoulder. Brühl scowled at my father, then glanced nervously toward Herbert Kalick. Obviously he interpreted my father's expression as being far too strong an expression of sympathy. My mother, who was crying, said in her soft, stupid voice: "You can see he doesn't know what he's doing, he doesn't realize – if he did, I would have to turn my back on him." "Go ahead, turn your back," I said.'

Hans was sentenced to dig a tank trap in the garden. It went across his grandfather's favourite flower bed, 'aiming directly at the copy of the Apollo of Belvedere, and I was looking forward to the moment when the statue would fall to my excavatory zeal. I rejoiced too soon: it was demolished by a small freckled boy called Georg. He blew himself and the Apollo up with a bazooka which he let off by mistake. Herbert Kalick's comment on this accident was a laconic: "What a good thing Georg was an orphan." '[14]

In *Hitler's Children* the Nazis' greatest crime was defined as 'the elimination of pity'. Herbert Kalick had no pity for the weak. Stefan, the older brother in Hans-Georg Behr's memoir *Almost a Childhood: Growing Up Amongst the Nazis*, had no pity for himself but pity for the Fatherland which he saw as having been grievously betrayed. His younger brother, the narrator, 'caught sight of Stefan sitting in his own room, but not doing anything, just crying.'[15] Stefan was very proud of being a student at a Napoli school, the schools for the children of high-ranking Nazis, and of the dagger of honour which he had won. As the news of the Russian advance reached the boys and their mother on their country estate, 'Stefan had just stood there all day saying nothing. Only out on the big meadow did he say, "Then I suppose I've lived for nothing." Then he fell silent again.' Some German soldiers in retreat came to the house. 'One soldier laughed at Stefan's dagger of honour and said he was a butcher in real life, and that thing would be of no use at all, and Stefan went back to his room in a bad temper.' Stefan 'laid out his Hitler Youth uniform on his bed, with the airgun and the dagger of honour crossed over it.'

The German soldiers left and Russian tanks arrived. The house was on fire and mother was screaming:

A little way off, in the middle of the path, lay a wrecked airgun, which was Stefan's, and on the left was the heap of sacks which made Mother scream so loud. Herr Kottnig got in the way, so you couldn't see it properly. But a leg was sticking out of one side of the heap, with a shoe on it. . . . When the boy asked more questions Herr Kottnig said Stefan had gone to meet the Russian tanks, wearing his Hitler Youth uniform and carrying the airgun, and he was only a child, 'but you don't see too well from a tank', and they had shot him, and then the tank ran over part of him.'[16]

After the war:

Mother was sad because she had to move to the inn, and the boy's sister was dead. That had happened some time ago, when the children were evacuated to the country and she was in the Allgäu, but Mother had only just heard about it, and now she had Elizabeth's things back. She had been just fifteen, and when the Yanks arrived she had bitten her capsule of cyanide, 'so as not to be raped by niggers', she wrote to Mother. Mother wept bitterly, which the boy didn't really understand, because Liesel had been dead for quite a while now, and she'd been very silly when she was alive. The boy didn't really like her at all, and Liesel had relished his dislike and needled him when she could. Now she was dead and Mother said, 'I have no one left but you.' Which wasn't a good thing, because you always got beaten when you stammered.[17]

The survivors of the Hitler Youth adapted as best they could, first to a divided Germany, and then to a reunited democratic Germany. But they had not forgotten that they had been betrayed. Some of them resolved never to do to others what had been done to them, but such a resolution requires a generosity of spirit which comes from being able to pity those who suffer without needing to judge how good or bad they had been. Not everyone can manage this. Some Germans felt that they could put things right by making some kind of reparation. Heinrich Böll argued that one of the reasons that post-war Germany achieved something of an economic miracle was that many Germans sought to make reparation and so find some inner peace by working hard: 'Ten years after the war it could seem as if everything was forgiven and forgotten. In a Calvinist kind of way the West Germans seemed justified by faith, faith in their own efforts; their material success demonstrated to the world that they were indeed of the elect.'[18]

The Calvinist elect are those people whose redemption by God is absolutely certain. Believers in the Just World can always bask in the illusion that their success is a proof of their goodness. This is a delusion much enjoyed by the rich. Some of Hitler's children created another kind of delusion. They had not been betrayed by the Nazis but rather the good Nazis had been betrayed by their wicked enemies. Some blamed themselves for failing Hitler, while others tried to rid themselves of their own pain by inflicting pain on those people such as children or migrants whom they saw as being bad or inferior.

There can be painful events in our childhood from which we can recover and grow stronger, but betrayal by someone who should care for us and whom we trust is not one of them. We may be able to work out a way to live with the memory of the betrayal without denying it or becoming crippled by self-hatred, but we lose forever our innocent joy in being alive. Often we can find ourselves carrying the burden of someone else's shame and guilt. In his novel *Some Hope*, Edward St Aubyn wrote about a five-year-old boy being raped by his father. He admitted to an interviewer that the boy was himself. He was reported as saying, 'It splits you in half. You can't accept that your father is doing this shameful thing to you and you take the shame upon yourself.'[19]

The same shame can be felt by one sibling betrayed by another. The betrayal may not be an act of sexual abuse. Some families are like war zones but without the blood. The victims know that their sibling adversary wants to annihilate them as a person, but they also know that what the adversary is doing is shameful and they take the shame upon themselves. I had always known that there were aspects of my family about which I could not speak to anyone outside the family. (I did not speak to anyone inside the family either.) It was not until I was an educational psychologist and working in child guidance clinics that I realised that, had child guidance clinics existed when I was a child, my family was the kind which would have been referred to one. It was another ten years before I started writing about my mother, and another ten years before I dared to speak openly about my sister. I did not realise that I was acting out of a loyalty based on shame until I happened to meet a relative of my brother-in-law who had visited Australia and stayed with my sister and her family. This woman told me that she had been greatly distressed by the way my sister and her husband disciplined their children. (They disciplined their children in the way that they had been disciplined by their parents, and in Australia then physical punishment was generally regarded as the best method of discipline, especially with boys.)This was the first time anyone had talked to me about my sister. I found myself torn between the relief that something hidden was now in the open and the fear of speaking to a stranger about what my mother called 'family business'. I said something briefly, and then the fear and shame prevailed. Perhaps somewhere deep down I still remembered what my sister had done to me for spoiling her autograph book.

## Siblings grown up

In the course of the many conversations I had with different individuals about their siblings I found that many people wanted to talk to me about their siblings, yet rarely did they do this easily. Again and again I was sworn to secrecy, and thus this book was deprived of many important stories. The person demanding secrecy would say 'I don't want my sister to find out', or 'My brother would kill me if he discovered I'd told you this.' Sometimes the story was about events in childhood, and sometimes about what was happening now. Sometimes the narrator linked the childhood and adult experiences, showing how the first led to the second. Often the events narrated were petty and mean, but they showed that the perpetrator regarded the victim with contempt.

Sometimes the person telling me their story would adopt a light, humorous tone, the kind I usually adopt when someone asks me about my sister. Sometimes the tone was cold and angry. One man said, 'When our parents died I ceased to speak to my brothers.' He did not tell me why, but I felt that he could not risk letting me glimpse his immense anger that hid a wound as deep and as painful as it was on the day it was inflicted.

Often the tone the person uses is one of great hurt. My friend and colleague Louise had told me that she had a sister whom she did not see very much because they had never got along together. She had also told me a little about her mother who was in her eighties, frail and occasionally forgetful but not seriously so. Then one day she told me that she had just discovered that, unbeknownst to her, her sister had taken power of attorney over her mother's affairs and was draining her mother's bank account into her own. Louise told me she was very worried about her mother, and that she had begun the legal process to have the power of attorney overturned. This was all very sensible, but the pain in Louise's eyes told of a much deeper hurt.

Louise had always expected that she would be the one who would look after her mother when she became incapable of living independently. Her sister lived a long way from them and had always shown little interest in caring for her mother, much less in caring for other people, whereas this was Louise's area of professional expertise. Moreover, Louise had all the attributes a carer needed. She was sympathetic, sensible, practical, knowledgeable, inventive, cheerful, amusing and encouraging. If ever I need a carer I would want someone like Louise. By her action her sister was not only depriving Louise of her rightful inheritance but also denying who Louise actually was. In effect, her sister was trying to annihilate her as a person. In the many months it took for the legal process to work its way through, Louise talked to me about what was happening to her. She said, 'It feels both physically and emotionally shattering.' She felt a profound sense of loss, which reawakened feelings of loss she had suffered when her father died, and when she discovered that her husband had betrayed her.

From many of the stories I was told but was forbidden to use it was clear that all the siblings in each particular family kept in touch with one another and together presented a front of a close, loving family. If I had told the story in this book I could have upset their way of operating as a family. Many, perhaps most, adult sibling relationships operate on the unstated principle that certain matters are never mentioned. One woman told me, 'When I'm with my sisters I'm like a swan, all calm and serene on top but paddling like mad underneath.' The television presenter and chat show host Jonathan Ross, who is one of six children, was quoted as saying, 'In big families you don't really communicate. There's always this big rush, scramble, noise, and it's all happy-sounding, but at the end of the day you're not really talking.'[20]

I found that many adult siblings might be prepared to talk about the betrayals they suffered at the hands of their siblings in childhood but they were very circumspect about talking about what happened once they had grown up. In the first volume of her autobiography Nawal El Saadawi wrote at some length about how badly her oldest brother had treated her. In the second volume, describing her adult life, she reported that, after her father died, she had become head of the family. She wrote:

> My father had carried the load of feeding nine children,
> their mother, his mother and a sister who was divorced
> and lived in the village with her. Now it was my turn
> to take over the load. Normally it should have reverted to
> my elder brother, but my young brothers and sisters held
> a meeting after the death of my father and decided
> that their sister Nawal be nominated as trustee over
> them. My father's pension was not enough to support
> all these young boys and girls, most of whom were still
> at school or university. I had to work to support them
> and to be able to care for my daughter Mona who
> continued to live with me after Ahmed Helmi and I
> were divorced.

She did not explain why the siblings had rejected her brother in favour of her. All she said was: 'My elder brother had graduated and was working in Tahrir Province.' She explained in a footnote that Tahrir Province was 'an agricultural college reclaimed from the desert about 60 kms from Cairo'.[21]

Acts of betrayal are simple and straightforward when the

purpose is to gain money or position or to save one's skin. Betrayals where the purpose is to preserve one's sense of being a person and perhaps destroy another's are far from simple. Much has been written about the relationship between Virginia Woolf and her sister Vanessa Bell. It is clear from all the written accounts that Virginia felt that her sense of being a person depended on her being close to Vanessa. Jane Dunn wrote: 'Virginia feared, more than anything, the loss of her adored Vanessa; her only sister and substitute mother. She was the focus of a fierce almost erotically possessive love, Virginia's sheet-anchor to life. "If you died, my life would be worthless," she wrote to Vanessa when she was in her late twenties and the intensity of that dependence never really left her.'[22] Yet, in order to preserve herself, Virginia betrayed Vanessa not once but twice. The first time was when, as a child, she felt that the close relationship Vanessa had with their brother Thoby was a threat to her. If Vanessa was close to Thoby she could not give Virginia the intense, single-minded attention that Virginia felt she needed. So Virginia decided to separate Thoby and Vanessa by making herself so witty, amusing and charming that Thoby would be drawn to her and away from Vanessa. Virginia used the same strategy when Vanessa fell in love with Clive Bell:

> For it was Virginia who felt the outsider: unwanted, left behind, disregarded. This was the feeling which had driven her in the nursery to break into the close relationship between Vanessa and Thoby, and seek to enchant this coveted brother with the weapons of wit and charm which his more responsible elder sister could never conjure. This old fear of being the outsider was to cause Virginia to repeat that plunder of Vanessa's necessarily exclusive relationship with Clive, and was to bring lasting pain to both sisters. To Clive she explained her double loss: 'Nessa has all that I should like to have, and you . . . have her.'[23]

When the Mitford girls were children they fought with one another as siblings do but closed ranks against outsiders. In adult life, politics divided them. Jessica (Decca) became a communist while Diana married Oswald Mosley, leader of the British Blackshirts, and Unity went to Germany and fell in love with Hitler. In the 1930s Diana and Unity visited Germany often and got to know Hitler whom they saw as a great leader. In England in the 1930s a significant number of members of the upper classes greatly admired Hitler, but Nancy Mitford was not one of them. The sisters' biographer Mary Lovell wrote that, when war was declared:

Nancy, who knew nothing of the reason for Diana's frequent visits to Germany – to obtain an [radio] airwave [for her husband's party] – was one of those who informed on her sister. On 20 June, nine days before Diana was arrested, Nancy admitted this to Mrs Hammersley: 'I have just been round to see Gladwyn[24] at his request to tell him what I know . . . of Diana's visits to Germany,' she wrote. 'I advised him to examine her passport to see how often she went. I also said I regard her as an extremely dangerous person. Not very sisterly behaviour but in such times I think it one's duty.'[25]

Diana was arrested at the same time as her husband and they spent much of the war years in Holloway Prison. Decca, who lived in the USA, decided that when she visited England she would not see Diana. She wrote:

I could not have borne [it]. When I was a small child she, seven years older, was my favourite person in the whole world. She was in all ways marvellous to me; she took me riding . . . taught me to speak French, encouraged me in the forbidden sport of 'showing off' in front of grown up visitors, was my staunch protectress against the barbs of Nancy, my ally in fights with Boud. I could see her in my mind's eye, a radiant beauty of seventeen shrieking at my jokes. Teaching me, helping me through childhood, in general being the best of all possible elder sisters.[26]

Don McCullin said in an interview, 'Betrayal is always a mistake.' He should know. As a war photographer he witnessed many acts of betrayal, but he also faced the issues of loyalty in his own life. He and his wife Christine had married at the beginning of his career, and she supported him and raised their children through all the years he put himself in terrible danger. He became famous and he betrayed her. He said that what happened with Christine was 'the most painful thing of all in a painful life. . . . It was a huge mistake. Betrayal is always a mistake. You cannot go around putting the blame on somebody else – when I knew I was making the wrong decision. I was beguiled by somebody else. It was a weakness in me. I became strong in some ways, and I became better informed in some ways. I was progressing with my photography – but at the same time I was losing some bits of integrity.'[27]

Don's integrity meant a lot to him, but the day came when he chose maintaining his integrity in preference to remaining close to his brother Michael. As children, they had been close and, despite the scrapes Michael got himself into in his teens Don remained loyal to him. He wrote that in the early 1960s Michael 'blazed the trail in Europe for football hooligans of later years'. In trouble with the Belgian police, he returned home. Don wrote:

> I didn't take seriously his flippant suggestion that he could always escape retribution, like a latter-day Beau Geste, by enlisting in the French Foreign Legion. People in deprived Finsbury Park were not accustomed to making gallant gestures of that sort. Yet this is precisely what he did. Not long afterwards, I received an official letter from the Foreign Office asking if I knew of my brother's whereabouts. It appeared that the Belgian authorities were anxious to extradite him. I put the letter straight in the fire.[28]

Michael stayed in the Foreign Legion but they each came to see war differently. 'It was perhaps the breadth of my experience that led Michael and me to differ. We had both been drawn to war by a sense of adventure, but its meaning for each of us had changed. To Michael war was a game, a passion. Although it still held excitement for me, most of the time I could think only of its horrors.' Don began his autobiography:

> Two brothers met on a desert battleground on a February day in 1970. The elder myself, covering my twentieth battle campaign as a photo-journalist; the younger, engaged in skirmishing with horse- and camel-mounted tribesmen of that remote African country, was my little brother Michael, then Sergeant, now Adjutant McCullin of the

French Foreign Legion. For the short hour in which I could touch down in this arid spot, we met only to disagree.

Later in the book he told the full story. The meeting in Chad 'seemed bizarre to me, in this era of high-speed jets and rockets, that there should be bush wars going on between tribesmen and Legionnaires. It also seemed an unequal war, between barely-armed primitives and some of the hardest soldiers in the world. Selective pacification, as they called it, seemed more like the sport of hunting men than any kind of political programme.' Michael gave him an elaborate hunting rifle, complete with telescopic sights. 'It must have been over six years since I had used a gun – I had stopped soon after I started taking pictures of war, when I got a better idea of what guns could do. He was upset by my attitude but I was incapable of accepting his gift.'[29]

Part of the meaning structure we call our self is a list, or several lists, of priorities. Thus we might put 'reading' at the top of one list and 'watching football' at the bottom, or we see 'being generous to family and friends' as being more important than 'saving for a pension'. Just what is contained in these lists and the order of the contents of each comes from our experiences. Don McCullin's experiences had led him to see his family and his relationship with his brother in the context of a wider humanity, and to feel a loyalty to those people who have no money, education or power to protect themselves from those who would destroy them.

Heinrich Böll had learned much the same thing from his family's experiences in Germany before the war. Böll's family were intensely loyal to one another but they did not subscribe to the values of *Gemüt*, the German word for a family loyalty which looks inward and excludes all others. Nazi propaganda used the concept of *Gemüt* to foster the belief that the Aryan race was superior to all other races. When Böll was born in 1917, Germany still had a Kaiser and was losing the Great War. His earliest memory was the return of Hindenburg's defeated army. The Kaiser was deposed and the Weimar Republic established. Böll's family lost their home in the financial turmoil of the Republic, and, by the time Hitler came to power, Böll was old enough to understand that the rise of Nazi Germany was the result of nationalist Germans joining the industrialists and bankers to support Hitler, and also what Böll called the 'blindness of the middle classes'.[30] His family were Catholic, and in 1933 they learned that the Vatican had signed the Concordat with Nazi Germany, and thus was the first state to give Hitler diplomatic recognition. Böll later wrote that at this point his family considered leaving the Church in protest, but did not do so because many Germans were leaving the Church and joining the Nazis. The family's attitudes put them in danger of arrest and imprisonment. What saved them was their mutual loyalty and their knowledge that the Nazi system attracted those who were easily corrupted. He wrote:

> By that time my father [a builder], insofar as he received any orders at all, had almost ceased working for churches and monasteries; almost all his orders were now government ones. And when those orders became even scarcer, he was urged to have at least one member of his family join a Nazi organization. A kind of family council was called, and my brother Alois became the victim of its decision, since, after some miserable receivership proceedings, he was officially the owner of the business. He was elected by the family to join the Storm Troopers. (To the end of his days he bore a grudge against us for this, and he was right: we should at least have drawn lots.) Of all the members of our family, he was the worst suited for that mimicry: the person least suited for a uniform I have ever known, and he *suffered*, he really suffered from those mob parades and route marches. I don't know how often he actually took part in those route marches – certainly not more than three times. Nor do I remember how often I went to see his platoon leader, a very recently converted former Communist who lived in a tiny attic above Tappert's drugstore at the corner of Bonner-Strasse and Roland-Strasse. There, on behalf of my brother, I would bribe that character – whom I remember as being depraved but not unfriendly – with a pack of ten R6 cigarettes, available in those days in nice-looking, flat, red packs, positively luxurious, to list my permanently absent brother as present. He did so,

and among our flippant variations of the Rosary decades we included the words: 'thou who hast joined the Storm Troopers for our sakes.' And the 'Full is Her right hand of gifts' was changed to: 'Full is thy right hand of R6's.'[31]

It is an old but true saying that you don't know who your friends are until you have suffered a disaster. This applies not just to friends but to siblings. Even when two siblings have always got along well together it can take a disaster to show just how strong the sibling bond actually is. When my friend Craig told me about what his brother Andy had done for him, I asked him to write a brief account of this because I felt that what Andy had done should be recorded somewhere. Craig wrote:

So, a story. My brother Andy arrived nine years after me and suddenly I had company. A bit young I know, so my job became the older brother who rocked his baby brother off to sleep most nights. Things happened; we grew up, had many ups and down that come to us all and then, on December 23, 2003, I was involved in a road accident. Cut from my clothes and helicoptered to an Intensive Care Unit in Birmingham, I had sustained all sorts of damage. Not that I knew. I was in a coma for the next two weeks. Which is how my brother saw me every day from Boxing Day on. He would drive from Peterborough to Birmingham (about 50 miles) to sit by my bed. Then, he would drive from the hospital to Shrewsbury (about 45 miles) to pick up Isabel, my partner and mother of our five kids) before returning to the hospital. Another sojourn, this time in Isabel's company, would be followed by a further round trip to take her home before calling in again at the hospital. A brief stay, and then finally, back to Peterborough. By my calculation that's three hundred miles a day to spend barely an hour sitting beside the bed of a man in a coma. I must have done something right when I used to rock him to sleep. And I love him.

Craig began his account with: 'Is this an exceptional story? I don't think so. I suspect siblings the world over act in wonderful ways but we only take note of the exceptions when brothers and sisters are unkind, cruel and unjust.' I think Craig is right. When her sister-in-law, her beloved brother's wife, developed breast cancer my friend Catherine showed as much concern as she would have shown to herself in that situation. When one of his brothers had a stroke Richard, like Craig's brother Andy, made long round trips, first to his brother's hospital and then to his home, to ensure that his brother had everything he needed. Then there are the acts of thoughtfulness which are part of the daily life of many siblings – meals cooked, shopping done, children minded, or something given with, 'I saw this in a shop and I thought you'd like it.'

We see the world in the way we have learned to see it. In our early years our family is our world, and so, when we encounter the world outside our family, we interpret that world in the way we have learned to interpret our family. We accept that leaders of the Church and state should be referred to as father or mother, and that those people who have the same nationality or religion as us can be seen as our sisters and brothers. Moreover, when we encounter people in positions of authority we can find ourselves re-enacting the particular kind of encounters we had with our parents, and with our friends and colleagues we re-enact our tussles with our siblings. Indeed, we can re-enact with different groups the siblings dramas of 'the good one' and 'the bad one'.

## The power of brotherhood

The idea of brotherhood has been around for as long as families have existed. All through the literature of the Christian Church the word is used to stress that the belief in God did not mean merely the relationship between a believer and God but a relationship between all fellow believers. Brotherhood is a key concept in Islam. Sheikh Ashraf Salah, speaking at the London Central Mosque on 31 May 2002, said:

> One of the greatest blessings of Islam is its admirable success in creating strong, warm, rich and durable bonds of love and brotherhood. It is this blessing of love and brotherhood that is the greatest source of sustenance for man, but few of us can honestly say that we have experienced true brotherhood. . . . Every Muslim should speak well to his brother. The tongue should sometimes

be silent and at other times speak out. As for silence, the tongue should not mention a brother's faults in his absence. Rather, you should feign ignorance. You should not dispute or argue with him, you should not criticise him, accuse him of anything or quiz him about his affairs. You should not be suspicious, for suspicion is the most untruthful report and suspicion leads to prying and spying. . . . We are also required to forgive our brothers' mistakes and failings, and help them overcome their shortcomings. . . . Love and cooperation are also some of the duties of brotherhood. One should relief [sic] his brother from discomfort and inconvenience. He should not discomfort his brother with things that are awkward for him. Rather, he should ease his heart of its cares and needs, and spare him from having to assume any of his burdens. . . . Moreover, Muslim brotherhood implies that you should pray for your brother and hope for him what you would hope for yourself. You should pray for him as you pray for yourself making no distinction between you and him. You should pray during his life and death that he may have all he might wish for himself, his family and his dependents.

In both Christianity and Islam the term 'brotherhood' was sometimes considered to refer only to men and sometimes to include women. Presumably it is the second meaning in Article 1 of the United Nations' Universal Declaration of Human Rights, which states: 'All human beings are born free and equal in dignity and rights. They are endowed with reason and conscience and should act towards one another in a spirit of brotherhood.' However, it seems that the actual experience of brotherhood is different for men and for women.

In the 1970s, members of the Women's Liberation Movement tried to persuade women generally to join the sisterhood, but somehow the idea did not catch on. Women have always looked after one another and have often banded together, usually very quietly, to protect themselves from men, but they could never elevate this practical bond into the semi-religious concept that many men have of brotherhood. Society has always made it clear to women that they must put their menfolk – father, brother, husband, son – ahead of their women friends. Women's

Liberation moderated this practice to a small degree, but while women can insist on their right to an occasional 'night out with the girls', few men have moderated their views of how women must respect a man's relationships with his male friends. Under the pretext of a sport or hobby, many men form relationships with one another which come first in their lives. No matter how important wives and children might be to such men, their mates come first. For such men the greatest crime a woman can commit is to shame him in front of his mates.

Evolutionary psychologists could argue that such bonding between men has arisen out of more than a shared interest or a desire to escape from nagging women. Elaine Morgan, a journalist who has specialised in anthropology, wrote:

> In many social species, there is also an ad hoc kind of brotherhood which operates when a group is confronted with a challenge. Adults, males in particular, will put any existing rivalries and frictions on hold and co-operate for the duration of the emergency. This instinct, described as male bonding, enables them to work together in hunting prey, as wolves and dolphins do, or in defending their territory against other bands of the same species. Within the band, it fosters the capacity to display loyalty – and that too is a eusocial instinct capable of evolving into something stronger and more permanent. [Eusocial means 'anything that fosters co-operation between individual organisms rather than conflict'.] Unfortunately, as compared to the goodwill derived from other biological roots, this one, being testosterone-based and adrenaline-fuelled, has a dangerous aspect. It needs an enemy, real or imagined, to activate it and sustain it.[32]

Groups define themselves in terms of who is excluded from the group. Thus a group of golfers is defined by those who do not play golf; a group of children is defined in terms of those who are not children. One striking feature of groups is that the strength of the bond between group members relates directly to the danger posed by those excluded from the group. Anyone who has worked in some kind of organisation would be familiar with the way a disparate collection of workers swiftly becomes a bonded group when a change of management produces a boss who in some way threatens the workers. Political leaders, from democratically elected prime ministers to the most totalitarian of dictators, will use the threat of an enemy, real or invented, to unite the people under his leadership.[33] There have always been brotherhoods united against a common enemy and such brotherhoods have often had political power, but perhaps never in our history has the concept of brotherhood so demanded our understanding until now.

The day after the two planes crashed into the Twin Towers television news teams roamed the USA finding people who looked like ordinary Americans and asking them to comment on what had happened. Almost to a man or woman these ordinary Americans asked, somewhat plaintively, 'Why do they hate us?' When home-grown British young men planted bombs in the London Underground the media worried away at the question, 'How could men who had grown up in this country and didn't come from deprived families do such a terrible thing?' A great many media pundits gave their answers to these questions, but of all the answers which I read none answered the first question with, 'No amount of goodness prevents disaster, even the disaster of someone hating you and wanting to destroy you.' Few answered the second with, 'If the group to which you've been assigned by others doesn't give you a sense of identity and self-worth you'll try to find one which does.'

It is possible to lead a life of comparative comfort and security and still feel empty and worthless. In contrast, many people who own very little can feel that their life does have significance because those around them treat them with respect, and because their life is rooted in a particular place where their family has lived for many generations. Unfortunately, the wars and conflicts of the twentieth century have displaced many millions of people. Some are refugees; some have successfully transferred themselves to another country where they can make a life for themselves. However, the experience of leaving one's homeland produces a feeling of dislocation and not belonging that can last for several generations. Thus succeeding generations can feel like strangers in a strange land, especially if their race or original nationality is not accepted by the inhabitants of their new country.

This was what the brothers Abd Samad and Zacarias

Moussaoui found in their own lives even though they were not born until after their family moved from Morocco to France. Zacarias is now infamous for being the twentieth hijacker who managed to miss his flight, and thus the only hijacker to be put on trial for the greatest act of terrorism ever perpetrated in the United States. At his trial the prosecution demanded the death penalty while the defence argued that Zacarias, being mad, welcomed the death penalty because that would make him a martyr. The jury denied him this and the judge handed down a life sentence.

His brother Abd Samad, who had no sympathy for extremist ideologies, wrote an account of their lives. His mother, Aïcha El-Wafi, publicly denounced him for doing this, principally because she insisted that she was a loving, devoted mother to her children and Abd Samad said that she was not.[34] Their parents were Moroccan but moved to Bayonne in France in 1965. They already had two daughters. Abd Samad was born in 1967 and Zacarias in 1968. Three years later their parents divorced. After that the boys saw their father only intermittently. Their mother moved to Mulhouse in Alsace and put the four children in an orphanage. Abd Samad wrote: 'I have very few memories of those grim childhood years, but they are dreadful ones.' When their mother managed to get a job and a place to live she brought her children home. According to Abd Samad family life was not happy. 'My mother didn't have much time for us; she always had other things to do. It would have been misguided to expect the slightest tender word from her or the merest gesture of affection. She didn't know how to do that. . . . So Zac and I kept ourselves to ourselves, giving one another support.'[35]

The family moved to a housing estate where they encountered racism at first hand. 'In our building lived the Kol family and the parents were very racist. When the Kols bumped into Zac and me, they called us, "dirty niggers". Not "dirty Arabs" but "dirty niggers". Probably because my brother and I are quite dark-skinned. They didn't make any distinction between Arabs and blacks; we were simply not whites.'[36]

Abd Samad saw Zacarias as 'an ideal younger brother. He was smart, clever and kind. He was a really nice boy. The nicest of our group, I think. He and I were really close, and we really liked one another a lot.' His mother agreed with him on this.

In an interview she described Zacarias as a 'sweet, affectionate child'. 'Zacarias was the child I never had any problem with. Even as a baby, he was a good, placid boy. He slept straight through until 6am. No one ever had a complaint to make about him at school.'[37]

Both boys were clever, but racism amongst the staff at their secondary school made it difficult for them to pursue their education. Zacarias took this very hard. 'When Zacarias was faced with humiliation, he reacted in a different way from the way I did. He locked himself away in his suffering, he nurtured it, it gnawed away at him silently. And when it was I who was the victim of racism, instead of him, the result was just the same: he suffered in his heart and soul, almost more than I did.'[38]

Aïcha insisted that although 'she spoke Arabic to the children they replied in French, saying, 'We're not in Morocco now, Mum, we're here now.' They celebrated both Christian and Muslim festivals because she says she wanted them to integrate.'[39] This was not how Abd Samad remembered his childhood. He reported that although their mother kept in touch with her family in Morocco, she did not teach the boys Arabic nor did she introduce them to Islam. She did not even celebrate the Muslim festivals and holidays. He wrote:

> Thus a void insidiously formed in us, an abyss which
> Zacarias and I would try to negotiate, but in different
> ways. Like many people of our generation, we were aware
> that we were not well acquainted with our original
> culture. We knew nothing about almost all the social
> codes of the Arab world. And yet we were not truly
> accepted in the country of our birth. Native French people
> rarely think twice about making us feel that we're not
> altogether 'like them'. This feeling gnawed away at us.[40]

Abd Samad realised that 'beneath his assertive exterior, Zacarias needed to be guided, supported and reassured by his teachers'. At his vocational school Zacarias had been given the support and supervision he needed but at university students were alone and had to make their own way. Zacarias found that difficult. Moreover, at university Zacarias learned about the Gulf War, what was happening in Bosnia, Algeria, Palestine, Afghanistan and Chechnya: 'Muslims were being persecuted all over the world. That disgusted us. Zacarias wasn't the only one to have this feeling. All Muslims of our age and even younger were shattered. They felt deeply and personally, in their very flesh, the injustice to which their religious brothers were victim.'[41]

Non-Muslims who have no religion or wear their religion lightly can find it hard to imagine these intense feelings of brotherhood and injustice. However, all of us have a group with which we identify. It need not be a religious or national group, but it is a group of people (and, for some people, animals) whose particular kind of suffering we see as being similar to our own. This is the group whose cause we support either actively or financially. Just how active we are in support of this group usually depends on how old we are. When we are young we may go on demonstrations to show our support for our group but most of us, as we get older, tend to write a cheque rather than demonstrate. Hilary Mantel, in reviewing a book about the French revolutionary Robespierre, remarked: 'The young dream of transcending their circumstances, of shaming the mediocrities around them; of saving lives, of being martyrs. When you have so much future before you, life seems cheap; perhaps you cannot fully imagine, as older people can, being extinguished, simply coming to nothing.'[42] Zacarias, being young, lost, lonely and dreaming of transcending his circumstances, was easy prey for those Muslims who wanted to enlist him for their extremist cause. He went to London and came back a changed man.

One of the witnesses for the defence at the trial of Zacarias was Abdul Haqq Baker, Chairman of the Brixton Mosque in London. When Zacarias first arrived in London he stayed at the Brixton Mosque and became friends with Abdul Haqq Baker who described Zacarias as being 'friendly, quiet, had a sense of humour, quite jovial'. However, after a year or so Zacarias began to change. The policy of the Brixton Mosque was adamantly against extreme dogma and actions. Zacarias began attending mosques where there were more extreme views. Abdul Haqq Baker described how, when he did attend the Brixton Mosque, Zacarias became 'increasingly arrogant and disruptive. He wanted a sense of belonging and there was frustration at the atrocities being committed in the Muslim world.' Abdul Haqq Baker told how he and Zacarias talked about this, and

Zacarias would ask him where the next jihad would be. 'He was actively seeking arenas for a jihad. One of his friends died in Chechnya, and he was seeking a similar fate. . . . He wants that martyr status.'[43]

Abd Samad saw the same changes in Zacarias. He wrote:

In the early stages of what can only be called an exile, we talked very often and he returned regularly to France. Then he changed. Gradually he became more aloof. He stopped telling me about the details of his life, he became taciturn. He had always been discreet, but now he became secretive. He no longer told me who he was meeting, or how he spent his days, and even less about what he lived off. A state of non-communication developed. He also changed physically. His features grew hardened. I misinterpreted all these changes. First and foremost I put them down to the problems he might be having living abroad. I didn't want to dramatise the situation, so I stuck strictly to the role of elder brother – accommodating, warm and patient. And I got it all wrong. Zacarias was in the process of ripping up his last roots. . . . Zacarias didn't call me any more and never came to see me – a deafening silence. I didn't understand how my younger brother had ended up finding it acceptable to strike us out of his life. It hurt me. I had always thought that our shared years of suffering had woven indestructible bonds. It was as if a part of me had been amputated. [In 1995] Zacarias went back to London where, so he said, he was going to get his MBS degree. The next time I saw him was in a photo, a few days after September 11th, 2001.[44]

Zacarias and Abd Samad had formed the kind of strong sibling bond that children do when they realise that there is no one to look after them except themselves. As they got older Abd Samad continued to fulfil his role as the older brother, but he also had commitments to his profession and to his wife, while Zacarias became increasingly rootless. He needed to belong in order to survive. He understood the importance of brotherly loyalty, and at university he encountered one vastly important Arab tradition, that of loyalty to your brothers. The Muslim extremists he had joined may have broken his connection with his brother but they did not destroy his habit of brotherly loyalty. Indeed, they used it to their own ends by directing Zacarias's loyalty to the brotherhood of his extremist Muslim group.

This kind of loyalty draws not just on the Muslim tradition of brotherhood but on a much older tradition, that of loyalty to the tribe. The Australian journalist Paul McGough, who knows the Middle East well, wrote that in Iraq, 'The tribes pre-date Islam. [They] are the foundation layer in Iraqi society – bedrock under the bedrock.'[45] The same can be said of all Muslim countries. Even if as refugees the members of the tribe have been dispersed, the concept of loyalty to the tribe remains strong.

The bonds of loyalty demand that each member of the tribe be good in the way that the tribe defines 'good'. Not to be seen as good is shameful. Paul McGough commented: 'For the tribes, pride and shame are issues of great importance.'[46] They are important for all of us, for pride and shame are the emotions of being validated and invalidated. Societies differ in how these emotions can be expressed. In Western societies people can be shamed by the behaviour of a sibling but they are not allowed to kill that sibling in order to restore the good name of the family. In Western societies people can feel shamed (invalidated) by the way another person has treated them and they can feel impelled to defend themselves by seeking revenge, but they are more likely to turn to law rather than murder to achieve this. Thus, if we refrain from priding ourselves on our superior virtue and instead look closely at our own emotions, we should be able to understand the young Iraqi man in Falluja who said:

> For Fallujians it is a *shame* to have foreigners break down their doors. It is a *shame* for them to have foreigners stop and search their women. It is a *shame* for the foreigners to put a bag over their heads, to make a man lie on the ground with your shoe on his neck. This is a great *shame*, you understand? This is a great *shame* for the whole tribe. It is the *duty* of that man, and of that tribe, to get revenge on this soldier – to kill that man. Their duty is to attack them, to *wash the shame*. The shame is a *stain*, a dirty thing; and they have to *wash* it. No sleep – we cannot sleep until we have revenge. They have to kill the soldiers.[47]

So important is our need to maintain our sense of being a person that we will use whatever is in our power to use to defend ourselves. If we view the world in a flexible way, with lots of ambiguities and uncertainties, we can usually arrive at an interpretation of a situation which allows us to defend ourselves without resorting to murder. We can deplore what someone has done to us and acknowledge our pain, while at the same time seeking to understand why our enemy has behaved as he did. For instance, if you value yourself and someone shows you very clearly that they do not like you, you can say to yourself, 'Anyone who doesn't like me is a fool, and I'm not going to waste my time on fools.' However, if we see the world in absolutes and certainties, we see the world solely in terms of good and bad. Our enemies are wicked and they must be punished. Karen Armstrong, once a nun and now an expert on fundamentalism said: 'It is important that we understand the dread and anxiety that lie at the heart of the fundamentalist vision. Only then will we begin to comprehend its passionate rage, its frantic desire to fill the void with certainty, and its conviction of ever-encroaching evil.'[48] A frantic desire to fill the void will inevitably lead to the most extreme of actions.

It is ironic that, at the time when the rich nations of the world have the military capability of destroying the human race a million times over, they are rendered almost helpless to defend themselves against a lone man (occasionally a woman) with a few sticks of explosive attached to his body. In her study of the economics of the Islamic jihad the economist Loretta Napoleoni pointed out:

> The importance of suicide missions is particularly
> striking in economic terms. A cost-benefit analysis
> shows suicide operations to be by far the most efficient
> form of terror attacks from a military point of view; they
> require relatively small amounts of money and can have
> great impact in terms of casualties and damage.[49]

Suicide bombers have not been brainwashed nor are they mad. Suicide is always the statement, 'If I can't live as the person I am I shall die as the person I am.' Islam has always condemned the suicide, but it has always lauded the martyr. Researching in Ramallah, the psychiatrist Nadia Taysir Dabbagh studied the records of a number of people who had committed suicide. These stories did not differ in their content and sadness from the stories of suicide the world over. Each person saw themselves as being in a difficult position with regard to their family and believed that the only solution was to kill themselves, even though this would bring shame to their family. Suicide may be a desperate attempt to validate yourself but it is also some kind of message, even an intended punishment, for the people left behind. This message may be, 'See what you made me do', or 'I reject you', or 'You don't care about me', or it may be 'Don't worry about me – you get on with your selfish lives.' The word 'selfish' is implied and the message usually worded as 'You'll be better off without me.' However, there is one situation where suicide need not be an act against the family, but this situation can exist only in societies where martyrdom is honoured. Nadia Taysir Dabbagh wrote: 'Suicide is seen as a private act condemned by society and religion, whereas martyrdom is seen as a public act which is exalted as being for the greater good.'[50]

People who are committed to the belief that the top priority in their life is to be good willingly choose martyrdom over happiness. They see martyrdom as the best way of testing themselves to see just how good they are – the greater the martyrdom, the greater their virtue. If you have nothing, no security, no home, but only your very life, then that is what you have to give in order to become a martyr. Not only can martyrdom restore your pride, it can restore your family's pride. Loretta Napoleoni wrote: 'Becoming a martyr is the highest moral achievement available to some of the refugees. Death, paradoxically, restores the dignity lost with the land, along with the political identity attached to it. Refugees are obsessed with dignity; like exposed bodies in a fully clothed society, they search frantically for something to cover their nakedness. Martyrdom is the best protection they can get: it ends a life of misery and grants social status, a very high one, something to be proud of for the entire family.'[51]

In all families, if one member of a family is honoured, then the family usually feels honoured. If one member of a family is in some way disgraced, then the whole family can feel disgraced. The disgraced family member has shamed the family, and often the family regards what the person has done as being unforgivable. Families who see the world in the inflexible categories of good and bad tend not to forgive, and they also tend to have long memories. As the years go by, succeeding generations in the family may forget that the disgraced, unforgiven person was actually a family member who was cast out by the family. All they may remember is that the descendants of the disgraced person are now the family's enemy, indeed the greatest enemy the family has ever had. Tucked away in their unconscious may be the knowledge that their enemy is part of their family or tribe, but all this unconscious memory does is to arouse the kind of passionate hatred and desire for revenge which siblings feel when one of their number betrays them. This is why conflicts between groups who share a common history and bloodline are more bitter and more resistant to reconciliation than those between two disparate groups.

In Northern Ireland the Protestants like to think that they are separate and distinct from the Catholics, and this is the way Australian Protestants used to think. The Australia I grew up in was just like Northern Ireland but without the Troubles, because Catholics in Australia were not discriminated against economically as they were in Northern Ireland. My Presbyterian family never knowingly engaged in any social intercourse with Catholics. When my cousin George married a Catholic girl, not only was the family shamed and horrified but they all knew that George was doomed. As it turned out, he had one of the longest and happiest marriages in my family. My parents' generation were never interested in family history because the family cupboards were crammed full of skeletons, but Protestants in Northern Ireland like Ian Paisley and his supporters have always insisted that they were descended from the English and Scottish Protestants who came to Ulster as part of the 'plantation' by James I in the early seventeenth century. The English settlers may not have been related to the Catholics in Northern Ireland but the Protestants from the Scottish lowlands certainly were. There is only a short stretch of water which divides Ayrshire from Ulster, and for centuries before the plantation the people on both sides crossed and recrossed this water, perhaps to settle or perhaps to trade. The stretch of water was very useful to cattle thieves who, according to recorded history, included my father's family, the Conns.

My mother's grandfather, James Freel from Donegal, would have been a Catholic when he was transported to Australia but it may have been that his behaviour in Australia towards his wife and children whom he deserted led his descendants to become staunchly Protestant. In Northern Ireland as in Australia marriages, or at least sexual intercourse, between Protestants and Catholics might have been a family scandal but they were not rare. A study of 'The influence of religion and birthplace on the genetic structure of Northern Ireland' showed that male members of the Church of Ireland (which is what the Church of England is called in Northern Ireland) tended to have a genetic structure somewhat different from male Catholics and Protestants, while male Catholics and Protestants were more similar.[52] This seems to suggest that the English who came to Northern Ireland were somewhat more likely to keep themselves separate than the original inhabitants who fought one another as only siblings can.

The differences between the Catholics and Protestants in Northern Ireland lie not so much in their genes as in the ideas in their heads. Ever since Henry VIII left the Catholic Church, Protestants and Catholics have entertained some less than flattering ideas about each other (i.e. the other side is the devil incarnate), but the division of Ireland into the Republic of Ireland and Northern Ireland in 1921 meant that the Catholics in Northern Ireland identified themselves as Irish or Northern Irish, while the Protestants there saw themselves as Ulstermen or British. During the Troubles these divisions in identification became more important, so that when psychologists asked people in Northern Ireland how they saw their social identity, nationality and religion were at the head of most people's list. However, ideas seem to be changing. 'In a study by Cassidy and Trew, psychology undergraduates (55 per cent Catholic, 45 per cent Protestant) at the Queen's University of Belfast were asked to rank the importance of six identities (family, friends, boy/girlfriend, university, nationality and religion). The majority of students assigned national and religious identity to the lowest two ranks (75 per cent and 72 per cent respectively).'[53] So for these students at least family and friends have become more important than religion and nationality. Perhaps the family feud is coming to an end.

Many people have tried to maintain their pride in themselves by claiming that they belong to a distinct and superior race. Alas, DNA research has shown that this is a delusion. The biologist Steven Rose wrote:

Modern genetic evidence demonstrates that whilst there are average genetic differences between human populations, these do not map on to socially ascribed 'racial' divisions. Thus no racial distinction is drawn between the populations of north and south Wales, yet there are small average differences in the genetic profile between the two populations of north and south Wales. And, conversely, genetically Polish Jews resemble their Catholic neighbours more closely than the do Jews from, for instance, Morocco.[54]

Meanwhile the conflict between Israel and Palestine continues to be extremely bitter with dreadful acts being committed by both sides, but this is not a conflict being waged by two distinct, unrelated groups. According to Jewish and Islamic traditions, Jews are descended from Isaac, son of Abraham, and Muslims from Isaac's half-brother Ishmael. There are a number of different versions of this story and there is no way of telling which one of them is true, but what does exist now is the scientific truth that Jews and Arabs share the same DNA. A report on the BBC World Service was headed 'Jews and Arabs "genetic brothers"'. It went on to say:

They may have their differences but Jews and Arabs share a common genetic heritage that stretches back thousands of years. The striking similarities in their biology have been revealed in a study of over 1,300 men in almost 30 countries world wide. . . . The study, published in the Proceedings of the National Academy of Sciences, found that Jewish men shared a common set of genetic signatures with non-Jews from the Middle East, including Palestinians, Syrians and Lebanese. These signatures were significantly different from non-Jewish men outside of the Middle East. This means that Jews and Arabs have more in common with each other, than they do with any of the wider communities in which they live.[55]

Another study by New York University confirmed a

remarkable similarity between Jewish and Palestinian genes. 'Jews and Arabs are all really children of Abraham,' said Dr. Harry Ostrer, director of the Human Genetics Program at New York University School of Medicine, who worked on the study. 'And all have preserved their Middle Eastern genetic roots over 4,000 years.'[56]

Certainly in many instances Israelis and Palestinians behave as family members do. Don McCullin, who spent considerable time in the Lebanon and the Middle East, said of the Palestinians: 'Dispersed in the Arab world, they seemed to me surprisingly similar to the Jews – hard-working, highly motivated, an intellectual elite providing a professional class for many another country.'[57] There was one extraordinary scene in Norma Percy's BBC TV series *Israel and the Arabs: Elusive Peace.* Anthony Zinni, the US Special Envoy to the Middle East in 2002, told the story of how he was watching the violence 'spiral out of control'. He called Jibril Rajoud, Palestinian Security Minister, and Giora Eiland, Major General of the Israeli Army and Security Chief, to a meeting. Anthony Zinni said:

> The first thing that struck me with a shock, when we
> got them together they knew each other. They hugged
> and they kissed each other. They told jokes and they
> laughed. It was a shock to me and I thought this'll go
> easier than I thought. We sat down at the table and as
> soon as we'd begun to negotiate they began screaming
> and getting at each other. I literally banged my fist on the
> table. I will not have any of this. We're not going to have
> any more of this screaming and yelling, or monologues.
> We're here to work. I told them I don't need to be here
> and I'm not staying if you can't move forward. And I
> will tell the world that you failed me. I was surprised
> because they had this sort of schoolboy look, like, okay.[58]

Every family in the world where there are at least two brothers has seen this scene enacted, with the father taking the Anthony Zinni role, using his authority to call the boys to order. Many sons find it necessary to defy their fathers in order to secure their sense of self, and they acquire an absolute way of thinking which prevents any reconciliation with their enemy, their brother. Other sons and daughters do learn the difficult skills of negotiation and compromise, and between them they create their own kind of forgiveness and reconciliation. However, whether in their adult life siblings choose to be enemies or to become friends, they remain tied by bonds of hatred and bonds of love in a lifelong relationship.

# Chapter 9

# A LIFELONG RELATIONSHIP

A sibling relationship may be lifelong but all too often, as the years go by, we can find ourselves not enjoying the comfort and pleasure that we find in a lifelong friendship. Instead, we feel the ineffable, poignant emotion of longing. Even in the most loving and close sibling relationship there can be feelings of longing for opportunities missed and happier times when the sun shone and the future was full of promise.

Temple Grandin, the animal scientist, talked about the emotion of seeking out what is needed where the animal becomes aware of a lack of something and strives to fill that need. We use the words 'needing' and 'longing' interchangeably but longing is different from needing. Needing is acutely felt and is directed at something fairly specific, while longing is more generalised, somewhat vague, often directed at something which is hard to define. A teenager may long to be famous but knows that he needs to pass exams or win some contest in order to transform himself into someone famous.

Needs point forward in time but longing can point to the past as well as to the future. When we are young just about all of our longings point to the future but as we get older increasingly our longings point to the past. We can long for many things but generally the longings that point to the past fall into two groups. We remember an event as being jangled, messy, broken, incomplete and we long to make it whole. We remember a broken or uncomfortable relationship, and we long for it to be smooth and loving. When people talked to me about their siblings such longings often revealed themselves. Some people talked of how a chance event led to the fulfilment of their longing; others told of a longing that was unfulfilled and painful. Some people declared that their relationship with a sibling was over, yet betrayed in what they said that their tie to that sibling was as strong as ever.

Ed Guiton was a mountaineer but it was an accident in a hotel bedroom which ended his career and left him in a wheelchair, almost totally paralysed. In his columns in the *Guardian* about the trials and tribulations of his new life he wrote: 'The accident reconnected me to my brother as we brushed aside the sullen estrangement we had allowed to creep over us.'[1] Eighteen months later he told me, 'My brother is almost two years older than me and, in the late 1940s and 1950s, we often had to share a bed as we were in a fairly large family. The rivalry between us was quite intense although we were close in other ways. In later life we drifted apart, though I have to say that most of the resentment was from me. Since my accident in 2000 Derek has been very supportive and we have become very close again and see each other regularly.'

No doubt Ed would have preferred that a far less catastrophic event had brought Derek and him together, but even the illest of winds can blow a little good sometimes. Not so for my friend Margaret who keeps in touch with me by email. I knew that she had been estranged from her mother and sister for some time, but in one email she said:

> My mother was loved by everyone but me. I have terrible guilt feelings that I didn't love her. She never did anything to make me feel like that. She came to live not far from me (but only for about eighteen months before she died). I couldn't bear to be alone with her and when I visited her (at home or in the hospice) I felt only relief when I left. And I feel I treated her very badly. My sister told me that too. We haven't spoken since (and that was four years ago). I tried to explain to my sister but she wasn't having any of it. It was her fiftieth birthday a few weeks ago. I figured fifty may be a watershed and so I sent her a birthday card and hoped she could forgive me and we could be friends. She sent the unopened card back. I feel very hurt at that, but that's her choice.

A woman who had been betrayed by her siblings and no longer had anything to do with them said to me, 'Trouble is they're inside me. I can't get away from them.' The American writer

Gertrude Stein and her brother Leo were always the closest of friends. Together they built up a splendid art collection and were amongst the first to recognise the genius of Matisse. But in 1915 they fell out, and Leo left Gertrude in Paris with her partner Alice Toklas and returned to the United States. They never spoke to one another. But they did see one another again. Leo and Alice each gave their description of this encounter. Brenda Wineapple, biographer of Gertrude and Leo, wrote:

> 'Gertrude I never saw after 1920,' said her brother Leo Stein in February, 1947, five months before his death. One day in Paris when they might have passed one another in the street, Gertrude Stein and Alice Toklas crossed to the other side. 'It was she who avoided me,' he remarked.

If this incident occurred, and probably some version of it did, Alice Toklas remembered it quite differently. She and Gertrude were sitting in traffic in their two-seater Ford, acquired in December 1910, on the Boulevard Saint Germain near the old church of Saint-Germain-des-Prés. Not moving in either direction, the traffic was the worst they had ever seen. Everybody had a car, Toklas recalled, army cars, secondhand cars, the cars foreigners were driving. And because all the traffic police had been killed at the front, she decided, leaving only a few ill-trained security police, she and Gertrude would just have to sit and listen to the honking and shouts. 'Three centimetres back and I can get through,' someone yelled, and some of the smaller cars, but not the Ford, moved forward.

Gertrude Stein suddenly stood and bowed, ever so slightly, in recognition of a man doffing his hat. 'Who was that?' Toklas asked. 'That was Leo,' Gertrude answered. Nothing further was said. But the look on Gertrude's face, Toklas observed, was 'compounded of something sardonic yet affectionate, and containing some regret, and a little love'.[2]

This complex mix of emotions is what many people feel about their siblings. They may have ceased to meet their sibling, or they may meet at family events and have a conversation composed of nothing but banalities with the occasional sly jibe. They may even perform the rituals that say to an outsider that this is a close family – a peck on the cheek, a hug, enquiries about the other's health and circumstances, yet each meeting seems to them to be incomplete and a lost opportunity to establish the kind of close relationship which they feel that somehow all siblings should enjoy.

The constant reiteration in the media and by politicians that the closeness of family members is of prime importance leaves many people feeling inadequate and guilty because they do not enjoy the close relationship with their siblings that seemingly most people enjoy with theirs. Even if they have established with their siblings a way of operating which on the whole works well they feel that they should try to make the relationship better. Sometimes, often at a point of family crisis, they manage to speak to their sibling and find that their sibling feels the same way as they do. Not all people are so fortunate.

Many people have tried to have the conversation with their sibling which will heal old hurts and establish mutual understanding only to find that their sibling refuses to engage and changes the subject to some trivial matter or leaves the room without speaking. Sometimes the conversation becomes a ferocious argument, often with tears, raised voices and much slamming of doors. The sibling who longs for reconciliation retires from the fray bruised, hurt and confused. Others find that any attempt at a conversation that would lead to reconciliation becomes no more than a replay of an old scenario, where the other person emerges as ever the victor and the peacemaker the victim, and nothing is achieved. Some people find themselves brooding over old hurts and blame themselves for not being able to forgive. It seems such a waste that we cannot enjoy an untroubled friendship with someone with whom we share a history. If only we could put things right!

If I were a proper psychologist, that is, someone who sees people as being no more than containers of dysfunctional cognitions and unhelpful traits but capable of learning functional cognitions and methods of restraining their unhelpful traits, I could give you Ten Tips which would enable you to create a relationship of unmitigated joy with your siblings. Alas, I am not a proper psychologist. I cannot help but be aware of the curious mystery of being a person, something we all experience as being very real and of immense importance, yet something which is totally dependent on the functioning of a lump of grey matter. I can never ignore the dilemma we live with throughout our lives, that the lump of grey matter creates a person who must live forever in his or her own individual world of meaning, yet in order to develop and survive the person must negotiate with other people, each of whom lives in his or her own world of meaning. Amongst these people are our siblings. We may grow up in the same house as our siblings but we live in different countries.

The curious mystery of being a person means that there are no firm rules for getting along successfully with other people. For instance, on the whole, if you are nice to other people they are likely to be nice to you, but then they might not be. They might take advantage of your niceness to cheat or harm you. The fact that you love someone does not mean that the person will love you. You cannot force people to love you or to want to spend time with you. I can only advise that if you are troubled by a longing to put things right with your siblings, it is worth trying to do so. If you succeed, that is wonderful. If you do not succeed, you can comfort yourself with the knowledge that at least you tried. However, trying and failing can be a comfort only if you understand why you failed.

Your attempt to put things right should not be rushed into but prepared for. In part this book is like the manuals that explorers used as they prepared for their journey into the wilderness. The explorers' manuals listed the necessary provisions. Here I list the ideas which were described in earlier chapters and which provide the necessary nourishment for your journey into the unknown. Next the explorers' manuals listed the dangers that an explorer might encounter. Here I shall list the dangers of competing to be good and that way of living which Freud called narcissistic, where the person is so wrapped up in himself that he sees other people as being no more than bit players in his own drama. Lastly, the explorers' manual described the goal and how the explorer would recognise it when he reached it. In my book, the goal is trust, and, if that cannot be found, at least you will have the understanding of why you failed.

## The six necessary provisions

### *First provision*

The first provision is an understanding of what forgiveness is. In a world where revenge is so often the basis for political action, forgiveness is lauded as a virtue. This shows a complete lack of understanding of what a virtue is. To act virtuously we have to make a choice of which of a number of possible actions we shall follow. Forgiveness is not a choice of action but an emotion that arises when we see that the person who injured us is no longer a threat to us. Forgiveness is the meaning, 'You are no longer a danger to me and I can understand and accept what you did.'

We can choose to act in a forgiving manner, but this does not mean that we feel the emotion of forgiveness. We can choose to strive to keep our hate and bitterness in check because those emotions damage us greatly, while seeking vengeance reinforces our hate and bitterness, and leads us into even more disasters. Parents who love their child and who choose not to seek vengeance on those who killed their child do not feel the emotion of forgiveness, although they may use the word forgiveness for what they are doing. The death of their child is an injury to their sense of being a person that will last for the rest of their lives because the child is irreplaceable. If you love your child, your child is a part of you, and so an attack on your child is an attack on you. If later the attacker expresses remorse for what he has done, the parent may feel a lessening of the anger he or she feels against the attacker and even be able to feel pity for the person who has repented, but the pain and the sadness will remain. When in Liverpool Anthony Walker, an 18-year-old black student, was viciously murdered by two white men, Michael Taylor and Paul Barton, Anthony's mother Gee Walker surprised many people by publicly forgiving her son's killers. It is not unknown for some Christians to make such a protestation of forgiveness in order to be seen as being very virtuous, but when Mrs Walker later explained the thinking behind her statement it was clear that she had given a great deal of thought to what forgiveness actually was. She said that if in the Lord's Prayer she prayed for God's forgiveness she would have to strive to forgive others, no matter how difficult that might be. When she said that she forgave the killers she was not saying she regarded them as no longer dangerous to her and could understand and accept what they had done. What she meant was that she did not want to feel anger, hate and resentment toward the killers because that tied her to them and harmed her. She strove to feel towards them, as she said, 'No anger, no bitterness, just pity,' because that would allow her to heal. 'I have to rise above the situation.' Such forgiveness, she said, is not a once-and-for-all action. 'It is a daily thing.'[3] She knew that she would never be able to leave Anthony's death behind her. She said, 'Our lives will never be the same again. How do you come to terms with the death of your child?'[4]

The feeling of forgiveness is possible only if the perpetrator of our injury recognises that we have suffered *and* takes responsibility for the act that led to our suffering. This is why siblings who wish to be reconciled need to have a conversation where old injuries are recognised and not denied, and the perpetrator takes responsibility for the act. Saying 'I'm sorry you are upset' is not taking responsibility for the injury. The perpetrator must be quite specific about what has occurred. A general 'sorry' is not enough.

We need to remember that most of us will do anything rather than take responsibility for our actions. We all have a range of ploys for pushing responsibility on to other people or other things. People who become experts in being good and who subsequently become depressed will often claim responsibility for the perilous state of the planet but resist taking responsibility for themselves, preferring to see themselves as a victim waiting for a saviour. They may claim that they had no choice but to become a martyr, or that they have an illness caused by a chemical imbalance or a depression gene. People with a volatile temper will often blame others for causing them to become angry, or claim that they inherited their bad temper from their parents and so they cannot be blamed for what they do, nor is there any way they can change what they do. If you have a sibling who has had a lifetime's practice in avoiding taking personal responsibility your chances of having a conversation that leads to reconciliation are extremely low.

## *Second provision*

Second, we need to understand what it is to be a human being, that is, a being who is constantly giving meaning to what is happening around him and inside him. These meanings are all that we can ever know. We see an object and at the same time as seeing the object we gives it a meaning, say, a car. We do not perceive and then create a meaning. *Perceiving is creating a meaning.*

We ought to grow up understanding this but we do not because our parents and teachers want us to believe that there is just one right way of thinking. If we think in the right way we will be loved and accepted; if we think in the wrong way we will be rejected and punished. As adults we might recognise that we have been duped by our parents and teachers, but at the same time we are surrounded by a vast number of 'experts' who insist that we are not active agents who interpret, decide and act but merely puppets pulled by the strings of our genes, or our traits, or by society, or by economics, or by planets millions of miles away. The idea that we are puppets can be seductive because we can then claim that we are not responsible for what we do. It can take considerable mental effort always to remember that the human world consists of the ideas generated by its inhabitants.

However, if we can remember this we have the key to understanding ourselves and other people. We can see how the sense of being a person is a structure of meaning, and how this structure is always in danger of being invalidated because each of the meanings is a guess about what is going on.

## *Third provision*

Third, we need to see how the structure of meaning is like an organism, growing and changing, and yet still containing its earliest meanings. Just as your bones are the bones you were born with, though older and bigger, so you are the child you once were. John Simpson captured this understanding when he compared himself at six and himself now:

I don't in any way resemble the large, sprawling figure I

was to become, but there are little details of similarity:
our big ears, our red lips.

The thing this six-year-old and I have most in common,
though, is that he and I see almost everything alike. The
same things frighten us, and the same things incline us to
take the same kind of risk. The same emotions sway us,
and bring tears to our eyes. We both hate the kind of
scenes that my father and mother seem to have most of
the time, and we both try to escape from them. I know
more than the six-year-old does, and can intimidate people
better than he can, and have endured things he would
never have survived. I would shock him, I suppose, with
my worldliness, and my occasional brutality, and my
willingness to put up with things that are second best.

But we each know how the other's mind works, because
it is essentially the same mind, whereas our legs and
faces and hands are not the same at all, merely similar.
I know what stories he likes, and he knows what stories
I like. He would recognize the thread of romanticism and
of pity that is common to us both, and the carelessness
and thoughtlessness too. He is me psychologically, in
a way he is not physically. I like him; I just hope he
would like me, and can't be absolutely sure he would.[5]

Because we hold ideas from our childhood we can still behave
in the ways we did then. Some of us remain children even though
our body is that of an adult. A father whose children were in
their twenties told me, 'Our children won't grow up until we're
out of the way.' He and his wife were in their fifties and very
healthy, so their children will be children for many years to
come. In Marina Lewycka's novel *A Short History of Tractors
in Ukrainian*, Nadia says: 'Every time I phone my father or my
sister, it is like crossing a bridge from the world where I am
an adult with responsibilities and a measure of power, to the
cryptic world of childhood where I am at the mercy of other
people's purposes which I can neither control nor understand.'[6]
We can be quite grown up when we are with friends and colleagues but as soon as we meet our siblings we can find ourselves reverting to childhood. A colleague told me, 'My brother
and I don't get on. When I'm with him I get so irritated. I think

it's because he reminds me of me in many ways. When we're with our mother we go back to being children, trying to get her attention. But we really don't want her attention. Ordinarily we prefer her not to pay too much attention to us.'

If we are not aware of when we look at the world with the eyes of the child we once were, we repeat the uninformed actions of that child. When Giles married again he found that when his two sons from his first marriage began to fight he and his partner Leonie would soon begin to argue about the boys, with Giles taking the side of the older boy and Leonie the part of the younger. Giles was the firstborn in his family and Leonie was the youngest in hers. Not surprisingly, they could not arrive at a sensible strategy for dealing with the boys' behaviour.

Fay said, 'Stephen and I are each the middle of three. When we were first together we'd have the most terrible fights. It was two hurt children fighting together. My children couldn't understand why we would fight like that. They don't have the hurts inside them that Stephen and I have.' Fay believed in talking things over but had difficulty in persuading Stephen to do this because he had always dealt with difficult situations by remaining silent. However, over the years they managed to recognise that they had been fighting old sibling battles and now they have ceased to do this.

### Fourth provision

Fourth, we must constantly remind ourselves that no two people ever see anything in exactly the same way. This means that different people have different priorities. If our prime purpose in life is our relationships with other people and our sibling's prime purpose is achievement, organisation and control, this does not mean that we are right and our sibling wrong, but just that our sibling is different from us.

### Fifth provision

Fifth, we need to remember that we learn many more things from our family than we are ever aware of learning. As children we assume that all families are like ours. Gradually we become aware that other families are not like ours, but more often than not we concentrate on the major differences and fail to recognise that each family has a style that the child learns. The frequency with which I am asked, 'But doesn't the way depression runs in families prove that there is a depression gene?' shows how rarely people are aware of how we learn the habitual attitudes of our parents. As adolescents we may have rejected our parents' attitudes but we have learnt them nevertheless. If you are a parent you will be able to recall your horror when you heard yourself saying to your child something that your parents had said to you and which you vowed you would never say.

When we leave home we develop a way of behaving which allows us to present ourselves as an adult in an adult world, but we do not forget our way of behaving when we lived with our family and tried to survive as a person. When we go home we encounter our family behaving in their usual way and we fall back into our childhood way of trying to survive our family style. Every family's style is always complex and subtle. When John Simpson went to a family funeral he became more fully aware of his family's particular style:

> This is a tribal gathering to mark the passing of a leading member, not a point-scoring session. Once again, the similarities begin to show themselves, rather than the elements of difference. The people here have a tone of speech, an attitude of mind, which is mocking and self-mocking, deprecating and self-deprecating.
>
> I have been aware of this tone a thousand times before: from my grandfather, my father, my uncle, my aunt, my cousins, stretching out across the lines of consanguinity. Somehow, at some distant time, someone introduced a thread of it into the complex pattern of the family's discourse, and it became dominant, so that it is the first thing you think about when my family comes to mind: that sharp banter, close to bickering, which falls short of spite only because the speaker so often turns the humour against himself or herself. I can hear them at it around me now, as they sit over the remains of the meal.
>
> 'To be honest, I feel nowadays I've got one foot in the grave and another on a banana skin.'

'The silly old thing – she's almost as stupid as I am.'[7]

Each member of the family develops his or her own version of the family style by selecting those ways of behaving which can serve as a defence against being invalidated by the family. Part of the family style always concerns what is allowed to be talked about and what is allowed to be remembered. Some members of the family will uphold the family's rules about what can be remembered and talked about, while other members of the family may challenge these rules. One man told me, 'I'm the family patriot and my brother is the rebel.'

### Sixth provision

Sixth, we must always bear in mind that we cannot help but remember things in our own individual way, and that what we do remember and forget has to do with validating ourselves as a person and warding off invalidation. Richard Benson discovered this when he set out to write the history of the family farm. As the eldest son, Richard should have taken on the job of running the farm but instead he became a journalist, while his sister Helen became a teacher. His brother Guy took over the job of working with their parents in what proved to be the futile struggle to hold on to the farm. Richard wrote:

> When I came to record it all, I found it easy enough to establish places and dates, but stunningly difficult to get anyone to agree with me on details. One of my most potent memories, for example, is taking charge of some ill pigs when I was about 17. I thought that by saving some of them I might redeem my klutzy image, and built them a special pen, and spent my spare time feeding them. They all died, and when I told my dad the last had gone, I realised that he had known that this would happen, and that he would have not let Guy, who was being trained seriously, persist in such a sentimental illusion; in short, it meant that everyone had realised before I did that I would be leaving.
>
> Did my brother, father or mother remember the sick pigs as a major turning point too? Er, no: they did not, in fact, remember them at all. The only person who did was Helen. She had helped me with them herself – only for me, in my

egocentric self-absorption, to subsequently forget about her. After months of this, and of the challenges to long-held ideas about family members and myself, I realised how separate we all are, in the end. It's quite a bleak feeling, and it means that you can only tell your own story, not everyone else's.[8]

Richard Benson discovered that what we remember most strongly are those events that related to us personally, either validating or invalidating ourselves. However, we often repress our memory of events that threatened to invalidate us completely and we resist other people's attempts to get us to remember. We need to be well aware of those events that threatened to invalidate our siblings, but we also need to be even more aware of those events that came close to invalidating us. Just in the way that Helen (Chapter 6) did not talk to her brothers about the death of their sister Miranda because she did not want to distress them, so your siblings mighty not talk about a family crisis for fear of distressing you. They may be doing this out of kindness, or they may want to think of themselves as being kind and thus being good.

## Competing to be good

When we are children we need adults to take care of us and to take responsibility for us. Thus it is in our interests to learn how to be good in the way the adults looking after us define 'good'. If we are to grow up and become adults and not merely children in adult bodies we have to learn how to take care of ourselves and to accept responsibility for ourselves. Part of taking responsibility for ourselves is knowing how to tolerate the uncertainty which is an integral part of life.

Many people do not want to take responsibility for themselves. They do not want to have to blame themselves when they make a mistake, and they want to avoid the unpleasantness of being uncertain and feeling helpless. They prefer that someone else, some parent-like figure, take responsibility for them. This figure may be the head of their family, or an older sibling, or God, or Allah, or a Power which controls some universal system such as karma, or a dictator, or the government, or simply them, the people with power and influence. The parent-like figure rewards them for being good, takes responsibility for them, and can be blamed when things go wrong. However, when we assume that someone else will take care of us, we enter into a contract where, in return for being looked after, we have to be good in the way that the person looking after us defines 'good'. But how can we know if we are sufficiently good unless we compare ourselves with other people in the way we compared ourselves with our siblings? Thus, by refusing to take responsibility for ourselves, we take into adult life the issues we encountered when we were children and competed with our siblings to be the goodest in the family. Many an ageing parent has had to suffer the ministrations of her children who are competing to be the best at looking after her while denigrating any sibling who fails to take part in the competition.

We should always remember that it is possible to be good without having to live as children being cared for and judged by a parent-like figure. If we take responsibility for ourselves we have to work out a code to live by. Through this we can judge how to balance our own needs against those of other people so that we can be a good citizen in the society in which we live. We do good not in the hope of gaining a reward and avoiding punishment but because it pleases us to do so. The majority of people who take responsibility for themselves choose to be good citizens because they know that their life will be more enjoyable if they live in a safe, law-abiding society.

Taking responsibility for yourself is never easy. To do so you need to have learned from your experiences of being invalidated that you actually cannot be wiped out as a person and that what is falling apart is not you but merely some of your ideas. Tom, an Australian with an Irish father and an Aboriginal mother, took responsibility for himself when he was in his teens and living at home became too difficult. He wanted to believe that there was a place for him in his family home but this idea proved not to fit the actual circumstances – the family home was no longer a safe place for him to live. From childhood to middle age the journey he made from living in a tent as a small child with his mother at La Perouse, Sydney, to his own hairdressing business in the wealthy suburb of Mosman was, in Australian terms, a far longer and more difficult journey than the traditional American journey from log cabin to White House.

Tom was one of 12 siblings and the only one who made a success of his life. He attributed his success to the fact that as a teenager he had recognised that he was gay. He told me, 'Being gay meant that I was an outsider. I could cope with being outside my family. I'd left school very early. I went into hairdressing because the happiest people I knew were hairdressers.' Deciding that he would be able to cope as an outsider and that he would seek a happy life for himself meant that he had the self-confidence to be responsible for himself. However, his success did not mean that he left his siblings behind. Because he understood how important it was to take responsibility for yourself, he tried to help his siblings do the same. Helping a person take responsibility for himself is a task which the most skilled of psychotherapists often finds impossible. Tom was distraught when the brother he was closest to killed himself, and angry when a sister threatened to blackmail him in order to get money from him. In a similar situation many siblings allow themselves to be blackmailed because they want to think of themselves as being good. Tom knew that there are times when we have to set aside our desire to be good because it is vital that we protect ourselves from harm. He acted immediately and decisively and foiled his sister's plan. Of course, Tom's life was not as simple and straightforward as my short account makes it sound. There were doubts, mistakes, uncertainty, false starts, attempts and defeats, victories and wasted time. That is what living is.

Max is a very intelligent and creative man who makes a success of whatever he undertakes. But there was one task that was beyond him. He knew from his own experience that it is possible to change your life for the better provided you take responsibility for yourself. He wanted his siblings to have the kind of happy life he enjoyed with his wife and children. He told me, 'I try so hard to sort my family out. I have a vision of what I think a family ought to be.' He could make his vision reality in his home with his wife and children but he could not achieve that for his siblings no matter what he did.

Seeing yourself as being looked after by some parent-like figure appears to offer some delightful pleasures, but these pleasures do not always eventuate. The contract 'You will look after me and I will be good' operates within the framework of the belief in the Just World. If you are good you will get your rewards. The belief in the Just World appears to promise to remove uncertainty from our lives, but it never lives up to its promise. When we are children we can hope that in the future our rewards will come, and we may plan our life around this belief, but in adult life the believers in the Just World are more likely to find themselves thinking, 'Why me? What have I done to deserve this?' than, 'This blessing is my reward for being good.' We might believe in the Just World but the world itself seems not to be privy to the Just World scheme.

Siblings who are very resistant to a reappraisal of their childhood may be engaged in lying to themselves about the functioning of the Just World. They might be telling themselves that their life is very happy, a just reward for all their goodness, and not wanting to acknowledge that what they actually feel is intense sadness and disappointment. Moreover, when siblings who believe in the Just World assess their life and compare it with the lives of their siblings, they can feel bitter that they have been denied the rewards they feel that they deserve, and envious of those siblings whom they see as having, quite undeservingly, much better lives than they do. Such bitterness and envy can be an insurmountable barrier to reconciliation.

As children we often protect ourselves against our siblings' cruelty by creating fantasies of revenge. Sometime indulging in such fantasies is enough to dissipate the child's need for revenge, and sometimes the fantasy becomes the basis of a work of art. Hans Christian Andersen's story 'The Red Shoes' concerns a little girl whose overweening vanity led to her valuing her red shoes above her concern for others and for her faith. Then an old soldier put a spell upon the shoes and condemned the little girl to dance without ceasing in the red shoes that were stuck fast to her feet. It was not until she had her feet cut off and she repented of her sin that she could find peace. Hans Christian Andersen named the girl Karen after his half-sister.

Fantasies of revenge usually take the form of the wicked sibling being punished, the nobility and goodness of the injured sibling displayed for all to see, and the wicked sibling begging the injured sibling for forgiveness. The biblical stories of Esau and Jacob, and of Joseph and his brothers are based on this plot. Jacob tricked Esau out of his birthright and his blessing. When eventually they met again Jacob 'bowed himself to the ground seven times, until he came near to his brother. And Esau ran to meet him, and embraced him, and fell upon his neck, and kissed him: and they wept.'[9] Joseph was his father Israel's favourite. When Israel gave Joseph a coat of many colours his siblings were jealous and hated him, even more so when Joseph told them about his dream. He said, 'For, behold, we were binding sheaves in the field, and, lo, my sheaf arose, and stood upright; and, behold, your sheaves stood round about, and made obeisance to my sheaf.' So his brothers sold him into slavery, dipped his coat in goat's blood and presented it to their father as evidence of Joseph's death. Joseph was taken to Egypt and sold to one of Pharaoh's officers. 'Joseph was a goodly person and well favoured' and 'his master's wife cast her eyes on him'. He managed to escape from that dilemma, and having correctly interpreted Pharaoh's dream of the seven fat cattle and seven lean cattle as the impending seven fat years and seven lean years, Joseph prospered. In the lean years his brothers came wanting to buy food. Joseph teased them extensively and then magnanimously 'he kissed all his brethren and wept upon them: and after that his brethren talked with him.'[10]

It seems that one of the biggest barriers to peace between Israel and Palestine is that many members of both sides can envisage peace only in terms of these Old Testament stories. Their opponents must admit their guilt, beg forgiveness and praise them for their magnanimity and goodness. This revenge plot does not allow for compromise where the opposing groups have to admit that there have been crimes and misdemeanours on both sides. If your sibling is operating on the revenge plot, and fears that any admission of personal guilt would be annihilating, then your saying to him, 'I know I wasn't perfect but there are faults on both sides' is not going to lead to a reconciliation.

When we enter into a contract to be good in return for being looked after, we divide ourselves in two. Instead of being one whole person we think of ourselves as being both the parent who sets standards and administers rewards and punishments, and the child who is sometimes obedient and sometimes naughty and rebellious. This way of thinking is often revealed in what people say about themselves, such as in, 'I thought I deserved a treat', and, 'I know it's wicked but I'll have a second helping.' (People who see themselves as a whole person say, 'I fancied this' and, 'Yes, I'd like a second helping.') Dividing ourselves in two, we can alternate between being the parent and being the child, often without realising that we are doing so. As the parent we can feel proud of our virtue and our power to punish the child, but as the child we can feel persecuted and so we rebel. Being the naughty child can be very pleasurable. One father told me, 'My sons compete in being bad.' No doubt they are fans of the immensely successful series of children's books about Horrid Henry with his brother Perfect Peter. Henry's creator, Francesca Simon, said of him, 'The humour comes from Henry's wants – that he wants something so desperately he will do anything to achieve it, and not think about the consequences. . . . He's thinking, I wanna go first – why shouldn't I go first, why should she go before me? He's just massive ego. . . . I think that why kids identify with him so – because we all think we'll be great if we were king of the world, and everyone did what we want them to do; it's stripping away the whole veneer of "you go first".'[11]

Being Horrid Henry can be an effective defence against adults whose demands that the child be good can threaten his sense of being a person with annihilation. A child or adult who never dares rebel loses touch with who they are and becomes a façade with seemingly no person behind the façade. However, adults who do not wish to take responsibility for themselves can enact a form of Horrid Henry which does them no good at all. They rebel against their inner parent and those people they can see as parents by resorting to excessive amounts of food, alcohol, cigarettes or drugs, or by refusing to follow a health or exercise routine not matter how ill they may become from such neglect.

The majority of ills that beset us in the developed world are not devastating diseases but chronic conditions with which we can live fairly successfully provided we take good care of ourselves. In the same way we can ward off many illnesses and ameliorate many of the conditions that can come with increasing age. We do not lack information about the necessity of a healthy diet, regular exercise and adequate sleep, nor about the dangers of a poor diet, nicotine and alcohol. If you have a chronic illness like diabetes or epilepsy, or you break your hip or develop allergic asthma, the medical profession will provide you with a programme which will help you maintain your health. However, such a programme needs to be followed daily. If you take responsibility for yourself and care about yourself it will seem good sense to do what you can to stay healthy, but if you have divided yourself into parent and child, it is easy to slip into Horrid Henry and refuse to do what the adults tell you. So you find yourself huddled with the other Horrid Henries in the smokers' group out in the cold, or abandoning your much-needed diet to enjoy the guilty pleasure of a cream cake. You can become the rebellious child who defies the adults that advise a programme of exercise to enable you to recover from an accident or keep your asthma under control. You can see any sibling who expresses a concern for your welfare as yet another interfering adult who must be defied.

Perhaps the saddest consequence of dividing yourself into parent and child is that you live only in the past and the future, worried that what you have done in the past will in the future bring the punishments you deserve. You can never live in the present, paying full attention to the present moment. Yet it is only in the present that we can be happy. Happiness is the emotion which says, 'Right now everything is wonderful.' Sometimes, living in the present goes beyond being keenly aware of the here and now and becomes the kind of experience which has been described as 'transcendent', or 'spiritual', or 'religious', or simply 'at one with nature and all that there is'. It is an experience that can come during meditation, or while looking at the sea, the mountains, the sky, or simply a flower. Some people call the experience 'being in touch with a Power greater than yourself'. However, this Power is not judging, rewarding and punishing you, but is simply there and it is part of you and you are part of it. In whatever way people describe this experience, there is general agreement that it is liberating and transforming.[12]

Buddhism has long recognised the necessity of being able to live in the present and called it *mindfulness*. Cognitive behaviour therapy has always been concerned with only the past and the future – the luggage from the past called 'dysfunctional cognitions' and the rewards that come from learning new cognitions. However, recently some CBT therapists have discovered mindfulness which has been defined as 'a way of paying attention with intention and without judgement to the present moment's experience'. Ways of teaching mindfulness have been developed where 'the central message is that paying attention fosters the ability to make wise choices'.[13] Taking responsibility for yourself means that you have to make choices and hope that they are wise ones.

Ceasing to compete over who is the goodest sibling in the family is part of taking responsibility for yourself. Helen told me how her relationship with her older brother James changed as she got older. She had said, 'My relationship with my siblings is very important in my life, in forming my personality.' Comparing herself with her older brother James she said, 'James is quite talented, always good at sport and music, always top of the class at school. Anything he turned his hand at he was better than me. I didn't feel there was anything I could make my own so as to make my own path, until I was eighteen and I went to Japan on my year out. That was completely different to anything he'd done. After that I was studying English at university, which was completely different from anything he'd done as well. There was a point where I realised you can't compare those things, or I don't have to. Doing my A Levels and making sure I got better grades than him, or the same grades as him was really, really important to me at that time, but by the time I took my degree, it wasn't important to me any more. I got a better degree than he did, and that doesn't really count for anything, so something has changed. I think our relationship improved so dramatically when he went to university and I went down to see him. Suddenly we were equals – not equals but on a much more equal level. I was staying with him, we could go to the pub together, and he'd introduce me to his friends like I was a real human being. Once he got to university, something changed when we didn't have to live with each other any more. There were a few more arguments, but we certainly didn't have physical violence any more.'

In taking responsibility for herself Helen did more than pursue interests different from those of her brother. She thought about what was happening in her life, just as she did when her sister Miranda died. She examined the question of God's benevolence and power in a world where suffering exists. One way of posing this question is to take the three statements, 'God is all good', 'God is all powerful', 'Suffering exists'. For two of these statements to be true the third must be false. People who want to believe in the existence of a Just World will say that we have to take God on trust and accept that He has mysterious ways. Helen saw this answer as a fudge and rejected it. In the same way, she recognised that her continued competition with her brother was based on her fantasy of defeating him and becoming Queen of the World. She knew that no one could be Queen of the World. She knew that if she were to take responsibility for herself she had to make a realistic assessment of the world in which she was one small part. She had to give up what Freud had called the fantasy of narcissism, where the person sees himself as being at the centre of a world where the only events which mattered were the ones which related to him.

## The narcissism of not liking yourself

Freud took the word 'narcissism' from the ancient Greek legend of Narcissus who was so in love with his own beauty that he remained lying beside a pool, admiring his reflection in the water. There he died and a beautiful flower, the narcissus, grew where he had lain. Freud's use of this term can be misleading for it can seem to imply that that those people who value and accept themselves are forever thinking about themselves, when in fact the reverse is true. When we value and accept ourselves we need to spend very little time worrying about what other people think of us. Instead, we can spend our time learning about other people and getting to know them. If we do not value and accept ourselves, we constantly worry about what effect we are having on other people. We always expect that people will not like us, and will think and talk about us in a most derogatory way. Our expectations prevent us from seeing what is actually going on.

It is a cruel irony that we cannot help but be the centre of our own world, yet if we do not strive to make that great leap of imagination into other people's worlds which we call empathy we cannot make good, lasting relationships with other people. Discovering how other people see themselves and their world can be very frightening because it robs us of our belief that the world is simply there and we see it as it is. The world is certainly there, but how it appears to us depends on us. Understanding this creates enormous uncertainty. Rather than accept this uncertainty, many people try to exclude anybody and anything that might suggest that their way of viewing the world is not absolutely right. The wars and conflicts that fill human history have been fought because each side insists that in religion and/or politics they are absolutely right and their opponents are absolutely wrong.

Similar battles go on in families. Toddlers may have a precocious ability to understand members of their family, but this is so they can keep themselves safe. Some toddlers retain this ability and elaborate it as they get older, perhaps because they need to survive, or because they find empathy interesting, or because it enhances their ability to form relationships. Toddlers' acts of empathy concern their own relationships with their family, whereas if we retain and elaborate our ability to empathise we can enter the worlds of people who know nothing of our existence, or even if they do know of our existence do not regard us as the most important person in their world. Many people discard their ability to empathise because they do not want to know that their picture of the world is not a picture of the world as it actually is. Neither do they want to confront the complexities and dangers involved in relationships and in life itself. By discarding this ability they mutilate themselves to a greater degree than if they had cut off one of their limbs, because they condemn themselves to a kind of lifelong loneliness since they never really get to know other people and thus feel close to them.

I know many narcissistic people who are warm and loving to me. I do not doubt their love, but when we meet, once they have greeted me most lovingly, I become their audience who can be relied on to respond to them with pleasure and applause. However, if I attempt to entertain them with some anecdote about me which does not directly involve them, their attention soon strays from what I am saying, and with a well-practised skill, they switch the conversation to their favourite topic, themselves. These are people who would claim that I am one of their dearest friends, but they have only the foggiest notion of what I do and who I am.

Such narcissistic people at least know that the only way to get people to like you is to be nice to them. Many narcissistic people do not know this. When someone talks to them about something that has no direct relationship to them their eyes glaze over. They reach for the television remote or walk out of the room. Being human, they need other people, but they blunder through relationships and wonder why people behave in ways that they do not expect. They form only very simple theories about why people behave as they do, perhaps by classifying all people according to their birth sign, or by deciding that one person is, perhaps, 'just like his father' and expecting the person to behave in every way as his father did.

When we are children and adults treat us in the cruel and careless ways that come close to annihilating us as a person, we have to defend ourselves. Just as in a war people who are under heavy attack from their enemy have to think only of themselves, so a child who is in the hands of inept or dangerous adults must think only of how to survive. As they get older, children in this situation might realise that they will be able to escape from this dangerous situation, but many do not. The source of his peril might have become an adult who can be escaped from or defied, but the child has taken this adult inside him. His peril is no longer the adult who loomed over him but the ideas in his head. He denigrates himself as the adults once denigrated him.

When we constantly denigrate ourselves, seeing ourselves as being bad and unacceptable, we cause ourselves a great deal of pain. We can deal with this pain in three different ways. The first, and the only way I would recommend, is that we realise that this way of thinking about ourselves is something that we learnt in childhood when we were learning to be good. As it is something learnt, we are free to change it. Second, we can continue to feel the pain but take pride in it because it is evidence of how good we are. Good people can never be good enough, so the pain is evidence that we are striving to be good, and thus we are superior to those people who do not realise how bad they actually are. Third, we can deny the pain by creating a fantasy

about how wonderful we are and what a happy and successful life we lead. Some narcissistic people create fantasies that,
in the range of possible fantasies, are quite modest. They see
themselves as successful in their work and family life, loved
by their family and liked by all who know them. They can be
wildly wrong in part or all of this, and they suspect this may
be so, but they have to be deaf and blind to any evidence that
their life is not what they fantasise it as being.

Some narcissistic people find a fantasy of a happy but quite
ordinary life entirely unsatisfactory. They have suffered too
many hurts and insults in childhood for their pain to be assuaged
by a fantasy of ordinary happiness. They need to be special, different from and better than all others. They fantasise that they
have some extraordinary talents, some special and perhaps secret knowledge, which makes them separate from and superior
to all others. For some who choose the defence of fantasy, being
a yet-to-be-discovered champion footballer, novelist, celebrity
is not enough. They have to be King or Queen of the World.
Some members of this group become psychotic: others become
dictators, prime ministers and presidents.

However, narcissistic people make a great contribution to the
lives of all of us. They make us laugh. If they are members
of our family, even as we bang our head against the wall in
frustration at what they do and say, we can laugh, and gossip
with those people who also find them funny. We laugh at their
overweening vanity, the way they delude themselves with their
self-serving fantasies, their lack of self-awareness, and the
blunders that follow from all this. Every comic novel, comedy
and television situation comedy has at least one narcissistic
person who lives in a world of his own and blunders about, not
understanding what other people are saying and doing, easily
falling for the tricks that other people play on him. Malvolio in
*Twelfth Night* and Gareth in *The Office*[14] might be centuries
apart in creation but they are as one.

Malvolio believes that his employer, the Countess Olivia,
values him much more highly than she actually does. He is
easily tricked into believing that she loves him and wants to
marry him. Having failed to learn much about Olivia, he is
unaware of Olivia's taste in men's apparel and, following the
trickster's advice to show that he returns her love, he wears

yellow stockings and cross-gartered, a way of dressing which she dislikes. Maria, Olivia's maid and author of these instructions, says of him, [He is] 'the best persuaded of himself; so crammed, as he thinks, with excellences, that it is his ground of faith that all that look on him love him'.

Malvolio would have dearly desired, had he known about such things, his own home page on the BBC website, just like that of Gareth of *The Office*. On this Gareth says:

> I was born 17th April, 1971. My star-sign is Aries. I had my horoscope done by my mum's friend Kath, who is an expert. She said a typical Aries is
>
> > Adventurous and energetic
> > Pioneering and courageous
> > Enthusiastic and confident
> > Dynamic and quick-witted
>
> This is exactly right. I am all of these things. I was a bit annoyed that she didn't mention intelligence but when I asked her if Aries was intelligent she said definitely. I was embarrassed to ask if Aries are good lovers because my mum was in the room, but the answer is yes.

As well as these extraordinary qualities, what marks Gareth out as very special is that: 'I am in the TA (Territorial Army). A lot of people think that those in the Territorial Army are not real soldiers. We are well trained, highly disciplined fighting machines ready for war. We are just not available during the week.'[15]

Even if you have not watched *The Office* you will know from Gareth's birth date that he is a grown man. His home page reads like that of a teenage boy. Narcissists like Malvolio and Gareth reveal a terrible naivety which makes us laugh at them, and sometimes want to punish them. The treatment that Malvolio receives – treated as being mad, locked in a dark room and mercilessly teased by the Clown – is cruel. Gareth is not treated cruelly by his colleague Tim, but he is teased, and is confused by Tim's teasing. Tim is not lost in a world of fantasy. His creator Ricky Gervais called him 'the voice of reason'.[16] Tim knows his limitations, but allows himself the hope that one day

Dawn, the receptionist, will leave her boyfriend for him. He recognises that Gareth needs his fantasy to survive, but his understanding makes him prey to pity, and pity is an uncomfortable emotion that can prevent us from taking a stand when perhaps we should do so. This is a dilemma familiar to those who have a narcissistic sibling.

The trouble with such compensatory fantasies is that they are very difficult to give up. For most of us, when life is not terrible, it is dull. Our life is not markedly different from that of the people around us. How can you be a distinctive individual amongst so many millions of people? If you suspect that in reality there is nothing distinctive about you, you can need a compensatory fantasy of being distinctive in some way just to get you through the day. If you are lucky you can find friends, or perhaps a partner, who can tolerate you living your fantasy. Television often portrays such partners as long-suffering wives (Margaret, wife of Victor Meldrew in *One Foot in the Grave*), less often as husbands (Richard, husband of Hyacinth Bucket in *Keeping Up Appearances*). Or you might be able to make an unspoken contract with your partner or friends where you tolerate their fantasies about themselves if they tolerate yours. The immensely popular television series *Cheers* and *Friends* are based on this formula.

But what if to compensate for the great hurts and insults in your childhood you need to go beyond being an outstanding individual and become King or Queen of the World? If you can persuade enough people to share your fantasy, so that they see you as the great leader and themselves as your devoted followers, then you do have a good chance of becoming famous, though infamy might follow not far behind. However, if you cannot persuade people to share your fantasy you are likely to be seen as being mad. When, in a manic state, a person becomes psychotic, he is treating as being real the fantasy of power and glory which he had created in order to defend himself from the pain of seeing himself as being bad and unacceptable.

The prison of a compensatory fantasy need not be a life sentence. In our teens we are all narcissists, but most of us get older and wiser. We know that we have to give up our teenage fantasies and learn how to empathise with other people, even though this means accepting that other people see the world differently from us. Alas some of us get older but no wiser. Perhaps one day Ricky Gervais will tell us whether Gareth, at a point of crisis such as being discharged from the TA, was able to give up his fantasy of being 'a highly disciplined fighting machine ready for war', or whether his way of recovering from such a loss was the one often used by old soldiers whose experience of war was not too terrible. Does Gareth turn into the pub bore whose stories of past exploits become more and more glorious as the years go by?

## Love and trust

If asked what they longed for in the adult sibling relationship perhaps most people would talk in terms of the expression of mutual love. However, the word 'love' carries a huge burden of people's expectations. According to John Lennon, it is all we need. But what do we mean by love? It is a positive emotion, something we can see as validating us, but there are huge variations in what we actually feel when we say, 'I love.' Our child, our lover and our sibling can elicit from us very positive feelings which we call love, but if we were to put into words the meaning of these different examples of love we would have to make some important distinctions between them. The love of a parent for a child and the love of an individual for a lover can be very passionate, but few people other than Virginia Woolf would say that their love for their sibling is passionate. The absence of passion in our love for our sibling can mean that we are not aware of this love at all.

Alain de Botton defined love from the point of view of the recipient. He said: 'To be shown love is to feel ourselves the object of concern. Our presence is noted, our name is registered, our views are listened to, our failings are treated with indulgence and our needs are ministered to. And under such care we flourish.'[17] This is the kind of love that can exist between siblings and neither may be fully aware of it because it has existed unremarked on for all of their lives. Perhaps they become aware of their love only when there is a crisis in the life of one of them. When we are children this is the kind of love we want from our parents and siblings. We love and long to be loved in return in the way which enables us to be certain that 'I exist and I am me, not the person other people want me to be.'

However, to maintain our love for a sibling, parent, partner or friend, we need from time to time some sign that the other person loves us. These signs maintain our love. In the absence of such signs we can hope that the other person loves us, and the fantasies that accompany the hope maintain our love. However, when the other person gives no sign at all of loving us and we give up our hope that they do, our own love dwindles and dies. In place of our love we feel indifference, an absence of both our love and the hate that accompanies love. When we love we become vulnerable to the hurts that the loved person can inflict, often unwittingly, and when we hurt we hate. When love disappears, the passion which inspired hate also disappears. Love cannot return to the place where indifference resides because what has been lost is not just the love but the trust which accompanies that love.

In the many conversations I have had with people, both women and men, who had discovered that their beloved partner had been unfaithful, what they talked about most was not love but the abuse of trust. 'He lied to me' is a more hurtful discovery than 'He loves someone else.' Many of the people who talked to me about the hurts their siblings had inflicted on them often included, almost in passing, an anecdote about how their sibling had stood up for them when they had been attacked by someone outside the family. In this action the other sibling seemed to be saying, 'I've got the right to beat you up but no one else can.' This kind of childhood relationship can become one in adulthood where each sibling knows that the other can be called upon in times of crisis. However, not all siblings enjoy the kind of relationship that becomes mutual trust in adulthood. With some siblings the lack of trust is irreparable. One of the siblings may hope that trust can be restored, but trust has to be mutual for the relationship to be good.

Stephen and his elder sister were sent to separate boarding schools and spent much of their childhood apart. They were not at all close, and he regretted this. When his sister's husband died suddenly Stephen felt it his duty to give his sister whatever help he could. He sat beside her at the funeral and stayed with her for a few days to help her with paperwork. He told me, 'My brother-in-law had stuff on his computer, particularly a book he was writing, that needed looking at, and my sister didn't know one end of a computer from another. So I sorted the computer for her, and I told her that there was a high risk, as I saw it, that she might actually wipe his computer with fiddling around, I made a copy of the book on a disk, and said to her, "If you need this, I've got it." I put it in my safe and forgot all about it. Then a couple of years later she asked me for the disk back – not because she'd lost it on her computer – it showed her ignorance, because I could have copied it, I could have done anything – but it was part of the process of removing my involvement in her life. And I was sad. It made me very, very sad, that, because I actually thought we'd had a closeness. Just being asked for the disk back, on one level seemed to imply a lack of trust. On another it was just shutting what may have been a little chink in the door, and it was just deliberately, quite explicitly closing it. You can think things have changed but they haven't.'

Trust, or the lack of it, is central to my relationship to my sister. My mother had a warning look for anyone who overstepped the mark that she had set. I knew this look only too well, and because it frightened me it must have seemed to me more menacingly strange than it actually was. My mother was pretty, yet suddenly her prettiness would vanish, her brows would lower, her eyes fix on the object of her displeasure, and her face would go black, a transformation which was as sudden as it was terrible. In my family any reference made to Mother's 'black look' was not an empty cliché.

If there is a 'black look' gene my sister inherited it, or perhaps, as the recipient of it, she learned how to do it and apply it to me. Any word or movement by me that did not suit her could earn this look, even when what I did was meant in the kindest way. When, as her bridesmaid, I stood beside her at the altar, I squeezed her hand in a somewhat sentimental but loving gesture as she was turning to follow the minister for the signing of the register. She responded to my gesture with her black look. I was shamed and worried that all the wedding guests had seen what happened.

I am no longer frightened of my sister's black looks even though I still manage to earn them. On my sister's eightieth birthday her family presented her and her husband with an album made up of photographs of them taken over the whole span of their lives. When my friend Nan and I went to visit her, my sister proudly showed the album to Nan who gallantly worked her way through it, while I explained who the people in the photographs were. When we came to her wedding photographs my sister told Nan, 'I didn't dress as a bride. I thought I wasn't pretty enough.' I had always known this and thought it sad, though my sister in her blue dress with black velvet trim and a perky little black hat did look very pretty. Then my sister told Nan something that made me feel even sadder. She said, 'You know, Mother wasn't interested in my wedding. She didn't help me arrange it.' Excited as I always am by the curious quirks of human nature I could not hold my tongue. I said, 'But Mother absolutely insisted that I had to be your bridesmaid. I didn't particularly want to do this and you had girlfriends I knew you'd prefer but I had to go with her on a really hot afternoon after school to buy a dress . . .' I let my voice trail into silence. Her black and threatening face demanded my silence. Nan and I dutifully returned to an inspection of the album and Nan, as ever, rescued the situation with a chatty, inconsequential remark.

I like to think that over the years I learnt to turn incidents like this into a humorous anecdote, but not long ago my son remarked on how unsettled I always was after a phone call from my sister. This was true. Even if the phone call had been seemingly quite ordinary, the moment I heard her voice I was on guard lest she say something that homed in on me, took me by surprise and left me feeling the hurt and loneliness of that little girl on the back seat of the car. I never felt that I could trust my sister.

The mistrust was mutual. As my sister aged she became softer and more kindly but she did not modify her need to keep everything under her control so that her view of her world was undisturbed. Uncertainty frightened her as much as it always did. She wanted to keep me as one of the figures in her landscape but she could not trust me because at any moment I was likely to say something that threw into question the picture she had made of her life and her world. She would always say that she wanted to see me, but her use of 'see' was literal. She wanted to lay eyes on me, but she did not want to enter into anything that might be called a conversation. I often joked to my son that, instead of visiting my sister, I should give her a life-size cardboard cut-out of myself, a representation of me which could be relied on not to speak.

Recently my sister and I met for lunch. That evening she phoned me and said, 'I've been meaning to ask you but I keep forgetting, do you want your books?' When our mother died my sister cleared out the family home and stored many of the contents in her own house. At lunch that day she had given me one of my first reading books. So I asked, 'You mean you've got more school books of mine?'

'No,' she said, 'they're those books of yours you gave me.' She meant the first editions of all the books I had written, each inscribed, 'To Myra, With Love from Dorothy.' She went on, 'I've got to get rid of them. You know we've put our name down for a unit.' This was an apartment in a retirement village. I said I did not want the books but wondered if any of her sons might like them.

She said, 'I don't think so. Andrew [her youngest] might. I could ask him.' She sounded very doubtful.

I said, 'You could give them to your local library.'

'You mean they'd like them?' Her doubt turned into incredulity.

'They might.' I think I may as well get that cardboard cut-out.

If there has been mutual trust in childhood, even though it might have disappeared in adult life, there is a reasonable chance that the mutual trust which two siblings had can be revived. However, achieving that may require an extraordinary effort, as the writer Rachel Simon found. Her book, *Riding the Buses with My Sister,* is an account of how it was only by spending a year with her sister Beth on her daily journeys on city buses that the two women found again the mutual trust they had enjoyed in childhood. (The Hallmark Hall of Fame movie made from Rachel Simon's book bears very little similarity to it. Whatever the book is, it is not sentimental, and Hallmark Films, like Hallmark Cards, are the epitome of sentimentality.[18]) What Rachel Simon found was that she could not overcome the guilt she felt about her relationship with her sister without changing herself. The book begins:

At six am on this winter morning, moonlight still bathes her apartment. She's already dressed: grape-juice coloured T-shirt and pistachio shorts, with a purple Winnie-the-Pooh backpack slung over her shoulder. I struggle awake and into my clothes: black sweater, black leggings. Beth and I, both in our late thirties, were born eleven months apart, but we are different in more than age. She owns a wardrobe of blazingly bright colours and can leap out of bed before dawn. She is also a woman with mental retardation.[19]

What Beth's family and her care team wanted was that Beth should have a job, one of the menial tasks which people with mental retardation are considered capable of doing. But Beth refused to work. Since early childhood, Beth had resisted doing what other people wanted her to do. One of her favourite phrases was, 'Stop bossing me around!' When she began living independently in her own small apartment she quickly exhausted its delights, but she discovered that her monthly bus pass enabled her to meet different people and to become friends with some of them. Rachel found her sister's pastime embarrassing and refused to discuss it with her. She wrote:

> I hadn't seen Beth in a couple of years. We stayed in touch through letters; once a week I'd scratch out a card, and in return she'd cascade fifteen back. Her letters consisted of two or three multicapitalized sentences sprawling down the page, sprinkled with periods, which she'd then fold into envelopes flamboyantly tattooed with stickers and addresses in fall-off-the page print. . . . I relished finding these treats populating my mailbox, whole colonies arriving in a single day. . . . But when I phoned her occasionally, the conversations were clumsy and joyless. She never volunteered information about herself, and when I divulged meagre scraps about myself, she made no effort to respond . . . . I didn't know what to say. After 'Hello', our dialogue rapidly disintegrated. Finally, resorting to the I'm-the-older-sister-you're-the-little-sister pattern I knew so well, I'd offer blandly, 'Did you hear about the Ninja Turtle mug giveaway at that fast food place?' 'How was your talk with Mom?' These queries would allow us to trudge ahead for a few minutes, Beth scattering monosyllabic

crumbs in my direction, me telling myself, Okay, it's boring, but it's brief. When we got off the phone, my shoulders would be as rigid as if I'd just marched into combat.[20]

At 39, Rachel's life was not as happy as she told herself she was. She had broken up with her partner Sam after he had asked her to marry him. She felt she could not make such a commitment. Now she filled her life with work. There were four siblings in Rachel's family, in order, Max, Laura, Rachel, and, just 11 months younger than Rachel, Beth. When Beth was seven months old she was diagnosed as mentally retarded. Their mother insisted that Beth should be a loved and respected member of the family, but perhaps blaming herself for Beth's condition she became depressed. Their father, a college professor, changed jobs, fell in love with a colleague and left the family. Their mother took up with a series of unsuitable men, culminating in her marrying a vicious criminal who forced the older children, now in their teens, out of the house. Then he and the mother, with Beth in tow, disappeared. The family did not know where Beth was, but finally the mother, frightened that her new husband would kill Beth, put her on a plane back to her father. When Beth returned she was no longer the lively, happy girl she had once been. She must have felt betrayed and abandoned by every member of her family.

Before the family fell apart Rachel and Beth had been very close. They would play together, 'and sometimes in the afternoons, she'll crawl with me into that quiet place under the house where Daddy piles the cut grass, and it smells fresh and green. We'll lie on the soft blades, and look up into the sunlight coming through the lattice between us and the outside, and one of us will surely spot it: the beautiful strands of a huge spider web in the corner, shining like diamonds in the sunlight. As we watch it sparkle, and point out how each thread runs magically into each other thread, she'll hold out her arm for me to tickle. I'll skim my fingers across her skin, and she'll say, "Oh, dee-lee-shus."'[21] As adults, when they met, 'We wrap our arms around each other, though I know it will be fast; Beth doesn't care to be touched, she has admitted to me, but hugs me because I like it.'[22]

One day Rachel's editor, having heard about Beth's fascina-

tion with buses, suggested to Rachel that she spend a day with
Beth on the buses and make this the topic for her next article.
So she did:

> Over that day I was touched by the bus drivers' compassion,
> saddened and sickened by how many people saw Beth
> as a nuisance, and awed by how someone historically
> exiled to society's Siberia not only survived but thrived.
> Indeed, the Beth I remembered from years ago had a
> heavy, ungainly gait; the Beth I saw now was not only
> nimble-footed, but her demeanour was exuberant and
> self-assured. I remembered my earlier objections to her
> bus riding, but they began to feel inexcusably feeble.[23]

The article was a great success and Beth was pleased. Then
Rachel got a letter from Beth's care team. Beth would like
Rachel to attend her annual plan of care review. At the end
of the day Beth asked Rachel to spend a year riding with her
on the buses and Rachel, not knowing where this would lead,
agreed.

At the plan of care review Rachel learned two things about
Beth. The first was that Beth was determined to live her life in
the way that she wanted. This was not the wilfulness of a child.
Beth had learnt that non-mentally retarded people can feel that
they know what was best for her, but they did not. They wanted
her to lead an organised life, achieving what she could with her
limited ability. Beth knew that this was not what she needed
in order to survive as a person. What she needed was people
and excitement. Riding the buses provided her with this. Getting what she needed gave her the self-confidence to acquire
the skills necessary for riding the buses. Rachel wrote:

> [Beth] was riding a dozen [buses] a day, some for five
> minutes, others for hours, befriending drivers and
> passengers as she wound through the narrow streets
> of the city and its wreath of rolling hills. . . she could
> navigate anywhere within a ten-mile radius, and, by
> studying the shifting constellations of characters and
> schedules posted weekly in the bus terminal, she could
> calculate who would be at precisely which intersection
> at any moment of any day. She staked out friendships all
> over the city, weaving her own travelling community.[24]

Second, Rachel learned that Beth had a rare eye condition where her corneas were becoming scratched and this was affecting her vision. She needed an eye operation, but she did not trust anyone. She fought off any dentist who tried to examine her teeth. She would not allow a nurse to come near her. Considering what her life had been, this was not unreasonable. The operation she needed required a general anaesthetic, followed by two days' rest with ice packs on her eyes. Beth told Rachel that she would not accept this, but by the time the operation was due she and Rachel had spent many months together. Beth allowed Rachel and her bus driver friend Jacob to take her to the hospital. Rachel wrote: 'Every minute, it seems that Beth lets down her pride a little more. Not only does she swiftly execute any instructions that the hospital personnel give her, she also requests that I join her in the room where she answers medical questions, gets her blood pressure checked, and is handed her hospital gown.'[25] But Rachel was not reassured. When a man came with the anaesthetic injection Rachel asked her to turn over and Beth said, 'I'll do it when I'm ready.'

I look at Jacob. We seem to agree, without even
speaking, and together we heave her onto her side as
if we're turning over a boat. She's laughing, enjoying
the attention. The man jams the shot in, and we
let her roll back, and then her fight is over.

It stays over as they put up the gurney side rails and
wheel her toward surgery, and I walk along beside her.
It stays over as I sit on a stool beside her in the holding
area, where the drug begins to take effect, and where I
reach across the rails and tickle her arm while we wait.

There, in this quiet corner of the hospital, stroking her
skin, I look into her eyes. They are so scratched and foggy,
so hard to see inside. Yet in this moment, they are also
stripped of all her defiance and foxiness and mischief. She
looks at me with a fullness of trust that I seldom see.

And something happens: the ice in my heart starts to
melt, and I feel a rush of love pour in. The sensation warms
and surprises me, and I wonder if she sees astonishment
in my eyes. She can't see much anyway and, besides, she's
drifting off to sleep. But somehow I'm sure she knows.[26]

How did Beth come to trust Rachel and Rachel to trust her? The answer lies in what Rachel did.

1  She tried to find out how Beth actually lived her life, not just what she did but why she did it.
2  She looked at Beth as person, and saw her in her own right and not as her kid sister.
3  She gave up making judgements about Beth and giving her advice.
4  Instead of focusing on what was wrong with Beth, Rachel saw how well Beth coped with her life, including the daily insults she received as a member of a despised minority.
5  She saw how successful Beth was at getting what she needed.
6  She reminded Beth of their childhood closeness, the physical intimacy of tickling, and of how Beth had once trusted her.
7  It was not until she felt that she had a good understanding of how Beth saw herself and her world that Rachel felt she could at the last moment take the responsibility for Beth having a vitally necessary operation.

This list might sound like the Ten Tips that a proper psychologist would give you. However, such Tips are not far removed from the advice in women's magazines that is very much along the lines of 'Brighten up last year's black sweater with a colourful scarf'. What Rachel did was to make some very profound changes in how she saw herself and her world. Letting down the barrier between herself and Beth might have enabled Rachel to let down the barrier between herself and Sam and marry him, but it did not create a perfect relationship of love and trust between her and Beth. Months after Beth's operation Rachel thought 'of all the things I don't know about Beth. After sharing bedrooms, buses, Donny Osmond, and thirty-nine years, I don't see the melancholy that Jesse [Beth's boyfriend] sees. I've long suspected it, but she never allows it to show. . . . I've always figured there must be some grief in her heart, but I don't know the things she censors. What she *must* censor, I correct myself, as we all do when we grow up and make ourselves distinct from our families. I love her, and at last I believe that she loves me too, but I know that in her eyes I will always be the big sister. It is both my bridge to her, and the moat eternally between us.'[27]

The eternal moat is not just between siblings. It exists between all human beings. We live in our own world of meaning and long to be close to other people, and as much as we long for closeness, we fear it, for closeness can threaten annihilation of our most precious possession, our sense of being a person. We cannot arrive at some eternal optimum balance of closeness and distance because relationships, like everything else in the universe, are in a constant process of change. We can try to make reality fixed and certain, but attempting this is the Buddha's definition of suffering. Happiness, the emotion which signals 'I am as I am, and things are as they should be', starts with accepting uncertainty and seeing it as good.

Whenever we feel that our sense of being a person is threatened with annihilation we need to remember that it is not we who are falling apart and disappearing but simply some of our ideas. These ideas need to fall apart and disappear because they are no longer a reasonably accurate picture of what is going on. We might have to endure a period of uncertainty while we work out better ideas, but they will come in time, and we shall find ourselves whole again – different but whole. Knowing this, we can survive the worst of crises, and, unlike Matisse, we can get a good night's sleep.

# NOTES

## Preface

1. Judy Dunn, *Sisters and Brothers*, Fontana, London, 1984.
2. Penelope Fitgerald, *The Knox Brothers*, Flamingo, London, 2002.
3. Richard Wollheim, *Germs*, Black Swan, London, 2004.
4. John Falkner, *My Brother Bill: An Affectionate Reminiscence*, Victor Gollancz, London, 1964.

## 1. Our greatest need: our greatest fear

1. Henri Matisse, M. A. Couturier and L. B. Rayssiguier, *La Chapelle de Vence: Journal d'une Création*, ed. Marcel Billot, Paris, 1993, p. 402, quoted in Hilary Spurling, *Matisse The Master*, Hamish Hamilton, London, 2005, p. 408.
2. Simone de Beauvoir, *Memoirs of a Dutiful Daughter*, Penguin, Harmondsworth, 1958, p. 207.
3. Hilary Spurling, *The Unknown Matisse*, Penguin, London, 1998, p. 59.
4. de Beauvoir, *Memoirs of a Dutiful Daughter*, op. cit., p. 29.
5. Ibid., p. 193.
6. Ibid., p. 184.
7. Ibid., p. 142.
8. Louis Aragon, *Matisse: A Novel*, quoted by Hilary Spurling in 'Matisse's Pyjamas', *New York Review of Books*, 11 August 2005, pp. 33–6.
9. *The Melbourne Age*, 15 February 2006.
10. S. C. Segerstrom and G. E. Miller, 'Psychological Stress and the Human Immune System: A Meta-analytic Study of 30 Years of Inquiry', *Psychological Bulletin*, vol. 130, no. 4, 2004, pp. 601–30.
11. BBC Radio 4, 2004.
12. *What Makes Alastair Campbell Run?* BBC1, 15 September 2004, reported in the *Guardian*, 16 September 2004.
13. J. D. Salinger, *Catcher in the Rye*, Penguin, London, 1994, p. 4.

14. Ibid., p. 178.
15. In Hermione Lee, *Virginia Woolf*, Vintage, London, 1999, p. 187.
16. Ibid., p. 725
17. Ibid., p. 173.
18. Justin Frank, *Bush on the Couch*, Regan Books, New York, 2004, p. 63.
19. Ibid., p. 64.
20. Antonio Damasio, *The Feeling of What Happens*, Vintage, London, 2000, pp. 199–200.
21. Antonio Damasio, *Looking for Spinoza*, Vintage, London, 2004, p. 170.
22. Temple Grandin and Catherine Johnson, *Animals in Translation*, Bloomsbury, London, 2005, p. 94.
23. Paul Broks, *Into the Silent Land*, Atlantic Books, London, 2004, p. 51.
24. Damasio, *The Feeling of What Happens*, op. cit., p. 318.
25. *New Scientist*, 24 July 2004, p. 8.
26. L. Terr, 'Childhood Traumas: An Outline and Review', *American Journal of Psychiatry*, vol. 148, 1991, pp. 10–20, quoted in Phil Mollon, *Remembering Trauma*, Wiley, Chichester, 1998, p. 34.
27. Damasio, *The Feeling of What Happens*, op. cit., pp. 43–6.
28. Patrick Tissington, 'Bravery is the Management of Fear', *Guardian*, 7 December 2004.
29. Damasio, *Looking for Spinoza*, op. cit., pp. 240–4.
30. Jean Améry, *On Suicide: A Discourse on Voluntary Death*, trans. John Barlow, Indiana University Press, Bloomington, 1999, p. 27, quoted in Lisa Lieberman *Leaving You: The Cultural Meaning of Suicide*, Ivan R. Dee, Chicago, 2003, p. 5.
31. Ibid., p. 153.

## 2. A relationship like no other

1. Diana Mosley, *A Life of Contrasts*, Gibson Square Books, London, 2003, p. 20.
2. Ibid., p. 20.
3. Ibid., p. 184.
4. Carole Angier, *Primo Levi: The Double Bond*, Penguin, London, 2003, p. xxii.
5. Fiora Vincenti, *Invito alla Lettura di Primo Levi* Mursia, 1973, p. 31, quoted by Angier, *Primo Levi*, op. cit., p. 46.
6. Angier, *Primo Levi*, op. cit., p. xiii.
7. Ibid., p. 45.
8. Ian Thomson, *Primo Levi*, Vintage, London, 2002.
9. Joan Fontaine, *No Bed of Roses*, William Morrow, New York, 1978, p. 7.

10. Ibid., p. 18.
11. Ibid., p. 102.
12. Ibid., p. 30.
13. Ibid., p. 145.
14. Ibid., p. 188.
15. Peter Parker, *Ackerley*, Farrar, Straus and Giroux, New York, 1989, p. 1.
16. Ibid., p. 44.
17. Ibid., p. 8.
18. J. R. Ackerley, *My Father and Myself*, Penguin, Harmondsworth, 1971, p. 76.
19. Parker, *Ackerley*, op. cit., p. 154.
20. Ibid., p. 156.
21. Ackerley, *My Father and Myself*, op. cit., p. 192.
22. J. R. Ackerley, *My Sister and Myself: Diaries (Oxford Letters and Memoirs)*, Oxford University Press, Oxford, 1990, p. 34.
23. Ibid., pp. 57, 58.
24. Ibid., p. 59.
25. Ibid., p. 62.
26. Ibid., p. 14.
27. Ibid., p. 21.
28. Victor G. Cicirelli, *Sibling Relationships across the Life Span*, Plenum Press, New York, 1995, p. 59.
29. Judy Dunn, *Young Children's Close Relationships*, Sage, London, 1993, p. 106.
30. Judy Dunn, *Sisters and Brothers*, Fontana, London, 1984, p. 142.
31. Dunn, *Young Children's Close Relationships*, op. cit., p. 89.
32. Judy Dunn and Robert Plomin, *Separate Lives: Why Siblings Are So Different*, Basic Books, New York, 1990.
33. Ibid., p. 16.
34. Peter Hepper, 'Unravelling our Beginnings', *The Psychologist*, vol. 18, no. 8, p. 476, quoting D. Querleu et al., 'Fetal Hearing', *European Journal of Obstetrics and Gynaecology*, vol. 2, 1988, pp. 191–212.
35. A. Gopnik, A. N. Meltzoff and P. K. Kuhl, *The Scientist in the Crib*, HarperCollins, New York, 2001, p. 28.
36. Ibid., p. 30.
37. Ibid., p. 29.
38. Ibid., p. 30.
39. A. N. Meltzoff 'Understanding the Intentions of Others: Re-enactment of Intended Acts by 18 month old Children', *Developmental Psychology*, vol. 31, no. 5, 1995, pp. 838–50.
40. Gopnik et al., *Scientist in the Crib*, op. cit. p. 38.
41. Dunn, *Sisters and Brothers* op. cit., p. 23.
42. Ibid., p. 30.
43. Gopnik et al., *Scientist in the Crib*, op. cit., p. 57.

44. Dorothy Rowe *Beyond Fear*, 2nd edn, HarperCollins, London, 2002, pp. 569–74.

45. P. E. Bebbington et al., 'Psychosis, Victimisation and Childhood Disadvantage. Evidence from the Second British National Survey of Psychiatric Morbidity', *British Journal of Psychiatry*, vol. 185, 2004, pp. 220–6.

46. Simone de Beauvoir, *A Very Easy Death*, trans. Patrick O'Brien, Andre Deutsch and Weidenfeld and Nicolson, London, 1965, p. 68.

47. Sue Gerhardt, *Why Love Matters: How Affection Shapes a Baby's Brain*, Brunner-Routledge, Hove and New York, 2004.

48. Peter Rose, *Rose Boys*, Allen and Unwin, Sydney, 2002, p. 19.

49. Ibid., p. 76.

50. Hilary Spurling, *Ivy When Young*, Allison and Busby, London, 1983, p. 33.

51. Ibid., p. 32.

52. Ibid., p. 47.

53. Ibid., p. 47.

54. Simone de Beauvoir, *Memoirs of a Dutiful Daughter*, Penguin, Harmondsworth, 1965, p. 5.

55. Ibid., p. 45.

56. Ibid., p. 13.

57. Ibid., p. 12.

58. Ibid., p. 39.

59. Dunn, *Sisters and Brothers*, op. cit., p. 19.

60. Ibid., p. 63.

61. Cicirelli, *Sibling Relationships Across the Life Span*, op. cit., p. 43.

62. de Beauvoir, *Memoirs of a Dutiful Daughter*, op. cit., p. 45.

63. Ibid., p. 44.

64. Ibid., p. 43, original emphasis.

65. Alexandra Fuller, *Don't Let's Go to the Dogs Tonight*, Picador, London, 2002.

66. Ibid., p. 182.

67. Temple Grandin and Catherine Johnson, *Animals in Translation*, Bloomsbury, London, 2005, p. 112.

68. Ibid., p. 122.

69. Fuller, *Don't Let's Go to the Dogs Tonight*, op. cit., p. 69.

70. Dunn, *Young Children's Close Relationships*, op. cit., p. 105.

71. Robert Plomin, *Separate Lives: Why Siblings Are So Different*, Basic Books, New York, 1990, p. 16.

72. Ibid., p. 16.

## 3. Two ways to experience existence

1. Dorothy Rowe, *Beyond Fear*, 2nd edn, HarperCollins, London, 2002.
2. Dorothy Rowe, *The Successful Self*, HarperCollins, London, 2002.
3. Dalton Conley, *The Pecking Order*, Pantheon, New York, 2004, pp. 188–90
4. BBC Radio 4, 8 May 2005.
5. Jane Austen, *Sense and Sensibility*, Penguin, London, 1995, p. 8
6. Ibid., p. 23.
7. Antonio Damasio, *The Feeling of What Happens*, Vintage, London, 2000, p. 138.
8. Ibid., p. 136.
9. Temple Grandin, *Thinking in Pictures*, Vintage Books, New York, 1985, p. 89.
10. Ibid., p. 132.
11. Ibid., p. 15.
12. Ibid., p. 88.
13. Ibid., p. 93.
14. Ibid., p. 193.
15. Quoted by Annie Murphy Paul in *The Cult of Personality*, Free Press, New York, 2004, p. 137; 'every individual is an exception from the rule', quoted in Robert I. Watson, *The Great Psychologists: From Aristotle to Freud*, J. B. Lippincott, 1963, p. 496; 'fitting such individuals into a rigid system is "futile"', Jung, *Psychological Types*, xiv; 'stick labels on people at first sight', ibid.
16. Paul, *The Cult of Personality*, op. cit., p. 134.
17. Andrew Butler, 'Reconceptualizing Research on Sociotropy and Autonomy' *Beck Institute Newsletter,* www.beckinstitute.org/jun 2000/research.html
18. A. T. Beck, 'Cognitive Therapy of Depression: New Perspectives', in P. Clayton and J. E. Barrett (eds), *Treatment of Depression: Old Controversies and New Approaches*, Raven Press, New York, 1983, pp. 265–90.
19. Butler, op. cit.
20. Dorothy Rowe, *Depression: The Way Out of Your Prison*, 3rd edn, Brunner-Routledge, London and New York, 2003.
21. Paul, *The Cult of Personality,* op. cit., p. 184.
22. Mark Twain.
23. Quoted in Leon Edel, *'William James: The Untried Years: 1843-1870*, Avon Books, New York, 1953, p. 59.
24. Ibid., p. 195
25. Ibid., p. 62
26. Ibid., p. 195.
27. Ibid., pp. 65–6.
28. E. Arnot Robertson, *Ordinary Families*, Collins Fontana Books, London, 1971, first published 1933.

29. Linda Simon, *Genuine Reality: A Life of Henry James*, University of Chicago Press, Chicago, 1998 pp. xviii, 258.
30. Rowe, *The Successful Self*, op. cit.
31. Linda Kreger Silverman, 'On Introversion', http://www.gifted development.com/Articles/On%20Introversion.html
32. Jill D. Burrass and Lisa Kaenzig, 'Introversion', http://cfge.wm. edu/documents/Introversion.html
33. Cordelia Fine, *A Mind of Your Own: How Your Brain Distorts and Deceives*, Icon Books, Cambridge, 2006, p. 15.
34. Marti Olsen Laney, *The Introvert Advantage: How to Survive in an Extrovert World*, Workman Publishing, New York, 2002 (www.the introvertadvantage.com).
35. Jerome Kagan and Nancy Snidman, *The Long Shadow of Temperament*, Harvard University Press, Cambridge, MA, 2004, p. 7.
36. Ibid., pp. 11–12.
37. Ibid., p. 218.
38. Ibid., p. 108.
39. *Pride and Prejudice*, op. cit., p. 135.
40. Robertson, *Ordinary Families*, op. cit., pp. 120, 127, 137.
41. Ibid p. 217.
42. Ibid., p. 288.
43. Juliet Mitchell, *Madmen and Medusas*, Penguin, London, 2000, p. 27.
44. Ibid., p. 41
45. In 1962 the Blessed John XXIII was Pope. He had been born in Bergamo.
46. Heinrich Böll, *The Clown*, trans. Leila Vennewitz, Penguin, Harmondsworth, 1965, p. 177.
47. Jonathan Brent and Vladimir Naumov, *Stalin's Last Crime*, HarperCollins, London, 2004, quoted by Gideon Haigh, *'Dry Rations', The Lure of Fundamentalism*, Griffith Review, no. 7, ed. Julianne Schultz, Griffith University, Meadowbank, Queensland, 2005, p. 238.
48. Hermione Lee, *Virginia Woolf*, Vintage, London, 1997, p. 173.
49. Angelica Garnett, *Deceived with Kindness*, Oxford University Press, Oxford, 1984, p. 19.
50. Ibid pp. 95–6.
51. Rowe, *Beyond Fear*, op. cit., pp. 442–96.
52. Tsitsi Dangarembga, *Nervous Conditions*, Seal Press, New York, 1989, p. 88.
53. Ibid., pp. 89–90.
54. Hilary Spurling, *Matisse The Master: A Life of Henri Matisse*, vol. 2, Hamish Hamilton, London, 2005, p. 115.
55. VW to VB [15 October 1931] *Letters, Vol. IV*, quoted in Jane Dunn, *A Very Close Conspiracy*, Virago, London, 2000, pp. 115, 225.
56. Garnett, *Deceived with Kindness*, op. cit., p. 33.

57. Spurling, *Matisse The Master*, op. cit., pp. 34–72.
58. Sallly Dickerson and Margaret Kemeny, 'Acute stressors and cortical responses', *Psychological Bulletin*, vol. 130, no. 3, 2004, pp. 355–91.

## 4. Competing to be good

1. Hans-Georg Behr, *Almost a Childhood: Growing Up Among the Nazis*, Granta, London, 2005, pp. 1–2.
2. Robin Dunbar, *The Human Story*, Faber and Faber, London, 2004, p. 100.
3. Ibid., p. 95
4. Anthony Fingleton, *Swimming Upstream*, Text Publishing, Melbourne, 2002, pp. 7, 96, 101.
5. Douwe Draaisma, *Why Life Speeds Up as You Get Older*, trans. Arnold and Erica Pomerans, Cambridge University Press, Cambridge, 2004, p. 45.
6. Bill Jones Production, Granada Television, 2005.
7. Orhan Pamuk, *Istanbul*, Faber and Faber, London, 2005, p. 15.
8. Ibid., p. 267.
9. Draaisma, *Why Life Speeds Up as You Get Older*, op. cit., p. 177.
10. Nawal El Saadawi, *A Daughter of Isis*, trans. Sherif Hetata, Zed Books, London, p. 28.
11. Ibid., pp. 58–9.
12. Ibid., p. 84.
13. Ibid., p. 86.
14. Don McCullin, *Unreasonable Behaviour*, Vintage, London, 2002, p. 143.
15. Ibid., p. 224
16. Ibid., p. 228.
17. Angelica Garnett, *Deceived with Kindness*, Oxford University Press, Oxford, 1984, p. 133.
18. *Guardian*, 27 April 2005
19. Virginia Ironside, *Janey and Me*, Fourth Estate, London, 2003, p. 271.
20. Temple Grandin and Catherine Johnson, *Animals in Translation*, Bloomsbury, London, 2005, p. 211.
21. Ibid., p. 112.
22. Melvin Lerner, *The Belief in a Just World: A Fundamental Delusion*, Plenum Press, New York, 1980.
23. Dorothy Rowe, *The Courage to Live*, HarperCollins, London, 1989.
24. Dorothy Rowe, *Wanting Everything*, HarperCollins, London, 1992, pp. 104–6.
25. 'God's been Mugged', *Guardian*, 6 June 2005.

26. *Guardian*, 2 April 2005.
27. Francis Wheen, *How Mumbo-Jumbo Conquered the World*, Harper-Collins, London, 2004, p. 297.
28. Ibid., p. 300
29. Jo Ann, Marjory and Joel Levitt, *Sibling Revelry*, Dell, New York, 2001, p. 191.
30. Ibid., pp. 191–2.
31. Erna Paris, *Long Shadows: Lies, Truth and History*, Bloomsbury, London, 2002, p. 71.
32. Judith Flanders, *A Circle of Sisters*, Penguin, London, 2002, p. 328.
33. E. Arnot Robinson, *Ordinary Families*, Collins Fontana Books, London, 1971, p. 33 (first published 1933).
34. Ibid., p. 185.
35. El Saadawi, *A Daughter of Isis*, op. cit., p. 63.
36. Ibid., p. 63.
37. Arnot Robinson, *Ordinary Families*, op. cit., p. 40.
38. McCullin, *Unreasonable Behaviour*, op. cit., pp. 7–9.

## 5. Power stuggles

1. Nicholas Stargardt, *Witnesses of War*, Jonathan Cape, London, 2005, p. 378.
2. Peter Rose, *Rose Boys*, Allen and Unwin, Sydney, 2002, op. cit., p. 120.
3. Ibid., p. 62.
4. Ibid., p. 119.
5. Ibid., p. 70.
6. L. P. Hartley, *Eustace and Hilda*, Faber & Faber, London, 1990, p. 35.
7. Ibid., p. 736.
8. Mary Lovell, *The Mitford Girls*, Abacus, London, 2002, pp. 22, 26, 54.
9. Fred Kaplan, *Dickens: A Biography*, Hodder and Stoughton, London, 1988, pp. 19, 309.
10. *Observer*, 1 May 2005.
11. Hans-Georg Behr, *Almost a Childhood: Growing Up Among the Nazis*, Granta, London, 2005, p. 39.
12. Ibid., p. 42.
13. Ibid., p. 78.
14. Ibid., p. 81.
15. Ibid., pp. 220, 223.
16. Ibid., pp. 261–3.
17. Ibid., pp. 263–5.
18. Dorothy Rowe, *Beyond Fear*, 2nd edn, HarperCollins, London, 2002.

19. Vernon Wiehe, *Sibling Abuse: Hidden Physical, Emotional and Sexual Trauma*, 2nd edn, Sage, Thousand Oaks, CA, 1997.

20. Fiona MacCarthy, *Eric Gill*, Faber & Faber, London, 1989.

21. Judith Flanders, *A Circle of Sisters*, Penguin, London, 2002, p. 130.

22. Ibid., p. 131.

23. Ibid., p. 131.

24. J. R. Ackerley, *My Sister and Myself: Diaries (Oxford Letters and Memoirs)*, Oxford University Press, Oxford, p. 21.

25. J. R. Ackerley, *My Father and Myself*, Penguin, Harmondsworth, 1971, p. 47.

26. Ackerley, *My Sister and Myself*, op. cit., p. 18.

27. Ibid., p. 13.

28. Personal communication, 21 October 2005.

29. 2 Samuel 13, 1:16.

30. Avishai Margarlit, *The Ethics of Memory*, Harvard University Press, Cambridge, MA, 2004, p. 122.

31. Lewis Carroll, *Alice's Adventures in Wonderland*, Macmillan, London, 1973, p. 130.

32. Peter Kingston, *Guardian Education*, 21 June 2005.

## 6. The death of a sibling

1.. Shelley Bovey, 'Only My Brother', *Independent*, 13 November 1996.

2. Ben Schott, *Schott's Original Miscellany*, Bloomsbury, London, 2002, p. 90.

3. Victor G. Cicirelli, *Sibling Relationships across the Life Span*, Plenum Press, New York, 1995, p. 190, quoting from H. Rosen 'Prohibitions in Mourning in Childhood Sibling Loss', *Omega*, 14, pp. 307–16.

4. Bovey, op. cit.

5. Justin Frank, *Bush on the Couch*, HarperCollins, New York, 2004, p. 4.

6. Ibid., p. 3.

7. Clare Jenkins and Judy Merry, *Relative Grief*, Jessica Kingsley Publishers, London, 2005, p. 101.

8. Ibid., p. 112.

9. Ethel Turner, *Seven Little Australians*, Hodder, Sydney, 1998.

10. Hilary Spurling, *Ivy When Young*, Allison and Busby, London, 1983, p. 115.

11. Judith Flanders, *Circle of Sisters*, Penguin, London, 2002, p. 13.

12. Cicerelli, *Sibling Relationships across the Life Span*, op. cit., p. 191.

13. Spurling, *Ivy When Young*, op. cit., p. 158.

14. Ibid., p. 115.

15. Ibid., p. 117.

16. Ibid., p. 142.
17. Ibid., p. 160.
18. Ibid., p. 244.
19. Ibid., p. 256
20. Tsitsi Dangarembga, *Nervous Conditions*, Seal Press, New York, 1989, p. 1.
21. Ibid., p. 10.
22. Judith Flanders, *A Circle of Sisters*, Penguin, London, 2002, p. 22.
23. Ibid., p. 61.
24. Ibid., p. 63.
25. Ibid., p. 231.
26. BBC2, 7 July 2005.
27. Sam Wollaston, 'Too Much, Too Young', *Guardian*, 6 July 2005.
28. Andrew Birkin, *J. M. Barrie and the Lost Boys*, Constable, London, 1979, p. 297.
29. J. M. Barrie, *Margaret Ogilvy*, Kessinger, Kila, MT, 2005, p. 5.
30. Ibid., pp. 7–17.
31. Jenkins and Merry, *Relative Grief*, op. cit., p. 112.
32. Jonathan Franzen, 'My father's brain', in *How To Be Alone*, Harper-Collins, London, 2004, p. 38
33. Hermione Lee, *Virginia Woolf*, Vintage, London, 1997, pp. 39, 115, 117–18.
34. Heinrich Böll, *The Clown*, trans. Leila Vennewitz, Penguin, Harmondsworth, 1965 pp. 16–18.
35. J. D. Salinger, *The Catcher in the Rye*, Pengin, London, 1994, p. 33
36. Ibid., p. 34.
37. Böll, *The Clown*, op. cit., pp. 22, 25.
38. Ibid., p. 31.
39. Ibid., p. 41
40. Ibid., p.43.
41. Salinger, *The Catcher in the Rye*, op. cit., p.61.
42. Ibid., p.107.
43. Ibid., p.182.
44. Ibid., p.104.
45. Ibid., p.155.
46. Böll, *The Clown*, op. cit., p.1.

## 7. A question of memory

1. Heinrich Böll, *What's to Become of the Boy? Or Something to Do with Books*, trans. Leila Vennewitz, Alfred A. Knopf, New York, 1984, pp. 3–6.
2. Richard Wollheim, *Germs*, Black Swan, London, 2005, p. 219.

3. Dalton Conley, *The Pecking Order*, Pantheon, New York, 2004, p. 10.
4. Daniel L. Schacter, *How the Mind Forgets and Remembers: The Seven Sins of Memory*, Souvenir Press, London, 2003, p. 9.
5. Lucy Mangan, *Guardian*, 30 November 2005.
6. Schacter, *How the Mind Forgets and Remembers*, op. cit., p. 152.
7. Ibid., p. 163
8. Wollheim, *Germs*, op. cit., p. 40.
9. Ibid., p. 181.
10. Schacter, *How the Mind Forgets and Remembers*, op. cit., p. 97.
11. Temple Grandin and Catherine Johnson, *Animals in Translation*, Bloomsbury Press, London, 2005, p. 194
12. Avishai Margalit, *The Ethics of Memory*, Harvard University Press, Cambridge MA, 2004, p. 168.
13. Schacter, *How the Mind Forgets and Remembers*, op. cit., p. 132.
14. John Simpson, *Days from a Different World*, Macmillan, London, 2005, pp. 92–3.
15. Orhan Pamuk, *Istanbul: Memories of a City*, trans. Maureen Freely, Faber, London, 2005, p. 265.
16. Gregg and Gina Hill, *On the Run: A Mafia Childhood*, Warner Books, New York, 2004, pp. 5, 30, 33.
17. Ibid., p. 69.
18. Ibid., p. 178.
19. Ibid., p. 180.
20. Ibid., p. 12.
21. Ibid., p. 18.
22. Ibid., pp. 11, 19.
23. Ibid., pp. 77, 155.
24. Ibid., p. 154, 204.
25. Ibid., p. 219.
26. Ibid., pp. 180, 229.
27. Ibid., 241.
28. Ibid., p. 244.
29. Dorothy Rowe, *Beyond Fear*, 2nd edn, HarperCollins, London, 2002, pp. 122–5.
30. *Observer*, 30 May 2004.
31. http://www.hearing-voices.org/
32. Rowe, *Beyond Fear*, op. cit., pp. 442–96.
33. Pamuk, *Istanbul*, op. cit., p. 265.
34. *Born Bad* was first performed at the Hampstead Theatre, London, on 29 April 2003.
35. Gaia Vince, 'Rewriting Your Past', *New Scientist*, 3 December 2005.

## 8. Loyalty and betrayal

1. E. Arnot Robertson, *Ordinary Families*, Collins Fontana Books, London, 1971 (first published 1933), p. 29
2. Diana Mosley, *A Life of Contrasts*, Gibson Square Books, London, 2003, p. 29
3. Elizabeth Jolley, 'My Sister Dancing', in *Sisters*, Drusila Modjeska ed., Angus and Robertson, Sydney, 1993, p. 174.
4. Doris Pilkington, *Rabbit Proof Fence*, University of Queensland Press, Brisbane, 2002.
5. Simone de Beauvoir, *Memoirs of A Dutiful Daughter*, Penguin, Harmondsworth, 1965, p. 98.
5. Tim Guest, *My Life in Orange*, Granta, London, 2004.
7. Dorothy Rowe, *Time on Our Side*, HarperCollins, London, 1994, pp. 93–160.
8. The History Channel and SBS, shown on Channel 4, 6 August 2005.
9. Nicholas Stargardt, *Witnesses of War*, Jonathan Cape, London, 2005, p. 32.
10. Henry Metelmann, *A Hitler Youth*, Spellmount, Staplehurst, 2004, p. 81.
11. Ibid., p. 175.
12. Stargardt, *Witnesses of War*, op. cit., p. 267.
13. Ibid., pp. 325–6.
14. Heinrich Böll, *The Clown*, trans. Leila Vennewitz, Penguin, Harmondsworth, 1965, pp. 18–19.
15. Hans-Georg Behr, *Almost a Childhood: Growing Up Amongst the Nazis*, Granta, London, 2005, p. 98.
16. Ibid., pp. 98, 104.
17. Ibid., pp. 123–4.
18. J. H. Reid, *Heinrich Böll: A German for His Time*, Oswald Wolff Books, Oxford, 1988, p. 75.
19. Rachel Cooke 'The Sins of the Father', *Observer*, 8 January 2006.
20. *Observer*, 18 December 2005.
21. Nawal El Saadawi, *Walking Through Fire*, Zed Books, London, 2002, pp. 55, 119.
22. Jane Dunn, *Virginia Woolf and Vanessa Bell: A Very Close Conspiracy*, Jonathan Cape, London, 1990, p. 100.
23. Ibid., p. 109.
24. Hubert Gladwyn Jebb (later 1st Baron Gladwyn) at the Ministry of Economic Warfare, 1940-42, Mary Lovell, *The Mitford Girls*, Abacus, London, 2002, p. 559.
25. Ibid., p. 325.
26. Ibid., p. 440.
27. *Guardian*, 6 August 2005.

28. Don McCullin, *Unreasonable Behaviour*, Vintage, London, 2002, p. 64.
29. Ibid., pp. 3–4, 132.
30. Reid, *Heinrich Böll: A German for His Time*, op. cit., p. 20.
31. Heinrich Böll , *What's to Become of the Boy? Or Something to Do with Books*, trans. Leila Vennewitz, Knopf, New York, 1984, p. 37.
32. Elaine Morgan, *Pinker's List*, Eildon Press, Leeds, 2005, pp. 214, 216.
33. Dorothy Rowe, *Friends and Enemies*, HarperCollins, London, 2000, pp. 313–86.
34. *Guardian* 21 April 2006.
35. Abd Samad Moussaoui, *Zacarias Moussaoui: The Making of a Terrorist*, trans. Simon Pleasance and Fronza Woods, Serpents Tail, London, 2002, pp. 5–6, 9.
35. Ibid., p. 9
37. Ibid., p. 9
38. Ibid., pp. 14, 69.
39. Ibid., p. 69
40. Ibid., p. 58.
41. Ibid., pp. 75, 79.
42. 'If You'd Seen his Green Eyes', *London Review of Books*, 20 April 2006.
43. BBC Radio 4, 20 April 2006.
44. Ibid., pp. 95, 114, 127.
45. Paul McGough, 'Mission Impossible: The Sheikhs, the US and the Future of Iraq', *Quarterly Essay*, Black Inc., Melbourne, Australia, issue 14, 2004, pp. 8, 11.
46. Ibid., p. 59
47. Ibid., p. 60, original emphases.
48. Deborah MacKenzie, 'End of Enlightenment', *New Scientist*, 8 October 2005.
49. Loretta Napoleoni, *Modern Jihad: Tracing the Dollars Behind the Terror Networks*, Pluto Press, London, 2003, p. 133.
50. Nadia Taysir Dabbagh, *Suicide in Palestine*, Hurst, London, 2005, p. 3.
51. Napoleoni, *Modern Jihad*, op. cit., p. 178.
52. J. H. Relethford and M. H. Crawford, *Annals of Human Biology* vol 25, no. 2, 1998, pp. 117–25.
53. Peter Bull, 'Shifting Patterns of Social Identity in Northern Ireland', *The Psychologist*, vol. 19, no. 1, 2006, pp. 40–3. K. Trew, 'The Northern Irish Identity', in A. J. Kershen (ed.) *A Question of Identity*, Aldershot, Ashgate, 1998, pp. 60–76.
54. Steven Rose, *The 21st-Century Brain*, Vintage Books, London, 2006, p. 95.
55. BBC News Sci/Tech, 10 May 2000.
56. History News Network, http://hnn.us/blogs/entries/12334.html

57. McCullin, *Unreasonable Behaviour*, op. cit., p. 217.
58. Norma Percy's BBC TV series *Israel and the Arabs: Elusive Peace* (Brook Lapping), 2005.

### 9. A lifelong relationship

1. 3 March 2004.
2. Brenda Wineapple, *Sister Brother: Gertrude and Leo Stein*, Bloomsbury, London, 1996, p. 1.
3. *Sunday* with Roger Boulton, BBC Radio 4, 16 April 2006.
4. *Women's Hour*, BBC Radio 4, 29 July 2005.
5. John Simpson, *Days from a Different World*, Macmillan, London, 2005, p. 347.
6. Marina Lewycka, *A Short History of Tractors in Ukrainian*, Viking, London, 2005, p. 41.
7. Simpson, *Days from a Different World*, op. cit., p. 408.
8. *Guardian*, 4 February 2006.
9. Genesis 33: 3, 4.
10. Genesis 45: 15, 37–45.
11. *Guardian*, 12 December 2005.
12. Dorothy Rowe, *The Courage to Live*, HarperCollins, London, 1989, pp. 35–7, 142–8, 266–80.
13. Julie Evans, 'Mindfulness from a Cognitive Therapy Perspective: Theoretical and Clinical Implications', *Clinical Psychology Forum*, vol. 258, 2006, pp. 5, 7.
14. Ricky Gervais and Stephen Merchant, BBC Television, 2005.
15. http://www.bbc.co.uk/comedy/theoffice/gareth
16. http://www.bbc.co.uk/comedy/theoffice/clips/rickyinterview/clip3.shtml
17. Alain de Botton, *Status Anxiety*, Penguin, Harmondsworth, 2005, p. 11.
18. http://www.rachelsimon.com/
19. Rachel Simon, *Riding the Buses with My Sister*, Hodder Headline, Sydney, 2003, p. 1.
20. Ibid., p. 9.
21. Ibid., p. 43.
22. Ibid., p. 13.
23. Ibid., p. 11.
24. Ibid., p. 2.
25. Ibid., p. 212.
26. Ibid., p. 213.
27. Ibid., p. 288.

# INDEX